Harvard Studies in Urban History

Series Editors: Stephan Thernstrom and Charles Tilly

Urban Growth and the Circulation of Information:
The United States System of Cities, 1790-1840

Allan R. Pred

HARVARD UNIVERSITY PRESS, CAMBRIDGE, MASSACHUSETTS, 1973

©1973 by the President and Fellows of Harvard College
All rights reserved
Printed in the United States of America
Library of Congress Catalog Card Number 73-76384
SBN 674-93090-8

For Sven and Ralph,
who can,
and would if they could

Acknowledgments

I am highly indebted to all those intellectual forebears whose ideas have been stored in the recesses of my mind, where they have freely mingled and coupled to give birth to the conceptual framework presented in this book.

Special thanks of a very different kind are much in order for Adrienne Morgan, who drafted my maps, and Glenn George, who served as my research assistant during the summer of 1969. I am also grateful to Gerry Karaska, editor of *Economic Geography*, and Les King, editor of *Geographical Analysis*, for publishing early versions of some of the material contained in these pages.

As always, I owe immeasurable gratitude to Hjördis, Michele, and Erik for their patience and love over the years while I have researched and written this work.

Contents

Figures

Maps

Tables

Urban Growth and the Circulation of Information: The United States System of Cities, 1790-1840

Introduction

Communications have enabled the social unit to grow, from the village to the town, to the modern city-state, until today we see organized systems of mutual dependence grown to cover whole hemispheres.
—Colin Cherry

How do large cities influence one another's growth? Although this question has broad ramifications, it has been only partially answered. In each major metropolitan complex of the United States the scale of problems involving race relations, poverty, municipal financing, local transportation, and environmental pollution is closely related to this question. In many countries of Europe and elsewhere the same question is directly linked to the political tensions deriving from pronounced regional inequalities of a social and economic nature. In economically unadvanced nations, where much urbanization and industrial development lies in the future, both short-range and long-range planning beg more complete answers to this question. Ironically, the very urgency that has attracted a vast contingent of social scientists and professionals to the solving of current problems in individual cities has prevented most of them from exploring the development processes of large sets of interdependent cities, or systems of cities.

The question of how large cities influence one another's growth is entangled with related questions of information circulation. Some argue that cities originate individually as communications nodes or foci of information exchange and accumulation. Their subsequent growth is highly correlated with the "intensification of *communication, knowledge* and *controls.*"[1] Within the present-day metropolis the concen-

1

tration of many economic activities, particularly administrative units, is encouraged by economies in the costs of collecting, processing, and transmitting information, as well as by the recognized role of knowledge in reducing uncertainty.[2] A system of cities, like any other sociocultural system, can be viewed "as a set of elements linked almost entirely by way of the intercommunication of information (in the broad sense)."[3] None of the economic actions and location decisions that underlie individual and collective urban growth can materialize unless preceded by information acquisition. None of the interurban commodity, capital, and human flows that are the outward expression of growth can transpire unless there is either the transmission of knowledge about demand, prices, and opportunities or some other form of information exchange. No modern multi-city business or public organization can coordinate its growth-generating day-to-day activities without maintaining a constant flow of information among its component units.

In this book I try to unravel the interrelationships between information circulation and certain aspects of the interdependent growth of large cities within a particular historical setting—the United States from 1790 to about 1840.[4] Although the time frame is limited, my principal concern is with general urban growth and locational processes, that is, with the identification of general feedback mechanisms which allow the components of specific patterns and structures at any point in time to have a nondeterministic impact on the components of subsequent specific patterns and structures, or system states.[5] Thus, the urbanization and information-circulation developments of 1790–1840 are not examined as an end in themselves but as a means to the broader end of better understanding the growth processes of all systems of cities. Because of the character of interurban information circulation before the telegraph, it is in some respects easier to pin down the relationships between information circulation and interdependent large-city growth for the 1790–1840 period than for subsequent periods of United States urban development. This work departs significantly from most urban histories, which have dealt with the growth and change of individual cities,[6] with transportation developments as they affect the success or failure of specific cities,[7] with comparative conditions in specified cities at particular times,[8] and with the history of American cities in general,[9] but seldom either with cities as members of a developing urban system or with urban growth as a process. However, my approach is related to the work of a handful of "new" economic historians who are concerned with the interplay between urban development and economic growth in the United States.[10] The approach is also in keeping with relatively recent pleas for the injection of social science theory, quantitative methods, and comparative analysis into urban historical research.[11] Most important, the problem dealt with in this work parallels two themes of increasing concern to geographers: the empirical and theoretical investigation of individual cities or groups of cities as systems,[12] and the conceptual and quantitative analysis of past urbanization and urban growth.[13]

The system of cities in the United States has been characterized in some respects by long-term stability. As Carl H. Madden noted, the "apparent conformity of the number and size of cities to the rank-size rule during the period [1790–1950] . . . portrays vividly the sense in which the growth of the system of cities in the United States can be viewed in one of its aspects as having been accompanied by stabilities or regularities."[14] In analyzing the rank-size relations of one hundred major American cities during the period 1790–1890, Fred Lukermann found much evidence of "stability" and noted that as the population spread westward, there was "a stable build-up of pattern," with "very little disruption of the urban configuration . . . except in the South and the extreme Northeastern margin [northern New England]."[15] In each of three regions that were well settled and economically integrated to some degree by 1840, there has been a long-term stability in the family of regionally dominant urban units. In each case, the units that are regionally most prominent today emerged as regional, or urban subsystem, dominants by 1840 at the latest. Moreover, the cities in question were identified as regional leaders before their populations had grown to more than a fraction of the totals now contained within their metropolitan counterparts.

In the Northeast (the area due north of the Potomac exclusive of western Pennsylvania, westernmost New York, and Washington, D.C.), the four largest urban complexes of the present day were already singled out in 1790.[16] At that time New York, Philadelphia, Boston, and Baltimore had populations ranging between .22 and 1.01 percent of their corresponding 1960 metropolitan-area totals. In 1790 these four cities were also the largest in the entire United States system of cities, and they remained so in 1840. In addition, by 1810 Providence and Albany had obtained regional rankings very similar to the fifth and sixth positions held by their 1960 metropolitan-area descendents (Table 1).[17]

In the area encompassed by the valleys of the Ohio and Upper Mississippi, the four largest cities of 1840 were identical with the central cores of the region's four leading metropolitan units in 1960 (Pittsburgh, St. Louis, Cincinnati, and Louisville). In three of the four instances the 1960 regional metropolitan rank had been attained in 1810 or 1820, when their populations ranged between .20 and .55 percent of their respective 1960 metropolitan area totals (Table 2). Likewise, the three largest urban complexes on the shores of Lake Erie as of 1960 (Detroit, Cleveland, and Buffalo) were clearly identified as such by 1830 or 1840, when their populations came to between .24 and .66 percent of their corresponding 1960 metropolitan-area totals (Table 3). The Lake Erie cities and the cities of the Ohio and Upper Mississippi valleys are assigned to different regional urban subsystems because in 1840 there were still limited economic linkages between northern and southern Ohio.[18] Today, the two groups of cities may be regarded as parts of one integrated subsystem.

Only in the South, where by 1840 a well-articulated regional urban subsystem had not begun to crystallize—that is, where interurban informational and economic ties were weak—has the subsequent long-term rank stability of cities not been impressive. In descending order the six largest Southern cities in 1840 were New Orleans, Charleston, Richmond, Mobile, Savannah, and Norfolk. In 1960 the New Orleans metropolitan area ranked behind the Atlanta metropolitan area, and the metropolitan heirs of the other five had all been surpassed by Birmingham and Memphis, as well as by Atlanta. Furthermore, Charleston had tumbled to seventeenth rank and Savannah to twentieth rank among the metropolitan areas currently found in what was the settled portion of the South in 1840.[19]

In light of this data, several questions arise about the growth of large

Table 1. Population and regional rank of leading Northeastern cities—1810, 1840, and 1960

City	1810		1840		1960 (metropolitan area)		A/B
	Population (A)	Rank	Population	Rank	Population (B)	Rank	
New York	100,775[a]	1	348,943[a]	1	14,759,429[b]	1	0.68[c]
Philadelphia	87,303[d]	2	220,423[d]	2	4,342,897	2	2.01[e]
Boston	38,746[f]	4	118,857[f]	3	2,589,301	3	1.50[g]
Baltimore	46,555	3	102,313	4	1,727,023	4	2.70[h]
Providence	10,071	7	23,171	6	816,148[i]	5	1.23
Albany	10,762	6	33,721	5	657,503[j]	6	1.64

Sources: U.S. Bureau of the Census, *Census of Population: 1960,* 1961, vol. I; George Rogers Taylor, "Comment," in David T. Gilchrist ed., *The Growth of the Seaport Cities, 1790–1825* (Charlottesville: University Press of Virginia, 1967), p. 39.
a. Including Brooklyn. New York's suburban population is included, as are Philadelphia's and Boston's, because the adjacent "suburbs," although not yet legally annexed, were physically and functionally integrated with their respective compact central cities.
b. New York and northeast New Jersey metropolitan area.
c. New York in 1790, which was second-ranked regionally and nationally, had a population that was 0.22 percent of its 1960 metropolitan area total.
d. Including Northern Liberties and Southwark (1810 and 1840); Kensington, Moyamensing, and Spring Garden (1840). e. In 1790, when Philadelphia was the nation's largest city, its population was 1.01 percent of its 1960 metropolitan area total.
f. Including Charlestown (1810 and 1840); Cambridge, Roxbury, and Dorchester (1840).
g. In 1790, when Boston's rank was identical with that of 1960, its population was 0.71 percent of its 1960 metropolitan area total.
h. In 1790, when Baltimore's rank was identical with that of 1960, its population was 0.78 percent of its 1960 metropolitan area total
i. Providence-Pawtucket metropolitan area.
j. Albany-Schenectady-Troy metropolitan area.

Table 2. Population and regional rank of leading Ohio and Upper Mississippi Valley cities, 1840 and 1960.

City	1840		1960 (metropolitan area)		
	Population (A)	Rank	Population (B)	Rank	A/B
Pittsburgh	31,204[a]	2	2,405,435	1	0.88[b]
St. Louis	16,469	4	2,060,103	2	0.80
Cincinnati	46,338	1	1,071,624	3	4.32[c]
Louisville	21,210	3	725,139	4	2.92[d]

Source: Census of Population: 1960, vol. I.
a. Including the "suburb" of Allegheny.
b. Pittsburg held its 1960 rank as early as 1810, when its population was 0.20 percent of its 1960 metropolitan area total.
c. As in 1960, Cincinnati held third-rank position in 1810, when its population was 0.24 percent of its 1960 metropolitan area total.
d. Louisville's 1960 rank was identical with its rank in 1820, when its population was 0.55 percent of its 1960 metropolitan area total.

Table 3. Population and regional rank of leading Lake Erie cities, 1840 and 1960.

City	1840		1960 (metropolitan area)		
	Population (A)	Rank	Population (B)	Rank	A/B
Detroit	9,102	2	3,762,360	1	0.24
Cleveland	6,071	3	1,796,595	2	0.34
Buffalo	18,213	1	1,306,957	3	1.39[a]

Source: See Table 2.
a. In 1830, when Buffalo was also the most important city on the eastern Great Lakes, its population was 0.66 percent of its 1960 metropolitan area total.

cities and information circulation. Why did rank stability set in among the largest cities of an urban system or subsystem under conditions of pretelegraphic information circulation? To put it another way, why does large-city rank stability usually set in relatively early in the development of regional urban subsystems and national systems of cities? This dual-faceted problem bears on other more limited questions, such as how and why New York came to dominate the entire American system of cities, or why the pattern of urbanization that had evolved by 1840 was so concentrated.

To answer such questions, I confined my study largely, but not exclusively, to nineteen important cities (Map 1). Although other Northeastern centers, such as Lowell, Portland, and New Haven, were larger than Cleveland and Detroit in 1840 and comparable in size to most other leading cities in the two western urban subsystems, they have never been regional dominants, and their current metropolitan-area populations are far below those of their western counterparts. Thus they are ignored. And although Chicago had by 1840 risen to first rank among cities on or near the western Great Lakes (its 1840 population of 4,470 representing .07 percent of that within its 1960 metropolitan area) and is today an excellent example of perpetuated subsystem dominance, it did not begin to accelerate in growth until the very end of the period under consideration. In 1830 it was no more than a village of about fifty inhabitants, and as late as 1839 its total exports were valued at only $38,843.[20] Therefore, the major Illinois center is also largely ignored.

During the period from 1790 to about 1840, the mechanization and far-flung extension of transportation helped domestic commerce to replace foreign commerce as the primary source of economic growth.[21] The period also witnessed a more than four-fold population increase, at the same time that the settlement pattern was edging westward, spearheaded by the establishment of frontier towns.[22] In 1790, 97.2 percent of the country's 3.9 million inhabitants lived in states bordering the Atlantic, the great bulk of them within fifty miles of the tidewater, whereas in 1840, those same states held only 62.6 percent of the 17.1 million population.[23] Although the much expanded population remained predominantly agricultural in 1840 (89.2 percent dwelling in what census authorities classify as "rural territory"), it had acquired a much higher degree of urbanized economic nodality than in 1790.[24] During the decades 1790–1800, 1800–1810, 1820–1830, and 1830–1840, "the rate of increase in the number of people living in cities was almost double that for the whole population and exceeded the urban growth rate attained in any post-Civil War decade."[25]

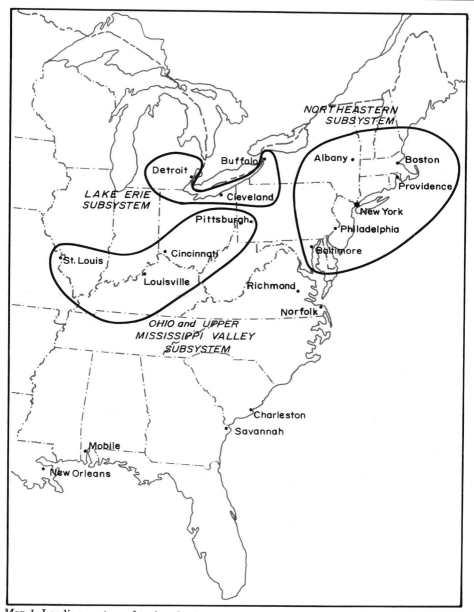

Map 1. Leading centers of regional urban subsystems and other important cities. The boundaries of the subsystems do not represent fixed regional boundaries. The economically integrated regions changed in configuration during the period 1790–1840, sometimes overlapped, and contained zones of regional transition. Rochester, for example, an important city of 1840, was located in a transitional zone between the Northeastern and Lake Erie urban subsystems.

The study opens with a survey of the basic characteristics of pre-telegraphic information circulation. Definitions are provided for two key, interrelated concepts: time-lag spatial biases and contact-array spatial biases in the availability of information. Among the various vehicles for the long-distance flow of information, newspapers are first treated. The types of information carried in the pretelegraphic press are described, as are the spatial biases in the availability of information from Europe. Based on a series of seasonally stratified newspaper samples, an analysis is offered of city-to-city variations in time-lag spatial biases in the availability of information during 1790 and 1794, 1817, and 1841. Locational variations in the availability of journalistic information are identified by comparing newspaper accessibility or "potential" maps for 1790, 1820, and 1840 with population accessibility maps for the same dates.

The role of postal services in the interurban circulation of information is next probed. General trends in the costs, clientele, and expansion of United States postal services are delineated, as are route developments and regional variations in service. Statistics on postal receipts in selected cities during 1822, 1840, and several intervening years both illuminate the urban concentration of the consumption of postal services and show the correlation of absolute urban population growth with absolute increases in the use of the mails. The concentration of foreign mail in New York is also reviewed.

To show the mutual influence of interurban commodity flows and long-distance information flows, the general characteristics of American domestic trade between 1790 and 1840 are given. With the aid of newspaper records of 1820 and 1840 shipping arrivals, matrices are drawn up to show the shipping interaction between the four largest Northeastern cities, between six major South-Atlantic and Gulf-Coastal ports, and between both groups of cities. The composition of freight movements associated with these matrices is described, as are the commodity flows between major Ohio and Mississippi Valley cities, and between the emerging principal ports of Lake Erie. Data on the tonnage of ships enrolled and licensed in the coasting trade supplement the evidence on New York's national dominance of interurban commodity flows.

The question of the effect of interurban travel on long-distance information circulation is not unrelated to that of interurban commodity flows, insofar as much of the travel by common carriers was associated with commerce. Travel-cost trends between 1790 and 1840 are described, as are the clientele of interurban common carriers and the passenger capacity of stagecoaches, sailing vessels, steamboats, and railroads. Annual travel-volume is estimated for selected urban pairs in the Northeast, in the Ohio Valley, and on Lake Erie. Long-run trends in the relative level of urban-pair interaction are discernible in cases where estimates are possible for several dates. The generally low level of interurban travel in the South is touched on, as are the estimated travel volume between New York and Charleston, and New York and Savannah. New York's position as the major node of interurban travel and travel-generated information is explored. A discussion of 1790–1840 interurban travel times includes specific data on travel-time reductions between several urban pairs.

At the heart of the work is a conceptual analysis of why large-city rank stability appears in the development of urban systems and subsystems. A necessary preliminary is a submodel of urban-size growth for the individual American mercantile city. It stresses the impact of transportation developments and agglomeration economies on the differential growth of cities. It is followed by an ideal-typical, nondeterministic model of the process by which large-city rank-stability set in for the United States system of cities and three of its regional subsystems between 1790 and 1840. The basic structure of the model is outlined, as are some of its most pertinent features: nonlocal multiplier effects, increases in commodity and human spatial interaction, and the influence of spatially biased information circulation on the exploitation of business opportunities. Inasmuch as another of the model's major components—the influence of spatially biased information on the diffusion of commercial and industrial innovations—is only partially consistent with existing theory, a revision of interurban diffusion theory is proposed. Disturbances to large-city rank stability and related models are also discussed.

The diffusion component of the model is then treated in a consideration of pretelegraphic patterns of interurban innovation diffusion. Three previous studies of particular pretelegraphic interurban diffusion processes are assessed. Then the diffusion of the cessation of specie payments during the Panic of 1837 is examined, with many of the paths of information and influence flow being identified. Synoptic pictures of several other interurban adoption sequences are exposed, as are prominent features of yet other pretelegraphic interurban diffusion processes. In all of these cases evidence is repeatedly found to support the proposed revision of interurban diffusion theory and thus the large-city rank stability model itself. Supporting evidence is also garnered from an inquiry into the 1790–1840 locational pattern of inventive activity, and from a survey of the data available on the disembarkation points of alien passengers and immigrants between 1817 and 1840. Last, a speculative detour is made on the highly localized diffusion of business attitudes and behavior patterns. The work has possible relevance to present-day locational and regional planning in both developed and newly developing economies.

The emphasis throughout this study on process rather than on unique urban history requires that broad conjectural elements be occasionally introduced where some readers might prefer extensive documentation of a single case. The process orientation also requires that conceptual loans be made from economics, social psychology, and the behavioral sciences in general. Such a departure from the groves of traditional academic geography is in keeping with the research trends of the times. The last decade or so has seen an almost complete obliteration of whatever clearcut boundaries existed between the various social and behavioral sciences. There has been an increasing tendency to employ identical or similar concepts and methodologies, and disciplinary cores are now more readily defined by the problems they select for study rather than by their monopoly over any theoretical or methodological territory. Hence, the process-oriented problem treated in these pages is clearly geographical, particularly insofar as it relates to the more general question of how and why human activities arrange themselves locationally as they do.

Pretelegraphic Information Circulation: A Prelude

In large cities there is more communication, both orally and by means of the press, among men possessed of knowledge, than in sparsely populated districts.
—Thomas Cooper (1826)

"What hath God wrought?" With the transmission of that message by Morse's electromagnetic telegraph over a line between Baltimore and Washington on May 24, 1844, a new chapter commenced in communications history. Prior to that date the long-distance movement of news and information was synonymous with human spatial interaction. Even the information contained in newspapers, journals, books, and other printed matter could circulate from place to place only if borne by foot or horse, or carried in vehicles or vessels under human guidance. In fact, the break with these slow-paced conditions was neither ubiquitous nor abrupt, for the diffusion of a skeleton network of telegraphic lines across the United States itself consumed many years.[1]

THE SPEED OF INFORMATION FLOWS

In an age when television images can be transmitted from the face of the moon through the enormous void of space to millions of instantaneously receiving sets, it may be difficult to comprehend fully the slowness with which even the most important information circulated in the United States and elsewhere before 1844. It is estimated that within half an hour 68 percent of the American population was aware of President John F. Kennedy's assassination.[2] In sharp contrast, a time lag of seven days occurred between George Washington's death on December 14, 1799, in Alexandria, Va., and publication of that news in New York City (Map 1.1).[3] The movement of significant news over the seas was no quicker in pretelegraphic times. For example, on December 24, 1814, the peace treaty ending the War of 1812 was signed. Two weeks later, on January 8, 1815, the battle of New Orleans was fought. Word of the latter event reached New York after twenty-seven days, while knowledge of the treaty was not received there from London until five days later, on February 11, or forty-nine days after the fact.

The sluggish pace of information flow becomes even more striking as one moves further back into eighteenth-century history. Repeal of the Stamp Act received royal confirmation on March 18, 1766, but the news did not reach New York until sixty-five days later. Reports of the battles of Lexington and Concord on April 19, 1775, although relayed by "express," did not reach New York for four days and were not published until April 25 in Philadelphia, May 9 in Charleston, and May 31 in Savannah.[4]

Although by modern standards information crawled over distances before the coming of the telegraph, there were undeniable advances in the speed of message movement during the 1790–1840 period. Since the long-distance spread of information was synonymous with human spatial interaction, the speed of transmission at any given date was a function of existing transportation technology. Thus, the construction of turnpikes, the adoption of the steamboat for passenger and freight purposes, and the initial diffusion of the railroad in the 1830s contributed to the increased rapidity of information dissemination. For instance, by 1830 it was possible for relay "expresses" to convey President Andrew Jackson's State of the Union address, with what was then viewed as "amazing speed," from Washington to New York in a record-breaking 15.5 hours, to Boston in over 31 hours, to Charleston in just under three days, and to New Orleans in approximately six days (Map 1.2). Seven years later the employment of new and speedier transportation facilities along some route segments reduced the express-delivery time of another presidential address to 11 hours to New York and about 24 hours to Boston.[5]

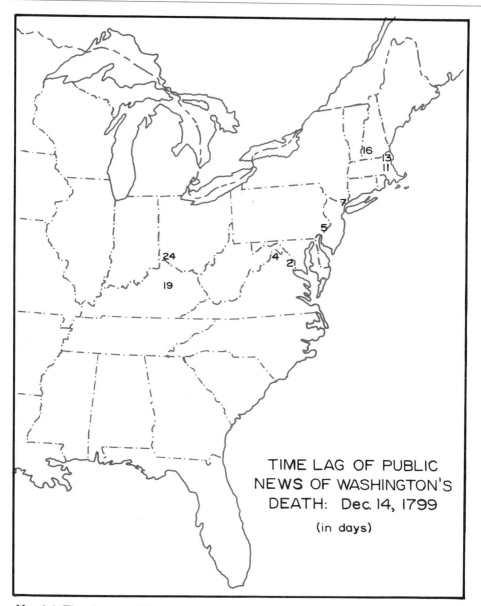

Map 1.1. Time lag in public news of George Washington's death, Dec. 14, 1799 (in days).

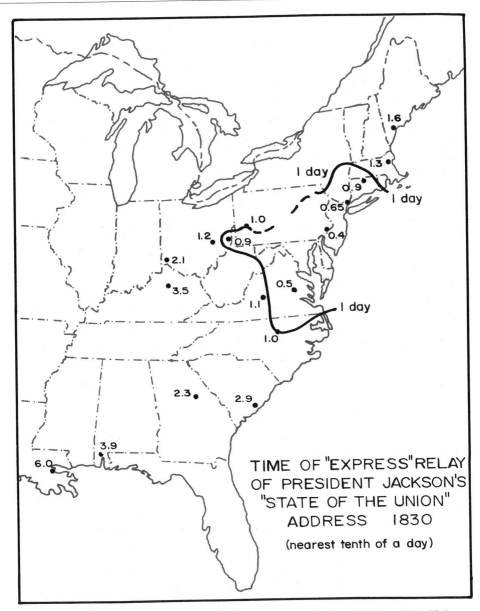

Map 1.2. Time lag in express relay of President Andrew Jackson's State of the Union address in 1830 (to nearest tenth of day).

SPATIAL BIASES IN INFORMATION AVAILABILITY

Regardless of the state of transport technology at any date, pre-telegraphic information circulation throughout the 1790–1840 period was characterized by a high degree of "spatial bias," that is, by an uneven and irregular as well as slow pattern of movement. The concept of spatial biases in information availability carries at least two connotations. One connotation springs from the time lag, or time-consuming, attributes of pretelegraphic information circulation. Hence, at a specific point in time (t_x) after an event that had occurred at an earlier time (t_e), public or private word of it was potentially available only to individuals dwelling within the irregularly shaped area around the source node over which it was feasible to travel or to ship mail and newspapers during the interval $t_x - t_e$. Therefore, the set of places where individuals could obtain news of the event more quickly than the average length of time required for all places in the circulation system can be said to have had a positive bias in potential information availability for that news, as well as for any other messages of identical locational origin. By the same token, the set of places where receipt absorbed a greater than average length of time can be described as having had a negative bias in potential information availability from the origin in question.

Pretelegraphic spatial biases in information availability can also be viewed from the perspective of specific places or cities. The resident population of every place in late eighteenth- and early nineteenth-century America had a unique array of nonlocal contacts. The aggregate nonlocal contact array, or information field, of an individual city dictated that its inhabitants were more likely to be exposed to non-redundant or new information from the places, normally nearby, with which contact frequency was high. The same city was less likely to acquire previously unencountered information from the places, normally relatively distant, with which contact frequency was low. Thus, for any given city, positive biases in information availability existed for the set of places with which it had an above-average frequency, or probability, of contact. Likewise, for any given city, negative biases in information availability existed for the set of places with which it had a below-average or zero contact probability.

Pretelegraphic informational spatial biases of the time lag and contact array varieties were often related to one another. In short, time was consumed as information progressed from one city to another through a network of dyadic linkages, or contact array elements. That is, the time lag between information origin in one city and receipt in another was related to the contact array of both places as well as of a varying number of intervening places. Consequently, the greater the frequency of direct or indirect contact between two cities at a given distance, the shorter the average time lag of information receipt vis-à-vis other places at the same distance.

Under both pretelegraphic and modern communications technologies there are three major categories of information circulation and acquisition that can be spatially biased. First is private information, or all information conveyed by person-to-person contacts, including face-to-face encounters and written exchanges (as well as telephone calls under modern conditions). Second is public information, or all messages circulated through printed media, spoken communication to an audience, and government sources (as well as radio, television, and film under modern conditions). By definition, information of this type reaches large numbers of people "without having its meaning altered by some third party (or parties)."[6] However, public information is frequently received in distorted form by individuals through a "two-step flow." That is, messages and "ideas, often, seem to flow *from* . . . print *to* opinion leaders and *from them* [as private information] to the less active sections of the population."[7] The third category is visual information, or individual visual observations and perceptions. Such information circulates in the sense that individuals carry it about with them from place to place. Visual information may also circulate as a result of its conversion to private or public information, in which case it is subject to time lag and contact array spatial biases. Otherwise, visual information regarding a physically fixed phenomenon is viewable as spatially biased insofar as its probability of acquisition decreases with increased distance from the source location.

All human decision-making behavior is to some extent dependent on the deciding unit's stock of information, whether intentionally or unintentionally accumulated. For all actors—whether individuals, coalitions, or organizations—can choose only from alternatives of which they are aware. Pretelegraphic spatial biases in information availability thus had far-reaching ramifications for the population growth of the nineteen regionally dominant cities focused on here. (Table 1.1). Certainly the pronounced time lag and contact array biases associated with pretelegraphic public, private, and visual information must have affected the economic actions and locational decision-making of urban merchants, investors, and industrial entrepreneurs. Theoretically, under

Table 1.1. Population growth of selected regionally dominant centers, 1790–1840.

Regional center	1790	1800	1810	1820	1830	1840
New York[a]	33,131	60,515	100,775	130,881	214,995	348,943
Philadelphia[b]	44,096	61,559	87,303	108,809	161,271	220,423
Boston[c]	18,320	24,937	38,746	54,024	85,568	118,857
Baltimore	13,503	26,514	46,555	62,738	80,620	102,313
Albany	3,498	5,289	10,762	12,630	24,209	33,721
Providence	6,380	7,614	10,071	11,767	16,833	23,171
Cincinnati	—	—	2,540	9,642	24,831	46,338
Pittsburgh[d]	—	1,565	4,768	7,248	15,369	31,204
Louisville	200	359	1,357	4,012	10,341	21,210
St. Louis	—	—	—	—	4,977	16,469
Buffalo	—	—	1,508	2,095	8,668	18,213
Detroit	—	—	—	1,422	2,222	9,102
Cleveland	—	—	--	606	1,076	6,071
New Orleans	—	—	17,242	27,176	46,082	102,193
Charleston	16,359	18,824	24,711	24,780	30,289	29,261
Richmond	3,761	5,737	9,735	12,067	16,060	20,153
Mobile	—	—	—	—	3,194	12,672
Savannah	—	5,146	5,215	7,523	7,303	11,214
Norfolk	2,959	6,926	9,193	8,478	9,814	10,920

Source: Census of Population: 1960, vol. 1; Taylor, "Comment," p. 39.
a. Including Brooklyn (1810–1840).
b. Including Northern Liberties and Southwark (1790–1840); Kensington and Spring Garden (1820–1840); Moyamensing (1830–1840).
c. Including Charlestown (1810–1840); Roxbury (1820–1840); Cambridge and Dorchester (1830–1840).
d. Including Allegheny (1830–1840).

pretelegraphic conditions the relative distribution of a particular city's trade origins and destinations is a surrogate for its relative distribution of nonlocal economic informational contacts in general.[8] This is so because pretelegraphic long-distance trade was almost always the outcome of information acquisition (through the press, mails, or business travel), while at the same time it served as a generator of information flows (again through the press, mails, or business travel). In particular, when trade was undertaken at the initiative of a purchasing importer, retailer, wholesaler, or industrial unit, the actual commodity shipment had to be preceded by some knowledge of and information exchange with the supply source. Similarly, when trade was initiated either by a middleman exporter of agricultural or industrial items, or by an urban production unit, the actual movement of goods had to be preceded by some knowledge of and information exchange with the marketing outlet. Moreover, pretelegraphic long-distance trading vessels themselves contributed to economic information flows by carrying letters and newspapers both privately and for the official posts.

Economic historians usually are justified in describing American regional or urban growth between 1790 and 1840 primarily in terms of trade. Yet such trade was as much the outcome of information flows as it was the generator of them. Therefore, in order to emphasize the intimate feedback mechanisms between interurban flows, interurban trade, and large-city growth, trade patterns are not immediately considered on the ensuing pages.

2

The Long-Distance Flow of Information
Through Newspapers

The most prominent activity in the cities of the early 1800s in addition to trade
was printing and publishing. Newspapers had developed to serve the needs of trade
for communications and announcements.
—Dorothy S. Brady

Aside from occasional journals, pamphlets, broadsides, and government publications, newspapers were the only regular pretelegraphic
communications medium through which news of distant origin could be
made locally available in the form of public information. Conversely,
newspapers were the only regular means by which locally originating
news could be disseminated as public information. Despite their near
monopoly of nonlocal public information, as well as their mounting
number and total circulation, newspapers had a very limited number of
subscribers and direct purchasers throughout the pretelegraphic age.
Although the diffusion of the daily paper and the penny press resulted
in a marked circulation increase during the 1830s (Table 2.1), as late as
1840 the number of newspaper copies encountered per capita during
the course of a year for the country as a whole was apparently less than
nine.[1] This figure, even if adjusted upward by the elimination of children and illiterates, adds significance to then existing newspaper information time-lags and the geographic concentration of publication.

TYPES AND FUNCTIONS OF INFORMATION CARRIED

"News from overseas was the great staple of colonial papers."[2] Early
eighteenth-century newspapers devoted little space to colonial domestic

Table 2.1. Growth of United States newspaper publication, 1790-1840.

Data category	1790	1800	1810	1820	1828	1835	1840	1840/1790
U.S. population (thousands)	3,929	5,297	7,224	9,618	12,237	15,003	17,120	4.4
Newspapers published	92	235	371	512	861	1,258	1,404	15.3
Newspaper editions per week[a]	147	389	549	759	—	—	2,281	15.5
Daily newspapers	8	24	26	42	49[b]	—	138	17.3
Annual circulation (thousands)	3,975[c]	12–13,000	24,577[d]	50,000[e]	68,118	90,361	147,500[f]	37.1
Annual newspaper copies per capita	1.0	2.4[g]	3.4	5.2	5.6	6.0	8.6	8.6

Source: U.S. Bureau of the Census, Historical Statistics of the United States, Colonial Times to 1957, 1960, p. 7; The American Almanac and Repository of Useful Knowledge, for the Year 1840 (Boston, 1840), p. 69; NWR 20, no. 25 (Aug. 18, 1821), 387; 47, no. 12 (Nov. 22, 1834), 184; "Daniel Hewett's List of Newspapers and Periodicals in the United States in 1828," Proceedings of the American Antiquarian Society 44 (1934), 365-396; Frederic Hudson, Journalism in the United States, from 1690 to 1872 (New York, 1873), pp. 770, 772; Alfred McClung Lee, The Daily Newspaper in America: The Evolution of a Social Instrument (New York: Macmillan, 1937), pp. 16, 718; S. N. D. North, History and Present Condition of the Newspaper and Periodical Press of the United States (Washington, D.C., 1884), pp. 45, 47.

a. Dailies were given a weight of six; triweeklies, three; semiweeklies, two; and weeklies, one.
b. Data probably incomplete.
c. Data actually for 1789.
d. This estimate, like most of the others in this row, is probably wanting in accuracy. However, it is consistent with a report that placed 1811 newspaper circulation at a total of 25,222,200. NWR 1, no. 7 (Oct. 19, 1811), 116-117.
e. The lowest figure of an 1821 estimate of 50-60,000,000.
f. This is a crude estimate arrived at by averaging an estimate of 100,000,000 in The American Almanac and an estimate of 195,838,673 in Hudson, Journalism in the United States, p. 772. The first figure seems conservative in view of the rapid growth of the penny press between 1835 and 1840, but the second was inflated by the inclusion of the annual circulation of 227 periodicals not classified as newspapers by the 1840 U.S. Census.
g. Based on an estimated total annual circulation of 12,500,000.

matters, and although Richard Merritt's content analysis of six colonial papers revealed an "increasing interest in things and events American" from 1735 to 1775, English and Continental news continued to dominate the columns of the post-Revolutionary War press.[3] For example, in 1794 only a few issues of one major Philadelphia paper had more column space allocated to American news than to European news.[4] Typically, the front page of a 1797 issue of a New York paper gave three of its five columns to "European Intelligence" and only a half-column to domestic news. For the next fifteen years news journals, whether published in Boston, Philadelphia, New Orleans, or elsewhere, continued to be primarily occupied with European matters.[5] Given the role of overseas trade in the national economy and the consequent concern with the state of foreign markets, shipping, and politics, the perpetual prominence of European items in the press of the Federalist era is understandable.

The ratio of foreign to national news in the American press through the first decade of the nineteenth century was only one symptom of the unintegrated nature of the domestic communications network to that date, or of the informational isolation of distant cities from one another.[6] For most of the eighteenth century this isolation was so great that even local news at times reached England before nearby colonies. However, with the War of 1812, which crippled foreign trade, American communications entered adolescence and began to develop into a well-integrated system. "The running story of that war, with its alternating defeats and victories, brought home to [newspaper] editors and readers the importance of domestic news."[7] Thereafter, domestic affairs more and more overshadowed accounts from Europe. By 1841 major dailies in New York, Philadelphia, and Boston made relatively few references to foreign developments. These same dailies set the pattern for most newspapers in the remainder of the country.

At various times the pretelegraphic newspapers allocated much space to literary items, political questions, war coverage, governmental proclamations, measures against yellow fever and cholera epidemics, and, in the case of the penny press of the mid- and late-1830s, racy and sensational matters. However, in terms of their impact on the economy in general and on urban locational decision-making in particular, three other characteristics of newspapers were especially noteworthy. These were their advertising function, their inclusion of shipping intelligence, and their listing of prices current and other commercial statistics.

Advertising. Initially, colonial newspapers contained very little in the way of advertising. But as population grew and the commerce of the Atlantic seaport towns expanded, advertising took command: "particularly after 1760, papers with as much as fifty percent advertising rapidly spread." The country's first daily, the *Pennsylvania Packet and Daily Advertiser*, set the pattern for its successors by giving advertising ten of the sixteen columns in its initial issue in 1784.[8]

During the half-century following 1790 the multiplying number of merchants, tradesmen, and manufacturers seeking new local and non-local markets caused the role of advertising in newspapers to be amplified both relatively and absolutely. At the onset of this period the name *Advertiser* began to appear frequently on newspaper mastheads. By 1800 twenty of the twenty-four dailies in existence bore it somewhere in their title. In the 1790s commercial announcements one column wide and mostly of a few lines in length usually occupied at least half of the four pages of such representative papers as Philadelphia's *Gazette of the United States and Daily Evening Advertiser* and the *American Minerva and New York Evening Advertiser.* As many as 350 insertions appeared per issue in the New York dailies of 1795.[9] After 1800, "some of the mercantile papers commonly sold four-fifths of their space, and sometimes nine-tenths of it; while even the [more] political papers were occasionally three-fourths advertising." For instance, *Poulson's American Daily Advertiser* of Philadelphia in 1800–1839 "averaged roughly twenty-two columns of advertisements in a 28-column sheet," and the *Morning Courier and New-York Enquirer* "frequently went to eight pages on Saturdays in 1829 in order to accommodate fifty columns of advertisements with a 56-column sheet." Three years later it was boasted that "the newspapers of the city of New York contain more advertisements than ALL the newspapers in Great Britain and Ireland!"[10] Very soon after their commencement the penny papers had 75 percent or more of their column space in advertisements.

The mounting demand for advertising space led simultaneously to a marked increase in newspaper size. Thus, the more commercial papers of the late 1830s became known as "blanket sheets," having eight or ten three-inch-wide columns, while their eighteenth-century fore-runners had measured only nine inches in width and fifteen inches in length.[11]

The cascade of advertisements in the early nineteenth-century mercantile dailies of the seaports included importers' announcements; listings of auctions, cargo-space availability, ship departures, and real estate sales; the offerings of commodity brokers; and the personal requests of lenders and borrowers. Other papers printed similar advertisements but inclined more to the insertions of retailers of dry goods, food, and other merchandise; patent medicine vendors; artisans and craftsmen seeking orders; and stage line (later railroad) companies making known their schedules and rates. Whatever the typical advertisement of a few lines referred to, "it is difficult for the modern business man to picture [the positive] results" obtained in the absence of competing electronic advertising media.[12]

Shipping Intelligence. From their inception, the first papers of Boston, Philadelphia, and New York devoted much of their limited domestic space to maritime reports. Such reports usually consisted of a few lines of local customs house entries and a dated list of shipping arrivals and clearances at other ports. Shipping intelligence of this nature was highly sporadic, irregular in composition, and often inaccurate, particularly with reference to shipping destinations. The press, for example, "could only report the destination listed at the customs house; but . . . ships often failed to dispose of their cargo at their first port of call and took it elsewhere to seek a more advantageous market."[13]

The prosperity of foreign trade during the 1790s led to an alteration in the journalistic treatment of marine intelligence. Coverage became more reliable and thorough, if still wanting, in certain papers that increasingly specialized in such information, such as Boston's *New-England Palladium*, the *Boston Gazette*, and the *New York Gazette*. Subsequent to the War of 1812 and the renewal of trade, shipping intelligence received yet greater emphasis in some papers. For example, in 1818 the *Pittsburgh Gazette* began a regular column reporting the arrival and departure dates of steamboats and other vessels. In 1815 the *New York Shipping and Commercial List* was founded, a paper whose primary function was the provision of shipping intelligence and whose pages provided the most detailed reports on nonlocal shipping arrivals and clearances available anywhere in the United States throughout the remainder of the pretelegraphic era. Moreover, with the *New York Journal of Commerce* and other New York dailies competing fiercely in the compilation of marine news, an 1830 newspaper editor could boast that New Yorkers "take it for granted that there is no other place in the country where the business of collecting ship-news is carried on with so much energy and industry as in the port of New York." In fact, he doubted "if any place in the world could rival it in this respect."[14]

Prices Current and Commercial Statistics. Closely related to the publishing of marine intelligence was the listing of wholesale prices and other commercial statistics of potential use to the mercantile community. Once again some of the earliest newspaper publishers in the colonial seaports were inclined to provide information of this kind.

Here, too, the upswing of trade in the 1790s, and the consequent increase in demand for information by importers, exporters, brokers, and other middlemen, engendered a more extensive and specialized journalistic treatment. Not only was more space allocated in already existing papers, but a relatively rapid succession of new journals was born whose primary function was to provide price quotations and other commercial information. For instance, in 1795 the *Boston Price-Current and Marine Intelligencer* made its first appearance, in 1796 the *New York Price-Current* was founded, in 1803 the *Baltimore Price-Current* was issued, and in 1804 came *Hope's Philadelphia Price-Current*. By 1815 these and other Atlantic coastal journals had largely taken the place of "long letters describing the state of the market and of printed prices current, both of which services the larger mercantile houses had furnished to their correspondents."[15]

As the economy of the Ohio and Mississippi valleys began to flourish, newspapers there also began to publish commodity prices. As early as 1801 the Cincinnati and Pittsburgh press provided New Orleans and Natchez prices. Local price lists, if somewhat crude, appeared with increasing regularity after 1816 in the weeklies of Pittsburgh, Louisville, and Cincinnati. However, it was not until 1825 that a specialized commercial daily was functioning in Cincinnati. In New Orleans current price quotations first became available in 1803 in *The Union or New Orleans Advertiser and Price-Current*.[16]

SPATIAL BIASES IN THE AVAILABILITY OF EUROPEAN INFORMATION

After about 1750 the few newspapers of the colonial seaports were usually three to six months behind in their reportage from Continental Europe. Just how great the hiatus was in any specific instance depended in part on the season, for North Atlantic navigation was at a virtual standstill during January and February, and in part on the whims of the prevailing westerly winds, which the small sailing vessels of the period were forced to combat by tacking, thereby adding several hundred miles to their voyage.

By 1790, the gap between newsworthy Continental happenings, for example, and their publication in Philadelphia newspapers was still in the vicinity of three months or more (Table 2.2). At this juncture most

Table 2.2. Average time lag between foreign events and Philadelphia newspaper publication, 1790.

City	Average time lag (days)
Liverpool	65.5
London	67.5
Brussels	76.0
Paris	80.8
Berlin	83.0
Dublin	87.5
Vienna	90.0
Warsaw	90.0
Stockholm	91.0
Copenhagen[a]	103.0
Madrid[a]	105.0
Constantinople[a]	147.0
Canton[a]	160.0

Source: Pennsylvania Packet and Daily Advertiser and the *Pennsylvania Journal and the Weekly Advertiser*, 1790 (48 seasonally stratified issues).
a. One datum only.

European news received in the United States had first been funneled through London, which in turn was generally two to six weeks behind in getting word from the various Continental capitals. Later, in the 1820s and 1830s, when the cotton trade with France assumed significance, the role of Paris as a news-source node was enhanced. Although certain vessels were by then somewhat larger and swifter—packets from Liverpool and London (Portsmouth) to New York averaging less than 38 days per westbound voyage from 1818 to 1832, whereas previously the average Liverpool-to-New York voyage had required 49.4 days— there were still occasions when eight or more winter weeks would pass in major cities without information from England. Thus, Hezekiah Niles complained from Baltimore in 1829: "This is the 17th January, and our [latest] European date is of the 9th November—or sixty-eight days since. We believe that never, since the establishment of the New York packets, have we been so long without news from Europe." And in 1840 his successor groaned: "We are nearly two months without information from Europe. Vessels from there have had long passages."[17]

Entry Points. By definition, all particular news from Europe arrived by ship, and therefore at some seaport, whence it spread to that seaport's hinterland and to other seaports and their hinterlands. Normally the distance factor was not particularly important in determining which place or places were most likely to receive any specific piece of European intelligence first. This was so since there is only a 13.6 percent difference between the distance of the shortest natural route from Liverpool to Portland and that from Liverpool to Norfolk; and all intervening ports along the Atlantic seaboard, with the exception of Baltimore, have considerably smaller distance-to-England differences. Given the chance addition to voyage lengths and times by vagaries of the weather, with everything else being equal, the probability of a port being first to acquire any specific news account was in large measure a function of the number of vessels arriving there per annum from Europe, divided by the total number of vessels arriving per annum from Europe at all points between Norfolk and Portland. In other words, the probability of a Northeastern or Mid-Atlantic port being an information entry point was essentially tied to its volume of foreign trade. However, this does not mean it is necessary to assume that all ships from Europe carried the same news in newspaper or private-information form, but merely that all such ships always carried some news in one form or another. Moreover, there were exceptions, such as the relatively infrequent winter situations when Charleston was first to be informed of some event by a vessel that either had crossed the Atlantic south of the more heavily trafficked lanes or was arriving from the West Indies.

If the probability generalization is accepted, then New York's informational superiority with respect to European matters as measured by the volume of yearly ship arrivals from Europe, even if not as pronounced as subsequently, appears to have been of much earlier origin than the normally accepted date of 1818. Although the data are not totally reliable, from 1796 the net revenue derived from duties on imported goods was greater in New York than in Philadelphia and all other ports. Furthermore, New York was responsible for the highest collection of import duties in 1792 and 1794; its shipping tonnage registered in foreign trade surpassed that of Philadelphia in 1794; and as early as 1791, 718 vessels from foreign ports entered New York's harbor, whereas only 595 sailed into Philadelphia.[18] By the first few years of the nineteenth century New York's import supremacy was well established. Import duties netted in New York for the four-year period ending March 31, 1805, amounted to $12.9 million, or roughly 30 percent of the total for all ports north of North Carolina. Comparable figures for New York's leading competitors were $7.8 million for Philadelphia, $6.4 million for Boston, and $3.9 million for Baltimore.[19] One decade later, with the British "dumping" goods accumulated during the War of 1812, the probability that New York would be the first to receive news from Europe had been raised to at least 44 in 100, if import duties are a valid indicator.[20]

Shortly thereafter, a new factor entered the equation, when New York's probability of gaining European intelligence before others began considerably to surpass its domination of the nation's import trade. Even though the city accounted for well over 50 percent of the annual value of all imports from 1830 through 1842, after 1822, and perhaps as early as 1818, New York was first to come into possession of the vast bulk of economic, political and cultural information arriving from England and the Continent.[21] This was primarily, but not entirely, owing to the growth of the city's packet services.

On January 4, 1818, the "Black Ball" line commenced a four-vessel monthly scheduled service between New York and Liverpool. In 1822, two rival lines went into operation on the same route. The Black Ball operators responded by adding four ships to their line and increasing the scheduled departures to two per month from each terminus. The total number of packet sailings per month thus stood at four each from both New York and Liverpool. The year 1822 also saw the initiation of packet service between New York and Le Havre. Thereafter, packet operations from the nation's "emporium" to Liverpool, Le Havre, and London grew steadily (Table 2.3).

Until 1838 and the coming of transatlantic steamship service, the New York packets—carrying "general news for the press; special information affecting the price of cotton or flour; regular mails; and official dispatches," —were able to provide the city with a near monopoly of first information encounters. One reason, other than speed, was that the Black Ball and other New York packet endeavors introduced the "line" to ocean navigation, "with several vessels under coordinated private management sailing in regular succession on specified dates between specified ports."[22] Hence, the packets offered a regularity, punctuality of departure, and reliability never previously known in the shipping world. Those consigning newspapers, mail, or any other manner of dispatch for transport across the Atlantic on a New York-bound packet were assured of precisely when their information would leave, as well as

Table 2.3. Growth of New York packet services, 1818–1840 (in ships).

| Year | Destination of ships | | |
	Liverpool	London	Le Havre
1818	4	0	0
1822	16	0	0
1825	16	4	12
1830	16	8	12
1835	16	10	14
1840	22	12	18

Source: Albion, *Square-Riggers on Schedule: The New York Sailing Packets to England, France and the Cotton Ports,* (Princeton: Princeton University Press, 1938), pp. 20-22, 33, 274; *NWR* 58, no. 2 (Mar. 14, 1840), 32.

where it would initially arrive. Those consigning information to any other westward sailing ship endured a considerable element of uncertainty as to when it would start on its way, as well as what would be its first port of call. In short, once the dependability and frequency of New York packet sailings became established, American importers and European exporters of information had ample reason to employ the ships of the Black Ball and its sister lines rather than other vessels.

Another key factor of the packet lines that contributed to New York's position of privilege regarding European news was the limited scope of packet development in competing ports. In 1822, for example, Thomas Cope organized a four-ship line with once-a-month service from Philadelphia to Liverpool; but by 1835 there were still only twelve arrivals of American ships at Liverpool from Philadelphia, all of them Cope packets, "which were apparently sufficient for the entire direct trade." The first Boston-sponsored packet venture to Liverpool, dating from 1823, met with even less success. "The lack of adequate return cargoes soon led to the failure both of this line and its successor, established in 1827, for the ships were often sent to Liverpool by way of Charleston in order to pick up cargoes, and that destroyed the regularity of service.[23] Although during their relatively brief existence the Boston packets were occasionally the first to bring news to American shores, this occurred only under exceptional circumstances, because of the much greater frequency of service to New York. Other ports were handicapped by having no vessels whatsoever plying the waters of the Atlantic.

The aggressiveness of New York journalists compounded the European news advantages provided them by the packet lines. Since the last decade of the eighteenth century some newspapers in Boston and New York had sought to expedite the publication of foreign news items by going out by boat to meet the incoming vessels and collect whatever newspapers and private information were available. In the early and mid-1820s, the demand for market information increased and the newspaper competition intensified. By 1830 there were forty-seven New York City newspapers, eleven of which were dailies. Thus, New York publishers began to take more elaborate measures to speed up the receipt of European reports. Wishing not only to score a scoop over competitors but also to keep abreast of developments, publishers were reluctant to await delivery of foreign newspapers and information to the city, because "even though a packet might have made a quick crossing, it was not uncommon for her to be delayed by fogs, calms, or adverse winds in the vicinity of Sandy Hook for many hours or even for several days. Consequently, the newsmen sent out small, swift craft to meet the incoming packets and take off the papers. Frequently a packet's news appeared in the New York papers two or three days before the ship herself finally reached the upper harbor."[24] The contest for breaking European news in New York escalated in the late 1820s and 1830s. Coalitions were formed among various newspapers in order to share the costs of retrieval; larger and swifter "clipper" schooners were built and purchased explicitly for the purpose; and these and other craft ventured as far as eighty or one-hundred miles out to sea to meet the incoming packets. In contrast, Philadelphia newspapers became so accustomed to being fed European fare by the New York press that, when weather conditions in the spring of 1830 considerably delayed the New York packet arrivals, no effort was made to secure information from a newly arrived overseas vessel tied up in the Delaware just below the city.[25]

In New York more than in any other American city, semaphoric "telegraphs" were employed. One of their main functions was to aid in the relay of information from packet to newspaper office. During the opening years of the nineteenth century New York merchants made use of "signal poles" on the eastern end of Staten Island "to give information of vessels arriving from sea."[26] In 1815 improvements were made in the signal pole operation, which had been temporarily halted by the War of 1812, and in 1821 packet operators put up a semaphore at the same site. "This semaphore . . . with various movements of its arms could spell out whole messages visible to the watcher with his telescope at the Battery." Semaphore relays were later extended to Sandy Hook and used to announce the approach of news boats. Crowds would subsequently surround the office of the *New York Journal of Commerce* or some other paper that operated news boats and await the appearance of an extra. The growing role of the semaphores in bringing news to New York is reflected by a report that the number of "telegraphed" vessels grew from 799 in 1824–1825 to 1,922 in 1833–1834.[27]

When the *Sirius*, *Great Western*, and other transatlantic steamers began entering New York waters in 1838, the relay system of packets and news schooners quickly became obsolete. On westward-bound passages, packet ships found it almost impossible to keep apace of the steamers. In 1839 the time consumed by 58 Liverpool-to-New York packet crossings ranged from 22 to 48 days, while the length of 15 steamship voyages from England varied from 13 to 21.5 days.[28] The speed of the steam-powered vessels caused the newspapers to forsake their schooners and to replace them with small boats, since they needed to venture no further than the Quarantine in the city's harbor. The steamers having usurped the informational function of the packets, further emphasized New York's role as the gateway for European news. Not until 1840, when Cunard's North American Royal Mail Steam Packet Company began to serve Boston, was there a significant break in the long-standing pattern of time-lag spatial biases in European information availability that so favored New York.

Domestic Circulation of Foreign News. Once in New York, information of foreign origin circulated outward from that city in a manner which was indistinguishable from the flow patterns associated with information of local origin or receipt. The ideal-typical, but by no means invariable, spatial pattern of foreign news dissemination from New York is summarized easily. (Map 2.1). Daily and other newspapers in Boston, Philadelphia, Baltimore, and much later the major Southern ports would reproduce verbatim or paraphrase a foreign story from a New York paper that normally had been secured through the mails. For example, as late as 1840 much of the foreign news carried by the *Philadelphia Public Ledger* was reprinted from the *New-York Herald* or the *New York Journal of Commerce*. More or less simultaneously, the press of Albany, New Haven, Hartford, and other urban places in New York's immediate hinterland would similarly copy their New York counterparts. In the second round, weeklies and other newspapers in the immediate hinterland of Boston, Philadelphia, Baltimore, and much later the major Southern ports would reproduce the item from the pages of a first-round recipient, except in instances where the mails allowed

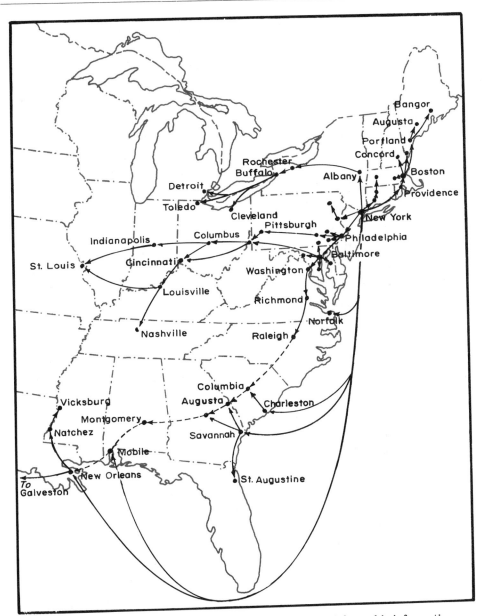

Map 2.1. Ideal-typical flow sequence of foreign and other pretelegraphic information from New York newspapers to papers in the rest of the country. Path directions do not necessarily represent actual routes. The trans-Allegheny pattern is for the 1820s and after. The dashed line from Raleigh to New Orleans represents the principal southern postal route, which gained in importance as a purveyor of New York newspaper information toward the close of the pretelegraphic era.

direct usage of a New York paper's account. Not long afterward, inland papers further south along the main postal route would mimic the New York journals. Sometime thereafter, newspapers in Pittsburgh, Cincinnati, Detroit, and other rapidly emerging cities to the west of the Alleghenies would reiterate the words of a New York, Philadelphia, or Baltimore daily. This was especially true in the 1820s and after, when the National Road and the spreading network of stage lines and canals eased the westward movement of information. By 1830 it could be stated: "European advices—from Havre in thirty days, and Liverpool in twenty-seven days, were lately received at Cincinnati via New York and Baltimore. A little while ago, the journey from Baltimore to Cincinnati, would have occupied as much time."[29] In the final stage, the smaller inland papers of the Middle West and South would ape the journals of the centers within whose sphere of influence they were situated, providing that the mails had not permitted direct plagiarism of a New York or other East Coast daily.

The increasing dependency of large-city papers on the New York press for European news is illustrated by the sources cited in *Niles' Weekly Register*, which was published in Baltimore from 1811 until the coming of the telegraph, except for a brief 1837–1839 interlude in Washington, D.C. In its first few years the paper's foreign affairs section was often preceded by a comment such as: "Just before this number went to press, we received London dates, via New York."[30] Although such references occurred over 50 percent of the time, they were by no means universal. Boston and Philadelphia were sometimes credited with providing information. On rarer occasions, Norfolk and Charleston were given as sources. Both during the confusion of the blockade in the War of 1812 and the years immediately following, it was most unusual for vessels arriving in Baltimore to be cited. After the commencement of packet operations in New York, reference to other cities noticeably declined. By 1820, an issue could state: "We take this opportunity to remark that on the present occasion, as is very often the case, we are chiefly indebted to the *New-York Commercial Advertiser* for this portion of our matter."[31] As the number of packet ships sailing to Le Havre increased in the mid 1820s, it became customary to observe that "London and Paris papers of late dates have been received at New York." Thereafter, virtually all foreign affairs material was attributed to the New York newspapers and packets, with increasing references to the "copious" volume of information received.

SPATIAL BIASES IN THE AVAILABILITY OF DOMESTIC INFORMATION

In colonial times even the major seaports existed in a state of extreme isolation with respect to domestic public information. For example, only fourteen and thirty-nine newspapers were published, respectively, in 1750 and 1780, and none of them appeared more than once weekly.[32] Furthermore, the mail service that carried these papers from editor to editor was highly irregular, with most mid eighteenth-century mails departing monthly or semimonthly. During 1790–1841 there were marked changes in the character of this isolation, which was synonymous with extreme spatial biases in information availability.

Time-Lag Surface Maps. To identify these changes, time-lag surface maps were constructed for individual cities at selected dates. Each map is based on a seasonally stratified sample of forty-eight issues of a local daily or dailies for the city and date in question. The only exception is the 1790 map for Boston, which in the absence of dailies was based on two semiweekly papers appearing a total of four days per week. In every case the sample consisted of the first two issues appearing in each month plus the two issues soonest to appear on or after the fifteenth of each month.

The news content of every sample edition was examined in its entirety. Wherever the date and location of a nonlocal event was indicated, which was not always the case with such items, the discrepancy in days between occurrence and publication was computed. After this operation was completed for a year's sample, the mean event-to-publication time-lag was derived for each recorded location. The means were then plotted on a base map, and isolines were drawn at five-day intervals by interpolation, with the occasional complementary use of physiographic, travel schedule, and postal service information.

It was necessary to stratify the samples seasonally because on early nineteenth-century postal and stagecoach routes service was usually more rapid from April 15 to October than during the remainder of the year. Even as late as the 1830s there were repeated complaints, for example, that the "mails have been much interrupted on the road between Philadelphia and Baltimore during the present winter."[33] Winter meant the freezing of the Hudson and the diminishment of New York–Albany interaction, as well as the occasional freezing of the harbors of Boston, Philadelphia, Baltimore, and other ports. Even in the absence of freezing, coastal vessels, which sometimes bore newsworthy information, arrived much less frequently in winter. Thus, Boston's coastwise shipping arrivals in May were four times those in January during the 1820s. The seasonal ebb and flow of the agricultural sector also brought varying time lags. For example, there was less frequent movement from New Orleans and the other cotton ports to New York in August and the early fall than at any other time of the year.[34] In consequence, random or unstratified samples might well have introduced statistical biases, with event-to-publication time-lags being excessively compressed or expanded.

The arbitrary selection for the maps of one or two papers at a given time and place need not have biased the data. Admittedly, it is likely that editors differed considerably in their selection of stories, and this may have been mirrored in paper-to-paper variations in the frequency with which specific nonlocal places were mentioned. However, such editorial preferences and prejudices should not have affected the time consumed from the occurrence of the nonlocal event to its local publication. Moreover, there is some danger that time lag means for particular nonlocal places might be distorted when based on a small number of values randomly clustered in one season. This danger is magnified if the news source is another paper that appeared only weekly. However, the possible impact of such distortions on the contour of isolines was usually offset by more broadly-based means obtained for other nearby places.

Time-Lag Surface Maps, 1790 and 1794. In absolute terms, the entire nation was still in a pronounced state of public-information isolation in 1790. Even in Philadelphia and Boston, which were then the first and third cities in the country, newspaper readers were at a considerable temporal remove from most nonlocal domestic events (Maps 2.2 and 2.3). This was equally true with respect to many occurrences in the

Map 2.2. Mean public-information time lags for Philadelphia in 1790. *Source: Pennsylvania Packet and Daily Advertiser* and *Pennsylvania Journal and the Weekly Advertiser,* 1790 (48 seasonally stratified issues). In this and subsequent public-information time-lag maps, dots represent places for which data were available.

Map 2.3. Mean public-information time lags for Boston in 1790. *Source: Columbian Centinel* and *Independent Chronicle,* 1790 (48 seasonally stratified issues).

nearby hinterland. For example, the mean time lag between events in Worcester and publication of their reports in Boston, only forty-two miles distant, was almost five days.

Once the 1790 situation is viewed from a comparative perspective a more meaningful picture emerges. While Boston and Philadelphia were roughly twelve days apart in public-information terms, they were much less isolated from each other than from other points at a similar physical distance from them inland.[35] For example, by the routes then utilized both Boston and Pittsburgh were roughly 330 miles from Philadelphia, yet the Pittsburgh-to-Philadelphia public-information time-lag was well over twice that prevailing between Boston and Philadelphia. In general, public information flowed most rapidly along an axis running diagonally from Baltimore to Philadelphia to New York to Boston. At the same time the inland, or westward, gradient from isoline to isoline was so steep that the four-day time gap between New York and Philadelphia was smaller than that between each of the cities and many more physically proximate areas normally considered to be part of their hinterlands.

The maps attest to the extreme informational isolation of the sparsely populated wilderness to the west of the Alleghenies, as in the time lag from Lexington, Kentucky, to Philadelphia. The remoteness of the area south of Richmond from the cities of the Northeastern seaboard is also reflected, as in the Charleston-to-Boston time-lag. In fact, in 1790 "such outlying papers as the *Augusta Chronicle* (Ga.) and the *Kentucky Gazette* (Lexington) were from one to two months late with their New York news, depending on weather and accidents."[36]

Within a very few years improved road conditions and faster, more frequent stage and postal services yielded some reduction in the absolute magnitude of spatial biases in domestic information availability. This is shown by a comparison between the five- and ten-day isolines for Philadelphia in 1790 and 1794 (Maps 2.2 and 2.4).[37] However, spatial variations in relative speed of information movement had been little altered.

The 1794 maps for both Philadelphia and New York again show that public information moved quickest along the Baltimore-Philadelphia-New York-Boston axis (Map 2.5). Within this corridor the speediest intelligence currents ran both ways between Philadelphia and New York.

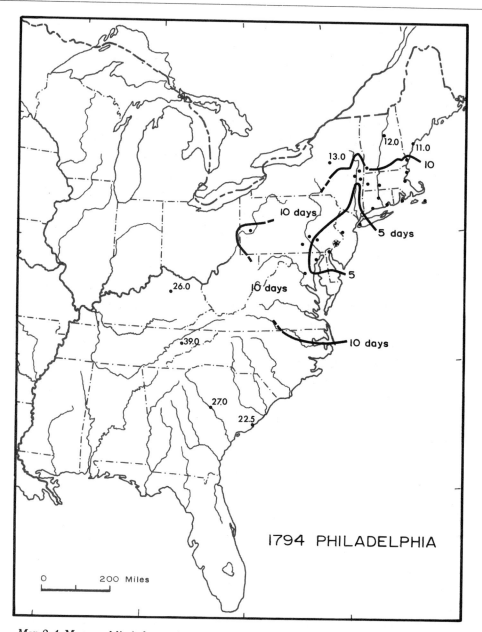

Map 2.4. Mean public-information time lags for Philadelphia in 1794. *Source: Gazette of the United States* and *Daily Evening Advertiser*, 1794 (48 seasonally stratified issues).

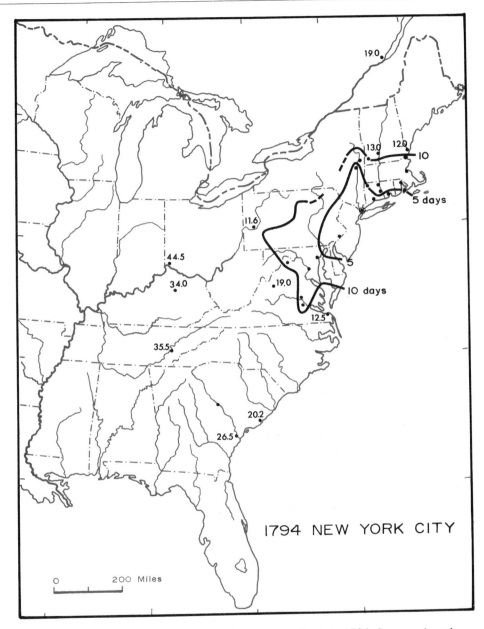

19.0

13.0 12.0
10

5 days

11.6

44.5
34.0

19.0

5

10 days

12.5

35.5

20.2

26.5

1794 NEW YORK CITY

0   200 Miles

Map 2.5. Mean public-information time lags for New York in 1794. *Source: American Minerva and New York Evening Advertiser*, 1794 (48 seasonally stratified issues).

41

106586

The time lag between these cities was reduced 60 percent in four years, falling from 4.0 to 1.6 days, while the Baltimore-to-Philadelphia interval had diminished only 40 percent, dropping from 6.0 to 3.6 days, and the Boston-to-Philadelphia gap had been shortened only 43.3 percent dropping from 12.0 to 6.8 days. Thus, public information flowed between the cities at the following approximate rates: New York-Philadelphia (both directions), 59 miles per day; Baltimore to Philadelphia, 27 miles per day; and Boston to Philadelphia, 47 miles per day. Although by then the channels of public information flow were also relatively efficient in the Hudson Valley (Albany-New York) and in southern Pennsylvania (Pittsburgh-Philadelphia), the New York-Philadelphia rates could not be matched anywhere else in the country, in part because of the superior travel and postal facilities between the two, in part because two cities with daily papers were nowhere more closely spaced. In sum, the resulting volume of information fed into them from their own hinterlands and from those of Baltimore and Boston indicate that at this early date New York and Philadelphia shared the crown of domestic public-information supremacy, with New York perhaps possessing the greatest positive spatial biases.[38]

Although spatial biases were somewhat smaller in 1794, extreme informational isolation still prevailed west of Pittsburgh, as shown by the Cincinnati-to-New York time-lag. Public information moved slowly from east to west as well as from west to east. For example, a Cincinnati weekly on January 11, 1794, carried Baltimore news that was fifty days old and a story from Portland, Maine, that was sixty-one days old. Similarly, the area south of Richmond remained at a tremendous informational distance from the major centers of the Northeastern seaboard. New York occurrences, as well as European news already obtained in New York, were almost certain to be three or more weeks old before they were publicly known in South Carolina, and still older before they had reached further south. Significantly, the public-information time gap between New York and Charleston, the largest city in the South, was by this time less than that between Philadelphia and Charleston, presumably because of the greater frequency of shipping interaction between the first pair of cities (cf. Maps 2.4 and 2.5).

Time-Lag Surface Maps, 1817. Time-lag surface maps were constructed for this date in part because of its halfway position between 1790 and the year in which the first telegraph line went into operation. In many respects 1817 was a turning point in the development of internal information movement and associated freight and passenger flows. It is generally accepted as the year in which the steamboat was proven a success on the waters of the Ohio and Mississippi Rivers. The increased frequency and speed of steam travel on western waters subsequently had great consequences for information transmission west of the Appalachians. The year 1817 was also a watershed in that it immediately preceded the 1818 completion of the National Road as far as Wheeling and the subsequent easing of east-west information flows. Furthermore, 1817 saw the start of construction on the Erie Canal, and, thereby, the identification of the Albany-Buffalo route as a major pathway of domestic information circulation.

By 1817 New York had clearly outdistanced Philadelphia and all other competitors and had established an informational hegemony (Maps 2.6 and 2.7). The area enclosed by New York's five-day isoline exceeded that encompassed by Philadelphia's, because its five-day information reach stretched farther southward as well as northward. Almost certainly, this was in some measure owing to New York's more frequent coastal exchange with Norfolk.[39] Because of more intense trade, New York's ten-day isoline embraced an exclave in South Carolina, and the city was informationally closer than Philadelphia to the other major centers of the Deep South. Despite its greater physical distance New York's mean information time-lag advantage over Philadelphia was 2.6 days to both Charleston and Savannah, and 6.5 days to New Orleans.[40] In effect, between 1794 and 1817 New York's time-lag isolines had been pushed out considerably, while those of Philadelphia and other cities had expanded more modestly.

Although time lags had not contracted as quickly as during the brief 1790–1794 interval, improvements in transportation and postal operations had further reduced the magnitude of spatial biases in domestic information availability throughout the country. Public information still flowed most swiftly along the Baltimore-Philadelphia-New York-Boston axis, which actually extended another thirty-six miles to Washington, the nation's capital since 1800. The Philadelphia-to-New York informa-

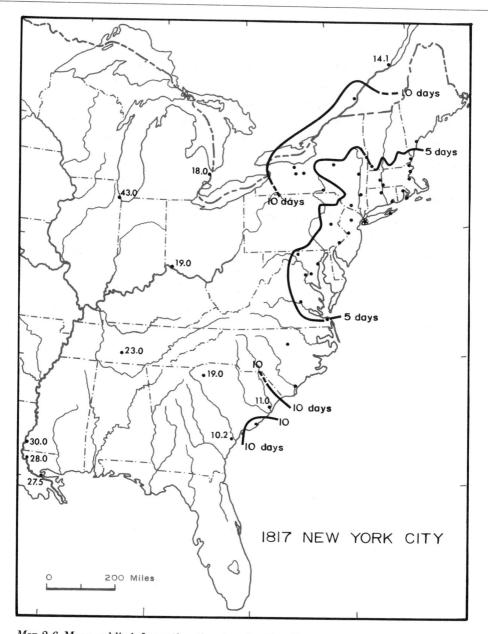

Map 2.6. Mean public-information time lags for New York in 1817. *Source: New York Evening Post*, 1817 (48 seasonally stratified issues).

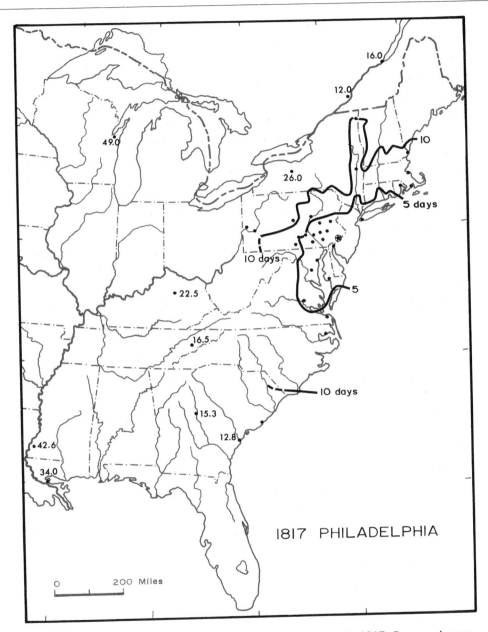

Map 2.7. Mean public-information time lags for Philadelphia in 1817. *Source: Aurora, General Advertiser,* (Philadelphia) 1817 (48 seasonally stratified issues).

tion time-lag had dropped 31.3 percent, from 1.6 to 1.1 days, largely because of the introduction of steamboats on the New York-to-New Brunswick leg of the route between the two cities. More dramatically, steamboats plying Long Island Sound had helped to chop the Boston-to-New York information gap 61.4 percent, from 5.7 to 2.2 days. In like fashion, the Baltimore-to-New York hiatus had shrunk from 5.6 to 2.1 days, or 62.5 percent.[41] But immediately to the south of Washington, the speed of news movement tapered off. From Baltimore to New York, information moved at approximately 94 miles per day, whereas news on its way to New York from Richmond flowed over the Richmond–Baltimore leg at roughly 72 miles per day. The absence of daily newspapers in all but a few places outside the Baltimore-to-Boston swath, plus the very limited extent of integrated stage and steamboat schedules outside that same belt, forced the news flows to be noticeably slower elsewhere.

One of the few other places where daily journalism flourished was Charleston. Yet a time lag map for that city reveals that spatial biases in domestic information availability were relatively extreme there as elsewhere in the area south of Richmond (Map 2.8). This was in part because the five-day isoline for Charleston compasses a much smaller area than that for Philadelphia and especially that for New York. More striking reasons were the slowness with which news traveled from other nearby southern centers and the city's remoteness from New Orleans. Although Savannah was not much farther from Charleston than Philadelphia was from New York,[42] the mean Savannah-to-Charleston time-lag was 3.5 days. In other words, information moved between the southern pair of cities at about 30 miles per day, and between the northern pair at about 91 miles per day. Similarly, public information from Augusta, which was only about 135 miles away, was delayed eight days on the average. Moreover, Charleston newspaper readers could expect their New Orleans information on prices and other matters to be from four to nine weeks old.[43] This tremendous degree of isolation from its sister port meant that Charleston was much closer informationally to places like Montreal and Portland, from which information was channeled to Charleston through New York. The positive northward distortion of Charleston's public-information field was also owing

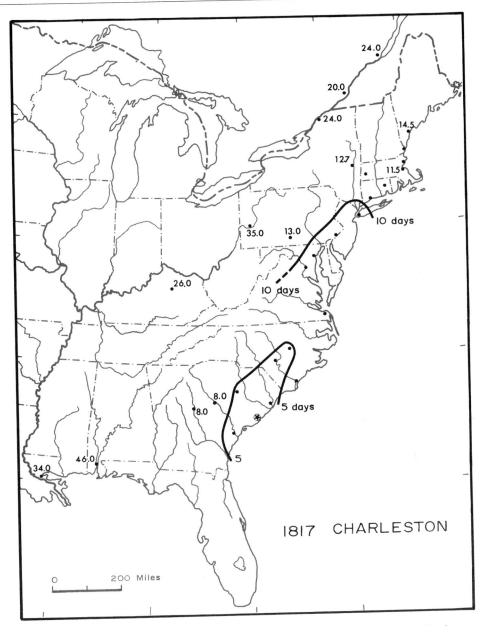

Map 2.8. Mean public-information time lags for Charleston in 1817. *Source: Charleston Courier,* 1817 (48 seasonally stratified issues). Owing to the wide range of data for New Orleans, the modal rather than mean value is given for that city.

to differences in frequency of coastal shipping interaction, for in 1820 Charleston had ninety-eight vessel arrivals from New York, but only seventeen from New Orleans.[44]

In 1817, most of the area west of the Alleghenies remained at a great informational distance from the more densely populated Northeast. Although Pittsburgh was closer to major coastal information sources than any other interior center, its time lag from Philadelphia was apparently no better in 1817 than it had been in 1794. Yet farther to the west some improvements were unmistakably evident. Detroit-to-New York and Cincinnati-to-New York public-information time lags now stood at 18.0 and 19.0 days respectively, and news flows in the opposite direction were of the same or larger dimensions.[45] Likewise, news from Knoxville and Lexington was made public in Philadelphia in 1817 with appreciably greater speed than it had been twenty-three years previously. Despite these improvements, the emerging Western centers were at least as isolated from one another informationally as the major North Atlantic seaboard ports had been in 1790. For example, Philadelphia-to-New York and Louisville-to-Cincinnati land distances were nearly identical, but the mean 1790 time lag between the former pair was 4.0 days, or just less than half that between the latter pair in 1818. Also, although the Pittsburgh-to-Cincinnati stage distance was less than that existing earlier from Boston to Philadelphia, the mean time lag between the former pair in 1818 was 12.2 days, which was almost indistinguishable from the 12.0 days between the latter pair in 1790.[46] This high degree of interurban isolation prevailed partly because Pittsburgh, Cincinnati, Louisville, Detroit, St. Louis and all other lesser interior urban foci were as yet without daily newspapers.[47]

Time-Lag Surface Maps, 1841. As the pretelegraphic era neared its end, the magnitude of spatial biases in domestic public information availability was constantly diminished by the spread of the railroad and other developments both inside and outside the newspaper world. Many of these advances only reinforced the news advantages of the Baltimore-Boston axis in general, and the informational supremacy of New York in particular.

One such innovation was news expresses. In 1833 the *New York Journal of Commerce* "established a horse express from Philadelphia to

New York, with eight relays, and by this means published the proceedings of Congress and all other Southern news one day in advance of their contemporaries." In the previous year a competitor, the *Morning Courier and New-York Enquirer*, had started an irregular express over the same route, but now unable to keep up with its rival, the *Enquirer* and other papers protested with sufficient vigor to force the *New York Journal of Commerce* to sell its operations to the United States Post Office, which then provided the same speedy service to all New York dailies. Dissatisfied with receiving its Washington dispatches no quicker than local rivals, the *New York Journal of Commerce* in turn extended a private express from the nation's capital. Twenty-four horses were employed over the 227-mile distance, usually completing the relay in about 20 hours and thereby providing news 12 to 48 hours before other New York papers secured the same information through the post. By 1835 much of the remainder of the New York press was benefiting from the railway mail service introduced over various segments of the Washington-to-New York route.[48]

News expresses were also established to the northeast of New York. In 1836 several of Boston's penny papers began running occasional expresses from Washington and New York in order to acquire major domestic and foreign stories more speedily. These expresses were shortly supplemented by the Post Office's "express mails," which conveyed clippings from one newspaper to another. Three years later, W. F. Harnden's privately operated package and mail express began serving papers in Boston and New York. Soon Harnden's use of steamboat and railroad lines enabled him to provide Boston editors with New York and Philadelphia papers within twenty-four hours of publication.[49]

Because of New York's expresses, its fleet of regularly scheduled packets to major Southern ports, its volume of business with the West and South, and the general aggressiveness of its editors, that city by 1841 dominated domestic public information flows far more than it had in 1817. In 1841 news quite often moved between pairs of cities over roundabout, lengthy paths that passed through New York. As early as 1833, the Baltimore-based *Niles' Weekly Register* reported: "News from Washington has been several times received at Charleston via New York; and we are sometimes indebted to New York papers for news from

Charleston." The *Norfolk Beacon*, published 229 miles southeast of Washington, copied Washington news "on two successive days from the *New York Journal of Commerce*, which it received by sea, before it had any advices from the capital." With striking regularity, Boston and Philadelphia papers credited the New York press for information originating in Charleston, Savannah, Mobile, New Orleans, and their respective hinterlands. (For a reasonably accurate ideal-typical picture of public-information flow from the South in the 1820s and 1830s, reverse the direction of all the South's arrows in Map 2.1.) In 1841 the *New Haven Herald* could claim: "Our Boston news now comes earliest by way of New York." Moreover, until the telegraph network had spread its tentacles extensively, Western newspapers were irked at the stranglehold exercised by the New York press over information of commercial significance.[50]

An English visitor of the late 1830s observed that Boston papers were "inferior in original intellegence to the papers of New York."[51] This superiority of New York over Boston and all other major cities is shown by a comparison of New York's time-lag maps for 1817 and 1841, as well as by juxtaposing New York, Boston, and Philadelphia maps for the later date. At the start of the 1840s, New York's five-day isoline encompassed an area resembling its 1817 ten-day isoline (Maps 2.6 and 2.9). By 1841, the city's ten-day isoline stretched about three hundred miles farther south along the Atlantic coast, and a similar expansion had occurred west of the Alleghenies and north of the Ohio River. New Orleans, which was almost four weeks away informationally in 1817, was now just shy of qualifying as a ten-day exclave.

In accord with its peripheral location, Boston's isolines of public-information delay did not extend as far south or west as those of New York (Map 2.10). This meant that news from afar was more often than not a day or more older there than in New York, through which it had usually passed. For example, the mean New Orleans-to-New York time lag was 10.6 days, that for New Orleans-to-Boston was 12.1 days; the mean Buffalo-to-New York time lag was 4.3 days, and that for Buffalo-to-Boston was 6.0 days. Philadelphia, with a somewhat more central location than New York, could not extend its ten-day isoline any farther south than could Boston (Maps 2.10 and 2.11), although its time gaps

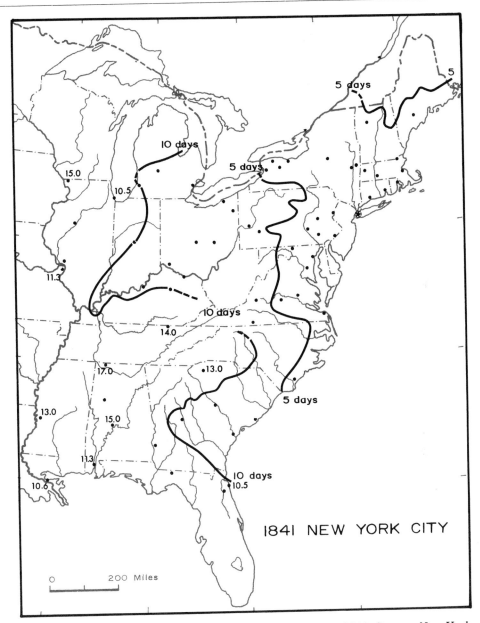

Map 2.9. Mean public-information time lags for New York in 1841. *Source: New York Daily Tribune,* 1841 (48 seasonally stratified issues).

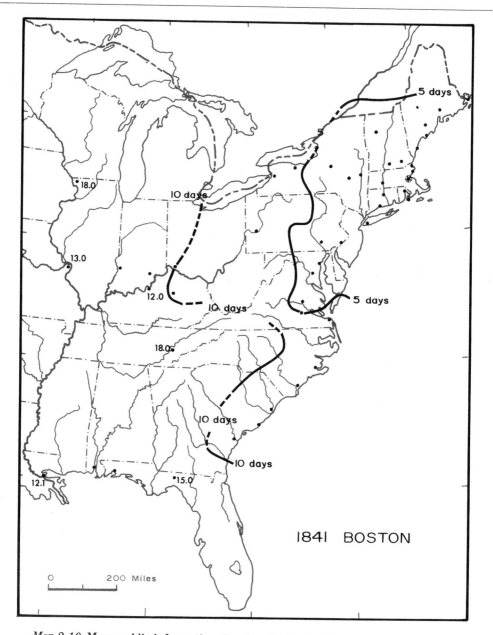

Map 2.10. Mean public-information time lags for Boston in 1841. *Source: Boston Evening Transcript*, 1841 (48 seasonally stratified issues).

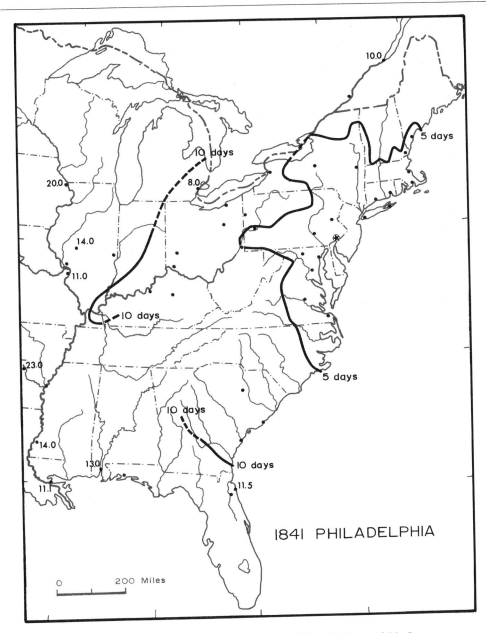

Map 2.11. Mean public-information time lags for Philadelphia in 1841. *Source: Philadelphia Public Ledger,* 1841 (48 seasonally stratified issues).

in the Midwest more closely resembled those of New York than those of Boston. The time lags from the South merely reflected the reliance of both Boston and Philadelphia papers on the New York press for information originating in that area.[52] Because of its linkages with Pittsburgh, Philadelphia held a small advantage over New York in the Ohio Valley. For example, having a 6.3-day informational separation from Cincinnati, Philadelphia enjoyed a 0.7-day headstart over New York. However, in the vicinity of the Great Lakes the tables were turned. For example, the 1841 mean public-information time lag from Cleveland to New York was 7.0 days, while that from Cleveland to Philadelphia stood at 7.7 days.

As it had been a quarter of a century earlier, the Baltimore-to-Boston axis was in 1841 the scene of the country's most rapid news transmission. Post-1817 improvements were not readily apparent from the Philadelphia-to-New York time lag, since the frequency of newspaper publication prevented its reduction to less than one day (from 1817 to 1841 the gap had decreased 0.1 day, to the minimum 1.0). At greater distances along the axis, advances were more evident. In 1841 Boston was informationally closer to Washington than Philadelphia had been to Washington in 1817 (2.8 days compared to 2.9 days). That is, information moved at a rate of approximately 174 miles per day over the entire length of the axis, which was nearly twice the rate prevailing in 1817 over the then most efficient Philadelphia-to-New York segment. Moreover, when news was deemed of unusual significance, it could be moved by railroad and steamboat relay at well below the mean rate: from Washington to New York in ten hours or less, and on to Boston in a total just under twenty-four hours, with an additional lag of a few hours before publication.[53] Despite the improvements in information movement between Washington and Boston, there were many areas where the five-day isolines for New York, Boston, and Philadelphia did not extend as far inland as might be expected (Maps 2.9 –2.11). This phenomenon occurred, except along the Philadelphia-Pittsburgh and Erie Canal routes, for a number of reasons. Probably the most important was the dependence of newspapers on one another in securing material for their respective columns, and the delay associated with the continued prevalence of weeklies and semiweeklies, as opposed to dailies, in the smaller cities in the hinterlands of the major ports.

By 1841 the South Atlantic Coast had come a long way from its position of informational isolation in the 1790s. The mean Charleston-to-New York time lag had dropped from 20.2 days in 1794 to 5.5 days in 1841. Charleston and Savannah began to be more integrated into the domestic information flow system with the commencement of packet service from New York in 1822 and 1824, respectively. In 1833 a line of expresses was established between Washington and Charleston, which sometimes permitted news to be carried the full distance in forty-eight hours. In the following year publishers in Augusta, Georgia, were able to procure New York and Charleston papers from Charleston in little more than the twelve hours required for the trains to cover the newly opened 136-mile railroad track from Charleston to nearby Hamburg, South Carolina. Shortly thereafter, steam-powered vessels started to convey information between Charleston and New York: "Sailing every Saturday from each port, they matched the sailing packets in frequency of service, and, when all went well, arrived in three days, which was just half the [existing] packet average and faster than the land mail route." In 1839, the news-bearing mails went from New York to Charleston, via the Wilmington and Raleigh Railroad in 3.5 days.[54]

Although New Orleans was still on the periphery of the domestic public information network, being ten or more days behind the events of Washington and New York, it no longer suffered from the extreme isolation endured in 1817. Here, too, as well as in Mobile, the introduction of regularly scheduled New York packet service in the 1820s was instrumental in contracting mean time lags. Packet voyage times were speeded up when specially designed "flat-floored" ships, relatively immune to Mississippi bars, were pressed into operation in 1831. A greater frequency of packet departures also hastened the flow of news information. Finally, in mid-1839 arrangements were completed between the postmaster general and the Georgia Railroad and Banking Company whereby New Orleans editors could obtain New York newspapers nine days after publication.[55]

Unlike the major South Atlantic and Gulf Coast ports, inland southern towns were still relatively inaccessible to public information in 1841. Some exceptions nevertheless emerged in the mid and late 1830s at places such as Montgomery, (Alabama), and Milledgeville, (Georgia), which were on the major post route to New Orleans. In most other instances, either the complete absence of a local paper or low accessibility to nonlocal papers was the reason for the absence of much public information.

In some respects the states of the Ohio Valley and the adjacent Midwest remained an informational backwater throughout the 1820s and 1830s. A Cincinnati paper could still complain in 1836 that "in winter, or in wet and frosty seasons of the year, the city is cut off from communication from every side; and is the worst, most difficult point to be approached of any of which we have any knowledge."[56] Nevertheless, by 1841 the tide of east-west trade, the multiplication of steamboat traffic, and the postal act of July 2, 1836, had greatly altered the mean time lags of Cincinnati and the other interior cities. The 1836 postal act empowered the postmaster general to "establish an express mail, in addition to the ordinary mail, on any of the post roads in the United States, for the purpose of conveying slips from newspapers in lieu of exchange newspapers."[57] In 1817, Western cities were much further removed informationally from New York than were Charleston and Savannah, despite the fact that most of them were physically closer to New York. But by 1841, Cincinnati and Detroit were on a more nearly equal footing with Charleston and Savannah (Table 2.4). Moreover, by this date Western towns that were neither directly on the Ohio nor on the shores of the Great Lakes were much less disadvantaged with respect

Table 2.4. Mean public-information time lags for New York, 1817 and 1841 (in days).

Public-information source	1817	1841	Percentage decrease
Charleston	8.2	5.5	32.9
Savannah	10.2	6.3	38.2
Cincinnati	19.0	7.0[a]	63.2
Detroit	18.0	7.5[a]	58.3

Source: New York Evening Post, 1817; New York Daily Tribune, 1841.
a. Since eastbound and westbound mails were of equal frequency, and since both Cincinnati and Detroit possessed daily papers in 1841, New York-to-Cincinnati and New York-to-Detroit time lags were presumably not significantly different from delays in the opposite direction.

to public information than were most of their counterparts in the interior of the South. The reason was apparently the greater preponderance of towns with newspapers in the West and, in consequence, the greater accessibility of Western papers to one another.

The growing coherence of public information circulation reflected by the outward wandering of isolines (Maps 2.2 - 2.11) is consistent with the increasing tendency for wholesale price changes in one city to be quickly reflected in other cities. Arthur H. Cole computed the average annual and monthly disparity of uniform groups of commodity indices for selected cities during the period 1816–1842. He found that the average annual disparity for New York, Philadelphia, Charleston, New Orleans, and Cincinnati fell from 9.3 for 1816–1830 to 4.8 for 1830–1842. The mean monthly disparity for the same five cities plummeted from 15.4 for 1816–1821 to 4.8 for 1830–1842. Although it is highly precarious to ascribe these disparity drops entirely to reductions in spatial biases in public information availability, it would be equally foolish to deny the leading role of this factor.[58]

Public-Information Accessibility Maps. Before the appearance of wire services, the individual newspaper's main source of domestic and foreign information was the columns of other journals. Thus, nonlocal newspaper circulation during the pretelegraphic period was comprised of two distinct components: circulation to other papers, and circulation to readers residing beyond the city of publication.

The practice of mutual journalistic plagiarism was of early origin. Almost as soon as newspaper publication had spread to several colonies, "printer-editors came to depend chiefly upon each other for their intercolonial news. By common consent they helped themselves to one another's news stories without credit, as they had appropriated the contents of foreign papers."[59] As newspaper publication became more widespread after 1790, the web of journalistic plagiarism also became more widespread and intricate. Most newspapers, when reporting major events, relied directly or indirectly on the coverage of the paper nearest to the source. Indirect exploitation, which was common, occurred when the reportage was directly purloined from the pages of a New York daily or some other large-city paper, which in turn had copied the story from the paper nearest the source. For lesser news, small-town papers customarily depended directly on the press of the city within whose hinterland they were situated and indirectly on the sources of that press. Conversely, small-town weeklies supplied large-city papers with hinterland news, although the small-town papers paid little attention to most local happenings, because their weekly appearance made it difficult for them to keep apace of local word of mouth. For example, from 1790 to 1815 and after, Boston's *Columbian Centinel* was a prime source of news for the newspaper publishers of eastern New England, "every one of whom relied upon it for matter to fill up the news department of his paper." Papers in the major urban centers also exchanged widely with one another and almost invariably with the New York dailies. Consequently, long chains of reference were commonplace, such as, "We learn from the *Albany Daily Advertiser* of yesterday from the *Buffalo Commercial Advertiser* of Saturday."[60]

The short- and long-distance exchange of copies between newspaper publishers continued to be of enormous importance until the 1840s. The chairman of the Senate Committee on Post Offices and Post Roads stated in 1832 that "all the useful intelligence" of large-city papers was reproduced "with but a few hours delay" in the local press of the "interior," a circumstance that was encouraged by the long-standing perogative of free postage.[61] Late deliveries and failure of the mails, therefore, usually left newspapers completely bereft of nonlocal information. For instance, the *Mobile Advertiser* of April 17, 1833, noted: "The failure of all the mails must plead our excuse for the barrenness of our columns today. We have no news from New York later than the 28th ultimo, being 19 days."[62]

Scattered data on the volume of newspaper mail provide the best clues to the part played by editorial exchanges in news dissemination. Although precise figures are lacking for the earlier portions of the 1790–1840 period, there is little doubt that newspaper mails accounted for a large proportion of all postal activities from the late eighteenth century onward. In 1803 Postmaster General Granger, when seeking to provide "every reasonable encouragement to those who will adventure in establishing and supporting regular lines of public carriages" to carry passengers and the mails south of Petersburg, Virginia, spoke of "the constantly increasing and enormous size of many of the mails on the great roads, owing principally to our extended and extending circulation of newspapers." Almost thirty years later a senator testified: "On Monday morning I saw the Southern mail as it was dispatched; there were twenty-one bags of newspapers, and all the letters did not fill as much as one bag."[63]

More specifically, the Philadelphia post office was reported to be sending out 162,040 newspapers every quarter in 1824. Although this only works out to nearly 12,500 copies per week, it must be considered a high total because of the very low circulation of papers prior to the birth of the penny press in the 1830s. The average circulation per issue of daily newspapers has been estimated at 800 for 1820 and 1,200 for 1830. As late as 1836, when the penny press was commencing publication in Philadelphia, "the united edition of all the daily newspapers [there] was between 7,000 and 8,000 copies per day," or about 45,000 copies per week.[64] The Philadelphia data would be even more revealing if it were disaggregated into postage-free exchange and postage-paid purchased subtotals. A better picture of the postal spread of newspapers from a single city emerges from an 1825 story in the *Richmond Whig:* "Between the 1st January last and the 31st March, 150,624 papers were sent from the city of Richmond, of which 110,848 are taken within the state, and the remaining 28,128 in different sections of the United States . . . The papers received [elsewhere] in exchange by the different printing establishments amount to 11,648"—or 896 per week. If it is assumed that all nonlocal papers took the editions of no more than one Richmond paper in order to procure information from that place, and if the weekly postal shipment of exchange papers is divided by six-elevenths (eleven being the total number of editions issued per week by the city's six existing papers—one daily and five weeklies), it may be estimated that as many as 486 of the country's approximately 730 papers were involved in the direct trade of public information with the press of the Virginia capital.[65]

Although data for New York City do not lend themselves to the same kind of manipulation, combined postage-free and postage-paid totals suggest that by the mid-1820s several hundred editors were receiving copies of New York papers, and that the number of such exchange recipients grew rapidly in the ensuing pretelegraphic years. The data also suggest that virtually all papers which were not involved in direct interchange indirectly acquired news from New York newspaper pages as a result of taking other papers. In 1828 it was estimated that nearly 40,000 newspapers were shipped weekly through the New York post office. Within five years this sum had multiplied several times over, for the *New York Gazette* claimed that "the number of newspapers passing through the post office amounts to one million per month."[66] By 1838 the postmaster general could note: "The mail which leaves New York daily for the South is believed to average nearly two tons in weight, more than a ton and a half of which is printed matter. At Baltimore it separates, and about half goes west and the other half south." Shortly before, the postmaster general had reported: "The number of newspapers, pamphlets, &c. paying postage, conveyed by mail annually, is estimated at about 25,000,000. The dead [undelivered] and free [exchange] newspapers may be about 4,000,000."[67] If exchange newspapers are estimated conservatively to have been responsible for roughly 3,000,000 of the "dead and free" total, and if that figure is divided by 312, the number of postal delivery days per annum, then the number of editorially exchanged papers in 1837 was close to 10,000 per day. Since the number of papers then existing in the United States was about 1,300, this would mean that the average newspaper office received seven or more exchange papers daily and that the composition of this bundle varied from day to day owing to the fact that most papers were not published on a daily basis (less than one in ten was then a daily). In all likelihood, this estimate falls far short of accounting for all actual journalistic exchange of information, for the 1836 Postal Act had established "express mails" which carried "slips" rather than entire issues from one paper to another.

As shown by the Philadelphia, Richmond, New York, and national data, the postal traffic in newspapers to nonlocal paying subscribers was considerable in the final pretelegraphic decades. The 1825 Richmond data are of particular interest, since they show over 2,100 purchased copies leaving Virginia each week. This suggests that large-city papers often had an extremely widespread readership, which is confirmed by an 1832 statement that over 14,000 newspapers were mailed weekly from Boston to places more than 100 miles distant, another 10,000 supposedly being dispatched by post to points within a 100-mile radius.[68]

The short- and long-distance movement by mail of large-city newspapers to inns, coffeehouses, and individual subscribers was encouraged by the preferential rates on newspapers that went into effect with the Postal Act of 1793, when Congress "avowedly undertook to encourage . . . [the growth of the press] as the most important disseminator of intelligence among the people." These rates, which remained in effect until 1845, were set originally at one cent for any distance up to 100 miles, and one and one-half cents for all distances beyond that limit regardless of size and weight. A later modification allowed papers to move over 100 miles for the one-cent charge provided they remained in the state of publication. The papers of the larger urban centers were especially favored by the size and weight provision. By the 1830s, when the major journals of New York and other cities were becoming larger and bulkier, "there was a great deal of complaint on the part of the publishers of interior newspapers that the postal laws already discriminated most unjustly in favor of the metropolitan newspapers. These . . . were carried long distances at the same rates of postage charged to the smaller local press, and they conveyed the latest news to the people of the interior towns earlier than the publishers in the latter, obliged to wait for their news for the arrival of the same papers, could republish and circulate it."[69]

Not all deliveries to subscribers outside the place of publication went through the postal system. Acknowledging a practice of decades, the 1825 Postal Act permitted individuals and firms holding mail transportation contracts to "carry newspapers, magazines, and pamphlets other than those conveyed in the mails." After 1835, ambitious papers increasingly availed themselves of railroads and steamboats for non-local distribution without the aid of the mails. At about the same time papers such as the *New-York Herald* and the *Boston Daily Times* began to extend their own carrier systems into neighboring urban communities—the former into Newark, Paterson, Albany, Troy, Hudson, Poughkeepsie, and even Philadelphia; the latter into Lynn, Salem, Worcester, New Bedford, and elsewhere. Yet more important were the special tri-weekly, semiweekly, or weekly editions "for country readers" put out by the large-city dailies and consisting chiefly of material from their own columns. By 1810 the publication of country editions had spread to 23 dailies. In 1820, 35 of the nation's 42 dailies had such rural editions, with no less than 20 emanating from New York, Philadelphia, and Baltimore.[70]

Given the preceding discussion, and particularly the observations on the extent of free editorial exchange, a measure of place-to-place variations in access to all U.S. newspapers would appear to serve well as a complementary indicator of public information spatial biases.

Geographical patterns of accessibility to population, demand, or any other unequally distributed phenomenon normally are shown on isarithmic maps by computing and plotting the "potential" for selected points in the area under consideration. The potential for any particular point, designated $_iV$, is equal to

$$\sum_{j=1}^{n} \frac{P_j}{d_{ij}},$$

where P_j is the population or value of the phenomenon at every other point and d_{ij} is the distance separating the particular point and every other point.[71] On such maps for 1790, 1820, and 1840, P_j was assessed for all counties having newspapers, with the value being set by the number of editions appearing weekly. Dailies were assigned a weight of six, triweeklies a weight of three, semiweeklies a weight of two, and weeklies a weight of one.[72] Intercounty distances were based on the population centroid of each county in 1960. These distances probably do not contain much distortion, both because of the relative stability of the centroids in most cases, and because any shift in the population gravity center of a specific county between the mapped dates and 1960 could add or subtract only a tiny percentage to most of its distances to other county centroids. Self-potential, or intracounty accessibility, was derived conservatively by plugging the mean of the particular county's two lengthiest perpendicular axes into the denominator. This had the effect of undervaluing the self-potential, and hence the total accessibility, of those counties dominated by a single physically compact city, such as New York or Philadelphia, where a considerable volume of local (intraurban) journalistic plagiarism was the rule.[73] For comparative purposes, all potentials for 1790, 1820, and 1840 were converted to a base, with New York's value in 1790 set at 100. The three dates were chosen for their spacing over the study period and for purposes of making comparisons with already existing population accessibility maps for the same years.

Public-Information Accessibility Maps, 1790. In 1791 Thomas Jefferson complained of the great commercial towns that, "though not 1/25th of the nation, they command 3/4 of its public papers." Although in fact only twenty-six of the country's ninety-two papers were in New York, Boston, Philadelphia, Baltimore, and Charleston as of 1790, Jefferson's statement was more accurate with respect to newspaper editions. With all daily papers being confined to New York, Philadelphia, and Charleston, and with most other papers in the five centers being semiweeklies or triweeklies, just over half of the 147 editions that appeared each week in the entire nation were accounted for by this quintet of ports. Moreover, just over a quarter of all other editions published per week originated in places closely tributary to New York, Boston, Philadelphia, and Baltimore.[74]

Hence, the highest levels of newspaper accessibility in 1790 occurred along the Baltimore-to-Boston axis (Map 2.12). Within this area, accessibility declined so rapidly from the New York-Philadelphia core that values at the northern and southern extremes were only one-quarter of those at the New York summit. Thus, as with the time-lag surface maps for 1790 and 1794, the public-information supremacy of Philadelphia and particularly of New York was clear-cut for both the Northeast and the country as a whole. The very low potential values of the entire South and the Western interior again vividly illustrate the great public-informational remoteness prevailing in those areas.

The extreme character of locational differences in accessibility to public information is further underlined by comparing public information accessibility with population accessibility for 1790 (cf. Maps 2.12 and 2.13). Quite plainly, public-information accessibility fell off much more quickly from New York than would be expected from the pattern of population accessibility. Eastern Massachusetts, with higher popula-

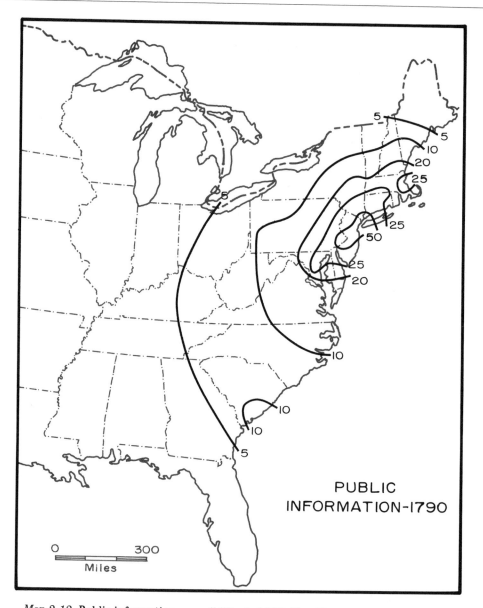

Map 2.12. Public information accessibility in 1790. New York=100.

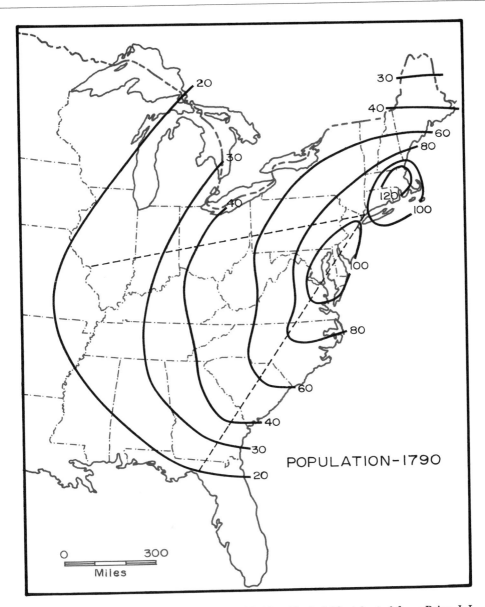

Map 2.13. Population accessibility in 1790. New York=100. Adapted from Brian J. L. Berry, *Theories of Urban Location* (Washington, D.C.: Association of American Geographers, 1968), p. 8. Transects correspond to those in Figs. 2.1. and 2.2.

tion potentials than New York, had a peak public-information accessibility in Boston only 47 percent that of New York. In heavily settled eastern Virginia, where newspaper publication was inhibited by the illiteracy of slaves and others as well as conservative attitudes toward printing, population accessibility stood at 80 percent or more of the New York standard, but public-information accessibility was only between 10 and 23 percent of that registered in New York. The accessibility values graphed for both a transect extending southward from New York and a transect stretching westward from the same place (Figs. 2.1 and 2.2) further illustrate extreme spatial biases in the availability of public information.

Public-Information Accessibility Maps, 1820. Despite the passing of three decades, most of the country in 1820 had failed to attain public-information accessibility measures comparable to those of New York in 1790. The public-information potential of New York itself had more than tripled during the same interlude (Fig. 2.1 and Map 2.14). The highest levels of newspaper accessibility remained within the strip adjoining the Baltimore-Boston axis. Even within this corridor there was a gap, consisting of large parts of Connecticut and Massachusetts and all of Rhode Island, where values were just shy of New York's in 1790. The Hudson Valley, eastern Pennsylvania, and northeastern Virginia accounted for most of the area immediately outside the Baltimore-Boston strip where the 1790 New York base value was either equaled or exceeded.

West of the Appalachians the isolation from domestic news was still considerable. Nevertheless, levels of news accessibility had advanced markedly over thirty years, owing largely to the relatively widespread diffusion of newspaper publication in western Pennsylvania and Ohio (Maps 2.15 and 2.16). Although potentials were far below the 1790 New York standard, the 1820 values of the newly identified western nodes of urban importance matched those of other major Atlantic ports in 1790. More precisely, Pittsburgh's 1820 potential was 74, compared to Philadelphia's 1790 score of 67; Cincinnati's 1820 potential was 54, while Boston's in 1790 was 47; and St. Louis' 1820 index of 32 was identical with Baltimore's in 1790.

In the South, 1820 public-information potentials continued to reflect pronounced spatial biases in the flow of domestic news. Almost

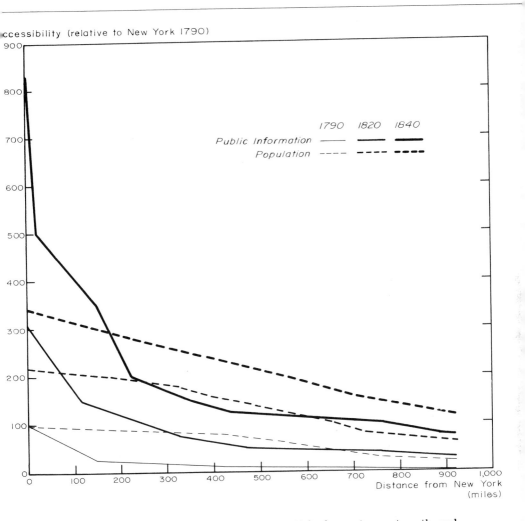

Fig. 2.1. Public information and population potentials along a transect southward from New York: 1790, 1820, and 1840. New York in 1790=100.

all of the Deep South had levels of news accessibility that did not measure up to half of New York's 1790 score, and virtually all of Alabama and Mississippi stood at less than one-third of that value. Only the vicinities of Charleston and New Orleans, where the daily press had established a firm foothold, could be characterized as islands of moderate accessibility in a sea of low accessibility.[75]

The magnitude of locational variations in accessibility to public

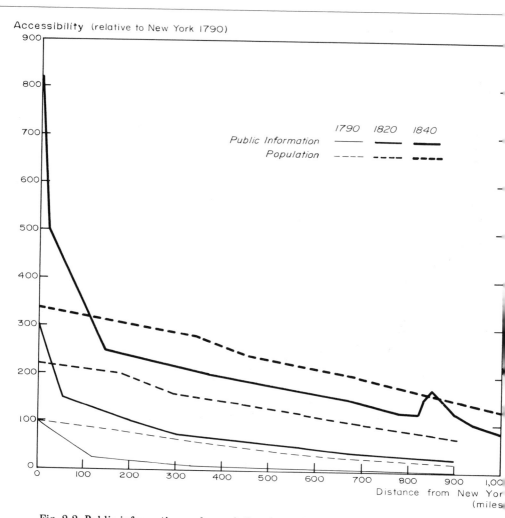

Fig. 2.2. Public information and population potentials along a transect westward from New York: 1790, 1820, and 1840. New York in 1790=100.

information are brought into sharper focus by a comparison with population potentials (Map 2.17). In contrast to the public-information potential situation, by 1820 substantial portions of the West and South had achieved population accessibility indices that equaled or surpassed those of New York in 1790. New York's now further entrenched nodal role in the dissemination of public information is summarized indirectly by the juxtaposition of public-information and population accessibility

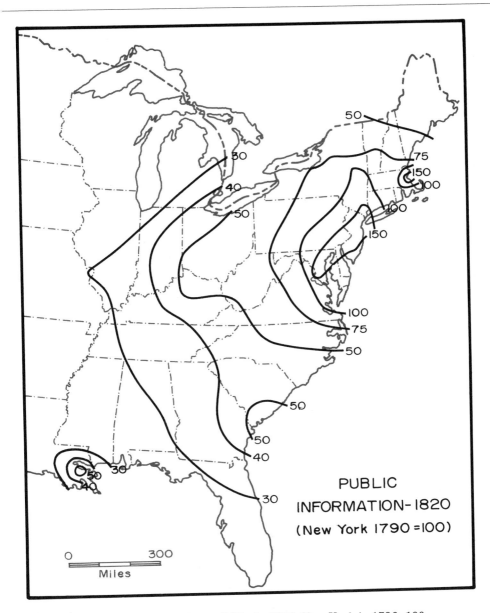

Map 2.14. Public information accessibility in 1820. New York in 1790=100.

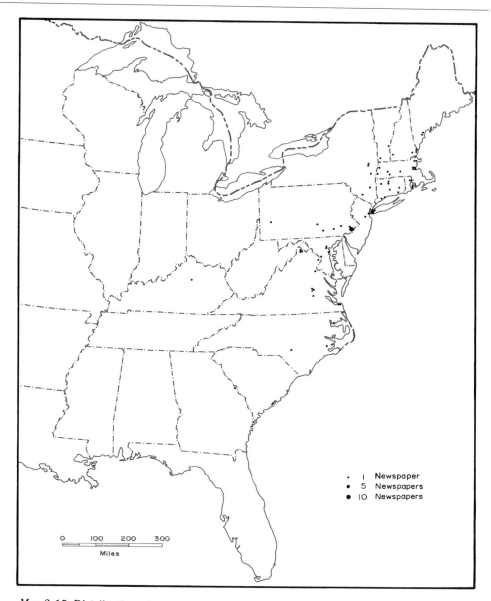

Map 2.15. Distribution of newspapers in mid-1790. There is no weighting for frequency of publication. *Source:* Clarence S. Brigham, *History and Bibliography of American Newspapers, 1690–1820* (Worcester: American Antiquarian Society, 1947), 2 vols.

Map 2.16. Distribution of newspapers at the end of 1820. There is no weighting for frequency of publication. *Source:* Brigham, *History and Bibliography of American Newspapers.*

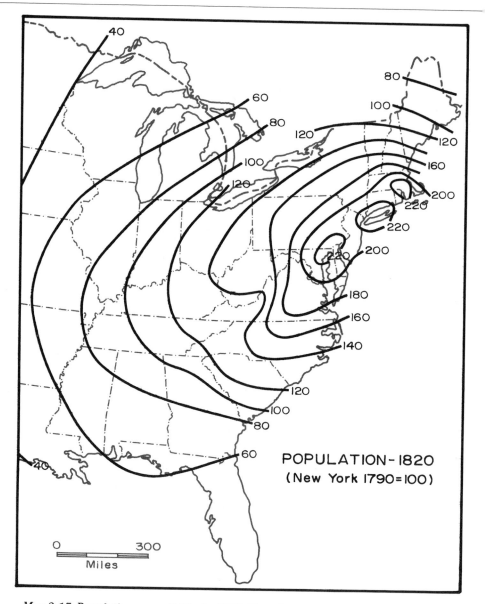

Map 2.17. Population accessibility in 1820. New York in 1790=100. Adapted from Berry, *Theories of Urban Location*, p. 8.

transects for 1820 (Figs. 2.1 and 2.2). Thus, except for a small area within less than one-hundred miles of New York, relative population potentials exceeded relative public-information potentials throughout the entire country. In other words, if New York values in 1790 are accepted as a measuring rod, public-information accessibility generally did not reach the levels that might be expected from population potentials.

Public-Information Accessibility Maps, 1840. In a superficial sense, the pattern of public-information accessibility was not much altered between 1820 and 1840. The belt of greatest public-information potential, with values now over 250, still paralleled the Baltimore-Boston axis (Map 2.18). However, this belt no longer had a slight discontinuity between New York and Boston. In addition, an area of quite high public-information accessibility (twice that of New York in 1790) surrounded the belt, with one lobe stretching westward parallel to the Erie Canal, and another following the other major path of east-west circulation, engulfing the Pittsburgh area, and penetrating Ohio.

The dominance of New York over the news circulation system was now complete (cf. Maps 2.18 and 2.19, and the 1840 transects in Figs. 2.1 and 2.2). The discrepancy between the public-information potentials of New York and other places was much greater than the discrepancy between corresponding population potentials, despite the fact that the measure of New York's public-information accessibility very likely is undervalued. New York's value would have been enhanced considerably if the foreign papers imported into the country through the city were figured in its total.[76]

A fuller integration of the Midwest into the general stream of domestic information exchange had come about by 1840. Nearly all of the substantially settled area west of the Appalachians had a degree of public-information accessibility that topped New York's in 1790 (Map 2.18). More important, zones of moderately high accessibility existed around Cincinnati, Louisville, and St. Louis, which along with Pittsburgh ruled the urban subsystem of the Ohio and Upper Mississippi valleys. The values attained in these zones slightly exceeded those for Boston, Philadelphia, and Baltimore in 1820, but fell below the 1840 levels of those same cities.

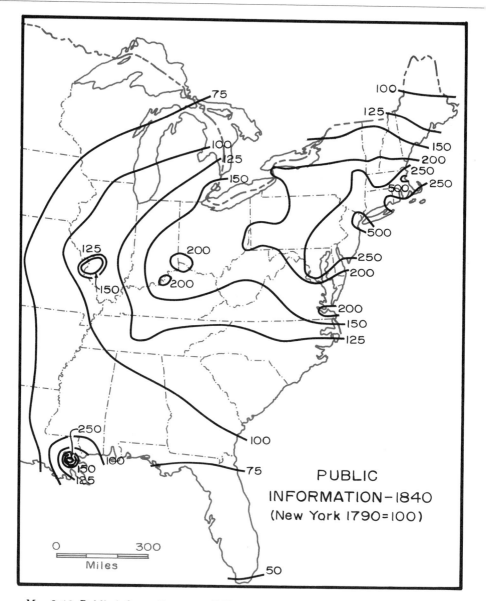

Map 2.18. Public information accessibility in 1840. New York in 1790=100.

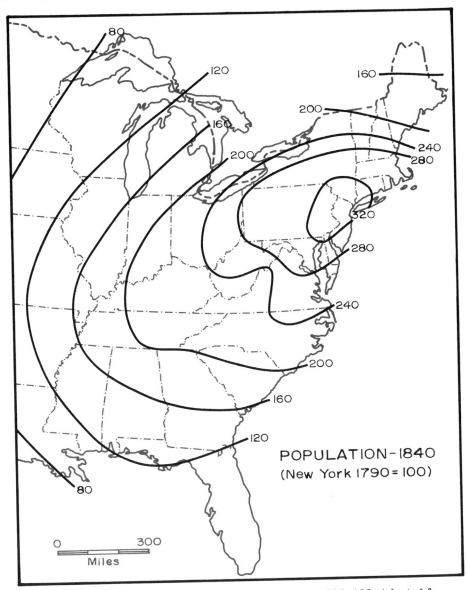

Map 2.19. Population accessibility in 1840. New York in 1790=100. Adapted from Berry, *Theories of Urban Location*, p. 9.

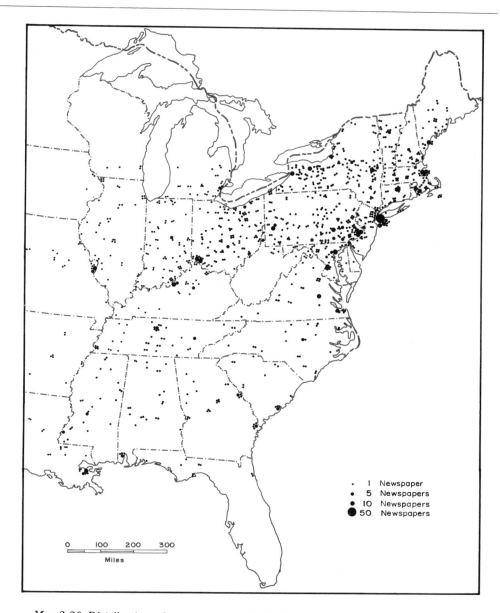

Map 2.20. Distribution of newspapers in 1840. There is no weighting for frequency of publication. *Source:* Sixth Census of the United States, 1840.

By 1840, parts of the South were fairly well incorporated into the public-information circulation system. New Orleans, by then a major source of daily papers as well as a leading entrepôt, possessed the highest potential outside the Washington-Boston axis.[77] However, much of the interior South and Florida, which was mostly unsettled, remained informationally isolated, at least from a relative viewpoint. Most of Alabama, Mississippi, about half of Georgia, and those portions of Louisiana more than seventy-five miles from New Orleans still had levels of public-information accessibility well below those of New York a half-century earlier—a situation in keeping with the sparse number of newspapers in that part of the country (Map 2.20).

3

Postal Services and Long-Distance Information Flows

There is no branch of the government in whose operations the people feel a more lively interest than in those of this department; its facilities being felt in the various transactions of business, in the pleasures of correspondence, and the general diffusion of information.
—Postmaster General John McLean (1828)

These three major functions of the United States Post Office, identified by its chief administrator in 1828, had characterized it since its creation in 1789 and were essentially identical with those of its earlier predecessors. A major portion of the information-diffusion role of colonial and United States postal services was accounted for by the delivery of newspapers to nonlocal editors and subscribers, especially after the mid-eighteenth century, when newspaper publication began to occur elsewhere than in the four largest port cities. Spatial biases developed in the availability of not only public information but also private information as a result of the pretelegraphic delivery of commercial and private correspondence by postal services. However, the postal services did not have a monopoly over the long-distance flow of private information. It was also circulated by travelers and migrants, and probably to a lesser degree by itinerant peddlers, craftsmen, preachers, and lecturers.[1]

EXPANSION, POSTAGE RATES, AND CLIENTELE

More than ninety years after the founding of its colonial predecessor in 1693, the United States Post Office was still a skeletal system. In 1785, more than once-a-week service existed only between New York and Philadelphia, and New York mails for Albany were as yet confined to fortnightly departures. That same year Congress ordered the immediate improvement of operations, as a consequence of which, significant advances were made prior to the federal era. Stagecoaches replaced postriders on the northern portion of the major route between Portsmouth and Savannah and on the New York-to-Albany route, both of which were now served three times a week in summer and twice weekly in winter. Philadelphia-New York service remained a step in front, as departures from both termini were increased to five times weekly. Numerous cross-posts, or minor post roads, were established. Such links ran from Boston and Portsmouth to Concord, New Hampshire, from Albany to Springfield, from New York to Danbury, Connecticut, and in Pennsylvania, from Philadelphia through Bedford, to Pittsburgh. Nevertheless, the volume of commercial and other private information moved through the mails was very limited. Postal receipts from 1785 to 1787 for the entire country ranged from $27,096 to $29,598, and quarterly data for the next two years indicate little annual increase. One unsubstantiated estimate for the year 1790, when the United States possessed only 75 post offices and 1,875 miles of post roads, puts the total number of letters carried at 265,545. This figure, if correct, would mean that scarcely one letter per fifteen persons was delivered over the full twelve-month period.[2]

During the fifty years between 1790 and 1840, the postal system was considerably fleshed out. The number of post offices, the mileage of postal routes, and total annual postage receipts all climbed rapidly (Table 3.1). Although these were spectacular developments, at the end of the period the use of the mails for transmitting private information over long distances was probably still confined to a relatively small minority of the total population, most of whom were involved in commerce.

Wesley Rich provided estimates from an 1855 source for the total number of letters carried annually by the United States Post Office from 1790 to 1829. According to these somewhat questionable data, the number of letters moved annually per capita was roughly 0.37 in 1800, 0.51 in 1810, 0.92 in 1820, and 1.09 in 1829. The total number of letters allegedly carried was 2.0 million in 1800, 3.9 million in 1810,

Table 3.1. Growth of United States postal services, 1790–1840.

Data category	1790	1800	1810	1820	1830	1840	1840/1790
U.S. population (thousands)	3,929	5,297	7,224	9,618	12,901	17,120	4.4
Post offices	75	903	2,300	4,500	8,450	13,468	179.6
Population per post office (thousands)	52.4	5.9	3.1	2.1	1.5	1.3	—
Miles of post routes	1,875	20,817	36,406	73,492	115,176	155,739	83.1
Postage revenues (thousands of dollars)	37.9	280.8	551.7	1,111.9	1,185.0	4,543.0	119.9
Postage revenues per capita (dollars)	0.01	0.05	0.08	0.12	0.14	0.27	27.0

Source: Historical Statistics, pp. 7, 497; Wesley Rich, *The History of the United States Post Office to the Year 1829* (Cambridge: Harvard University Press, 1924), pp. 182–184; *HCSR* 3, no. 27 (Dec. 30, 1840), 430; Timothy Pitkin, *A Statistical View of the Commerce of the United States of America* (New Haven, 1835), pp. 338–339.

8.9 million in 1820, and 13.7 million in 1829. With data put forward by the post office itself, a presumably more reliable estimate can be arrived at for 1837. The annual report of the postmaster general for that year stated: "the whole number of letters delivered from the post offices of the United States . . . was 29,360,992. For free letters and dead letters may be added at least 3,000,000 more." Counting both free and dead letters, the amount of correspondence carried, while apparently substantially increased, still did not total more than 2.05 letters per capita per annum. In other words, as pretelegraphic times drew to a close, the volume of mail was sufficient to provide each adult inhabitant with approximately one piece of correspondence every third month.[3]

There is much evidence that the major share of private correspondence was accounted for by shipping merchants, commission merchants, brokers, factors, retailers, and other commercial agents. Postmaster General McLean indicated in 1828 that, "every year, no inconsiderable amount of the active capital of the country, in some form or other, passes through the mail." Earlier Adam Seybert had suggested that the country's commercial prosperity went hand-in-hand with the rapid increase in the number and length of well-regulated post roads. The operations of numerous merchants, such as Baltimore's Robert Oliver, bore out the role of the posts in the gathering of commercial information and the execution of business. An 1840 article claimed: "By far the greater portion of postage is paid on business letters, and it is the increase or diminution of this branch of correspondence, which mainly occasions an augmentation or declension of the revenues of the [Post Office] Department."[4]

Postage rates must have been an important factor in curtailing the use of the mails for private-information transmission outside the business community. Given the wage and income levels of farmers and laborers during the period, these rates in all likelihood loomed quite high, perhaps even prohibitive, to most individuals. The stamp fees established by Congress in 1792, even though lower than before, began at six cents for a communication of one sheet that was destined for another post office within 30 miles. Charges were then graduated by distance zones, with the scale reaching a peak of 25 cents for all distances in excess of 450 miles. Until after the introduction of the telegraph, double rates were assessed for two-sheet letters, triple rates for three-sheet letters, and quadruple rates for "packets" enclosing four or more sheets. In 1799 the rates were slightly raised, eight cents per sheet now being charged in the first 40-mile zone; and in 1815 a short-lived 50 percent increase went into effect. The fees introduced the following year remained unchanged until 1845. These ranged from six cents per page for the first 30 miles to 25 cents for distances over 400 miles. From 1794 on, extra charges were placed on intraurban delivery, with the proceeds going to the letter carrier.[5]

That these rates were perceived as costly by the vast majority of the population may be deduced from wage and income data. For example, daily wage rates for nonfarm labor in the United States as a whole stood at approximately $1.00 in 1800, $0.75 in 1818, and $0.85 in 1840; monthly wage rates for nonslave agricultural labor were roughly $10.00 in 1800, $9.30 in 1818, and $10.40 in 1840; and total annual income per capita in 1840, exclusive of persons employed in commerce and their dependents, varied from a low of $32 in Iowa to a high of $102 in Rhode Island, with the national mean being roughly $55.[6]

Regardless of whether the pretelegraphic usage of postal services was income elastic or not, there was still a considerable subpopulation that was precluded from sending private information through the mails, simply because of the illiteracy rates prevailing at the time. In 1840, the earliest date for which nationwide data are available, census authorities reported that no less than 22 percent of the population over 20 years old was illiterate—a figure that is usually regarded as too low.[7]

ROUTE DEVELOPMENT AND REGIONAL VARIATIONS

There was a tremendous 83-fold expansion of the postal route network from 1790 to 1840, as partly indicated by the main post roads existing in 1804 and 1834 (Maps 3.1 and 3.2). Yet one pretelegraphic postal route mile was not automatically equal with another, since there were important differences in road quality, means and speed of conveyance, and frequency of service. In the early nineteenth century, "many post roads were scarcely more than bridle paths, while others, such as the Boston Post Road out of New York through coastal Con-

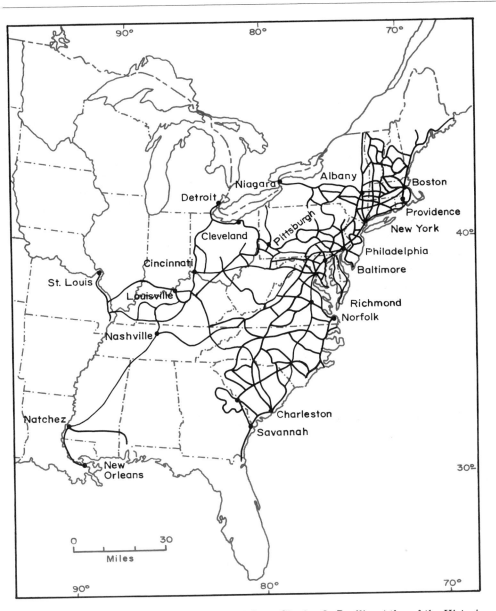

Map 3.1. Main post roads, 1804. Adapted from Charles O. Paullin, *Atlas of the Historical Geography of the United States* (Washington, D.C.: Carnegie Institute of Washington and the American Geographical Society of New York, 1932), plate 138J.

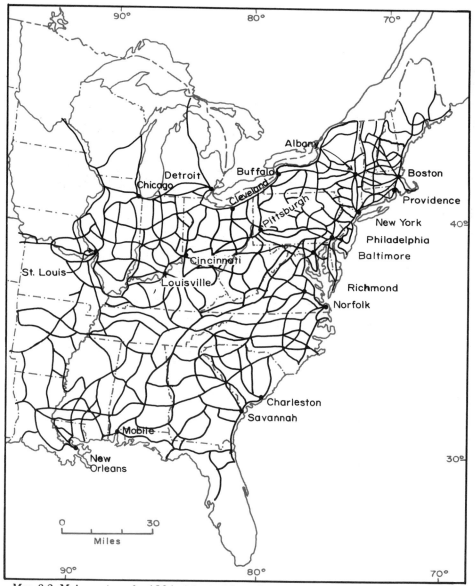

Map 3.2. Main post roads, 1834. Adapted from Paullin, *Atlas*, plate 139K. This map does not give a full picture of network expansion between 1804 and 1834 because of the double standard employed by its compilers, who allowed "main" post roads to include "the roads on the frontier in regions where there was but a single post road," while at the same time showing "only the most important roads" in densely populated areas such as New England.

necticut, were heavily traveled by coach and post riders" and were usually, but not invariably, less treacherous. Thereafter, because of the spread of turnpike construction, the authorization granted to the post-master general in 1815 to contract steamboat lines to carry the mails, the modest inception of railroad usage by the post office in 1834, and the appearance of express services two years later, the speed and dependability discrepancies between the best and the poorest routes became even more pronounced.[8]

On most routes, an increased volume of mail and improved service went hand in hand. Typically, newly established routes were served by individual postriders. Then, as the mails became too heavy to be carried on a single horse, they were transported either by means of a pack horse, led by a rider on horseback, or in a sulky or two-wheeled mail cart. With increasing volume they were sent by the regular stagecoach, which usually ensured swifter and safer deliveries. As late as 1840, very few routes benefited from carriers superior to the stagecoach. In 1835, when the long transition to railroad service had just commenced, the annual transportation of mails amounted to 7,817,973 miles by horseback and sulky, 16,874,050 miles by stages and post coaches, 906,959 miles by steamboat, and 270,504 miles by railroad. By 1840, the westward spread of the postal network had brought about a sizable increase in the annual transportation of mail by horse-powered means (12,182,445 miles by horseback and sulky, 20,299,278 by stage and post coach), while expanded railroad and steamboat mail service, combined (3,889,053 miles) accounted for little more than ten percent of the mileage total. Since a large share of the steamboat and railroad postal routes had twice-daily services, it is apparent that well over 90 percent of the 1840 routes were still dependent on the horse.[9]

In light of the preference given to the New York-Philadelphia link before 1790, as well as the known dimensions of public-information time lags, it is to be expected that the routes along the Wasington-Boston axis consistently had the quickest, most frequent service. At about the same time that mails were first being sent by steamboat to and from New York along the Hudson and the Long Island Sound, as well as to New Brunswick on the route to Philadelphia, it was observed: "The mail runs daily between all the great towns, and the commercial cities of the United States; twice a week to the capitals of each state, which are not commercial, and once a week to other places. The usual rate of travelling is forty miles per day on the cross roads, and from sixty to one hundred and twenty in twenty-four hours between the great commercial towns; from Philadelphia to New York, Baltimore and Washington city, the speed is greater, being at the rate of about seven miles per hour." This route superiority between the major centers of the Northeast was compounded by the employment of steamboats on the Trenton-Philadelphia leg of the New York-Philadelphia route. Further advantages were gained in 1819, when the Union Line of steamboats and stages was contracted to carry mail between Baltimore and Philadelphia, and again, in the mid-1820s when steamboats between Providence and New York were departing several times per week.[10]

A rapid-fire series of postal improvements along the Washington-Boston axis commenced in 1832, by which date twice-daily direct service existed between New York and Philadelphia in addition to a line of wayside deliveries along the same route. In that year "express" mails were provided between New York, Philadelphia, and Washington, with the New York-Philadelphia contract calling for speeds of 15 miles per hour and use of the partly opened Camden and Amboy Railroad. In 1834, mail was carried on the completed portion of the Boston and Providence Railroad, thereby hastening connections with the daily steamboat to New York, and a special New York-Philadelphia mail was instituted, with the overland portion being carried by rail. The following year, the New York-Philadelphia "express" mails were upped to a twice-daily schedule, the opening of the Wilmington and Susquehanna Railroad enabled twice-daily Washington-Baltimore service, and the New York-Providence steamboat deliveries were extended to Sunday. The net result was that mails could regularly be moved between Philadelphia and Boston in the remarkable time of 36 hours, with occasional claims of Washington-to-Boston service in 39 hours. From 1836 on, through mail between New York and Philadelphia was conveyed entirely by railroad, whether or not it was designated "express." Finally, in 1840 a new arrangement was made to speed New York-Boston mails via the rail services connecting New London, Norwich, and Worcester, which included facilities for en-route letter sorting by postal clerks. At that time the states through which the Washington-Boston axis passed were responsible for half of the annual postal transportation by railroad and steamboat.[11]

Perhaps the best indication of the relative speed and frequency of postal operations along the Washington-Boston axis is the repeated evidence of inferior service from the major cities of this axis to the leading centers in their respective hinterlands. A case in point is Philadelphis's postal connections in 1794. In that year, while mails for New York were departing five times weekly, it was advertised: "The mail for Lancaster, Yorktown, Carlisle, Shippensburg, Chambersburg, Bedford, Greensburg and Pittsburg closes every Saturday precisely at half past 11 in the morning. The mail for Reading, Lebanon, Harrisburg and Carlisle closes every Tuesday at 3 o'clock in the afternoon." Forty years later, shortly after the twice-daily Philadelphia-New York service had been speeded up by the railroad, the daily mail service to Lancaster was reduced to thrice weekly. As for Boston, in 1834 departures from that city for New York via Providence or New Haven were not matched in frequency on any of the Hub City's other thirty-one hinterland postal lines except those to its Cambridge suburb, Portsmouth, and Waltham, the latter only nine miles distant. Furthermore, postal shipments from New York to Albany and points west on the Erie Canal route, while numerous, were substantially fewer than those to Philadelphia. The picture, however, was not always one-sided. For example, by 1836 Boston had two railroad mails daily to and from Lowell.[12]

Despite the comparative superiority of postal links between Boston and Washington, operations along their lengths were not always reliable. During the 1790s, especially in wintertime, the New York-Philadelphia stage deliveries were at times wanting in regularity. In 1805 it was reported: "Philadelphia mails from New York are delayed, because the ferry boats to Paulus Hook N. J. have been frequently compelled to return to New York on account of floating ice." As late as 1835, *Niles' Weekly Register* noted: "We have had two failures of the mail east of Philadelphia, in the present week." Especially prior to railroad and steamboat connections, complaints were often lodged regarding the Baltimore-Philadelphia posts. The postmaster general noted in 1825 that, "during a considerable part of the winter and spring seasons of the year, when the weather is mild, the great mail route between [Philadelphia and Baltimore] . . . is so bad, as to render the rapid movement of the stages upon it impracticable." These conditions continued in the 1830s. In 1832, it was lamented that "the mails have been much interrupted on the road between Philadelphia and Baltimore during the present winter." Two years later, with some rails in operation, distress was expressed in Washington over the three days required for the newspaper-bearing mails to arrive from New York. Slow, late, and infrequent mails were nevertheless a much more common problem in the rest of the country. In some places the snail and the mud-turtle were popular symbols of the post office.[13]

Owing largely to the executive and congressional view that political unity depended on a well-informed populace, policies were developed in the 1790s to ensure that the developing postal network would not lag far behind the spread of settlement into the West and South. By 1810, Postmaster General Habersham could write: "Cross-roads are now established so extensively that there is scarcely a village, court house or public place of any consequence but is accommodated with the mail." By 1794, roads had been put through to Danville, (Kentucky), and Knoxville, (Tennessee); and as of 1812, nearly every road west of the Alleghenies had been constructed as a post road with some measure of assistance from federal funds.[14]

Despite post-road construction and the rapid multiplication of post offices, private information moved very slowly through the mails west of the Appalachians for most of the 1790–1840 period, although the larger cities had somewhat better service by the end of that time. Initially, conditions were primitive. Mail stages were not known in Ohio, Kentucky, and Tennessee until 1806 and 1807. In 1805, the mails between Cuyahoga (Cleveland) and Detroit were borne by "two faithful, enterprising hardy young woodsmen." The speed and frequency of the mails, even where stages were used, were such that in terms of private information, western urban settlements for a long time remained fairly well isolated from one another, as well as from the major eastern ports.[15]

Indications of the West's remoteness from the East in this regard are abundant. In 1798, "the schedule time of the mails from Philadelphia, the national capital, to Danville, Kentucky, was 17 days. From Philadelphia to Lexington, Kentucky, the time was supposed to be 19 days, though it often took much longer, up to 31 days, on account of bad roads and bad connections." In 1807, Cincinnati received mail once a week from the Ohio capital, Chillicothe, which in turn obtained mail from the east fortnightly. Not until 1816 did St. Louis obtain an irregular weekly postal link with the East; and in 1820, with service improved, a local paper stated: "we now have regular arrivals from . . . Washington to Baltimore in twenty [days], Philadelphia twenty-one, New York twenty-two, and Boston twenty-four." In 1818, the opening of the National Road to Wheeling facilitated matters somewhat, bringing with it thrice-weekly postal contacts between Ohio Valley ports and eastern centers. Stage deliveries along the physically arduous Washington-Wheeling route, however, continued to suffer long delays and even complete losses. In 1822, the postmaster general was forced to explain to inquiring legislators that "the failures and delays have been caused by the danger, difficulty, and impracticability . . . in crossing the Monongahela River at Brownsville, Pennsylvania; and that delays have sometimes been occasioned by some smaller streams in Maryland, but those have not caused any failures." Sixteen years later, another postmaster general, also called upon to provide "information in relation to the route's irregularities and failures," could only alibi: "for most of the failures there is no remedial power short of that which governs the seasons and controls the elements." As late as 1837, when the post office was boasting of recent dramatic improvements in delivery times, express mails from New York consumed 3.6 days in reaching Cincinnati and 4.3 days in reaching Louisville, if they succeeded in remaining on schedule. In both cases the ordinary mails, by which most private correspondence was sent, were about one day slower, and no further notable time reductions occurred until some time after the telegraph, when direct railroad ties with the Atlantic seaboard were completed.[16]

Quite early the postal route from Buffalo to Cleveland to Detroit, as well as the routes serving Pittsburgh, Cincinnati, Louisville, and St. Louis, came to have the same kind of relative intraregional superiority as that possessed by the Washington-Boston links in the more densely settled East. However, these Western routes were always years and sometimes decades behind their Eastern counterpart in the absolute quality of service offered. That is, while better connected with one another postally than were most other lesser frontier urban settlements, the leading centers of the Lake Erie and the Ohio and Upper Mississippi Valley urban subsystems were by comparison with the East informationally isolated from each other well into the 1830s. In 1814, when there were three mails per week between Albany and Buffalo, there was only one post weekly from Buffalo to Cleveland and Detroit. This was scheduled to take 6.9 days for the first leg alone, but seldom arrived without considerable delay because of the dreadful road conditions. By 1832, Buffalo-Cleveland posts departed daily, and Cleveland and Detroit exchanged mail three times weekly. Although there were dozens of other postal routes in northern Ohio at the time, the only other daily service in that area was between Cleveland and Pittsburgh. Likewise, Detroit's connecting route with Cleveland was the only one in all of the Michigan Territory to operate on a thrice-weekly basis. This movement was still confined to stages, which meant that it was hampered both by the mucky road through the Black Swamp between Toledo and Lower Sandusky and by the "fearful and horrible" road south of Detroit. Relief was not provided until the steamboats of Lake Erie were drafted for postal service.[17]

In 1816, once-a-week mail to St. Louis from Louisville and Cincinnati was six days in coming. Thus, a Cincinnati businessman who did not properly time the sending of a letter might not have it delivered in St. Louis for twelve or thirteen days, and might not receive a reply for over three weeks. Similar isolation existed between Pittsburgh and Cincinnati or Louisville, for in 1817 the Pittsburgh-Louisville stage mail was announced as a seven-day venture in each direction. Here, too, by 1832 the superior frequency of service to and from the region's leading cities was well established. In western Pennsylvania, where over sixty routes were concentrated, only those from Pittsburgh to Cleveland and from Pittsburgh to Wheeling functioned daily. Similarly, in southern Ohio the only daily mails proceeded from Wheeling to Cincinnati via Columbus, from Wheeling to Louisville via Maysville, Kentucky, and from Cincinnati to Louisville via Georgetown, Kentucky.[18] Although the time-saving potential of steamboat mails was early recognized, their costs discouraged the post office from completing arrangements until long after steamers had proven themselves commercially successful on the Ohio. It was 1831 before a thrice-weekly steamboat mail was established to connect both Louisville and Cincinnati with a land mail route from the East at a point on the Ohio about 150 miles east of Cincinnati. This line was apparently put on a daily schedule the following year, but by 1837 daily service was in evidence only between Louisville and Cincinnati. Despite the natural opportunity afforded by Lake Erie and the Ohio River, Ohio and Kentucky in 1840 accounted for less than 6 percent of the nation's annual postal transportation by steamboat and railroad, although at the same date the two states possessed well over 13 percent of the country's total population.[19]

Although Virginia, the Carolinas, and the Savannah Valley of Georgia were fairly well-populated long before the area to the west of the Appalachians, there, too, private information moved slowly via the mails for much of the 1790–1840 period.[20] As Wesley Rich indicated: "This part of the country had always lagged behind the other parts in the development of its roads and consequently of its mail service. We find [from the 1790s on] many references in the letters of the Postmaster General to irregular service and delays and interruptions of the mails in the South." Stage mails were not introduced in the South until 1797, and then only as far south as Petersburg, Virginia. Speed and frequency of service were particularly inferior on the main route from Petersburg to Augusta, Georgia, and on the Southern cross-posts. Although deemed a continuation of the nation's major post road, the Petersburg-Augusta route via Raleigh, North Carolina, and Columbia, South Carolina, did not obtain stage services until 1803, and it was many years before deliveries were made daily. The contrast between service on this route and that extending northward beyond Washington was constantly reflected in the press. As late as 1829, Hezekiah Niles stated from Baltimore: "We have latterly received more than 1500 letters a year from the states east and north of the Susquehannah, and except because of the violent robberies of the mail that took place, do not think that our loss has amounted to more than one in 500 . . . We cannot speak thus of the south and southwest generally . . . we send the REGISTER with more certainty to most distant places east, and with far more assurance of its safe arrival, than if to proceed 50 miles south of the Potomac." Over a decade later, it was reported: "The southern papers complain loudly of the repeated failure of the mails. In Charleston the Chamber of Commerce has taken the subject in hand." Similarly, in Norfolk, which like Charleston was served by a branch post line, the local *Phoenix* noted in 1841 that "the irregularity of the Mails has thrown the editorial corps upon their *wits*."[21]

Because of the slowness of Southern posts, private information of a commercial nature from the North was often conveyed outside of the mails, either by boat from New York to Charleston and Savannah, or overland by privately hired riders. Thus, in 1825 a newspaper in Fayetteville, North Carolina, a town on the major Petersburg-Augusta route, recounted that the postmaster general "has given notice to the mail contractors in this place, that he will shortly make it their duty, on occasions of great importance to the commercial community, to send express mails on their lines, at the rate of 11 miles an hour, and thus, by affording to all the news of important changes in the markets, to put a stop to the system of speculation which has lately been so extensively practised by individuals of one commercial town on those of another who were not possessed of the same means of information." Elsewhere than on the principal route to Augusta and on points served by the cross-posts to Norfolk, Wilmington, Charleston, and Savannah, conditions were still worse. It has been said of the situation in the early 1830s that for the remote districts, "particularly those in the mountains and the pine-barrens, the mails ran seldom, if at all, and stages never."[22]

In the lower South, from Augusta as far as New Orleans and beyond, postal connections were extremely poor. Mails to New Orleans over frequently altered routes passing through unsettled areas and Indian country began soon after the Louisiana Purchase. In 1806 this hazardous service was put on a weekly basis, but real improvements were long in coming. In 1824, when some mails from Washington to New Orleans went by way of Abingdon, Virginia, Knoxville, Tennessee, and Natchez, Mississippi, on a 24–25 day schedule, the road used was considered uniformly bad except for the part passing through the Indian country. Other mail was forwarded from Augusta via Montgomery and Mobile, from whence it was forwarded by steamer over the final 170 miles. "This route was considerably shorter . . . and the [Post] Office calculated it could be negotiated in 19 days if the necessary bridges [or ferries] were provided." This extension of the major North-South route was not promoted to thrice-weekly status until 1830, and even then mail shipments from Washington to New Orleans took a minimum of 14 days if all went well.[23]

Clearly, the postal isolation of the major Southern cities from the leading centers of the Northeast was equal to, and in the case of New Orleans in excess of, that of the Ohio Valley and Lake Erie ports. Moreover, there were no direct postal links between Charleston or Savannah and New Orleans or Mobile. Hence, major Southern cities were more remote from one another by letter than were cities of the Western interior. In 1835, the much improved indirect mail service from New Orleans to Charleston still must have been more than eight days in passage, for the listed time from the Louisiana hub to Columbia, South Carolina, was 7 days and 16 hours, and cross-posts from Columbia to Charleston were scheduled to consume another 16 hours.[24] Ultimately, some highly perceptible advances were made in the speed and quality of services to the Northeast. In 1836, express mails were extended to New Orleans, which soon cut delivery times from New York to about 9 days. In 1839 the Wilmington and Raleigh Railroad signed a contract with the post office that enabled mail from New York to reach Charleston in 2.6 days under the best of conditions, and in 3.5 days when because of weather or darkness, the boat connection at the Wilmington, North Carolina, terminus could not cross the bar at the mouth of the Cape Fear River (from 1826 through 1835 the New York-Charleston mail had taken well over 6 days). In 1839, rail arrangements in Georgia permitted the regular New York-New Orleans mail run to be completed in 9 days, thereby obviating the need of an express mail.[25]

URBAN CONCENTRATION OF POSTAL ACTIVITY

Whatever regional variations may have existed in the speed, frequency, and reliability of postal services, the most important aspect of spatial biases in the availability of postally conveyed private information throughout the entire 1790–1840 period was the extremely disproportionate urban concentration of mail origins and destinations. In consequence of the commercial dominance of postal usage, most of the meager revenue of the United States Post Office in 1790 (Table 3.1) "was derived from letters passing from one seaport to another." As was observed in an 1834 Senate report: "A commercial and manufacturing community have more correspondence and of course contribute a greater proportion of the resources of the [post office] department than an agricultural people."[26]

The pretelegraphic concentration of postal volume in cities may be surmised from existing data on receipts, or the "gross amount of letter and newspaper postage," collected at individual post offices for scattered dates between 1822 and 1841. The chief virtue of these postal receipt statistics is that the figures for the same place at any two dates are roughly comparable, owing to the more or less unaltered structure of postage rates between 1816 and 1845. While basic rates remained unchanged during this interval, triple rates were formalized in 1836 for letters and newspaper clippings delivered by "express mails." Thus, a specific volume of receipts at a given post office after 1836 would in all probability represent a somewhat smaller number of letters than the same income at the same office at an earlier date.[27]

The principal shortcoming of the data derives from the difficulty of using them to make accurate place-to-place comparisons of the amount of private information moving by mail. Postages rates were fixed by distance, with the post-1816 charge for the last zone, 400 miles or over, being $0.25 per sheet. Yet since it cannot be assumed that the percentage distribution of mail by rate zones was identical for any pair of cities, it also cannot be assumed that an equal level of postage receipts for two or more cities indicates an equal volume of business and personal correspondence. In particular, cities in the relatively low population accessibility areas of the South and West were likely to have much higher than normal percentages of their mail destined to places in their most expensive rate zone; that is, the number of letters sent per $1,000 of receipts was almost surely lower in such cities than in the major Northeastern urban centers with higher accessibility (Maps 2.18 and 2.20). The danger of equating receipts with mail volume is borne out by the case of Boston in 1834–35, when its postage receipts ($82,134.41) ranked third in the country, and were roughly two-thirds those of second-place Philadelphia ($122,334.19). Yet it was then asserted: "As it respects [mail] tonnage, Boston is greatly ahead of Philadelphia . . . and is second only to the great commercial emporium—New York."[28] The difficulty of making interurban comparisons of postage receipt data is further compounded by the impossibility of breaking down individual totals into subtotals for letter postage receipts and newspaper postage receipts.[29]

Despite the impossibility of making consistent one-to-one translations from local postal receipts to local mail volume, it is possible to draw several general conclusions from the available data (Tables 3.2 and 3.3). In total terms, if not in per capita terms, New York and the other major Northeastern ports dominated private information exchange through the mails in the final pretelegraphic decades. During earlier decades, when postal services had been much more limited, their domination was even more pronounced. In 1791, for example, when the postage revenue collected for the entire country was less than half that garnered by New York City in 1822, post offices in the four leading Northeastern ports brought in substantially more than 50 percent of the national total.[30] In the early 1820s, when New York had little more than 1.5 percent of the nation's population, the city accounted for about 8.5 percent of all postal receipts.[31] From 1826 onward, New York was consistently responsible for 10.0 or more percent of the country's postal receipts. In both the early 1820s and the early 1840s, as well as at every intervening date for which data has been found, New York, Philadelphia, Boston, and Baltimore took in close to one-quarter or more of United States postal receipts, although the four cities had only 3.92 percent of the nation's population in 1820, and 4.94 percent in 1840. (Actually, in 1826–27, 1828–29, 1829–30, 1830–31, 1831–32, and 1832–33 the postal receipts of the four ports exceeded 25 percent of the country's total). These figures are consistent with both the alleged preeminence of commerce in generating mail and the dominance of New York and its three sister ports over the nation's commerce during this period.[32]

The location quotients for the major cities of the Western interior and the South (Tables 3.2 and 3.3) indirectly suggest that these places usually dominated private information flows through the mails at the regional level to a degree at least equal to the Northeastern ports.

Table 3.2. Postal receipts for selected major cities, 1822.

Location	1820 population	1822 postal receipts	Percentage of 1820 U.S. population (A)	Percentage of 1822 U.S. postal receipts (B)	Location quotient B/A[a]
United States	9,638,453	$1,108,309.84	100.00	100.00	1.00
New York[b]	152,056	94,367.90	1.58	8.51	5.40
Philadelphia[c]	108,809	77,048.57	1.13	6.95	6.16
Boston[d]	54,024	51,739.04	.56	4.67	8.33
Baltimore	62,738	41,442.79	.65	3.74	5.75
Albany	12,630	11,033.51	.13	1.00	7.60
Providence	11,767	8,816.27	.12	.80	6.52
Rochester	3,120	2,161.70	.03	.19	6.03
Portland	8,581	5,349.80	.09	.48	5.42
New Haven	7,147	6,467.52	.07	.58	7.87
Springfield, Mass.	3,914	1,164.58	.04	.11	2.59
Hartford	4,726	5,883.11	.05	.53	10.83
Portsmouth, N.H.	7,327	3,355.17	.08	.30	3.98
Worcester	2,962	921.91	.03	.08	2.71
Cincinnati	9,642	5,759.11	.10	.52	5.16
Louisville	4,012	5,245.06	.04	.47	11.37
Pittsburgh	7,248	6,726.46	.08	.68	8.07
St. Louis	3,700	2,570.32	.04	.22	6.04
Wheeling	1,200	1,799.01	.01	.16	13.35
Lexington	5,279	4,609.92	.05	.42	7.60
Nashville	4,366	5,043.02	.05	.46	10.05
Buffalo	2,095	1,335.45	.02	.12	5.54
Detroit	1.422	1,237.63	.01	.11	7.57
Cleveland	606	309.82	.006	.03	4.45
New Orleans	27,176	23,251.98	.28	2.10	7.44
Charleston	24,780	27,254.39	.26	2.46	9.57
Richmond	12,067	17,635.13	.13	1.59	12.72
Mobile	1,935	2,051.86	.02	.19	9.22
Savannah	7,523	16,727.85	.08	1.51	19.39
Norfolk	8,478	6,528.09	.09	.59	6.70

Source: See Table 1.1; U.S. Senate, *Letter from Postmaster General Transmitting Statements Showing the Amount of Postage Received at Each of the Post Offices of the United States and the Territories Thereof, During the Year 1822*, Executive

Table 3.2 (continued)

Paper No. 95, 18th Cong., 1st sess., 1824; *NWR* 22, no. 6 (Apr. 13, 1822), 96; 24, no. 22 (Aug. 2, 1823), 352; Richard C. Wade, *The Urban Frontier: Pioneer Life in Early Pittsburgh, Cincinnati, Lexington, Louisville, and St. Louis* (Chicago: University of Chicago Press, 1964), pp. 60, 201; Pitkin, *Statistical View*, p. 539.

    a. Here and in Table 3.3, B/A was actually arrived at by computing the compound fraction:

$$\frac{\dfrac{\text{Local postal receipts}}{\text{Local population}}}{\dfrac{\text{U.S. postal receipts}}{\text{U.S. population}}}$$

    b. New York and its boroughs as constituted under the act of consolidation in 1898.
    c. Including suburbs (Kensington, Northern Liberties, Spring Garden, and South-wark).
    d. Including suburbs (Charlestown and Roxbury).

Table 3.3. Postal receipts for selected major cities, 1840–1841.

Location	1840 population	1840–41 postal receipts[a]	Percentage of 1840 U.S. population (A)	Percentage of 1840–41 U.S. postal receipts (B)	Location quotient B/A[b]
U.S. population	17,069,435	$3,005,370.15[c]	100.00	100.00	1.00
New York[d]	391,114	337,983.37	2.29	11.25	4.91
Philadelphia[e]	220,423	171,987.83	1.29	5.72	4.48
Boston[f]	118,857	100,894.53	.70	3.36	4.82
Baltimore	102,313	85,296.92	.60	2.84	4.74
Albany	33,721	31,125.04	.20	1.04	5.24
Providence	23,171	17,748.60	.17	.59	4.35
Rochester	20,191	18,244.96	.12	.61	5.14
Portland	15,218	4,580.97	.09	.15	1.71
New Haven	12,960	10,518.74	.08	.35	4.61
Springfield, Mass.	10,985	4,025.51	.06	.13	2.08
Hartford	9,468	10,272.84	.06	.34	6.16
Portsmouth, N.H.	7,887	1,955.50	.05	.07	1.41
Worcester	7,497	4,195.15	.04	.14	3.18

(continued)

Table 3.3 (continued)

Location	1840 population	1840–41 postal receipts[a]	Percentage of 1840 U.S. population (A)	Percentage of 1840–41 U.S. postal receipts (B)	Location quotient B/A[b]
Cincinnati	46,338	38,177.21	.27	1.30	4.80
Louisville	21,210	21,754.64	.12	.72	5.82
Pittsburgh	21,115	25,610.34	.12	.85	6.89
St. Louis	16,469	26,145.33	.10	.87	9.02
Wheeling	7,885	2,330.02	.05	.08	1.68
Lexington	6,997	8,602.35	.04	.29	6.98
Nashville	6,929	10,912.77	.04	.36	8.94
Buffalo	18,213	11,729.08	.11	.39	3.67
Detroit	9,102	5,257.75	.05	.18	3.28
Cleveland	6,071	8,962.96	.04	.30	8.38
New Orleans	102,193	78,188.02	.60	2.60	4.35
Charleston	29,261	45,156.35	.17	1.50	8.76
Richmond	20,153	31,343.81	.12	1.04	8.82
Mobile	12,672	34,643.39	.07	1.13	15.17
Savannah	11,214	20,149.50	.07	.67	10.21
Norfolk	10,920	10,553.51	.06	.35	5.49

Source: See Table 1.1; U.S. House, *Letter from the Postmaster General, Transmitting a Statement of the Nett Revenue at Each Post Office in the United States for the Year Ending on the 30th June, 1841*, Document No. 65, 27th Cong., 2nd sess., 1842.

a. The figures in this column represent net postal receipts, whereas those given in Tables 3.1 and 3.2 represent gross postal receipts. Thus, there is a discrepancy between the United States total shown here and that shown for 1840 United States postage revenues in Table 3.1. Net receipts were apparently determined by deducting from gross receipts the salaries paid to the local postmaster and his employees.

b. See note a in Table 3.2.

c. Excluding receipts collected at twelve Canadian offices.

d. New York and its boroughs as constituted under the act of consolidation in 1898.

e. Including suburbs (Kensington, Moyamensing, Northern Liberties, Spring Garden, and Southwark).

f. Including suburbs (Cambridge, Charlestown, Roxbury, and Dorchester).

Statewide data reveal that St. Louis was responsible for 42.5 percent of Missouri's postal receipts in 1840–41, but for only 4.3 percent of its 1840 population. Similarly, in 1840–41 the New Orleans post office took in 79.9 percent of Louisiana's postage, but the Crescent City accounted for only 28.9 percent of the state's 1840 population. However, the extremely high postal receipt-to-population ratios registered by many of the interior and Southern cities, such as Louisville, Wheeling, and Savannah in 1820, and St. Louis, Mobile, and Savannah in 1840, were very likely inflated by the crucial commercial links existing between them and their relatively distant and larger Northeastern counterparts. That is, these cities almost certainly sent a comparatively small number of letters per $1,000 of receipts, owing to the large share of their mailings being charged the maximum 400-mile rate.

Finally, there was an extremely close relationship throughout the 1820–1840 period between absolute urban population growth and absolute increases in postal receipts. When 1822–1840 receipt increases were tested against 1820–1840 population increments for the selected cities, a correlation of .9921 was obtained (R^2 = 98.42 percent).[33] In extreme cases this meant that the city with the largest population growth—New York—had far and away the largest postal receipt increases, while the city with the smallest absolute population expansion—Portsmouth, New Hampshire—actually had an absolute decline in postal receipts.[34] Since the wholesaling-trading complex was the major source of urban-size growth during these years, the high correlation is also consistent with the part ascribed to commerce in generating mail.

The little data available on the actual mail volume of individual cities is quite revealing, if far from conclusive. In 1828 it was reported: "Between fifty and sixty thousand letters are sent through the [New York post] office every week." If the weekly volume is set at 55,000, then the annual total, barring marked seasonal variations, would be 2,860,000 letters. When juxtaposed with the only available national estimate of letters carried during 1828, which set them at 12,785,072, this figure indicates that New York apparently accounted for 21.6 percent of the country's letter origins. This crude approximation seems to clash with postal receipt data, which shows the New York post office bringing in no more than 11.8 percent of the national total. The two percentage figures can be partially reconciled by allowing that a very large relative share of New York's post was destined to its immediate hinterland, as well as to cities such as Philadelphia, Boston, and Albany in the city's intermediate postal-rate zones. This would still permit an absolutely large mail traffic with distant Western and Southern cities. The possibility that the 1828 report was an exaggeration appears diminished by an 1833 claim by the *New York Gazette* that "the amount of letters received at the [New York] post office for the last six days . . . [was] 109,620." Of this total, about 86,000 letters were of domestic origin. If it is assumed that one domestic letter was sent for every one received, then the 1828–1833 increase in New York letter origins by approximately 56 percent would not appear to be very inconsistent with the 49 percent increase of New York postal receipts over roughly the same five-year span.[35]

A much lower weekly volume of postage-paid mail was reported for New York in the spring of 1838 (Table 3.4). At that time commercial activities were in the doldrums, so that one would expect postal volumes to be off. Regardless of whether or not the 1838 figure puts the lie to the 1828 and 1833 estimates, it convincingly demonstrates

Table 3.4. Letters charged with postage in five major cities during one week, 1838.

City	Letters	Week ending
New York[a]	42,734	June 13
Philadelphia[b]	20,193	June 17
Baltimore	9,776	June 13
Richmond	3,032	June 16
Washington, D.C.[c]	2,325	June 9

Source: U.S. Senate, *Report from the Postmaster General*, Executive Document No. 1, 26th Cong., 2nd sess., 1840, p. 490.

a. Only Manhattan Island, which legally constituted New York at the time.

b. Apparently including only suburbs not possessing separate post offices. Because of the omission of certain Philadelphia and New York suburbs, ratio comparisons cannot be drawn with the population and postal receipt data in Table 3.3.

c. Owing to Executive and Congressional privileges, most of the mail emanating from Washington, D.C., went free of postage.

that the absolute number of letters generated by New York was far ahead of other major centers.

THE CONCENTRATION OF FOREIGN MAIL IN NEW YORK

New York's time lag advantages over other places with respect to public information of European origin were matched by her time lag advantages in the availability of private information of European origin. However, neither type of advantage explains the city's apparent contact array biases, that is, the highly disproportionate concentration of foreign mail destinations within the city.

New York's time lag advantages in the receipt of private information from Europe through the mails were of considerably earlier origin than the establishment of her clear-cut public informational advantages. Because of its central location, New York was chosen in 1755 to serve as the western terminus of the four-vessel brig line established by British postal authorities to carry American-bound mails on a regular basis. The New York vessels continued to run until after the Revolution, when another special line of ships was put briefly into operation to carry mails between New York and France. Service to Britain continued to function except for postponement during the War of 1812. Thereafter, "the little brigs kept up their work until 1828, when they finally succumbed before the superior service of the various packet lines." Until the coming of the Black Ball packets, which immediately began to siphon off the mail volume of the British ships, there was no guarantee that New Yorkers would always be first to receive privately conveyed information, for much correspondence went outside the regular mail on vessels that were frequently faster than the postal brigs.[36]

The volume of mail from England and the Continent funneled through New York to the country as a whole grew steadily as the speed, punctuality of departure, and general reliability of the growing packet service became generally known and as official arrangements became institutionalized—until in 1840 the British government discontinued employing the New York packets and instead entered into contracts with the Boston-bound Cunard Line. In 1821 a single packet could deliver over 5,500 letters, a figure that was raised to between 6,000 and

7,000 letters in 1826. In 1830 the single-day delivery record climbed to 8,000, only to be surpassed by a count of 9,539 in 1836 and nearly 12,000 in 1840. A very high percentage of this mail was directed to destinations within New York itself, a percentage that held with remarkable consistency over the years (Table 3.5).[37]

It may be reasonably disputed that there is an element of deception in the figures that show New York City as then constituted receiving a volume of mail twenty or more times that of its share of the national population.[38] This was because not all international correspondence was carried through the regular mails. Merchants sometimes found it convenient to forward written messeges on their own vessels, which may have meant that a good deal of mail left and entered the country from ports other than New York during the 1820s and 1830s.[39] However, New York merchants themselves sometimes sent and received mail via their own ships and other vessels not sailing for the packet lines.[40] Thus, any argument that the destination data are incomplete would have to apply for both New York and the rest of the country. Moreover, if most international correspondence had to do with commercial affairs, then New York's high relative frequency of postal contact with Europe was

Table 3.5. Destinations of European mail arriving in New York, 1821–1838.

Date	Total letters arriving	Number destined for New York	Number destined for rest of U.S.	Percentage destined for New York
Single day, February 1821	5,533	2,191	3,342	39.6
Jan. 1– Dec. 31, 1834	420,359	183,855	236,504	43.7
Single day, February 1836	9,539	4,532	5,007	47.5
Jan. 1– June 30, 1838	249,548	101,848	138,700	42.3

Source: NWR 19, no. 26 (Feb. 24, 1821), 432; 48, no. 3 (Mar. 21, 1835), 42; 50, no. 1 (Mar. 5, 1836), 4; 54, no. 23 (Aug. 4, 1838), 367.

Table 3.6. New York's share of United States foreign trade, 1821–1838 (in millions of dollars).

Year	Total U.S. imports	Imports via New York	Total U.S. exports	Exports via New York	New York imports and exports as a percentage of U.S. foreign trade
1821	62	23	64	13	28.6
1834	126	73	104	25	42.6
1836	189	118	128	28	46.1
1838	113	68	108	23	41.2

Source: Robert Greenhalgh Albion, *The Rise of New York Port, 1815–1860* (New York: Charles Scribner's Sons, 1939), pp. 390–391.

not inconsistent with the city's share of the country's foreign trade (cf. the final columns of Tables 3.5 and 3.6). The 1821 incongruity may be owing to the unrepresentativeness of the single-day data, to the possibility that the New York packets had not as yet captured foreign trade from other ports to the same extent as in later years, or to some other factor that is not immediately apparent.

Interurban Commodity Flows and
Long-Distance Information Circulation

By 1800 the metropolis [of New York] had outdistanced its rival American cities
in the field of commerce.
—Sidney I. Pomerantz

The key relationships between trade patterns and interurban information flows acquire particular significance from the fact that most long-
distance trade in the pretelegraphic United States, whether involving
agricultural products, raw materials, or manufactured goods, was in
some sense interurban. At some point in their journey from ultimate
origin to ultimate destination, goods usually moved either from one
port city to another, or from an urban collection center to an urban distribution center. One exception occurred in those sparsely settled areas
where farmers moved their own produce over considerable distances,
such as down the Ohio and Mississippi Rivers, to a final urban market.
However, this exception was limited, partly because the items taken by
farmers to places such as New Orleans often passed through wholesaling
channels and then moved to other towns or cities. Also, as population
densities increased, individual long-distance agricultural shipments
rapidly decreased. At first, the single farmer was replaced by the
local storekeeper, who did much of his local business by barter, and
who assembled many small produce lots that were shipped "to a central
market [city], where they were consigned to a commission merchant
or to the merchant's wholesale supplier." From that point in local
development, the interurban component of agricultural trade normally
became increasingly dominant. "Before 1820 in those parts of the
East enjoying good transportation facilities, and by the 1830s in many
areas of the West, the principal purchasers of farm products offered for

sale, even in the small towns, were [urban-based] produce buyers and forwarders."[1]

In view of the interurban character of most pretelegraphic long-distance United States trade, and the fact that trade is generally both a product and a generator of information flow, a picture of the contact-array spatial biases in information availability for the coastal, river, and lake cities involved can be obtained from port-by-port shipping arrival data and related descriptive materials on coastal trade and shipping on inland waterways. Such materials, however, must be seen against a back-drop of the general characteristics of domestic long-distance trade from 1790 to 1840.

LONG-DISTANCE DOMESTIC TRADE

Relation to Foreign Trade. The decade 1810–1820 has been called "the great turnabout" in American economic development. The two prior decades had marked a high point in the country's dependence on foreign trade, after which, exports changed in character and declined in relative importance vis-à-vis domestic trade. In 1793 foreign commerce had been greatly stimulated by the outbreak of the Napoleanic Wars. The hostilities allowed neutral American shipowners and merchants to capture much of the West Indian trade previously held by the British, French, and Spanish. As a result of the burgeoning of this carrying and re-export trade and the export of domestic products, "the economic development of the United States was tied to international trade and shipping" between 1793 and 1808, at which point a sharp decline was brought on by passage of the Embargo Act in response to repeated British and French seizures of United States vessels. Foreign trade expansion was also rebuffed by the Nonintercourse Act of 1809, for-bidding commercial relations with Britain and France, and by the British blockade during the War of 1812. There was a marked revival in the absolute volume of foreign trade subsequent to the war, particularly as a result of increasing cotton shipments: from 1820, cotton exports annually accounted for one-third or more of the total value of the United State's exports, and from 1835 through 1840, cotton's share did not dip below 50 percent. However, events had turned the country in upon itself economically. By 1825, the year in which shipments overseas reached their highest peak since 1818, the per capita value of exports was less than it had been before the Revolutionary War. Even in leading mercantile centers such as Boston, Philadelphia, and Baltimore, the per capita value of exports had declined sizably since the Embargo Act (Table 4.1).[2]

Although per capita export data give some indication of the growing relative importance of domestic trade, they do not shed light on the exact magnitude of domestic trade increases. Unfortunately, only fragmentary statistics exist on domestic coastal, inland waterway, and overland trade. It is therefore quite difficult to draw a clear picture of the mounting relative and absolute importance of such trade. However, an imperfect glimpse is obtained by comparing the gross tonnage of ships employed in foreign trade with that of ships employed in coastwise and internal trade (Table 4.2).

Although tonnage figures grossly reflect "the great turnabout" of 1810–1820, they fail to do justice to the growing relative importance of domestic trade, for a number of reasons. First, one ton of shipping employed in foreign trade was not fully comparable to one ton of shipping employed in coastal and inland waterway trade. The distances involved in foreign trade were much greater than those involved in domestic shipping. Therefore, the number of spatial interactions, or trade volume, per ton per annum was almost certainly larger in the

Table 4.1 Exports per capita in real terms for major mercantile cities, 1800–1825.[a]

Year	Boston[b]	Philadelphia[b]	Baltimore	New York[b]
1800	$162	$139	$196	$160
1810	131	86	68	117
1820	85	45	62	85
1825	71	76	38	175

Source: Gordon C. Bjork, "Foreign Trade," in Gilchrist, Growth of the Seaport Cities, p. 56.

a. Export values from federal returns, deflated according to the Warren-Pearson Wholesale Commodity Index, with 1790 = 100.

b. Including suburban population.

domestic than in the foreign case. Second, while there was no way in which foreign-trade vessels could escape registration, some domestic-trade vessels could be exempted. For example, not all coastal vessels of less than twenty tons were required to secure a government license— although admittedly, many of the boats under twenty tons that partook in domestic shipping must have been involved in local rather than long-distance interurban trade. Moreover, vessels registered for foreign trade often moved from one American port to another between Atlantic crossings. Finally, tonnage figures for ships cannot fully represent domestic trade expansion because they ignore overland trade.

It is nevertheless safe to conclude that until the second decade of the nineteenth century, long-distance information circulation had a large external component, that is, a significant share of the long-distance interurban flow of information had its origin or its destination overseas. But thereafter, the internal component acquired increasing primacy. This conclusion is also consistent with the ratio of foreign news to domestic news contained in the American press until after the War of 1812.

Long-Distance Versus Short-Distance Domestic Trade. The small amount of domestic trade that occurred prior to the second war with Britain was overwhelmingly dominated by short intraregional move-

Table 4.2. Documented tonnage of United States vessels employed in foreign and domestic trade, 1790–1840 (in thousands of gross tons).

Kind of trade	1790	1800	1810	1820	1830	1840
Foreign	346	667	981	584	538[a]	763
Coastwise and internal	104	272	405	588	517[a]	1,177
On Western rivers	—	—	—	27	33	118
On Great Lakes	—	1	2	4	11	54

Source: Historical Statistics, pp. 445–446; William N. Parker and Franklee Whartenby, "The Growth of Output Before 1840," in *Trends in the American Economy in the Nineteenth Century* (Princeton: Princeton University Press, 1960), p. 203.
a. The decline in tonnage during 1820–1830 is presumably attributable to the removal of defunct vessels and other "ghost tonnage" from the Treasury records during 1828–1830.

ments: "In becoming politically independent of England, the old thirteen provinces developed little more commercial intercourse with each other in proportion to their wealth and population than they had maintained in colonial days . . . Each group of States lived a life apart." As of 1800, except for the highway to Pittsburgh, "no road served as a channel of commerce between different regions of the country. In this respect New England east of the Connecticut was as independent of New York as both were independent of Virginia, and as Virginia in her turn was independent of Georgia and South Carolina." West of the Alleghenies, where less than 10 percent of the country's population was settled, the Ohio River was the main artery of traffic. But the valley of the Ohio "had no more to do with that of the Hudson, the Susquehanna, the Potomac, the Roanoke, and the Santee, than the valley of the Danube with that of the Rhone, the Po, or the Elbe." The country's local internal trade at this date occurred mainly between the leading seaports and their immediate hinterlands: between Boston and easternmost Massachusetts, between Philadelphia and both the Delaware Valley and southeastern Pennsylvania, between Baltimore and the shores of Chesapeake Bay, and between New York and both the Hudson Valley and Long Island.[3]

Immediately after the War of 1812 the settled areas to the west of the Alleghenies remained as commercially isolated as in 1800, but the Northeast and South began to indulge in an expanding volume of long-distance trade, including the southward redistribution of European imports from New York and other ports. This trade was the result of the South's growing commitment to cotton and the Northeast's increasing specialization in commerce and foreign exchange. Long-distance trade took on continually larger dimensions not only between places in the regionally differentiated Northeast, South, and West, but also intra-regionally, that is, between the largest cities of the Northeast, the Ohio and Upper Mississippi valleys, and Lake Erie. All this transpired in the wake of the vigorous development of internal transportation. The 1820s saw the completion of the Erie and other important canals, as well as the diffusion of the steamboat on the Western rivers, the Great Lakes, and along some coastal shipping lanes. The 1830s witnessed the stepped-up pace of canal construction, with the total mileage of operating canals leaping from 1,277 in 1830 to 3,326 in 1840, and the most important additions occurring in Pennsylvania and Ohio. Canals such as the Delaware and Raritan considerably shortened the shipping distances between New York, Philadelphia, Baltimore, and other Atlantic ports (Map 4.1). The 1830s also witnessed the nascence of the steam railroad, with total trackage growing to somewhere in the vicinity of 3,000 disjointed miles (Map 4.2). However, during the 1830s the rail lines chiefly aided "local rather than regional or interregional commerce."[4]

Not only did transportation improvements of the 1820s and 1830s greatly amplify the significance of long-distance trade, but they also brought about a reorientation in the direction of lengthy commodity flows. When the Ohio Canal was completed in 1833, "a part of the surplus grain of Pennsylvania, Kentucky, and southern Ohio, which formerly had been shipped down the Mississippi River, was diverted to the eastern route via [the Erie Canal] to the coast."[5] Because of the incompleteness of the statistics, however, there has been considerable debate over the South's self-sufficiency in foodstuffs, and the related volume of interregional agricultural flow from the West to the South, so that it is difficult to assess how much overall redirection occurred in the 1830s.[6]

The most important feature of domestic interregional trade in the quarter-century following the War of 1812 was the coastwise exchange of goods between the Northeast and the South. The South sent its basic staples northward, and to a much lesser degree up the Mississippi to the West, and in return for its cotton, tobacco, sugar, and rice received finished goods of both foreign and domestic origin from the Northeast, which also exported such goods to the West. By 1836, "over four-fifths of the tonnage coming to tidewater over the Erie Canal came from western New York State and less than one-fifth came from western states." This discrepancy indicates that the West-Northeast trade was still relatively unimportant in comparison to the Northeast-South exchange, although it may also be deceptive in that some Western produce moved to the Northeast by way of New Orleans. Nevertheless, the 1839 consumption of Northeastern imports in the South has been put at perhaps four times that in the West.[7]

Coastal and Inland-Waterway Transport Vis-à-vis Long-Distance

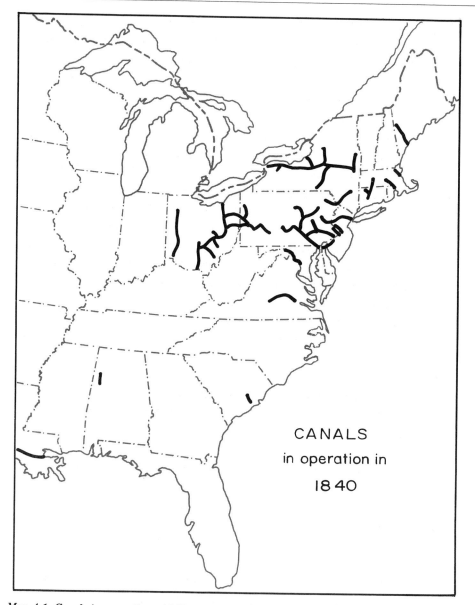

Map 4.1. Canals in operation, 1840. Adapted from Emory R. Johnson, T. W. Van Metre, G. G. Heubner, and D. S. Hanchett, *History of Domestic and Foreign Commerce of the United States* (Washington, D.C.: Carnegie Institution of Washington, 1915), II, 228.

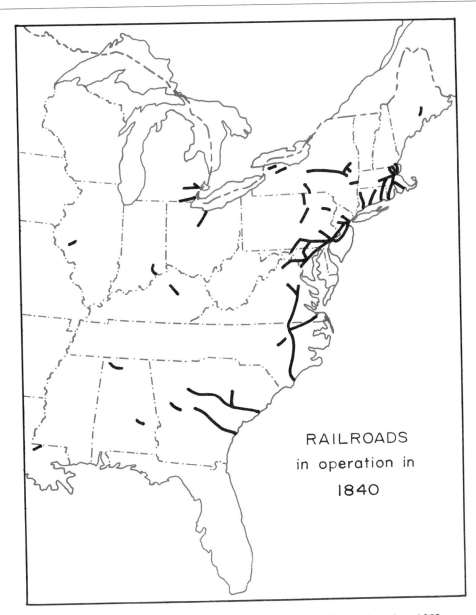

Map 4.2. Railroads in operation, 1840. Adapted from Paullin, *Atlas*, plate 138L.

RAILROADS

in operation in

1840

Overland Trade. In post-1815 interregional trade, little long-distance commodity movement went by overland means of transportation. Instead, the Northeast-South trade was virtually synonymous with coastwise shipping, and the Northeast-West trade was dominated by canal. After the mid-1820s the West-South trade and Great Lakes shipments took place almost entirely in steamboats and other waterborne vessels. The commanding role of water transport in long-distance domestic trade is suggested by the importance of coastal shipping alone. Israel Andrews "estimated in 1852 that the coasting trade accounted for half the total flow of internal commerce in both tonnage and value." This fraction must have been much larger prior to 1840, when the inland waterway trade of the West was absolutely and relatively smaller and when railroad shipments were insignificant.[8] It may be safely assumed that the share of coastwise trade in total domestic trade loomed even larger before the War of 1812, although during that war the British blockade gave long-distance overland trade a brief period of glory. In the 1790s, "the proximity of the great part of the population to the seacoast made it cheaper and more convenient to carry on the [little] interstate trade that did exist by means of small sailing-vessels plying along the coast."[9]

The limited role of overland transportation in long-distance domestic trade was owing to its costliness. From 1800 to 1819, freight charges for shipment by wagon varied from time to time and place to place between 30 and 70 cents per ton-mile.[10] A sharp decline in wagon haulage charges first occurred in association with the general price deflation of 1819–1821: "Before 1819 westward from Philadelphia and Baltimore they [rates] had ranged from 30 cents a ton-mile to more than double that figure. During 1822 they were quoted as low as 12 cents." Thereafter, until the 1840s, charges apparently followed general price trends to a degree, although in some cases road and turnpike improvements may also have contributed to rate reductions: "A Pennsylvania estimate of 1824 gives the cost of turnpike transportation in that state as little more than 13 cents a ton-mile. At the time when railroads were first introduced [in the early 1830s], 20 cents a ton-mile appears to have been regarded as the average wagon charge."[11] In 1839 an engineer-economist estimated that overland transport costs were 15 to 20 cents per ton-mile by turnpike, 10 to 15 cents by macadam road, and 2.5 cents by railroad. Despite the appearance of lower rates, the railroads were of little help to long-distance overland freight costs because frequent and highly expensive transshipments were necessary between independent lines, whose termini were often separated by considerable distances (Map 4.2).[12]

Although these costs suggest that cheap commodities could not move overland for long distances without raising their prices to unmarketable levels, the prohibitive magnitude of absolute wagon ton-mile rates cannot be appreciated fully unless juxtaposed with water-transport rates. An 1816 Senate Committee Report indicated that the cost of importing a ton of goods from Europe was about $9.00, or roughly the cost for moving the same ton of goods 30 miles overland. At the same period "the mere charge for carting wheat to Philadelphia equaled its whole selling price if it were drawn 218 miles; for corn this was true for a distance of 135 miles." Fifteen years later it was stated: "A barrel of flour can be shipped from Philadelphia to Liverpool . . . for fifty cents, while, on a turnpike road from Pittsburgh to Philadelphia, a tenth of the distance, it would cost five dollars." On the opening of the entire length of the Erie Canal, transport costs between Buffalo and Albany supposedly fell 90 percent. At the same time the Columbus *Ohio State Journal* noted: "It takes thirty days to transport goods [overland] from Philadelphia to this place, and costs five dollars per hundred. From New York city to this place [via the Erie Canal] twenty days, and costs two dollars and fifty cents per hundred." During the late 1820s vessels moving flour from Albany down the Hudson and around to Providence and Boston usually assessed a tariff of $4.50 per ton, "but sharp competition often lowered the charge to $2.50 per ton. By comparison teamsters demanded $10 a ton just to haul goods the 45 miles between Boston and Providence." Similarly, as a result of the steamboat, during the 1820s and 1830s "the reduction in upstream river freights was so much greater than the decline of wagon rates that any article of unusual weight or bulk could be shipped more economically to Cincinnati from the eastern seaboard . . . by way of New Orleans." Finally, canal rates, which were considerably higher than those imposed by coasting vessels, were on the average about 1.5 cents per ton-mile in 1839, or less than one-tenth the overland cost absorbed in most instances.[13]

However, these costs did not entirely prevent pretelegraphic long-distance overland trade other than during the War of 1812. Prior to the opening of the Erie Canal, turnpike routes westward from Philadelphia and Baltimore had served as arteries for long-distance wagon shipments: "It is estimated that in the early 1820s the Pittsburgh Pike [from Philadelphia] carried about 30,000 tons of goods annually, the National Road [from Baltimore] about 10,000 tons." Little of this commerce moved from West to East, for it was comprised overwhelmingly of manufactured items of Eastern and English origin: "High valued manufactures always could bear the burdensome overland transport costs from the East; it was western produce that could not absorb the charges eastward." The relative importance of westward overland flows of manufactured items nevertheless diminished after the Erie Canal had become functional and the steamboat had become ubiquitous throughout the Ohio-Mississippi system. For a while, conditions were such that, "owing to the relative cheapness of eastbound wagon carriage compared to the westbound [in 1826 the Pittsburgh-to-Philadelphia rate per 100 lbs. was $1.00–$1.12½, the Philadelphia-to-Pittsburgh rate was $3.00], it would actually have cost less to ship heavy goods a complete circuit from Philadelphia around by New Orleans and Pittsburgh and return than to pay the charge for the westward overland carriage by the Pennsylvania road."[14] It is the very costliness of such overland trade that justifies the use of coastal and inland-waterway shipping data for individual cities as an indicator of the long-distance contact-array biases in information availability of those same cities.

ATLANTIC AND GULF COAST PORTS

Commodity Flows Between Major Northeastern Cities. The growth of economic exchange between the South and Northeast during the first four decades of the nineteenth century often obscures the fact that there was a considerable volume of goods movement between the four leading cities of the Northeast. In both 1820 and 1840, the four cities in question—Boston, New York, Philadelphia, and Baltimore—were the largest cities in the Northeast as well as the largest centers in the country. Contrary to Walter Christaller's central place theory, which would permit the direct flow of goods only from New York to each of the three centers immediately below it in the urban-size hierarchy, and from Philadelphia to the roughly equal-sized Boston and Baltimore, coastal interaction occurred in both directions between every possible pair of ports (Tables 4.3 and 4.4). The extent of this interaction was great in relative as well as absolute terms, despite the fact that in both years there was a depression.[15] In 1820 and 1840 New York and Boston each provided more arrivals for Philadelphia than any other port inside or outside the Northeast. In those same two years New York and Boston each accounted for more arrivals in Baltimore than any other

Table 4.3. Coastal shipping arrival matrix for major Northeastern cities, 1820 (in number of vessels).[a]

Place of arrival[b]	Place of departure			
	New York	Philadelphia	Boston	Baltimore
New York	—	100	101	54
Philadelphia	68	—	72	12[c]
Boston	91	43	—	72
Baltimore	38	13[c]	56	—

Source: NYSL, 1820 (all 104 issues).

a. No distinction was made in the data source between ships, brigs, schooners, and sloops. Because of the variations in carrying capacity of these different types of vessel, therefore, the arrival totals are only crude indications of the volume of shipping interaction between the four ports.

b. The number of arrivals recorded for any pair of ports was not equal at both termini; for example, there were 100 at New York from Philadelphia, but only 68 at Philadelphia from New York. A key reason is that vessels were generally recorded as arriving from their last port of call rather than from their port of origin. In this table and others, shipping arrival data are used in preference to shipping departure statistics, because ships that were required by law to register at the local customhouse on arrival were not required to do so when clearing port unless laden with so-called "debenture goods." Thus, there were often considerable discrepancies between the local annual totals for shipping arrivals and shipping clearances. For example, in 1830 2,938 coastwise arrivals were recorded in Boston, but only 2,216 coastwise clearances. Despite having fewer omissions, the post-1815 arrival statistics published by newspapers were far from being complete. However, most arrival omissions involved either fishing vessels or local short-distance traffic in wood, lumber, sand, and stone carried by small vessels. *HMM* 15 (July 1846), 38; 6 (February 1842), 184; *HCSR* 2, no. 6 (Feb. 5, 1840), 95; 3, no. 24 (Dec. 9, 1840), 383; Edward C. Kirkland, *Men, Cities and Transportation: A Study in New England History, 1820-1900* (Cambridge: Harvard University Press, 1948), 7.

c. On other forms of trade between Baltimore and Philadelphia, see note 27 in this chapter.

Table 4.4. Coastal shipping arrival matrix for major Northeastern cities, 1840 (in number of vessels; weighted arrivals in parentheses).[a]

Place of arrival	Place of departure			
	New York	Philadelphia	Boston	Baltimore
New York	—	210[b] (333)	335 (577)	175 (290)
Philadelphia	233 (370)	—	90 (172)	5 (9)[c]
Boston	245 (388)	191 (320)	—	107 (178)
Baltimore	144 (250)	4 (6)[c]	67 (124)	—

Source: NYSL, 1840 (all 104 issues); Albion, Rise of New York Port, pp. 303–307, 408–409.

a. Most vessels employed on major United States coastal shipping routes at this date fell into one of four general categories of progressively larger average size and carrying capacity. "The sloop, which was generally the smallest type, had a single mast, supporting a large fore-and-aft sail. The schooner likewise had fore-and-aft sails, generally with two masts but occasionally . . . with three. The brig had two masts but was square-rigged; that is, each mast supported several sails which crossed from side to side of the vessel instead of being fore-and-aft. Finally, the full-rigged ship had three masts, all of which were square-rigged." Albion, Square-Riggers, p. 13. Arrivals, all of which were specified by vessel type, were weighted as follows: ships 4.0, brigs 2.0, schooners 1.5, and sloops 1.0. Yet the weighted arrivals also give only a crude indication of shipping interaction between the four ports, since it was impossible to take into account vessel-to-vessel variations in the value of cargo carried.

b. The number of Philadelphia arrivals in New York was actually much greater, although precisely how much is difficult to ascertain. The boarding officer of the Revenue Department who prepared the statistics did not include the "many" coal-laden schooners from Philadelphia, which were "never boarded, (owing to the remoteness of the points at which they come in)." HMM 4 (February 1841), 196.

c. On other forms of trade between Baltimore and Philadelphia, see note 27 in this chapter.

port in the country. Likewise, in 1820 and 1840, New York, Philadelphia, and Baltimore were among Boston's four most important shipping arrival origins (in both years the outsider being New Orleans, the country's fifth largest city). In 1840, Baltimore, while less important than Boston and Philadelphia in New York's coastal trade, still ranked fifth among New York's domestic-arrival origins (both New Orleans and Mobile surpassed it in that respect, owing to the scale of the cotton trade). Only between Philadelphia and Baltimore, separated by an extremely roundabout route to the south of Cape Charles, was the volume of through coastal shipping interaction relatively small.

The coastal commodity flows crisscrossing between New York, Baltimore, Boston, and Philadelphia were of three basic types: agricultural or raw material production from the hinterland of the port of origin, manufactures produced in the port of origin or its hinterland urban dependents, and redistributive shipments. The last type included goods originating at one port and sent to a second to be reshipped out of the region, and goods originating outside of the region and reshipped from one of the four ports to another.

During the period 1820–1840, Boston receipts included flour, corn, oats, and other grains from Baltimore, Philadelphia, and New York, both for its own use and for the shoe- and textile-producing towns in its hinterland.[16] Also unloaded at Boston's docks were hides and leather from Baltimore, Philadelphia, and New York for the boot and shoe industries near Lynn (a considerable volume of the hides coming through New York from the West and Latin America being tanned first in New York before moving on to Boston);[17] an increasing volume of Lehigh, Schuylkill, and Lackawanna anthracite coals from Philadelphia;[18] a variety of foreign imports from New York; and steam engines and miscellaneous manufactures from Philadelphia.[19] During the 1820s and 1830s commodities arriving by coastal shipping at Philadelphia included shoes from Boston for local and nearby consumption, textiles and shoes from Boston to be resold to Western merchants,[20] and English dry goods and other foreign imports from New York.[21] From 1820 to 1840 New York's coastal receipts included shoes and textiles from Boston, the lion's share of which was forwarded to the West or South by local merchants;[22] mackerel and surplus foreign imports from Boston; diverse industrial commodities from Philadelphia, many of which were reshipped to Southern ports;[23] increasing amounts of coal from Philadelphia;[24] flour from Baltimore (of decreasing importance after the opening of the Erie Canal); and coffee and tobacco from Baltimore (the tobacco was processed in New York both for domestic redistribution and for export to Europe). Finally, coastal acquisitions at Baltimore during this period included leather products from Boston, a varied mix of foreign imports from New York, and on occasion, manufactured goods from Philadelphia.

Additional commodity flows occurred between Boston, New York,

Philadelphia, and Baltimore by means other than coastal shipping. Most of this additional traffic occurred by canal rather than by overland transport, which was prohibitively costly except over very short distances and where limited stretches of railroad had appeared in the 1830s. The Delaware and Raritan Canal, completed in 1834 across New Jersey from New Brunswick to Bordentown, provided an important new commodity-exchange route between New York and Philadelphia. In 1840, 172,120 tons of merchandise were barged between New York and Philadelphia, an impressive sum in view of the fact that the coastal trade between the two metropolises was put at 60,000 tons in 1823 and 212,000 tons in 1830.[25] Much of the New York-bound traffic consisted of Schuylkill coals that came via Philadelphia and Lehigh coals originating on the Lehigh Canal.[26] Another canal, the Chesapeake and Delaware, completed in 1830, drastically reduced the water distance between Baltimore and Philadelphia and further discouraged coastal-shipping trade between those two cities. In 1838, 131,769 tons were carried along this route, at least 50 percent of which moved between the two large cities, including coal, hardware, and dry goods westward from Philadelphia, and raw and manufactured tobacco eastward from Baltimore.[27] In addition, coastal arrivals in New York from Providence often contained merchandise of high value per unit weight from Boston, via the short 42-mile land route to Providence, served by railroad after 1835.[28]

The interurban commodity traffic within the Northeast was not exhausted by the various permutations of trade between Boston, New York, Philadelphia, and Baltimore, for each of the four major cities had an important commerce with cities in its own interior and coastal hinterlands. Boston had the "down East" trade with the coastal havens of Maine and with its more proximate ports, such as Salem and Portsmouth. Baltimore had the Chesapeake Bay commerce, the downstream Susquehanna River trade carried out by thousands of small river craft (upstream navigation was not possible), and turnpike traffic with the western and southern portions of the Susquehanna Valley. Upon completion of the Chesapeake and Delaware Canal and the Union Canal to the Susquehanna below Harrisburg, "Philadelphia seems to have wrested much of the earlier [Susquehanna] river trade from Baltimore."[29]

Philadelphia also had trade with points along the Delaware River and its tributaries, as well as commerce with areas west of the city—from 1794 by way of the Lancaster Turnpike, extended to the Susquehanna in 1803; from 1828 by the Union Canal; and especially after 1834, upon completion of the "Mainline" of canals and railroads, with places as far west as Pittsburgh.

New York had a flourishing coastal trade with Providence, Bridgeport, New Haven, New London, Norwich, and lesser Connecticut and Rhode Island ports; a smaller but still sizable coasting commerce with Maine, consisting mainly of the import of lumber, granite, and other building materials; and above all, an intense riverine traffic with Albany and such smaller Hudson Valley centers as Poughkeepsie, Newburgh, and Kingston. Long before the 1825 opening of the Erie Canal, the flow of flour and grain from Albany to New York and of imports and manufactures in the opposite direction was of large dimensions. Soon after the Erie commenced operations and the tonnage moving through its locks had begun to be measured by the hundreds of thousands, the Hudson River traffic involved over 1,000 vessels.[30] Since Albany was the fifth-ranking Northeastern city in 1830 and 1840, it is significant that the Erie Canal also generated a heavy movement of sloops and schooners between Boston and Albany.[31]

Commodity Flows Between Major South Atlantic and Gulf Coast Ports. Unlike the situation prevailing in the Northeast, with few exceptions the major cities of the South carried out a comparatively small absolute volume of commodity exchange with one another throughout the pretelegraphic period (Tables 4.5 and 4.6).[32] The six cities in question fell into two groups, those generally labeled the "Cotton Ports"—New Orleans, Charleston, Mobile, and Savannah—and the remaining two Virginia centers, Richmond and Norfolk. Since all the ports save New Orleans were small by Northeastern standards, even though large by Southern standards, and since the principal export of four of the six ports was cotton, there was little reason for them to attain high absolute levels of seaborne commodity exchange. Even in relative terms, when an adjustment for population is made, the levels of commercial interaction between pairs of Southern ports were not really comparable with those between virtually every major Northeastern pair (Table 4.7).

Table 4.5. Coastal shipping arrival matrix for major South Atlantic and Gulf Coast ports, 1820 (in number of vessels).

| Place of arrival[a] | Place of departure | | | | | |
	New Orleans	Charleston	Rich-mond	Mobile	Savannah	Norfolk
New Orleans	—	10	0	2	1	1
Charleston	17	—	7	1	10	5
Richmond	3	2	—	0	1	2
Mobile[b]	0	0	0	—	0	0
Savannah	4	6	2	0	—	1
Norfolk	3	10	3	3	7	—

Source: NYSL, 1820 (all 104 issues).
a. Listed in order of 1840 population.
b. Although Mobile was one of the South's leading cities in 1840, in 1820 it was a town of less than 2,000, which explains its apparent lack of shipping interaction with major Southern ports.

Table 4.6. Coastal shipping arrival matrix for major South Atlantic and Gulf Coast ports, 1840 (in number of vessels; weighted arrivals in parentheses).[a]

| Place of arrival | Place of departure | | | | | |
	New Orleans	Charles-ton	Rich-mond	Mobile	Savan-nah	Norfolk
New Orleans	—	16 (28)	2 (3.5)	56 (111.5)	10 (16.5)	2 (4)
Charleston	24 (47)	—	11 (18)	3 (5.5)	8 (15)	2 (8)
Richmond	3 (5.5)	0	—	1 (1.5)	0	0[b]
Mobile	106 (253)	4 (8)	4 (8.5)	—	3 (12)	1 (4)
Savannah	16 (27)	10 (18)	0	0	—	3 (8)
Norfolk	8 (15)	9 (14.5)	4 (6)[b]	0	5 (10)	—

Source: NYSL, 1840 (all 104 issues).
a. See note a in Table 4.4.
b. In 1840 some freight was carried between Norfolk and Richmond on regularly scheduled passenger vessels whose arrivals were not recorded in the data source.

Table 4.7. Relative level of intraregional shipping interaction between pairs of ports, 1840.[a]

Port pair	Weighted interactions per thousand capita[b]
Northeast	
New York–Boston	2.06
Philadelphia–Boston	1.45
Baltimore–Boston	1.37
New York–Philadelphia	1.24[c]
New York–Baltimore	1.20
Philadelphia–Baltimore	.05[d]
South	
New Orleans–Mobile	3.17
Charleston–Savannah	.82
Savannah–Norfolk	.82
New Orleans–Charleston	.57
Charleston–Norfolk	.56
Mobile–Savannah	.50
New Orleans–Savannah	.38
Charleston–Richmond	.37
Charleston–Mobile	.32
Richmond–Mobile	.30
Richmond–Norfolk	.19
New Orleans–Norfolk	.17
Mobile–Norfolk	.17
New Orleans–Richmond	.07
Richmond–Savannah	0.0

Source: Tables 4.4 and 4.6.

a. Because of the grossness of arrival data for 1820, no relative levels of interaction were computed for that year.

b. The number of interactions per thousand capita for each port pair (I_{ij}) was determined by the expression:

$$I_{ij} = \frac{A_{i \to j} + A_{j \to i}}{P_i + P_j/1,000}$$

$A_{i \to j}$ is the number of weighted arrivals at port j from port i; $A_{j \to i}$ is the number of weighted arrivals at port i from port j, and P_i and P_j are the populations of the two ports.

c. The high relative level of interaction between New York and Philadelphia was obtained despite the absence of data regarding interaction via the Delaware and Raritan Canal.

d. Direct coastal shipping activity between Baltimore and Philadelphia was kept at a very low level in 1840, in part because of the considerable traffic moving between the two cities via the Chesapeake and Delaware Canal.

The only exception, and a glaring one, was the two-way traffic between New Orleans and Mobile.

The very low absolute level of shipping trade between major Southern cities is strikingly apparent from another perspective. In 1820 the only port to receive vessels from another port with more than once-a-month frequency was Charleston, which had 17 arrivals from New Orleans, averaging one every 22 days. In 1840, in only five of thirty possible instances were arrivals at a given Southern port from another given Southern port in excess of one per month. At New Orleans, boats arrived on an average of once every 22.8 days from Charleston and once every 6.6 from Mobile. New Orleans arrivals at Savannah averaged one every 22.8 days, at Charleston one every 15.2 days, and at Mobile one every 3.4 days.[33]

The ramifications of the limited commercial interaction between leading Southern cities apparently were two-fold. First, the slow movement of information between most of these places, as evidenced in newspaper-information time lags and postal services, was not likely to have been much hastened or supplemented by seaborne information. Second, since commerce was generating little information exchange between most of the six Southern ports in question, it is highly probable that most of the economic information of distant origin received by any one of them came from outside the South. For example, in 1840 there arrived at Charleston's docks 1,740 ships, brigs, schooners, sloops, and steamboats from points beyond South Carolina, of which 279 were of foreign origin and 1,461 from domestic points, but, apparently only 48 came from other major Southern ports (Table 4.6).[34]

The limited trade between the leading Southern ports consisted mainly of a few items. New Orleans shipped flour and corn, received via the Mississippi, in roughly equal volumes to Gulf Coast ports, especially Mobile, and to South Atlantic ports, especially Charleston and Savannah.[35] New Orleans also provided sugar, molasses, and some tobacco for its sister ports in the South, although for all three products the traffic was quite insubstantial until the mid or late 1830s (Table 4.8). During the 1820s and 1830s Mobile shipped fluctuating amounts of cotton to the New Orleans market when it could not be sold directly to Northeastern and foreign ports. In 1838–1839, for example, 22,920

Table 4.8. Sugar and molasses exports from New Orleans to major Southern ports, 1835–1836 and 1839–1840.[a]

Total exports and destination	Sugar		Molasses	
	1835–1836	1839–1840	1835–1836	1839–1840
Total exports[b]				
Hogsheads	5,677	45,511	1,012	8,937
Barrels	3,138	5,978	9,289	42,926
Charleston				
Hogsheads	1,066	1,583	0	0
Barrels	149	88	326	2,844
Richmond[c]				
Hogsheads	0	1,923	0	89
Barrels	0	179	202	1,694
Mobile				
Hogsheads	3,997	2,194	0	38
Barrels	513	315	3,831	3,867
Savannah				
Hogsheads	90	722	0	117
Barrels	0	0	237	1,309
Norfolk				
Hogsheads	3	819	128	50
Barrels	0	553	27	971

Source: HMM 3 (November 1840), 456; HCSR 3, no. 17 (Oct. 21, 1840), 264–265.
a. Years commence Oct. 1 and end Sept. 30.
b. Excludes exports to upstream Mississippi Valley points.
c. Incudes exports to Petersburg, Virginia.

of the 310,021 bales of cotton leaving Mobile were bound for New Orleans.[36] Of minor importance were grain shipments from Richmond to Charleston and Savannah.

Commodity Flows Between Major Southern and Northeastern Ports. The coastal trade between the Northeast and the South was an outstanding feature of domestic trade following the War of 1812. On the whole, the interregional exchange between leading Southern and Northeastern ports completely overshadowed that between the Gulf Coast and South Atlantic ports (Tables 4.9, 4.10, and 4.11). The absolute volume of traffic moving from New York and Boston to each individual

Table 4.9. Coastal shipping between major Southern and Northeastern ports, 1820 (in number of vessels).

From Northeast to South

| | Place of departure | | | |
Place of arrival	New York	Phila- delphia	Boston	Balti- more
New Orleans	40	12	19	10
Charleston	98	38	46	27
Richmond	74	15	23	9
Mobile[a]	1	1	2	0
Savannah	86	22	41	14
Norfolk	111	29	17	2

From South to Northeast

| | Place of departure | | | | | |
Place of arrival	New Orleans	Charles- ton	Rich- mond	Mobile	Savannah	Norfolk
New York	81	103	167	29	125	79
Philadelphia	41	29	37	5	20	26
Boston	44	29	52	4	15	11
Baltimore	21	12	1	0	11	1

Source: NYSL, 1820 (all 104 issues).
a. See note b in Table 4.5. It is possible that, because of Mobile's small size, the NYSL did not try to acquire complete data for it. This is suggested by a report that of 280 shipping arrivals in Mobile during 1819, 73 were from "Atlantic ports"—a term that may have included both Southern and European cities. NWR 16, no. 14 (May 29, 1819), 240.

Southern port was far greater than that moving between any Southern ports except New Orleans and Mobile. Also, the absolute level of commerce between Philadelphia and Baltimore, on the one hand, and individual Southern ports, on the other hand, was generally somewhat higher than that between Southern ports. For instance, in 1840, Baltimore and Philadelphia arrivals at Savannah were more important than those from Southern ports, and Baltimore and Philadelphia dockings at Charleston outnumbered those from every Southern port save New

Table 4.10. Coastal shipping between major Southern and Northeastern ports, 1840 (in number of vessels; weighted arrivals in parentheses).[a]

From Northeast to South

Place of arrival	Place of departure			
	New York	Philadelphia	Boston	Baltimore
New Orleans	189 (637)	20 (51)	137 (363)	7 (19)
Charleston	198 (460)	19 (31.5)	44 (121)	25 (42)
Richmond	222 (346.5)	1 (1.5)	34 (52.5)	2 (3)[b]
Mobile	187 (482)	24 (36)	68 (199.5)	18 (27)
Savannah	125 (363.5)	35 (63.5)	78 (182)	22 (43)
Norfolk	105 (167.5)	2 (3)	36 (56)	10 (16)[b]

From South to Northeast

Place of arrival	Place of departure					
	New Orleans	Charleston	Richmond	Mobile	Savannah	Norfolk
New York	270 (862)	125 (282)	116 (189)	193 (420.5)	101 (212.5)	122 (188)
Philadelphia	39 (83)	4 (7)	4 (6.5)	10 (19)	13 (21)	4 (6)
Boston	168 (500.5)	37 (77)	24 (37)	61 (145.5)	29 (54)	37 (57)
Baltimore	60 (128.5)	26 (42)	3 (7.5)[b]	7 (11.5)	20 (36)	0[b]

Source: NYSL, 1840 (all 104 issues).
a. See note a in Table 4.4.
b. Some freight was carried between Baltimore and Norfolk, and between Baltimore and Richmond, on regularly scheduled passenger vessels whose arrivals were not recorded.

Table 4.11. Relative level of interregional shipping interaction between pairs of Northeastern and Southern ports, 1840.

Port pair	Weighted interactions per thousand capita[a]
New York–New Orleans	3.32
New York–Mobile	2.49
New York–Charleston	1.96
New York–Savannah	1.60
New York–Richmond	1.45
New York–Norfolk	.99
Boston–New Orleans	3.99
Boston–Mobile	2.63
Boston–Savannah	1.82
Boston–Charleston	1.34
Boston–Norfolk	.87
Boston–Richmond	.64
Philadelphia–New Orleans	.42
Philadelphia–Savannah	.36
Philadelphia–Mobile	.24
Philadelphia–Charleston	.15
Philadelphia–Norfolk	.04
Philadelphia–Richmond	.03
Baltimore–New Orleans	.72
Baltimore–Savannah	.69
Baltimore–Charleston	.64
Baltimore–Mobile	.33
Baltimore–Norfolk	.14[b]
Baltimore–Richmond	.09[b]

Source: Table 4.10.
a. See note b in Table 4.7.
b. See note b in Table 4.10.

Orleans. Furthermore, in most instances the relative level of shipping interaction between the Southern ports and New York and Boston was very high, while the level prevailing between the Southern ports and Baltimore and Philadelphia was usually no higher than that prevailing between the Southern ports themselves (Table 4.12).

New York's so-called cotton triangle provided the most significant

Table 4.12. Cotton exports from Mobile and New Orleans to major Northeastern ports, 1821–1841 (in bales).[a]

		Destination		
Year	New York	Boston	Philadelphia	Baltimore
From Mobile				
1821–22	29,376	3,134	1,219	—
1823–24	14,999	967	352	—
1829–30	29,322	3,995[b]	—	—
1830–31	31,342	—	—	—
1831–32	22,513	7,125	0	0
1832–33	19,472	4,637	0	0
1833–34	14,809	10,521	0	0
1834–35	36,052	14,884	0	0
1835–36	42,264	11,830	0	0
1836–37	31,775	8,210	0	0
1837–38	47,168	7,870	0	0
1838–39	59,176	13,721	735	685
1839–40	34,067	19,823	2,758	759
1840–41	51,621	27,168	2,843	2,656
From New Orleans				
1821–22	28,873	7,279	10,688	2,831
1822–23	26,640	5,699	5,638	799
1823–24	28,520	7,842	3,381	1,250
1824–25	51,810	7,439	3,260	1,733
1825–26	36,839	11,903	5,172	3,053
1826–27	37,207	9,415	9,265	3,155
1827–28	38,486	20,006	9,921	2,744
1828–29	20,009	12,333	3,440	1,164
1829–30	30,915	13,686	4,277	1,580
1830–31	55,737	36,327	10,607	5,750
1831–32	24,955	25,078	4,607	1,614
1832–33	31,497	28,868	7,239	4,743
1833–34	15,938	25,947	3,368	1,701
1834–35	50,978	42,928	7,918	989
1835–36	29,604	37,084	7,428	1,128
1836–37	24,734	38,409	6,022	2,978
1837–38	39,352	40,271	8,526	6,148
1838–39	62,691	49,242	6,150	3,450
1839–40	47,941	54,367	6,482	3,111
1840–41[c]	55,930	81,626	5,721	4,832

Source: NWR 24, no. 2 (Mar. 15, 1823), 21; 27, no. 10 (Nov. 6, 1824), 149; 39, no. 11 (Nov. 6, 1830), 183; *HMM* 3 (Nov. 1840), 454; 5 (Nov. 1841), 472; 10 (May 1844), 425; 13 (Nov. 1845), 422; Albion, *Rise of New York Port*, p. 101.

a. Unless otherwise noted, years commence Oct. 1 and end Sept. 30.
b. Calendar year 1830.
c. Year commencing Sept. 1 and ending Aug. 31.

component of the interurban commodity flow between the South and Northeast.

At the three corners of the "cotton triangle" were the cotton port (Charleston, Savannah, Mobile, or New Orleans), the European port (generally Liverpool or Havre), and New York. On this triangular course there were two distinct major movements.

Many vessels, usually the majority, actually sailed around the three sides. They carried cotton directly from the southern port to Europe;[37] returned to New York with general freight or immigrants; and finally returned southward on the coastwise run with freight or in ballast . . .

[New York] was much more vitally concerned, however, with the alternative course which utilized only two sides of the triangle, eliminating the normal direct run between, say, New Orleans and Liverpool. A considerable part of the cotton and other products was carried to Europe by way of [New York] . . . even though that involved some two hundred extra miles and the extra charges for loading and reloading. This gave [New York's European packets] . . . their eastbound cargoes. In return, an even larger proportion of the European goods reached the South by travelling the two sides of the triangle via . . . [New York] instead of going direct from a European port to a cotton port.[38]

Although New York's cotton trade dated back to 1785, the cotton triangle was not in real operation until the early nineteenth century. At that time, some of the city's merchants began to imitate one another, both in the stationing of factors and commission agents in the South (in order to purchase cotton either directly from the planter or from his agent at a major port), and in the extending of credits to Southern retailers and wholesalers who were themselves forced to sell on credit to cotton growers until the annual crop had been harvested or sold.[39] By 1811, New York merchants had acquired a strong grip on the cotton re-export trade, providing Liverpool with 15,000 bales, or more than the combined total of over 6,000 bales supplied by Philadelphia, Boston, and Baltimore.[40] After the War of 1812, New York maintained its leadership in channeling the cotton traffic to the Northeast and Europe, although Boston captured a larger share of New Orleans's cotton exports during most of the late 1830s and early 1840s. The shipping entrepreneurs of New York consolidated the city's position after 1822 by establishing regularly scheduled packet lines to the major cotton ports much like those operating to Liverpool, Le Havre, and London

(Table 4.13). The speed and reliability of these packets, which carried most of the trade between New York and the four Cotton Ports, played a key role in providing New York with a time lag advantage in the acquisition of Southern economic information.[41]

Northeastbound trade within the cotton triangle was not confined to cotton. Thus, even when Boston merchants were most active on the New Orleans cotton market, New York still dominated the total trade with New Orleans. For the quarter ending June 30, 1839, for example, New Orleans had coastwise exports whose value was placed at $8,036,726, of which $3,437,740 went to New York, $1,906,607 to Boston, $869,036 to Philadelphia, and $607,807 to Baltimore.[42] Vessels from New Orleans to New York carried lead from the mines of Galena, Illinois; pork, flour, bacon, and other agricultural products that had been floated down the Mississippi from the interior; as well as tobacco, sugar, and molasses (Table 4.14). Hides and rice occasionally supplemented cotton shipments from Mobile, Charleston, and Savannah to New York. Vessels moving southerly within the cotton triangle carried

Table 4.13. Growth of New York's Cotton-Triangle packet services, 1825–1840 (in ships).[a]

	Port served			
Year	New Orleans	Charleston	Mobile	Savannah
1825	12	8	0	6
1830	12	8	6	6
1835	12	8	6	8
1840	20 (24)[b]	8	6 (24)[b]	3[c]

Source: Albion, *Square-Riggers*, pp. 35, 55, 57, 274; *NWR* 58, no. 2 (Mar. 14, 1840), 32.

a. Excluding brigs and schooners in regular service.

b. There is a discrepancy between the number of packets reported by Albion and by *NWR* (latter figures in parentheses), perhaps because the counts were taken at different times of the year, or because of Albion's refusal to reckon in brigs and other smaller vessels.

c. Between 1835 and 1840 several packet ships on this run were transferred to the New York–New Orleans run, owing to the overexpansion of Savannah services, the silting in the Savannah River, and the greater profitability of trade with New Orleans.

Table 4.14. Tobacco, sugar, and molasses exports from New Orleans to major Northeastern ports—1830–1831, 1835–1836, and 1839–1840.[a]

Commodity	Total exports[b]		New York		Boston		Philadelphia		Baltimore	
	Hhds.	Bars.	Hhds.	Bars.	Hhds.	Bars.	Hhds.	Bars.	Hhds.	Bars.
Tobacco										
1830–31	21,240	0	13,099	0	3,970	0	2,193	0	882	0
1835–36	19,329	0	9,516	0	2,894	0	2,167	0	775	0
1839–40	13,980	0	7,185	0	3,219	0	2,764	0	520	0
Sugar										
1835–36	5,677	3,138	126	13	49	0	122	71	0	0
1839–40	45,511	5,978	18,893	598	951	327	8,629	134	8,192	325
Molasses										
1835–36	1,012	9,289	721	1,693	0	0	0	935	0	314
1839–40	8,937	42,926	3,511	15,179	811	4,463	962	3,321	1,267	6,042

Source: HMM 3 (November 1840), 455–456; HCSR 3, no. 17 (Oct. 21, 1840), 264–265.
a. Years commence Oct. 1 and end Sept. 30.
b. Excluding exports to upstream Mississippi Valley points. New Orleans' foreign exports of tobacco often surpassed her domestic shipments, but her foreign export of sugar and molasses was usually negligible.

a variety of imported and domestic merchandise that was bound either for direct consumption in the individual cotton port and its immediate hinterland, or for redistribution up the Mississippi for Western store-keepers. The items shipped from New York included imported goods such as Yorkshire woollens, Lancashire cotton goods, Birmingham hardware, Sheffield cutlery, French ribbons, laces, and wines, and books and other items from London. The domestic manufactures shipped from New York included furniture, coarse textiles and sheetings from New England factories, readymade clothing and soap from New York, boots and shoes from Massachusetts, harnesses and saddlery from Newark, and occasionally in the 1830s, steam engines, machinery, and locomotives. New York also forwarded flour, cheese, potatoes, onions, carrots, apples, and other foodstuffs for both urban consumers and rural planters and slaves especially in and around Charleston.[43]

Other commodity flows between major Southern and Northeastern cities had certain stereotypical characteristics. In return for Boston's considerable cotton imports (Table 4.12),[44] destined in large measure for Lowell and other textile towns, its procurements of corn and flour from New Orleans, Richmond, and Norfolk,[45] and its lesser imports of coal from Richmond (about 5,160 tons in 1839)[46] and of lead, pork, lard, and other products via New Orleans (Table 4.14), Boston sent out vessels to leading Southern ports principally carrying New England cotton goods, boots, and shoes, as well as foreign manufactures. Philadelphia reciprocated for its cotton imports by shipping local and foreign manufactures, vegetables and other foodstuffs to New Orleans, Mobile, Charleston, and Savannah.[47] Philadelphia had little exchange with Richmond and Norfolk, however, because the coal and agricultural products exported from those two Virginia ports were not in demand in southeastern Pennsylvania. Baltimore sent corn and other grain products to Charleston and Savannah, as well as textiles, other manufactured items of local origin, and miscellaneous imports to Norfolk and all four Cotton Ports. In addition, New York's trade with Norfolk and Richmond largely involved the northward shipment of coal, flour, and tobacco from Richmond[48] and an assortment of forest and agricultural products from Norfolk, as well as the southward movement of much the same array of goods as shipped to the Cotton Ports.[49]

INTERIOR RIVER AND LAKE PORTS

Commodity Flows Between Major Ohio and Mississippi Valley Cities.
Not unlike the case of the Northeast, the focus usually placed on interregional trade often obscures the importance of intraregional commodity movements between the largest cities of the Ohio and Upper
Mississippi valleys. The interurban commerce of the Old Northwest was
not confined to the shipment of Western products from Cincinnati,
Pittsburgh, Louisville, and St. Louis to the South and Northeast via
New Orleans, along with the movement of Southern staples and Northeastern and European manufactures in the opposite direction. On the
contrary, there was a noteworthy exchange of goods between Cincinnati, Pittsburgh, Louisville, and St. Louis. It consisted of agricultural
products or raw materials from the hinterland of the river port of origin,
products brought into the West through one of the four major cities
and redistributed intraregionally through the other three cities, and of
manufactured goods either from the port of origin itself or from some
lower order city directly dependent on it. Unfortunately, available
source materials are not adequate for summarizing this traffic in the
form of an arrival matrix.

The largest volume of trade between any two upper Mississippi and
Ohio ports, at least during the 1820s and 1830s, was apparently between Cincinnati and Louisville, the two major cities (Table 1.1) which
were located closest to one another. Again in direct contradiction of
Christaller's central place theory, which would allow for the direct flow
of goods only from the larger Cincinnati to the smaller Louisville, this
economic interaction was two-way.[50]

The relative importance of the Cincinnati-Louisville traffic is apparent
from a juxtaposition of total steamship arrivals at Louisville with the
known steamship service between the two centers. In 1819 the first
regularly scheduled steamboat between Cincinnati and Louisville was
put into operation, making once-weekly round trips over the 131-mile
route. At that date Louisville's total steamship arrivals were probably
somewhat less than 100, for the earliest available total is 196 for 1823.
By 1826, regular Cincinnati-Louisville service was on a thrice-weekly
basis, and five years later daily departures were available from each

terminus. In 1826 Louisville steamship arrivals were likely somewhere in the vicinity of 600, based on an interpolation of 1824 and 1829 totals, and in 1831, when Louisville had a greater steamship traffic than New Orleans, they most likely surpassed 1,100. If there were 38 weeks of ice-free operation, this would mean that in both years regularly scheduled vessels from Cincinnati alone accounted for about one-fifth of Louisville's steamboat arrivals, or roughly 114 arrivals in 1826 (3 x 38) and 228 arrivals in 1831 (6 x 38). The total percentage accounted for by Cincinnati steamers must have been much higher, for a large volume of freight also moved between the Ohio and Kentucky cities by unscheduled steamboat. A total of 25 steam vessels plied the waters between those cities in 1834, for example, each weighing 200 tons or more, which meant that they belonged to the largest-size class in operation. The magnitude of the Cincinnati-Louisville traffic is further indicated by a report that of "733 arrivals at Cincinnati during a seven and one-half month's period in 1827–28, nearly half were from Louisville."[51] Moreover, Cincinnati-Louisville traffic was not confined to steamboats, although by the late 1820s they accounted for the lion's share of the trade. Earlier, large numbers of small unpowered boats moved downstream from Cincinnati to Louisville, both since early steamboats had difficulty in navigating the Upper Ohio, and because, until the 1829 opening of the Louisville and Portland Canal, upstream movement beyond Louisville was obstructed by the Falls of the Ohio except when the water was very high.

Even after the opening of the Louisville and Portland Canal, Louisville retained much of its role as a transshipment point and remained a gateway to and from the South.[52] There was a mounting volume of goods flowing from Cincinnati to Louisville, with Cincinnati's total exports growing from approximately $1,000,000 in 1826 to $9,000,000 in 1839. The traffic was largely comprised either of pork and pork products, flour, and whiskey, most of which was headed ultimately for New Orleans or points beyond, or of locally produced steam engines, mostly destined for steamboat use, and southbound sugar mills and cotton gins.[53] The goods forwarded to Cincinnati by the shippers and middlemen of Louisville consisted mostly of Southern staples, mainly cotton, tobacco, sugar, and molasses, locally processed tobacco and hemp, and imports from beyond the South acquired via New Orleans, such as dry goods and coffee.

The interurban commerce of Pittsburgh and Cincinnati was also of great magnitude, if somewhat less than that between Cincinnati and Louisville. During the same 1827–1828 span, when Louisville answered for almost half of Cincinnati steamboat arrivals, Pittsburgh was providing one-third or perhaps more of Cincinnati's steamboat dockings.[54] For much of the pre-1840 period, the downstream traffic from Pittsburgh to Cincinnati was apparently larger than that moving in the opposite direction. In 1825, for instance, the first year for which data are available, Pittsburgh exported 15,250 tons of merchandise to Ohio and Mississippi River points and imported 7,190 tons in return. By 1839, Pittsburgh's downriver shipments had climbed to 84,915 tons, while her upriver imports had grown to 63,943 tons.[55] Probably the most important class of goods shipped from Pittsburgh to Cincinnati was the high-value-per-unit-weight manufactures from the Northeast and abroad, which could tolerate the high costs incurred in having to be transported from Philadelphia either entirely overland or, after 1834, by rail and canal.[56] Dry goods, queen's ware, and other "fine merchandise" were the principal items in this class of manufactures.[57] The city's own growing number of factories were themselves increasingly responsible for exports to Cincinnati. Locally manufactured shipments included iron and iron products (nails, castings), hardware, glass, and paper.[58] A third class of Pittsburgh-to-Cincinnati shipments encompassed both processed and unprocessed raw materials from the valleys of the Monongahela and Allegheny Rivers, such as timber and wood products, coal, and salt.[59] The smaller volume of goods moving upstream from Cincinnati to Pittsburgh, though diversified, principally included pork and pork products (especially after 1834 when it became possible to forward these items to Philadelphia via the Mainline), butter, cheese, and commodities of Southern origin.[60]

A third set of important trade relationships existed between Louisville and Pittsburgh. By 1835 the traffic between the two cities warranted the establishment of a twelve-vessel steamboat line offering daily sailings, and in the ensuing two years, two similar Louisville-Pittsburgh lines went into service. "Before 1830, fully three-fourths of all steamboats arriving at Pittsburgh were from Louisville," often via Cincinnati. In 1837 no fewer than 525 of Pittsburgh's 1,810 steamboat arrivals originated in Louisville.[61] Shipments from Louisville to Pittsburgh greatly resembled those from Louisville to Cincinnati; that is, Southern staples, foreign coffee, and locally processed hemp and tobacco predominated. In like fashion, the freight from Pittsburgh to Louisville was nearly identical with that shipped from Pittsburgh to Cincinnati, the most important items being manufactures from the Northeast, products from Pittsburgh's own factories (in this case including steam engines, cotton gins, other machinery, and textile products), and processed or unprocessed raw materials from Pittsburgh's immediate hinterland.

In addition to conducting a considerable commerce with one another, the merchants of Pittsburgh, Cincinnati, and Louisville transacted much business with St. Louis. Because St. Louis was less populous than its three Ohio River sisters (Table 1.1), and because the area it served was later in being settled, there was a slight lag before the volume of trade between the Missouri city and Pittsburgh, Cincinnati, and Louisville assumed major proportions. It was 1831 before the total number of steamboat arrivals in St. Louis surpassed the figures reached by Louisville in 1824 and Cincinnati in 1825. By 1837, the trade justified 109 steamboat sailings from Pittsburgh to St. Louis, many by way of Cincinnati or Louisville, as well as the operation of a regularly scheduled six-boat line between the two cities. Lead and furs were the most important commodities moving from the St. Louis wharves to the three infant metropolises of the Ohio Valley. Shipments westward to St. Louis basically involved familiar commodities: local and Northeastern manufactures from Pittsburgh, processed pork as well as agricultural implements and other local industrial products from Cincinnati, tobacco and hemp from Louisville.[62]

All this interurban trade occurring intraregionally within the Ohio and Upper Mississippi valleys took place alongside the interregional flows funneled via New Orleans. Although considerable controversy surrounds the dimensions of this interregional trade, its bare essentials can be outlined without becoming involved in the debate. During much of the 1820s, roughly 3,000 flatboats from Louisville or points further up the Ohio descended annually to New Orleans. However, these vessels, which had an average carrying capacity of perhaps 40 tons, were not all functioning on an interurban basis, for many farmers continued, as in earlier pioneer days, to take their own flatboats downstream, thereby avoiding either direct or indirect contact with merchants in the intervening river ports.[63] Although as late as 1840, "nearly a fifth of the freight handled on the lower Mississippi went . . . principally by flatboat," the over-all commerce of the Mississippi and Ohio had seen interurban steamers [exceed] the flatboats between 1820 and 1830 in terms of both business transacted and freight hauled.[64] By 1834 at least 60 percent of the steamboats of 200 tons or more on the Ohio-Mississippi system were running from Cincinnati and Louisville to New Orleans, or from St. Louis to New Orleans. As many as 140 trips were made annually on the Louisville-New Orleans route by these steamboats, and another 50 or 60 trips were made by smaller steamers over the same route.[65]

Until the breakthrough of steamboat freighting services, upstream long-distance interurban traffic from New Orleans was very limited. In 1817, shortly before "the steamboat became the exclusive carrier of upstream shipments of all descriptions," the slowness and costliness of upstream movement were such that "about twenty barges, averaging one hundred tons, afforded the only facilities for transporting merchandise from New Orleans to Louisville and Cincinnati."[66] Once the steamboats had established their upstream monopoly from New Orleans, the items they primarily purveyed to Louisville, Cincinnati, Pittsburgh, and St. Louis were: Southern cotton, sugar, and molasses; foreign tea and coffee; and some Northeastern and European manufactures, the latter largely from New York. In addition to the much debated shipments of pork products, flour, corn, and other foodstuffs, the trade moving to New Orleans from the three Ohio River ports and St. Louis included whiskey, tobacco, lead, steam engines, cotton gins, sugar mills, and other manufactured items.[67] It may be argued that Louisville, Cincinnati, Pittsburgh, and St. Louis provided New Orleans with at most about one-third of its annual receipts of $16.2 million during the period 1823–1825, and between 25 and 30 percent of its annual receipts of $44.1 million during the period 1836–1840.[68] As suggested by the flow of goods from New Orleans to the leading Northeastern cities, a good deal of the pork, bacon, flour, corn, tobacco, and lead originating in Pittsburgh, Cincinnati, Louisville, and St. Louis continued on its way beyond New Orleans and terminated its interurban movement in New York, Boston, Philadelphia, or Baltimore.[69]

Commodity Flows Between Major Lake Erie Ports. The interregional trade of the relatively well-settled portion of the West oriented toward the eastern Great Lakes helped to propagate interurban, or intra-regional, flows among that region's major centers—Buffalo, Cleveland, and Detroit. In a crude sense, the intraregional relations of Cleveland and Detroit with Buffalo were not unlike those of Pittsburgh and Cincinnati with Louisville, with Buffalo serving both as an exit for agricultural products, headed mostly to New York, and an entrance for merchandise, chiefly from New York, in much the same way that Louisville functioned as a gateway for New Orleans. However, inter-urban commodity flows between Buffalo, Cleveland, and Detroit were somewhat later in acquiring stature, because in 1840, two of the three cities were still of approximately the same size as their Western river counterparts had been in 1820. Until shortly before 1820, Buffalo was no more than a "village isolated from the main stream of commercial activity," and in the early 1820s, when Detroit was still engulfed in a frontier atmosphere, the annual trade volume of that Michigan city sel-dom surpassed $100,000. As late as 1825, the total value of goods exported from Cleveland barely topped $50,000.[70]

Nonetheless, even before Lake Erie trade had reached an appreciable scale, the regionally dominant pattern of flow between Buffalo, Cleve-land, and Detroit was being established. In 1817, "a regular line of waggons and packets" was established between Detroit, Buffalo, and New York, and in the following year the first steamboat to ply the Great Lakes was put into operation between Buffalo and Detroit. Of the one steamboat and seven schooners arriving in Detroit during a nine-day period in 1820, three were directly from Buffalo, one directly from Cleveland, and three from "Ohio ports," which may have included Cleveland. This was a far cry from conditions attaining in 1835, when Buffalo had a total of 720 steamboat arrivals and when on a single day three steamboats, 32 schooners, and one brig departed the port for Cleveland and Detroit. By the mid and late 1830s, with the Ohio Canal feeding Cleveland, and several roads as well as the short Michigan Central Railway penetrating westward from Detroit, these three mutually interacting cities held undisputed hegemony over their once serious competitors, such as Sandusky, Ohio, Monroe, Michigan, and Dunkirk and Oswego, New York, (the latter fronting Lake Ontario). In fact, by 1839, 50 of the 61 steamboats operating on Lake Erie, Lake Michigan, and Lake Superior belonged to operators in Detroit (20), Cleveland (17), and Buffalo (13). At the same time, 196 of the 225 sailing vessels functioning on the same lakes were owned by interests in Detroit (83), Buffalo (59), and Cleveland (54).[71]

For some time the most essential feature of interurban trade on Lake Erie was the movement of manufactures and foreign imports from Buffalo to Cleveland and Detroit. Until the opening of the Erie Canal, the volume of this flow, which originated for the most part in New York, was limited. Before that time, demand was not great around Lake Erie, and the cost of reaching the area was out of proportion to the value of many goods. (The 1817 charge for freighting one ton from Manhattan to Buffalo, for example, was $100, or about 25 cents per ton-mile.) However, within only a few weeks of the opening of the canal at Buffalo in October 1825, a lively lake trade between Buffalo and Cleveland rapidly sprang up. Thus, whereas Cleveland had waterborne imports of just over $130,000 in 1825, in 1830 the corresponding total was just shy of $1,000,000, and the city had established itself as an important distribution center. Westward shipments from Buffalo to Cleveland and Detroit continued to outweigh those in the opposite direction until perhaps as late as 1835. Only two years earlier, Cleveland's waterborne domestic imports (about $4.7 million) had been more than triple her waterborne domestic exports ($1,544,000). In the 1830s Detroit, too, was "considerably more active as a receiving center for eastern merchandise, foodstuffs, and immigrants than as an exporting market." The tables had turned by 1836, when 54,219 tons of freight passed eastward over the Erie Canal from Western states, while 38,893 tons of merchandise were barged on the canal en route to points west of Buffalo.[72]

The big boost to commodity traffic going from Cleveland to Buffalo was the opening of the Ohio Canal. As soon as that canal was completed, "a part of the surplus grain of Pennsylvania, Kentucky, and southern Ohio, which formerly had been shipped down the Mississippi River, was diverted to the eastern route to the coast, and as early as 1838 the receipts of wheat and flour at Buffalo were greater than the receipts at New Orleans." The expansion of Cleveland's outgoing shipments was indeed abrupt, for the total nearly doubled in value from 1831 to 1833. By 1840, Cleveland's merchants were forwarding about 2,000,000 bushels of wheat and 500,000 barrels of flour, "with Buffalo receiving the great bulk." In the same year Buffalo received a total of 1,005,000 bushels of wheat and 597,142 barrels of flour. Corn, wool, and ashes were among the other products shipped from Cleveland to Buffalo.[73] The interurban commercial exchange between Buffalo, Cleveland, and Detroit further included shipments from Detroit to both Buffalo and Cleveland of furs, peltry, and salt that had originated in the upper Great Lakes; shipments from Detroit to Buffalo of Michigan wheat and flour, especially during the late 1830s; and shipments of agricultural products of shifting composition from Cleveland to Detroit.[74]

One conclusion that can be drawn from the pattern of long-distance trade throughout the country is that New York had emerged as a national hub for interurban commodity flows, playing a vital role in the Northeast's interregional trade with the South and West as well as in the intraregional trade of the Northeast itself. The tonnage of New York ships "enrolled and licensed" in the coasting trade at various dates provides evidence as to New York's prominent position in the national network of interurban commodity flows. On the surface it would appear that from 1800 on, New York accounted for roughly one-fifth or more of the total tonnage employed in domestic trade (Table 4.15). And even when New York's percentage of the national total dipped to a low of 18.0 in 1840, the city's absolute shipping capacity completely overshadowed that of any other single port, its total being almost equal to that of its four nearest rivals—New Orleans, Boston, Philadelphia, and Baltimore (Table 4.16). Moreover, the 1840 data underplay New York's coastal shipping role on at least two scores. For one thing, New York's shipping capacity was inadequate to meet local demand. As an 1827 observer noted: "In commercial relations strictly her own, she, in fact, employs a considerable amount of the tonnage of other cities." Seven-

Table 4.15. Documented tonnage of New York vessels employed in coastwise trade, 1793–1840 (in thousands of gross tons).[a]

Year	New York vessels (A)	National documented total in coastwise and internal shipping (B)	A/B
1793	14	122	11.1
1800	54	272	19.9
1810	88	405	21.7
1816	117	522	22.4
1821	122	615	19.8
1829	151	509[b]	29.7
1840	211	1,177	18.0

Source: Adam Seybert, *Statistical Annals: Embracing Views of the Population, Commerce, Navigation . . . of the United States of America* (Philadelphia, 1818), pp. 323–324, 329–330; *Historical Statistics*, p. 445; *NWR* 24, no. 22 (Aug. 2, 1823), 350–351; U.S. Senate, *Commerce and Navigation of the United States*, Executive Document No. 76, 21st Cong., 2nd sess., 1831, p. 271; U.S. House, *Commerce and Navigation of the United States*, House Document No. 122, 26th Cong., 2nd sess., 1841, pp. 284–285.

a. Includes all "enrolled and licensed" vessels, "licensed" vessels under 20 tons used in the coastal trade, and steam-powered vessels. For the legal status of both "enrolled and licensed" and merely "licensed" vessels, as opposed to vessels "registered" to indulge in foreign trade, see Joseph Blunt, *The Shipmaster's Assistant, and Commercial Digest* (New York, 1837), pp. 10–22.

b. Shipping tonnage data prior to 1829 were not very trustworthy, owing to the inclusion of "ghost tonnage" (see note a in Table 4.2).

teen years hence, another authority commented: "The tonnage belonging to the people of Boston is not . . . altogether confined to her own port, but it is well known that one-third of the commerce of New York, from the year 1839 to 1842, was carried either upon Massachusetts' account, or in Massachusetts' vessels."[75] Second, much of New York's tonnage "registered" in foreign trade occasionally undertook coasting voyages. This condition is highly significant since New York's almost 204,000 tons of "registered" shipping represented 26.7 percent of the nation's foreign-trade vessels.[76]

In view of the impact of the relative distribution of any place's trade origins and destinations on its contact-array and time-lag spatial biases in the availability of information, it is now possible to formulate

Table 4.16. Documented tonnage employed in domestic trade at major coastal, river, and lake ports, 1840 (in gross tons).

Port	Coastwise and internal shipping	Steam-powered vessels
New York	211,011	34,754
Boston	62,975	1,874
Philadelphia	51,676	4,899
Baltimore	41,254	8,846
New Orleans	77,537	54,757
Charleston	13,456	3,984
Norfolk	11,680	1,016
Mobile	8,547	3,714
Savannah	7,409	5,049
Richmond	3,396	0
Cincinnati	12,052	12,052
Pittsburgh	12,000	12,000
St. Louis	11,259	11,259
Louisville	1,592	1,592
Detroit	11,231	3,232
Cleveland	9,515	4,290
Buffalo	4,916	4,916
U.S. Total	1,176,694	198,184

Source: U.S. House, *Commerce and Navigation*, pp. 284–287.

a number of hypotheses. First, information flows must have been quite frequent and relatively rapid between New York, Philadelphia, Boston, and Baltimore, between Pittsburgh, Cincinnati, Louisville, and St. Louis, and between Buffalo, Cleveland, and Detroit. Because of the West's late settlement and delayed start of large-scale commerce, in the cases of both the four Western river cities and the three Lake Erie ports the speed and frequency of contact must have been decades out of phase with the rates prevailing among the Northeast's four major cities. Second, in general, information exchange between the largest Southern cities must have been relatively infrequent and slow. Contacts between Southern cities and New York, however, were probably sufficient in many instances to cause specific messages to pass from one Southern city to another via Manhattan. Finally, in its role as "The Great Commercial Emporium of the Confederacy," New York must have acted as the principal node of the nation's information circulation system. All three of these assertions are consistent with the evidence on public-information time lags, public-information accessibility, and postal services.

5

Interurban Travel and Long-Distance Information Circulation

It is a common observation that the amount of travel from one important commercial place to another in our country has lately increased in an astonishing degree. The mere growth of our population is not sufficient to account for this effect, for the increase of population has been infinitely short of the increase of travel. It must be owing, therefore, to the reduction of fare and the greater speed of the passage.
—A New York City Newspaper Editor (1827)

In the absence of modern communications media, the pretelegraphic intercity traveler played a vital role in the long distance spread of information. He could verbally communicate new or redundant information from his city of residence, or from other points along his route, to individuals in the places to which he journeyed. Similarly, he could bring back new or redundant private information to his home city. Upon his return, he could also convert newly acquired visual information or perceptions into either verbal or published form, that is, into private or public information. In addition, information acquired while away could influence the returning traveler to adopt a material innovation, thereby converting the information into visual form for fellow urban residents. Moreover, interurban travel was often intimately related to other forms of long-distance public and private information circulation, since stagecoaches and other common carriers were often entrusted with the postal transport of letters and newspapers.

Because of the variety of ways in which interurban travel contributed to pretelegraphic information circulation, figures on the volume of travel between specific urban pairs should provide one means of determining spatial biases in the availability of information at various dates.

Unfortunately, such data are quite scanty, difficult to locate, and not infrequently of questionable reliability. Nevertheless, when the limited statistics on the volume of interurban travel are juxtaposed with information relating to travel costs and journey times, they are of help in interpreting the growth of large American cities.

INTERURBAN TRAVEL COSTS

For the bulk of the country's population, the real costs of interurban travel by common carrier were prohibitively high between 1790 and 1840. However, exceptions did exist for trips of a very short distance or over a few post-1820 steamboat and canal routes where low fares prevailed for those willing to tolerate discomfort. There was also a long-run tendency for charges to decline (Tables 5.1 and 5.2).

Just how expensive the interurban travel fares were for most Americans is best illustrated by re-examining prevailing wages. Daily wage levels for nonfarm labor in the United States as a whole were approximately $1.00 in 1800 and the period 1812–1815, $0.75 in 1818 and the period 1830–1832, and $0.85 in 1840. During that same four-decade span, monthly wage rates, including board, for free agricultural labor ranged from $10.00 in 1800 to $8.50 in the early 1830s, and up to $10.40 in 1840.[1] Expenses were high even for the better-rewarded nonfarm laboring class. The cost of fares alone would have required that the average urban worker sacrifice ten days' wages to travel from Boston to New York in 1802, seven days' pay to journey from New York to Albany in 1813, and twenty days' earnings to move from Philadelphia to Pittsburgh in 1812.

These fares were regarded at the time as very high by foreign visitors, and although most of them fell during the quarter-century following the War of 1812, interurban travel remained expensive for the common worker. For example, around 1840 roughly six days' wages were required to purchase a one-way ticket from Boston to New York, and at least seven days' earnings were needed to cover passage from Philadelphia to Pittsburgh. Only when passengers were willing to be crowded onto the open decks of the larger vessels, or when entrepreneurs were forced to slash fares because of competition, was intercity travel rela-

Table 5.1. One-way travel fares between selected major urban pairs, 1790–1840 (in current dollars).[a]

Urban pair	Year	Cost
New York–Boston	179?	21.00
	1802	10.00–?
	1817	13.00
	1822	13.00
	1825	11.00[b]
	1826	7.50[c]–11.00
	1827	7.50[c]
	1832	11.00[b]
	1834	7.50–8.50[c]
	1835	5.50–6.50[d]
	1840	5.00–7.00[d]
New York–Philadelphia	179?	9.00
	1796	6.00
	1802	5.00–6.00
	1816	5.50–10.00[c]
	1817	5.00[c]
	1820	5.00[c]
	1821	4.00[c]
	1826	3.00–5.00[c]
	1829	1.25[e]–4.00
	1836	2.00[f]–5.00[d]
	1838	3.00–4.00[d]
	1839	3.00–4.00[d]
	1840	3.00–4.00[d]
Philadelphia–Baltimore	179?	10.00
	1796	6.00
	1826	4.00[c]
	1839	4.00[d]
	1840	4.00[d]
New York–Albany	1797	7.00
	1813	7.00[g]
	1816	7.00[g]
	1817	7.00[g]
	1823	5.00–6.00[g]
	1824	2.00[g]
	1829	0.50–1.00[g]
	1838	0.50–3.00[gh]
	1840	1.00[g]

(continued)

Table 5.1 (continued)

Urban pair	Year	Cost
Philadelphia-Pittsburgh	1812	20.00
	1836	6.00[i]-10.00
Pittsburgh-Cincinnati	1823	12.00[j]-15.00[gj]
	1836	2.50-10.00[gj]
Cincinnati-Louisville	1819	12.00[j]
	1823	4.00[j]-6.00[gk]
	1839	1.00[f]-4.00[gj]
Cincinnati-St. Louis	1836	4.50[f]-10.00[gj]
	1839	4.00[f]-12.00[g]
Louisville-New Orleans	1816	125.00[gk]
	1817	75.00[j]-125.00[gk]
	1818	70.00[j]-120.00[gk]
	1819	75.00[j]-125.00[gk]
	1829	8.00[f]-10.00[fgk]
	1832	6.00-?[fgk]
	1839	30.00-50.00[gk]
	1839	25.00-40.00[gj]
Buffalo-Detroit	1818	15.00[g]
	1821	18.00[g]
	1838	8.00[g]
Charleston-Savannah	1802	5.00
	1839	5.00
Charleston-Mobile	1840	65.00[m]
New York-Charleston	1802	55.00
	1817	25.00[g]
	1839	40.00[d]

Source: ARJ 3, no. 44 (Nov. 8, 1834), p. 689; *Badger & Porter's Stage Register*, no. 4 (1826), 3, 6, 11; no. 6 (1826), 3, 15, 18, 19; no. 65 (1836), 19, 30; *HCSR* 2, no. 22 (May 27, 1840), 338; *HMM* 25 (August 1851), 243; *NYSL*, May 24, 1816; *NWR* 10, no. 23 (Aug. 3, 1816), 381; 20, no. 18 (June 30, 1821), 288; 25, no. 6 (Oct. 11, 1823), 95; 26, no. 21 (July 27, 1824), 336; 32, no. 13 (May 26, 1827), 224; 36, no. 23 (Aug. 1, 1829), 366; 37, no. 5 (Sept. 26, 1829), 70; 56, no. 7 (Apr. 13, 1839), 98-99; 56, no. 18 (June 29, 1839), 288; 58, no. 16 (June 20, 1840), 256; Henry Adams, *The United States in 1800* (Ithaca: Cornell University Press, 1955), p. 10; Ralph H. Brown, *Historical Geography of the United States* (New York: Harcourt Brace, 1948), p. 282; J. S. Buckingham, *America: Historical, Statistic, and Descriptive* (New York, 1841), 182; Frank Haigh Dixon, *A Traffic History of the Mississippi River System*, National Waterways Commission Docu-

Table 5.1 (continued)

ment no. 11, (Washington, D.C., 1909), pp. 26–27; Seymour Dunbar, *A History of Travel in America* (Indianapolis: Bobbs-Merrill, 1915), I, 329, 398–399; II, 404–405; III, 743, 799–800, 971, 994–995; Alice Morse Earle, *Stage-Coach and Tavern Days* (New York: Macmillan, 1901), p. 270; Louis C. Hunter, *Steamboats on the Western Rivers* (Cambridge: Harvard University Press, 1949), p. 420; Kirkland, *Men, Cities and Transportation*, I, 23, 55; Balthasar H. Meyer, ed., *History of Transportation in the United States Before 1860* (Washington, D.C.: Carnegie Institution of Washington, 1917), pp. 74–77; F. A. Michaux, *Travels to the West of the Allegheny Mountains* (London, 1805), p. 24; John H. Morrison, *History of American Steam Navigation* (New York: W. F. Sametz, 1903), pp. 59, 169, 170, 218, 227–229, 270, 285–286, 370.

    a. By stagecoach unless otherwise specified.

    b. Cheaper routes were available by stagecoach and steamboat.

    c. By stagecoach and steamboat.

    d. By railroad and steamboat. Entirely by railroad for Philadelphia–Baltimore in 1839 and 1840.

    e. Special low rate during a brief period of intense competition between rival carriers.

    f. Special low rate for deck passengers.

    g. Entirely by steamboat.

    h. Special high fare on "the most elegant boats."

    i. By railroad and canal packet boat.

    j. Downstream rate, which was usually lower than the upstream fare because of the smaller amounts of time and fuel consumed.

    k. Upstream rate.

    m. By stagecoach, steamboat, and railroad, including meals for four days.

tively cheap in 1840. At that time one could sail from New York to Albany for less than one day's salary.

The cost of interurban travel was made more burdensome for the vast majority of Americans because of the time consumed on long-distance trips. Unless journeying by boat, the intercity traveler had to reckon with the expenses of overnight stops at roadside inns. He also had to purchase meals unless, as on some steamboat routes, these costs were included in the price of his tickets. The magnitude of these additional outlays varied, but seldom did they total less then one dollar per day, and generally they had the impact of adding several days' wages to the cost of the trip. In 1796, passengers on the three-day stagecoach trip from New York to Baltimore paid an additional $2.25 per day for bed and meals; in 1812, such expenses on the six-day Philadelphia-Pittsburgh trip were $7.00; and in 1840 the 3.3-day trip from New York to Richmond involved about $6.00 in extra expenses.[2] In many cases, high

Table 5.2. Cost of travel per passenger mile between selected major urban pairs, 1790–1840 (in cents).[a]

Urban pair	Year	Cost
New York–Boston	179?	9.4
	1802	4.3
	1840	2.0–2.8
New York–Philadelphia	179?	9.9
	1817	5.0
	1840	3.3–4.4
Philadelphia–Baltimore	179?	10.0
	1826	3.3
	1840	3.3
New York–Albany	1797	4.6
	1823	3.4–4.1
	1840	0.7
Philadelphia–Pittsburgh	1812	6.7
	1836	1.5–2.5[b]
Pittsburgh–Cincinnati	1823	2.7–3.3
	1836	0.6–2.2
Cincinnati–Louisville	1819	9.0[c]
	1839	0.7–3.0[c]
Louisville–New Orleans	1817	5.3[c]
	1817	8.8[d]
	1839	1.8–2.8[ce]
	1839	2.1–3.5[de]
Buffalo–Detroit[f]	1818	4.1[g]
	1838	1.9[g]
Charleston–Savannah	1802	4.7
	1839	4.7
Charleston–Mobile	1840	8.2[g]
New York–Charleston	1802	6.0
	1839	5.0[h]

Source: Table 5.1; H. S. Tanner, *The American Traveller* (Philadelphia, 1836); Samuel Mitchell, *Traveller's Guide Through the United States* (Philadelphia, 1838).

a. Computed on the basis of current route distances. Unless otherwise indicated, the difference between new and old route lengths was not especially great.

b. This relative reduction in costs is exaggerated, since the old stage route was 296 miles, while the newer canal-railroad route was 394 miles.

c. Downstream rate.

d. Upstream rate.

e. Cheaper deck rates were available.

f. Via Cleveland.

g. Excluding that portion of the fare covering meals.

h. This relative reduction in costs is understated, since the old sea route was 900 miles, while the newer land-sea route was 795 miles.

expenses along the way probably acted as a deterrent to interurban travel by foot or self-owned horse, especially since journeys by these means were apt to take a longer time. However, if boarding expenses are taken into account when calculating the cost of travel, then the long-run reduction in this cost (Table 5.1) was even greater, because travel times, and thereby food and bed costs, were greatly reduced between 1790 and 1840.

Interurban travel not only was generally expensive, but was particularly so between those South Atlantic and Gulf Coast cities that were isolated informationally and economically from one another. One account in the early nineteenth century indicated that a 70-mile stage-coach trip from Charleston cost $15, or 21.4 cents per mile. Differences between the cost of interurban travel in the South and elsewhere were still quite pronounced around 1840. In fact, in 1839 fares apparently jumped in price per-mile as soon as one moved south of Baltimore. Whereas costs per passenger mile between Boston and Baltimore varied from 2.0 to 4.4 cents, depending on the stage of the journey and how comfortably one chose to ride, they rose to 5.4 cents per mile for the trip from Baltimore to Richmond, and 6.0 cents per mile between Portsmouth (Norfolk) and Charleston.[3] The comparatively low incomes of most Southerners made it even more difficult to travel from one city to another. As of 1840, the average annual income of nonagricultural workers in the South Atlantic states stood roughly at $232, while the corresponding figures for the Middle Atlantic and New England states were respectively $348 and $466.[4]

CLIENTELE OF INTERURBAN COMMON CARRIERS

In the face of high fares and other travel expenses, long-distance interurban travel was usually out of the question for all but businessmen and the economic elite. The only major exceptions were migrants, who especially after the breakthrough of the steamboat could travel on a few major routes at special low fares without worrying about the costs of a return trip.

The businessmen traveling from city to city, or from small town to major city via another urban center, were of several types. Probably the most important group, at least in terms of numbers, consisted of retailers. Normally these persons made annual or semiannual wholesale purchases of merchandise. Often they also made arrangements for the sale of agricultural produce received as payment in kind. In the early 1820s it could still be reported: "In the United States there are no commercial travellers; consequently, the shop or store keepers are obliged to repair to the large towns, to procure the different articles they may want. There is, therefore, always a great concentration of persons at the principal seaports, to purchase groceries, woollens, cotton goods, &c." At least until the 1820s, "the market was too scattered to make it economical for the wholesale middlemen to seek out the retailers. Consequently, the retailers to obtain supplies had to go to the wholesale markets [of the Northeast]. This they ordinarily did twice a year, in the fall before transportation became too difficult and again in the spring when the winter stock had been disposed of and transportation was again not so difficult." Southern storekeepers journeying northward usually deferred their visits until early summer, when both business was slack and the weather tended to be bad at home. In the 1820s and 1830s the "improvements in transportation brought by turnpikes, steamboats, canals, and railways, coupled with industrial progress and an increase in population, caused interior cities to develop as wholesale markets . . . The development of these markets encouraged [some interior] retailers to obtain their supplies in these cities [primarily Cincinnati, Pittsburgh, Louisville, St. Louis, Buffalo, Detroit, and Cleveland] rather than in the seaboard markets." At the same time a growing number of Northeastern and Southern general-store owners and other retailers continued to flock to New York, Boston, New Orleans, Philadelphia, and Baltimore.[5]

Auctions were particularly important in attracting retailers to major cities between the War of 1812 and the early 1830s. Auctioneers, who acted for a principal and did not acquire title to the goods they sold, were able to sell exceptionally large lots of merchandise and thus frequently could offer lower prices than other wholesalers.[6] Although auctions had earlier been of some importance, their halcyon days followed the War of 1812, when foreign merchants, who had been shut out of the American market by the government's restrictive policies before and during the war, found that the quickest and most profitable method of selling accumulated goods "was to have an agent accompany the merchandise and place it in the hands of an auctioneer upon arrival." The auction sales of foreign merchants soon became highly concentrated in New York, where local legislation was more favorable to such activity than in Boston and Philadelphia. The number of retailers drawn to New York by its auction halls is suggested by the growth of the city's commodity auction sales from almost $3.5 million in 1818 to $23.7 million in 1835. In 1827, New York's sales, exclusive of domestic dry goods, corresponded to over 25 percent of total United States imports. By comparison: "At a semi-annual sale held in Boston in 1829 it was estimated that sales at auction of domestic goods amounted to about $1,300,000." Most important, in terms of the amount of information gathered and disseminated as a result of auction activities, retailers sometimes attended these sales "for many days, and even for weeks together."[7]

Another major group of interurban business travelers consisted of wholesaling merchants and their agents. Among these were Northeastern wholesale commission merchants who journeyed intraregionally and out to urban centers in the West and South in order to sell textiles or other local and hinterland specialities. This type of venture was not especially common until the 1830s, at which time there was also a significant increase in the movement of Western wholesale agents to New York and other Northeastern "commercial emporia." These persons usually were intent on making large-scale acquisitions of Northeastern and European manufactures. Agents of merchant houses in New York, Boston, and elsewhere also traveled southward in order to make cotton purchases; and particularly in the late 1820s and 1830s there was some two-way traffic between Northeastern domestic produce merchants and Western produce buyers and forwarders. In addition, agents were sent out by importers and others with the task of collecting unpaid debts. Finally, factors and other nonlocal agents occasionally either made a trip to the home city of their merchant employers or received visits from those same employers.[8]

Manufacturer's selling agents, particularly from the textile industry, comprised a third group of businessmen employing interurban common carriers. Although such agents had been in operation as early as 1803, they were few in number until the 1830s. Their increase went hand-in-hand with the expansion of domestic textile production and was instrumental in the decline in importance of auctions.[9] Members of the economic elite also resorted to the stagecoach lines and other inter-urban carriers when vacationing or visiting relatives, who frequently also served as business partners or contacts.

During the decades following the War of 1812, migrants to the West who did not have the energy, means, or time to journey by foot or horse found it increasingly possible to utilize common-carrier services on a few routes, owing to the provision of cheap accommodations. Although they normally passed through several cities on their westward journey, the contribution of migrants to interurban information circulation must have been comparatively small in proportion to their numbers, for most of them had rural destinations, many were moving from rural surroundings in New England or elsewhere, others of European origin did not speak English, and virtually all were one-way passengers.

The cheapest per-mile fares available to westward-destined migrants in the 1820s and 1830s were on the usually jammed decks of the steamboats plying between New York and Albany, between Buffalo, Cleveland, and Detroit, and down the Ohio and Mississippi Rivers. Regarding the steamboats of the Ohio and Mississippi, whose fare conditions were not unlike those on the other two routes, Hunter noted: "Not only was the cost of deck passage low, but the spread between deck and cabin fares was remarkably wide and was seldom equaled in other modes of transportation in that day. Deck fare was frequently only one-fifth or one-sixth of the cabin fare; sometimes it rose to as much as one-third or one-half."[10] Packets and barges on the Erie Canal and on the Mainline between Philadelphia and Pittsburgh also carried migrants comparatively cheaply, often at the snail's pace of 1.5–2.0 miles per hour. Shortly after the opening of the Erie Canal, one journal commented: "Emigration is powerful to the West. The vessels on Lake Erie are hardly able to carry the passengers and their goods." By 1837, it was estimated that 94,500 through passengers were annually carried on the canal's "line" boats.[11]

INTERURBAN TRAVEL VOLUMES

Passenger Capacity of Common Carriers. As long as the stagecoach
was the principal means of passenger conveyence between any pair of
cities, the volume of interurban travel was bound to be restricted. The
stagecoach had a limited carrying capacity which, along with its slowness,[12] meant high labor and maintenance costs per passenger mile.
These high costs necessitated the high fares that prevailed. Although
the specific carrying capacity of the often uncomfortable stagecoach
varied in time and place, it seldom exceeded eleven passengers. Apparently, the types of stagecoach most commonly employed prior to
about 1820 carried six to nine passengers. Thereafter, the "ordinary
stagecoach" is reported to have had room for nine passengers inside and
one outside. On a few selected routes where demand was high and road
conditions were relatively good, the passenger capacity of stagecoaches
may have been slightly greater. Thus, at the turn of the nineteenth
century an English traveler reported that he journeyed from New York
to Philadelphia in a "clumsy and uncomfortable machine" which held
twelve persons, including the driver.[13] Road conditions themselves were
important in limiting the carrying capacity of stagecoaches, for the
larger the vehicle, the greater the likelihood of its becoming bogged
down or having other maneuvering difficulties on poor roads.

Until after 1790 there were practically no good roads in the United
States. In the immediately ensuing decades the mileage of roads that
were accommodating to stagecoaches steadily increased. Nevertheless,
the state of the roads "varied in different sections of the country, at
different seasons of the year, at different times during the period . . .
and apparently with the degree of prejudice or irritability of those who
travelled over them."[14] The most important road developments conducive to stage travel occurred between the mid-1790s and mid-1820s
in the form of turnpike construction, especially in New England, New
York, New Jersey, Pennsylvania, and Maryland. Conditions on these toll
roads, which were usually chartered by the state governments and built
by private stock companies, were praised by visiting transportation
authorities.[15] Despite advances, roads bearing stage traffic between
major cities frequently remained wanting in quality. For example, in

1830 a correspondent of the *Boston Courier* reported that the stage route between Boston and Albany was "extremely rough and hilly." In 1840 the road from Buffalo to Detroit had a notoriously bad reputation, and throughout the 1820s and 1830s there were complaints of the "wretched condition" of the National Road from Baltimore westward.[16] However, it was in the South that road conditions in general were poorest. In 1808, Secretary of the Treasury Albert Gallatin noted that "South of the Potomac few artificial roads have been undertaken." Thirty years later, despite sporadic road-building surges in South Carolina, the roads in the South "suitable for vehicles were still few and far between when compared with similar highways in the North."[17] Hence, road conditions curtailed the volume of interurban travel possible by stagecoach in the South even more so than in the rest of the country.

For some time after 1790, sailing vessels provided an important alternative to stagecoaches for making journeys between the leading coastal cities. Until turnpikes became widespread in the Northeast, travel by water, "despite its hazards and delays, was comparatively expeditious." As late as 1817, "a large part of the travel between New England and the Middle [Atlantic] States" was accounted for by small coasting vessels. By the 1790s, travel from New York to nearby and distant Atlantic Coast ports via sloops and other seacraft "was well established and frequent." During the Federalist era, "constant traders" carried passengers fairly regularly from Boston to New York, Philadelphia, Baltimore, and Albany, and at the same time, "almost all travel between the South and North was . . . undertaken by way of the sea."[18] Following the War of 1812, when the British blockade had forced passenger traffic by sea to a halt, the role of sailing vessels in interurban travel dwindled gradually in significance. This was owing partly to road improvements and increased stagecoach use, partly to the growing use of steamboats.

Although figures to show the passenger numbers carried by "constant traders," or packets, during their halcyon days are difficult to find, it is clear that their capacity was not great. These vessels were usually small and almost invariably allocated the largest portion of their space to hauling freight. One of the few accounts available of coastal packets fully loaded with passengers indicates that two vessels departing from

Charleston for New York in 1825 carried, respectively, 88 and 76 travelers. Although such relatively large numbers may occasionally have sailed at the same time, the total passenger volume carried by constant traders on most interurban routes often was inhibited by several circumstances, including the fact that departure dates were less frequent and more unreliable than those of stagecoaches. Travelers were also discouraged by the possibility of weather-caused delays at sea, for coastal packets often "put into harbor at the slightest sign of danger."[19]

The steamboat was the first means of transportation to facilitate interurban travel on a truly large scale. Its impact was confined to travel between urban pairs that were separated in whole or in part by water. Fulton's *Clermont* first carried passengers between New York and Albany in 1807. In 1809 steamboats began transporting passengers on two portions of the New York-to-Philadelphia route—from New York to New Brunswick and other New Jersey points on the Raritan River, and from Bordentown to Philadelphia. Following the War of 1812, steamboats were put into passenger operation between New York and New Haven, Providence, and other Long Island Sound ports, with connecting stagecoach service to Boston. In the 1820s and 1830s steamboats grew in importance as passenger movers along the Atlantic Coast, on the waters of the Ohio and Mississippi, and between Buffalo, Cleveland, and Detroit.

Although the earliest steamboats apparently did not carry passengers in much greater numbers than their sailing competitors, technological improvements in the steam engine soon allowed larger vessels to be built. "The passenger lists of twelve steamboats arriving at Louisville from New Orleans in the early twenties averaged forty-one cabin and 209 deck passengers." At roughly the same time, Hudson River steamers frequently carried between 200 and 300 passengers, and steam-powered vessels arriving at Detroit from Buffalo had 200 or more persons on board. In 1836, 308 passengers were carried on the *Carroll* when it commenced operations on the Chesapeake Bay portion of the route between Philadelphia and Baltimore. Two years later the *Neptune*, in service between New York and Charleston, "could amply and comfortably accommodate with separate bed and board more than 200 passengers, and carry as many more who did not need separate beds, on her decks." At the same time, one could sail from New York to Albany on a steamboat bearing "between four and five hundred passengers." In the summer of 1839 the *New York Journal of Commerce* could write: "The number of people moving about at this time is wonderfully great. The *Massachusetts*, from Providence, came in yesterday morning with near six hundred passengers."[20] This revolution in the carrying capacity of individual vessels reflects only partially the impact of improved steamboat technology on interurban passenger flow, for during the 1820s and 1830s steamboats became faster as well as larger. Increased speeds meant faster journeys, a greater number of trips per annum for each vessel, and the possibility of spreading out fixed costs, all of which contributed to the fall in fares and costs.

The 1830s witnessed one other significant change in the passenger capacity of interurban transport media. As of 1830 there were only 23 miles of railroad track operating in the United States. One decade later this total had grown to at least 2,818 miles. With the exception of the coal roads of Pennsylvania and some of the shorter lines of the West and Deep South (Map 4.2), most of the new trackage was oriented toward the existing pattern of interurban passenger traffic up and down the Atlantic Coast. Thus, most of the railroads operating in southern New England in 1840 connected to the Long Island Sound steamboat lines, which devoted a major share of their efforts to passengers moving between New York and Boston. Most of the lines in New Jersey, southeastern Pennsylvania, and Maryland were either primarily concerned with the movement of passengers between New York, Philadelphia, Baltimore, and Washington, or provided feeder services to that same mainstream of traffic. The lengthy route extending southward from Fredericksburg, Virginia, to connecting steamboats at Wilmington, North Carolina, served the travel of businessmen between New York and other major Northeastern cities, on the one hand, and Charleston and the other major Cotton Ports on the other hand. In addition, the disjointed railroads leading west from Albany eased travel between New York and Buffalo, Cleveland, and Detroit. On these few selected routes, horses were frequently the first source of motive power, but single steam-powered locomotives were soon able to draw in excess of one hundred passengers at once. Moreover, it was often the case that, even when incomplete, a railroad "seemed only to aid in encouraging travel, so that twice as many stages were needed on the uncompleted portion as were formerly used on the whole route."[21]

New York and Philadelphia. The most important traffic route in the East and thereby in the entire country was that between New York and Philadelphia, which evidently experienced a sharp and steady increase in the number of passengers moving over its length from 1790 to 1840. At the outset of the 1790s, a total of twenty-four ferry-connected stages—twelve in each direction—ran weekly between New York and Philadelphia.[22] If it is assumed that the vehicles employed had a somewhat smaller capacity than those used a decade later and that they did not always carry a full load, it follows that each stage on the average carried about six passengers. This yields a total of 144 one-way passengers per week and around 7,500 journeyers per year. There is no comparable gauge for approximating the number of passengers transported by competing sailing vessels, but on the basis of the frequent newspaper mention of passenger-bearing coastal traders and packets, it does not seem too unreasonable to assume that the numbers involved were about one-third those moved by stagecoach, or 2,500. The total traffic between New York and Philadelphia in 1790 can therefore be set at about 10,000 (Table 5.3), exclusive of the wealthy who traveled in their own carriages and those moving on foot or horseback. Since the number sailing around Cape May may have been as low as 20 percent of the stagecoach traffic volume or as high as 50 percent of that figure, the range of the estimate can be placed at 9,000 to 11,250.

Apparently the increasing economic interdependence between New York and Philadelphia during the early Federal period led to more than a doubling of passenger traffic between the two cities by 1804. As of that date, a "Diligence Stage," a "Commercial Coachee," and a "United States Mail Stage" operated daily except Sundays in each direction between both cities.[23] Since these stagecoaches could seat a maximum of 11 persons, it is assumed that an average of 9 passengers was carried on each of the 36 weekly one-way trips.[24] This would put the mean number of stage travelers per week at 324, and the annual total at somewhat above 16,800. In the absence of any precise data, it is again assumed that the passenger volume sailing between the two hubs was one-

Table 5.3. Estimated common-carrier travel volumes between New York and Philadelphia, 1790–1840.

Year	Estimated one-way trips $(t_{NY \to P} + t_{P \to NY})$	Combined population of New York and Philadelphia[a] $(p_{NY} + p_P)$	One-way trips per thousand New York and Philadelphia capita[b]
1790	10,000 (9,000–11,250)[c]	77,227	130 (116–146)
1804	22,500 (20,100–25,250)[c]	148,475[d]	151 (135–170)
1816	33,900 (29,800–36,100)[c]	219,045[d]	155 (136–165)
1828	80,000	348,950[d]	229
1833	120,000	434,196[d]	276
1840	200,000	569,366	351

Source: Sidney I. Pomerantz, *New York: An American City, 1783–1803: A Study of Urban Life* (New York: Columbia University Press, 1938), p. 163; *New York Daily Advertiser,* May 22, 1804; *NYSL,* May 24, 1816; Wheaton J. Lane, *From Indian Trail to Iron Horse: Travel and Transportation in New Jersey, 1620–1860* (Princeton: Princeton University Press, 1939), pp. 195, 201–202, 289; George Armroyd, *A Connected View of the Whole Internal Navigation of the United States* (Philadelphia, 1830), p. 99; *NWR* 30, no. 12 (May 20, 1826), 201; 35, no. 1 (Aug. 30, 1828), 4; *HCSR* 2, no. 10 (Mar. 4, 1840), 146; Taylor, "Comment," p. 39.

a. New York population includes Brooklyn. Philadelphia population includes Kensington, Moyamensing, Northern Liberties, Spring Garden, and Southwark.

b. Computed by the compound fraction:

$$\frac{t_{NY \to P} + t_{P \to NY}}{(p_{NY} + p_P)/1{,}000}$$

c. Range given in parentheses owing to imprecision of data. See text.

d. Interpolated from nearest census-date populations.

third that moving by stagecoach, or over 5,600. This results in a total traffic volume of roughly 22,500. Again allowing that the number traveling by sloop and schooner may have been anywhere between 20 and 50 percent of the stagecoach sum, the range of the estimate can be set at 20,100 to 25,250.

Although the War of 1812 had stunted normal economic activity, another large gain in New York-Philadelphia passenger traffic apparently was registered by 1816. Four different stagecoach lines were offering 58 coaches per week, 29 going in each direction. These vehicles had steamboat connections between New York and New Brunswick or Elizabethtown and between Philadelphia and Trenton.[25] Again on the assumption that an average of nine passengers traveled on each one-way trip, the weekly mean was 522 New York-Philadelphia riders, and the annual stagecoach volume was about 27,100. Since considerable savings in time had by then been gained on the combined stagecoach-steamboat trip, the sailing packets must have begun to lose a share of the traffic between the nation's two leading urban centers. Consequently, it is assumed that the sea-route traffic was around 6,800, or only one-fourth of that moving by steamer and stage. This puts the one-way passenger total in the vicinity of 33,900. If it is allowed that the number of sloop and schooner travelers actually fell to as little as 10 percent of the steamboat-stagecoach traffic, or came to as much as one-third that traffic, the range of the 1816 estimate becomes 29,800–36,100.

Although the passenger traffic between New York and Philadelphia expanded considerably from 1790 to 1816, its most pronounced up-surge began in the following period, when the steamboats employed on the route became more numerous, larger, faster, and cheaper. By 1829 an expert on internal communications of the United States could state that about 80,000 passengers had passed between New York and Phila-delphia in the previous year. Given the scattered accounts of as many as 600 persons flowing between the two cities in one day, this estimate does not appear to be an exaggeration.[26]

Further momentum to the growth of the New York-Philadelphia traffic was provided in 1833 by the opening of the first stretch of the Camden and Amboy Railroad, which tied up with already existing steamboat services. In its first year of operation this link transported almost 110,000 passengers across New Jersey (Table 5.4). Inasmuch as the People's Line of stages at first offered vigorous through-traffic com-petition to the new means of conveyance, it may be estimated conserva-tively that the total New York-Philadelphia traffic in 1833 was at least 120,000.[27] Except for a brief setback in 1837, the number of travelers using the Camden and Amboy grew steadily from 1834 to 1839. In the following year a new rail alternative became available, which provided through trains from Jersey City to Philadelphia (Map 4.2). It involved three railroads (the New Jersey, a new branch of the Camden and Amboy, and the Philadelphia and Trenton) and included a specially built bridge over the Delaware at Trenton. "This route was about 3

Table 5.4. Through passengers carried by the Camden and Amboy Railroad, 1833–1840.

Year	Passengers
1833	109,908
1834	105,418
1835	147,424
1836	163,731
1837	145,461
1838	164,520
1839	181,479
1840	162,690

Source: HCSR 2, no. 10 (Mar. 4, 1840), 146; 6, no. 12 (Mar. 23, 1842), 185; HMM 2 (April 1840), 347.

miles longer than that by the Camden and Amboy, but the change from water to rail and from rail to water on the latter route proved very speedily a distinct handicap."[28] Hence, the drop-off in through traffic on the Camden and Amboy in 1840 quite likely was more than offset by travel on the new alternative. If it is assumed that the growth of combined traffic from 1839 to 1840 was comparable to that for the Camden and Amboy alone from 1838 to 1839, an estimate is obtained of about 200,000 New York-Philadelphia passengers for 1840 (Tables 5.3 and 5.4).

Although there may be a wide margin of error in several of these absolute estimates, it is nevertheless clear that the amount of information exchange via travel between New York and Philadelphia became relatively more intense between 1790 and 1840, for during that half-century the number of one-way trips per thousand New York and Philadelphia capita grew from between 116 and 146 to roughly 351.[29] In other words, travel volumes between New York and Philadelphia expanded 2.4 to 3.0 times faster than would be expected from their combined population growth, and travel-generated information circulation between the two cities probably grew to at least the same degree. These figures should not suggest that all travel between New York and Philadelphia was undertaken by residents of the two fledgling metropolises. However, each traveler, regardless of his city of residence or his ultimate travel destination, was a potential bearer of information to one or more New York or Philadelphia inhabitants.

New York and Boston. For most of the 1790–1840 period, several alternative New York-Boston routes were available, most of which passed through either Providence, the sixth largest city in the Northeast in 1830 and 1840, or other places of importance, such as New Haven, Hartford, and New London. The services available over these routes, unlike those between New York and Philadelphia, apparently involved considerable way-traffic. This fact makes the estimation of New York-Boston travel volumes hazardous and extremely difficult.

It was not until the spring of 1793 that stagecoaches first operated daily, except Sunday, between New York and Boston. Every other day the vehicle making the trip in 1793 was a more expensively priced "limited" coach, admitting only four passengers. Although the slower stages running on other days were somewhat larger because of way traffic to New Haven, Hartford, and lesser centers, it cannot be assumed that New York-Boston coaches averaged more than four through passengers per trip. Thus, with six stages operating per week in each direction the number of one-way New York-Boston passengers per week should have averaged about 48. This would mean that in 1794, the first full year of daily operations, no more than 2,500 travelers were involved. However, the traffic between New York and Boston may have reached twice that sum because businessmen frequently sailed the entire distance or took the New York-Providence leg of the journey by water. If the volume of sailing traffic was as low as half that by stagecoach, the one-way New York-Boston passenger total in 1794 can be estimated as having fallen between 3,750 and 5,000 (Table 5.5).[30]

The New York-Boston travel volume experienced a boom following the War of 1812. Regular New York-New Haven steamer operations began in the spring of 1815, and in 1816 the Sound Steamboat Line advertised the commencement of new services, "with the steamers *Fulton* or *Connecticut* leaving New York five days a week for New Haven, while the *Connecticut* continued three days a week on to New London." Stages connected to and from Boston at both New Haven and New London. In 1822, when steamboats began operating from New

Table 5.5. Estimated common-carrier travel volumes between New York and Boston, 1794 and 1834.

Year	Estimated one-way trips $(t_{NY \to B} + t_{B \to NY})$	Combined population of New York and Boston[a] $(p_{NY} + p_B)$	One-way trips per thousand New York and Boston capita[b]
1794	3,750–5,000	65,051[c]	58–77
1834	84,250–96,100	367,458[c]	229–261

Source: Oliver W. Holmes, "Levi Pease, The Father of New England Stage-Coaching," Journal of Economic and Business History 3 (1930–1931), 241–245, 256; Dunbar, History of Travel, I, 187–188; ARJ 3, no. 44 (Nov. 8, 1834), 689; Badger & Porter's Stage Register, no. 65 (1836), 4, 18, 22, 29, 30; Tanner, American Traveller, p. 43; Mitchell, Traveller's Guide, pp. 60–61; Taylor, "Comment," p. 39.

a. 1834 New York population includes Brooklyn. 1834 Boston population includes Cambridge, Charlestown, Roxbury, and Dorchester.

b. Computed by the compound fraction:

$$\frac{t_{NY \to B} + t_{B \to NY}}{(p_{NY} + p_B)/1,000}$$

c. Interpolated from nearest census-date populations.

York to Providence, Providence became the major funnel through which New York-Boston passenger traffic passed. From the start, the number of connecting stagecoaches shuttling between Providence and Boston varied from 15 to 25 per sailing day. When the steamboat monopoly previously existing on Long Island Sound was declared unconstitutional in 1824, there was an immediate mushrooming of steamboat links between New York and Boston. By 1826, two steamer lines were operating directly to Providence, and four others provided stagecoach tie-ins with Boston: two via Hartford, one via New London, and one via New Haven.[31]

In 1834 it was claimed that the "Annual amount paid for the conveyance of [steamboat] passengers between Newport, Providence, and New York, at $6 per passenger, is about $475,000." If this was correct, roughly 79,000 passengers were involved. Since the combined population of Providence and Newport was then about 8 percent that of New York and Boston, it would seem safe to guess that 75 to 90 percent of

the 79,000 passengers, or 59,250 to 71,000 persons, were moving
between the two larger cities via Providence. A conservative estimate
would put the entire New York-Boston travel volume at least 25,000
higher, owing to the steamboat-stagecoach trips that were still made
daily via New Haven, Hartford, New London, or Norwich, giving a grand
total of 84,250-96,100 passengers (Table 5.5).[32]

Although specific passenger estimates cannot be made for the years
after 1834, it is evident that business travel continued to soar between
Boston and New York. In 1835 the Boston and Providence Railroad
began competing with the four Boston-Providence stagecoach lines. On
the New York-Providence steamboats 200 to 300 passengers per trip
was the rule, and before the decade was out, twice that number could
be carried on a single voyage. Providence began to lose its primacy as a
steamboat terminus for the New York-Boston traffic in 1837, when
"New York business men built a railroad from Providence to Stoning-
ton, [Connecticut], where it connected with their Sound steamers from
New York. By reducing the water trip, this meant a quicker through
connection." Numerous travelers were also using the Boston and
Worcester Railroad to make the New York-Boston journey via Norwich
and Worcester. Nevertheless, revenue statistics for the Boston and
Providence Railroad indicate that its number of full-length passengers
probably was close to 150,000 by 1839.[33]

The traffic estimates suggest that from 1790 to 1840 the amount of
information circulating between New York and Boston as a result of
travel increased considerably in relative intensity as well as absolute
volume. Since the number of one-way trips between the two cities grew
several times faster than would be expected from their combined population increase, it is probable that the amount of information exchanged
grew accordingly.

Philadelphia and Baltimore. On the surface it would appear that the
1790-1840 growth in relative intensity of passenger traffic between
Philadelphia and Baltimore was much greater than that between either
New York and Philadelphia or New York and Boston (Table 5.6).
As of 1796 there were 14 "water-stages" running weekly between
Philadelphia and Baltimore—seven in each direction—via a route that in
all but the winter months included sections over water, from Phila-

Table 5.6. Estimated common-carrier travel volumes between Philadelphia and Baltimore, 1796–1839.

Year	Estimated one-way trips $(t_{P \to b} + t_{b \to P})$	Combined population of Philadelphia[a] and Baltimore $(p_P + p_b)$	One-way trips per thousand Philadelphia and Baltimore capita[b]
1796	4,300	75,883[c]	57
1818	30,000	164,009[c]	183
1839	190,000	314,659[c]	604

Source: J. Thomas Scharf and Thompson Westcott, History of Philadelphia, 1609–1884 (Philadelphia, 1884), III, 2,156, 2,161; NWR 16, no. 22 (July 28, 1819), 357; Meyer, History of Transportation, pp. 392–393; Taylor, "Comment," p. 39.

a. Includes Kensington, Moyamensing, Northern Liberties, Spring Garden, and Southwark.

b. Computed by the compound fraction:

$$\frac{t_{P \to b} + t_{b \to P}}{(p_P + p_b)/1,000}$$

c. Interpolated from nearest census-date populations.

delphia to New Castle, Delaware, and from Frenchtown, Maryland, to Baltimore.[34] If, as in the New York-Philadelphia case of 1790, an average of six passengers per stage is assumed, then the weekly Philadelphia-Baltimore passenger traffic can be set around 84, and the annual travel volume for 1796 can be estimated at 4,300. Since the all-water alternative around Cape Charles and up Chesapeake Bay was extremely circuitous, being at least four times the distance, it appears unnecessary to make allowances for additional passengers.

Here, too, the years following the War of 1812 witnessed a burgeoning of travel volumes. By 1815, steamboats had replaced small sailing vessels on the Philadelphia-Delaware portion of the route. Soon three steamboats were employed on the Chesapeake Bay leg of the trip, and no less than eighteen stagecoaches were shuttling between New Castle and Frenchtown. A reliable source stated that in 1818 "there were about 30,000 full passengers" between Philadelphia and Baltimore.[35]

Philadelphia-Baltimore travel continued to spiral in the 1820s and was given additional momentum in 1833 when the New Castle and Frenchtown Railroad opened. Three years later that railroad and its connecting steamboat services had competition from both a combined steamboat-canal linkage and a stagecoach line. In 1838 the steamboat was largely replaced by the Philadelphia, Wilmington and Baltimore Railroad. The following year the same railroad carried 213,650 passengers.[36] Since Wilmington was the only intermediate stop of consequence, and since its population was well under 3 percent of the combined populations of Philadelphia and Baltimore, probably at least 190,000 through passengers moved between the two terminal cities in 1839. It is not likely that any exaggeration arises if this figure is used as a measure of the total Philadelphia-Baltimore travel volume (Table 5.6), for in the same year some passengers continued to opt for the route of the New Castle and Frenchtown Railroad.

Whereas the absolute number of one-way trips apparently multiplied over 44 times from 1796 to 1839, the number of trips per 1,000 Philadelphia and Baltimore residents expanded more than sixfold during the same period, presumably having a corresponding effect on information circulation. This impressive growth was not entirely owing to the increased economic interdependence of the two cities. Unquestionably, a good percentage of the message-bearing travelers between both places were either New York and Boston businessmen on their way to attend to matters in Baltimore and other Southern cities, or were Baltimore and Southern merchants who were continuing beyond Philadelphia, most often to New York. In addition, large numbers of those passing between Philadelphia and Baltimore were bound to or from Washington, D.C.[37]

Other Major Northeastern Cities. The other most important interurban corridor of passenger flow in the Northeast was that between New York and Albany. By the opening of the nineteenth century, stagecoaches along this route were of secondary importance in the passenger-carrying business to the "scores of sloops" that sailed the Hudson River during the months when it was ice-free. Upon the *Clermont's* initial voyage with twelve through passengers in 1807, the sloop began to fade in importance. The number of New York-Albany steamboat sailings quickly grew from 24 in 1807 to 66 in 1809, and by 1816 eight steamboats were involved in the interurban Hudson traffic.[38] The task of appraising the number of passengers carried by these and subsequent steamboats, however, is seriously complicated by their heavy way-traffic to intervening river ports, including Peekskill, Newburgh, Poughkeepsie, Kingston, and Hudson.

The significance of the New York-Albany travel route was greatly magnified in 1825 when the intrastate monopoly of the North River Steamboat Company ended and the Erie Canal was opened. Thereafter, the New York-Albany travel volume became increasingly dominated by New York-bound merchants from Rochester, Buffalo, Cleveland, Detroit, and the West in general; by New York businessmen moving in the opposite direction; and by hordes of migrants with rural and urban destinations in the West. By 1832 a cautious analyst of New York-Albany steamboat traffic could arrive at an estimate equivalent to 182,400 passengers. One year later, another assessment yielded 189,000 steamboat passengers and 15,300 stagecoach travelers during the winter months. These 1833 figures average out to 720 one-way trips per 1,000 New York and Albany inhabitants (cf. Tables 5.3, 5.5, and 5.6). This exceptionally high ratio is accounted for in great part by the fact that none of the other urban pairs examined so far had a comparable stream of migrants flowing between them. By 1840, 24 large steamboats were devoted to bearing migrants and merchants between New York and Albany.[39]

Especially after the Mohawk Valley route from Albany had been established as the major pathway to the West, travel between Boston and Albany flourished. Not long after the opening of the Erie Canal, eight stagecoach companies linked the two cities. By 1827 there were "two daily and nine tri-weekly stage lines running [from Albany] to Boston, making an average of six and one-half coaches daily, besides extras which may be put in the route for private parties or to care for any overflow from the regular coach." These lines operated over various roads and carried such a volume of way traffic that it is almost impossible to estimate their through Boston-Albany traffic. In 1834 several of the lines provided connections with the recently completed Boston and Worcester Railroad. Despite this improvement, it is quite possible that in the late 1830s the majority of travelers from Boston to Albany and points westward were making the journey via Providence and New York.[40]

Once the steamboat became common on Long Island Sound in the 1820s, most businessmen traveling between Boston and Philadelphia presumably did so by way of New York. However, prior to that time merchants often sailed between the two cities, either directly or by way of Providence. During the first decade of the nineteenth century the Philadelphia-Boston packets sailed whenever a sufficient quantity of freight had accumulated, but by 1815 demand was adequate to permit more regular scheduling. The Boston and Philadelphia Steamboat Company was organized in 1832. However, its two steamers apparently were devoted primarily to trade, and there is no indication of the volume of their passenger business.[41]

Major Cities of the Ohio and Upper Mississippi Valleys. In 1817, "the whole passenger and freight traffic of the Ohio River was handled by twenty barges . . . and a hundred and fifty keel-boats."[42] With the ascendancy of the steamboat on Western rivers in the 1820s, travel volume boomed between Pittsburgh, Cincinnati, Louisville, and St. Louis. A few scraps of evidence suggest that the low steamboat fares (Table 5.2), which were particularly conducive to migrant travel, raised the relative intensity of interurban passenger flow between these four cities to a very high level by 1840.

Regularly scheduled steamboat passenger service in the West was pioneered in 1819 with one trip per week in each direction between Cincinnati and Louisville. If, in accord with the carrying capacity of vessels at the time, an average load of 80 to 100 passengers per trip is assumed, then during the first full year of operation, lasting about thirty-eight ice-free weeks, the Cincinnati-Louisville traffic should have ranged between 6,000 and 7,600 (Table 5.7).[43] "Favored by the heavy traffic and short distance between Cincinnati and Louisville, thrice-weekly service between these ports was in effect by 1826, and five years later regular daily departures from each terminus were offered."[44] By 1840 an observer could maintain that the two steamers in regular Cincinnati-Louisville service carried "at an average" 125 passengers on their daily through voyages. If accurate, this means that approximately

Table 5.7. Estimated common-carrier travel volumes between major Ohio Valley cities, 1820–1850.

Urban pair	Year	Estimated one-way trips	Combined population	One-way trips per thousand capita[a]
Cincinnati–Louisville	1820	6,000–7,600	13,654	438–555
Cincinnati–Louisville	1840	57,000	67,548	850
Pittsburgh–Cincinnati	1850	89,828	183,297[b]	490

Source: Morrison, History of American Steam Navigation, pp. 228, 230; Israel Andrews, Report . . . on the Trade and Commerce of the British North American Colonies, U. S. Senate Document No. 112, 32nd Cong., 1st sess., 1853, pp. 660–661.

a. Computed by compound fractions of the type given in Tables 5.3, 5.5, and 5.6.
b. Pittsburgh population includes the subsequently annexed municipality of Allegheny.

1,500 were transported weekly, and about 57,000 persons made the trip during the ice-free season.[45] Many of these travelers evidently had begun their journey in Pittsburgh or elsewhere and were bound for New Orleans or St. Louis. Others came from New York and Boston via the Erie and Ohio Canals.

Passengers were able to move by once-monthly keelboats between Pittsburgh and Cincinnati as early as 1794, when both were little more than villages in the wilderness. Although the Pittsburgh-Cincinnati traffic grew considerably during the 1820s and 1830s, with 538 departures of passenger- and freight-bearing steamers from Pittsburgh for Cincinnati and Louisville in 1837, regularly scheduled service apparently did not acquire any permanence until the early 1840s.[46] Because of this lack of regularity, as well as the fact that boats leaving Pittsburgh usually called on Cincinnati, Louisville, and other intervening points, it is difficult to estimate travel volume for 1840 or any earlier date. However, a reliable source indicates that in 1850 Pittsburgh-Cincinnati steamboats carried 89,828 travelers.[47] A substantial share of this travel volume and that of earlier dates involved businessmen and others who either were continuing beyond Pittsburgh to major Northeastern centers, or were passing through Pittsburgh from the Northeast to points as distant as New Orleans. Nevertheless, even if the number of one-way trips per 1,000 Pittsburgh and Cincinnati residents had doubled from 1840 to 1850, the relative intensity of passenger exchange between the two at the former date must have been quite high considering the distance separating them (449 miles via the Ohio River).

Travel volumes between St. Louis and Louisville are also not easily pinpointed. However, it is clear that they were relatively large by the 1830s, for by 1832 the St. Louis Times could advertise simultaneously eight steamboats for Louisville and Cincinnati.[48]

The relative intensity of traffic between Cincinnati and Louisville, and between Pittsburgh and Cincinnati, is not be misconstrued, for in both instances the ratios are inflated by large volumes of migrants. Thus, the relative intensity of travel-linked business information flows between both urban pairs is very likely to have been well below that suggested by the one-way trip ratios.

Buffalo, Cleveland, and Detroit. The small stream of steamboat passenger traffic that came into being on Lake Erie in 1818 was swollen several times over within a very short period of time following the opening of the Erie Canal. From 1825 to 1830 the number of arriving and departing "steamboats and vessels" at Buffalo leapt from 359 to 2,052, while the number of passenger-bearing steamboats putting in at Cleveland went from 21 to 448 during the same five-year interval.[49] By 1825 it was reported that about 300 migrants and other passengers per week were arriving in Detroit. Thus, assuming thirty weeks of operation, roughly 9,000 travelers arrived by water at Detroit from Buffalo and Cleveland. Since steamers between Buffalo and Detroit normally called at Cleveland, the volume of traffic between any two of the three cannot be established.[50]

In 1830 traffic was sufficient to warrant a daily line of Buffalo-Detroit steamboats. Three years later, a total of 61,480 persons was carried by eleven steamers operating on the Great Lakes. If it is estimated conservatively that only 30,000 of these travelers made through Buffalo-Detroit journeys, with the remainder moving between those two cities and other ports, including Cleveland, then the number of one-way trips per 1,000 inhabitants of Buffalo and Detroit would still have been as large as 1,890 (cf. Tables 5.3 and 5.5–5.7).[51] In 1837 a Detroit businessman asserted that over 180,000 persons annually arrived and departed his city by steamboat, most of them via Buffalo and Cleveland. Given Detroit's population of less than 9,000, this assertion might appear astronomical. However, it is consistent with a newspaper report of "more than three thousand persons" sailing westward from Cleveland on a single day, with the fact that 525 steamboat round-trips were completed between Buffalo and Detroit in 1841, and with Israel Andrews' report of 369,430 passengers arriving and departing Detroit in 1850.[52]

In short, in both absolute and relative terms the volume of travel between Buffalo, Cleveland, and Detroit was very large by the mid-1830s—at least by pretelegraphic standards. Moreover, as in the Ohio Valley, the westbound passenger flow must have considerably outweighed eastbound flow, owing to the number of migrants involved. Insofar as the dominating migrant component was partly European, the travel ties of Buffalo, Cleveland, and Detroit with New York must have been strong, for the overwhelming majority of European immigrants entered the country through New York. As the other major component of the Buffalo-Cleveland-Detroit passenger traffic consisted of businessmen en route to or from New York, the importance of travel and information links with the nation's largest city is quite evident.

Major Southern Cities. Throughout the period 1790–1840 travel volumes between major Southern cities were generally very limited in comparison to the interurban passenger flows in other parts of the country. Not only did road conditions curtail the volume of travel possible by stagecoach in the South, but limited economic relationships and the lengthy detour around Florida discouraged travel by sea between New Orleans and Mobile, on the one hand, and Richmond, Norfolk, Charleston, and Savannah on the other. "A view of the general system of [Southern passenger and freight] transportation just prior to the railroad era, say in 1830, would show that, except for the introduction of steamboats upon the chief rivers, no great change in the character of either vehicles or avenues had resulted." In the mid-1830s travelers still marveled at the limited amount of traffic south of Richmond.[53]

As late as 1836, Southern interurban travel was largely confined to movement between the most closely spaced major urban pairs: Richmond and Norfolk, Charleston and Savannah, New Orleans and Mobile. No regularly scheduled passenger steamboats connected any but these three city pairs. To go from Richmond or Norfolk to Charleston by stagecoach still required that a change of vehicle be made in Raleigh, North Carolina, or Columbia, South Carolina. Likewise, no through stagecoach service existed from Charleston or Savannah to New Orleans or Mobile.[54] Only in 1839, with the completion of the Wilmington and Raleigh Railroad, was movement between Richmond and Charleston greatly facilitated. No real improvement between Charleston and Mobile came about until 1840, when a thrice-weekly mongrel line began operations, covering 460 miles by steamboat, 210 by coach, and 21 by rail, with a steamboat connection from the Alabama port to New Orleans. Both of these new services catered not so much to internal Southern travelers as to businessmen going to and from New York, Philadelphia, and Baltimore.[55]

In contrast to the dearth of passengers between the Southern cities themselves, a well-established travel network existed between those centers and New York, Philadelphia, Baltimore, and Boston long before the Wilmington and Raleigh went into operation. Baltimore had steamboat service to Norfolk in 1819, and by 1825 had regularly scheduled packets transporting both freight and passengers to Charleston, Savannah, and New Orleans. Another steamboat line to Norfolk and Richmond was also shortly available. Before the War of 1812 Philadelphia had "constant traders" to and from Norfolk, Richmond, Charleston, and Savannah. In the 1830s Philadelphia's passenger connections with the South included steamers to Norfolk and multiple-media routes to Mobile and New Orleans. Bostonians could also make travel accommodations to the major South Atlantic ports prior to the War of 1812, but in the 1820s and 1830s some of this traffic, as well as that to New Orleans and Mobile, went via New York.[56]

The most significant flow of travelers for the major Southern cities was with New York. Early in the nineteenth century New York had "constant traders" carrying cargoes and passengers back and forth to Charleston, Savannah, New Orleans, and Richmond. Coastal packet lines of a permanent nature were established in 1822 to Charleston and New

Orleans, and in that same year "a steam brig that plies with passengers and freight" was inaugurated to Norfolk. By 1832 at least thirty-two ships were running from New York to New Orleans, Charleston, Mobile, and Savannah (Table 4.14). Numerous other smaller vessels also carried travelers between New York and the major Southern ports. In the mid-1830s these "minor" packet lines provided six schooners to Norfolk and nine to Richmond. In addition, there was much business travel between New York and the South that went and came via Philadelphia and Baltimore.[57]

Coastal travel in the South was heaviest in the summer, "when large numbers sought to avoid the unhealthy and uncomfortable heat of the Southern cities. Charleston and Savannah society tended to move northward en masse." Businessmen from Charleston, Savannah, Mobile, New Orleans, and some of the inland cities "took advantage of the fact that trade was apt to be stagnant at home and came to New York to combine pleasure with business while replenishing their stocks."[58] It is clear, expecially in view of the great distances to New York, that the number of passengers going in both directions was relatively large. However, there are sufficient clues to make only one New York-Savannah estimate and two New York-Charleston estimates.

A Bostonian writing in 1825 stated that the number of passengers from Charleston and Savannah to and from New York amounted yearly to almost 10,000, a figure roughly equivalent to 19,000 one-way trips in 1824.[59] This claim may have been inflated, but if it is allowed to include those whose journey to or from New York was via other cities, it should be acceptable as the total number of New York-Charleston and New York-Savannah travelers. Two alternatives are open for apportioning the 19,000 one-way trips. One is to assume that they were divided in proportion to the 1824 populations of Charleston and Savannah, which would yield about 14,800 one-way trips between New York and Charleston, and about 4,200 such trips between New York and Savannah (Table 5.8). The other is to assume, on the basis of Charleston's 8-6 advantage over Savannah in the number of packet ships serving New York (Table 4.14), that the split went 10,900 to 8,100 in favor of New York-Charleston one-way trips. As of 1836, one New York-Charleston passenger steamer sailed from both places every

Table 5.8. Estimated common-carrier travel volumes between New York, Charleston, and Savannah, 1824–1836.

Urban pair	Year	Estimated one-way trips	Combined population[a]	One-way trips per thousand capita[b]
New York–Savannah	1824	4,200–8,100	171,962[c]	24–47
New York–Charleston	1824	10,900–14,800	191,491[c]	57–77
New York–Charleston	1836	26,000–32,500	325,036[c]	80–100

Source: Albion, Square-Riggers, p. 75; Badger & Porter's Stage Register, no. 45 (1836), 30; Buckingham, America, I, 167; Census of Population, 1960, I, pt. A, 1–67.
a. New York populations include Brooklyn.
b. Computed by compound fractions of the type given in Tables 5.3, 5.5, and 5.6.
c. Interpolated from nearest census-date populations.

Saturday. The carrying capacity of the vessels involved was over 400.[60] Assuming that the pronounced seasonal variation in demand kept the average trip load down to 250 passengers, or 500 one-way travelers per week, a total of 26,000 passengers is obtained for the entire year. If it is further assumed that the numbers still making the New York–Charleston journey by cargo-bearing packets were sufficient to compensate for any error and to augment this figure by one-fourth, the annual total would be 32,500 one-way trips. However gross these estimates may be, it appears that the relative growth of New York–Charleston travel volume—and thus of travel-generated information circulation—was greater than would be expected from their combined population expansion figures.

The Primacy of New York. In terms of absolute numbers of passengers, the most important interurban travel links in the United States near the end of the pretelegraphic period were those between New York and Philadelphia; New York and Boston; New York and Albany (and on to Buffalo); Philadelphia and Baltimore; Cincinnati and Louisville; Pittsburgh and Cincinnati; Buffalo, Cleveland, and Detroit; and New York and the Cotton Ports. In four of the eight instances, New York was directly involved. In two other instances (Philadelphia-Baltimore and Buffalo-Cleveland-Detroit), there was a sizable component that had

New York as its ultimate origin or destination. Even in the remaining two cases (Cincinnati-Louisville and Pittsburgh-Cincinnati), there were more than a few who were either coming from or going to New York. Thus, insofar as absolute data best reflect the volume of travel-generated information entering and leaving a city, at the national level New York clearly dominated the long-distance circulation of information via travel. This position of primacy apparently was attained early in the 1790–1840 period; and by the 1820s, those thronging to and from New York included a growing share of the country's travelers to points abroad, as well as Southern and Western retailers and merchants, Northeastern businessmen in general, and European immigrants.

The tremendous amount of information channeled through New York by travelers is beyond measure, but it is at least suggested by an 1828 claim that the city annually had a minimum of 320,000 passenger arrivals and departures by steamboat alone.[61] This avowedly conservative estimate appears more credible when placed in the context of a reliable report that during the year ending July 1851, more than "two million passengers were carried on New York's three main steamboat routes."[62] New York's position as the nation's major focus of travel-generated information circulation almost certainly was reinforced by the railroad developments of the 1830s. During that decade it was stated that "all past experience has shown that the travel in this country, particularly on routes connected with its commercial metropolis [New York] increases annually, in a ratio far beyond that of its business population, and in no case is this increase so high as when connected with the establishment of steamboats and railroads."[63]

Frequent accounts of the difficulty of obtaining hotel or boarding-house space serve as an indicator of the upsurge in passenger traffic to New York following the opening of the Camden and Amboy Railroad. For example, an 1833 periodical reported: "the influx of strangers in that city is unprecedented . . . The steamboats and stages arrive in all directions crowded with passengers. Some of the principal houses have turned away from fifty to a hundred a day. On one day of last week a gentleman was unable to get into any of the hotels in Broadway, and at one house twenty-five persons slept in a single room."[64] By the late 1830s it was estimated that on any one date New York had a "floating population" of domestic and foreign visitors that totaled "about 50,000," the "greatest number of these . . . engaged in commerce or trade, with a due admixture of professional men."[65] If this was approximately correct, and even if, as is unlikely, the average length of stay for traveler's to New York was as much as four weeks, then the number of persons annually passing through the city was at least 650,000. By the same reasoning, the number of one-way trips originating and terminating in the city surpassed 1,300,000—exclusive of those made by the city's own resident businessmen.

INTERURBAN TRAVEL TIMES

The rapid increase in travel volume was associated with a comparatively high frequency of communication between specific urban pairs, giving them highly positive contact-array spatial biases in the availability of information. The transport improvements that contributed to this increase in interurban travel volume also brought about drastically reduced travel times on the same routes and thereby enlarged the time-lag spatial biases in information availability held by the cities involved. The scale of improvements in travel time between 1790 and 1840 is indicated in part by the "rates of travel" from New York in 1800 and 1830 (Maps 5.1 and 5.2).[66] However, because of the information advantages that resulted from interurban travel-time reductions, a closer examination is called for.

Rapid travel was at a premium along the principal interurban routes of the Northeast. Even though average speeds were only around fifteen miles per hour in 1840 on the common carrier routes between New York and Philadelphia, New York and Boston, Philadelphia and Baltimore, and New York and Albany, travel times between these major cities had been reduced to from one-fourth to less than one-eleventh of what they were in 1790 (Figs. 5.1–5.4, Table 5.9). Thus, over a period of fifty years the mean reduction in travel time per year, or the rate of "time-space convergence," among these leading centers ranged as high as over 100 minutes per year in the New York-Albany case.[67] In other words, travel times improved in the 1790–1840 interval from a substantial 12.4 minutes per route mile in the New York-Philadelphia

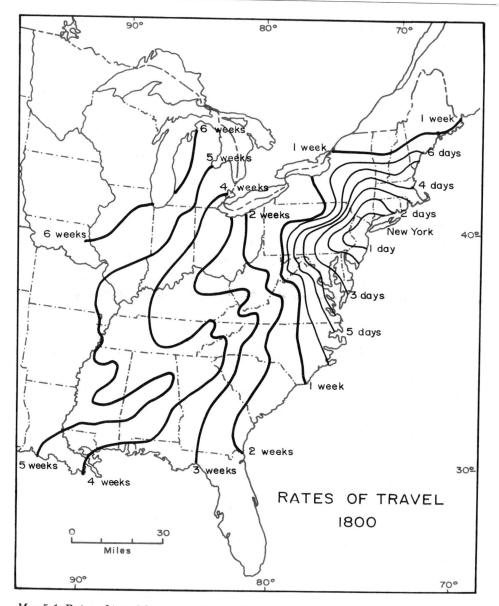

Map 5.1. Rates of travel from New York, 1800. Adapted from Paullin, *Atlas*, plate 138A.

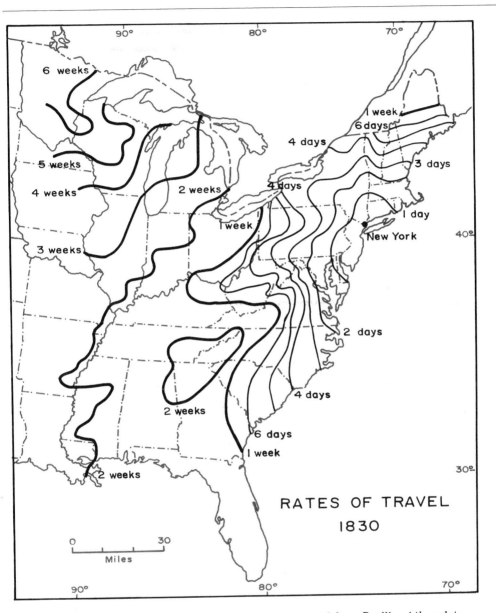

6 weeks

5 weeks

4 weeks

3 weeks

2 weeks

2 weeks

1 week

4 days

4 days

4 days

1 week

6 days

1 week

6 days

4 days

3 days

1 day

New York

2 days

40°

30°

RATES OF TRAVEL
1830

0   30
Miles

90°   80°   70°

Map 5.2. Rates of travel from New York, 1830. Adapted from Paullin, *Atlas*, plate 138B.

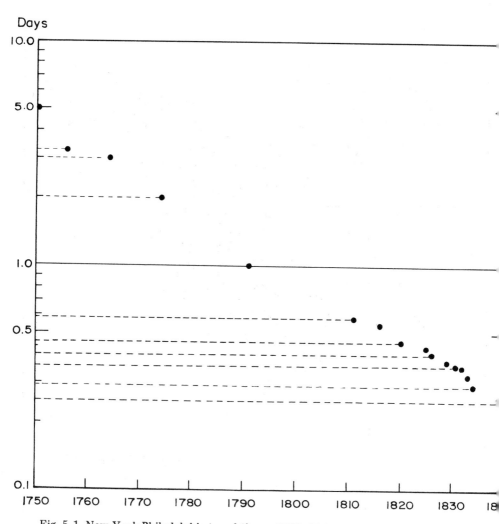

Fig. 5.1. New York-Philadelphia travel times, 1750–1840.

Source: HCSR 2, no. 22 (May 27, 1840), 338; *New York Gazette and General Advertiser*, Aug. 5, 1834; *New York Mercury*, Jan. 3, 1774; *New York Packet*, July 7, 1791; *NWR* 10, no. 23 (Aug. 3, 1816), 381; 19, no. 9 (Oct. 28, 1820), 142; 28, no. 10 (May 7, 1825), 147; 30, no. 11 (May 13, 1826), 185; 36, no. 19 (July 4, 1829), 301; 36, no. 23 (Aug. 1, 1829), 361; 41, no. 11 (Nov. 19, 1831), 225; 43, no. 17 (Dec. 22, 1832), 268; 45, no. 5 (Sept. 28, 1833), 68; 56, no. 7 (Apr. 13, 1839), 98; Dunbar, *History of Travel*, 1, 182, 184; Lane, *From Indian Trail to Iron Horse*, p. 194; Scharf and Westcott, *History of Philadelphia*, III, 2,159, 2,160.

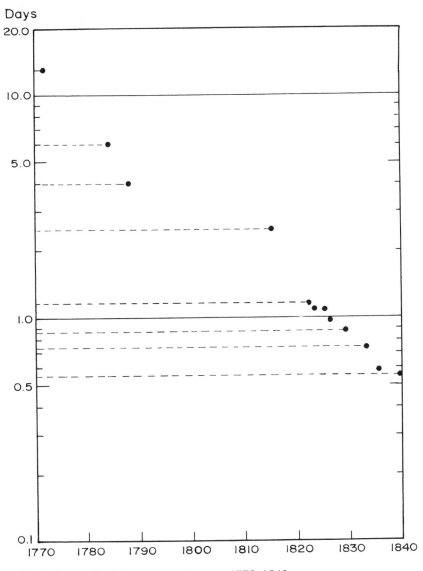

Fig. 5.2. New York-Boston travel times, 1772–1840.

Source: HCSR 3, no. 18 (Oct. 28, 1840), 277; *NWR* 24, no. 12 (May 24, 1823), 178; 28, no. 10 (May 7, 1825), 147; 30, no. 11 (May 13, 1826), 185; 36, no. 10 (May 2, 1829), 148; 40, no. 18 (July 2, 1831), 315; 44, no. 13 (May 25, 1833), 193; U.S. Senate, *History of the Railway Mail Service*, Executive Document No. 40, 48th Cong., 2nd sess., 1885, pp. 9, 20; Adams, *United States in 1800*, p. 8; Albion, *Rise of New York Port*, p. 146; Dunbar, *History of Travel*, I, 188; III, 743; Earle, *Stage-Coach and Tavern Days*, p. 278; Holmes, "Levi Pease," pp. 241, 256.

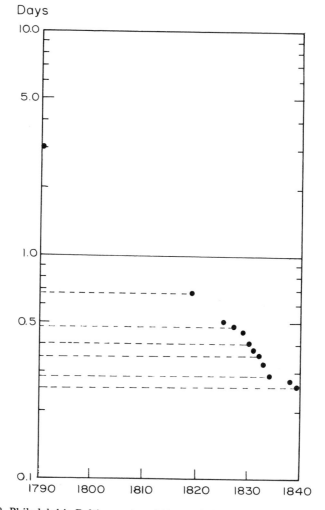

Fig. 5.3. Philadelphia-Baltimore travel times, 1790–1840.

Source: NWR 16, no. 22 (July 28, 1819), 357; 28, no. 10 (May 7, 1825), 147; 36, no. 17 (June 20, 1829), 286; 36, no. 19 (July 4, 1829), 302; 38, no. 16 (June 12, 1830), 293; 42, no. 7 (Apr. 14, 1832), 111; 43, no. 5 (Sept. 29, 1832), 70; 44, no. 9 (Apr. 27, 1833), 133; 44, no. 15 (June 8, 1833), 236; 46, no. 8 (Apr. 19, 1834), 119; 52, no. 23 (Aug. 5, 1837), 368; 56, no. 7 (Apr. 13, 1839), 99; *Pennsylvania Packet and Daily Advertiser* (Philadelphia), Oct. 16, 1790; Dunbar, *History of Travel*, I, 191; Buckingham, *America*, I, 182. Travel in 1790 was often even slower than indicated here.

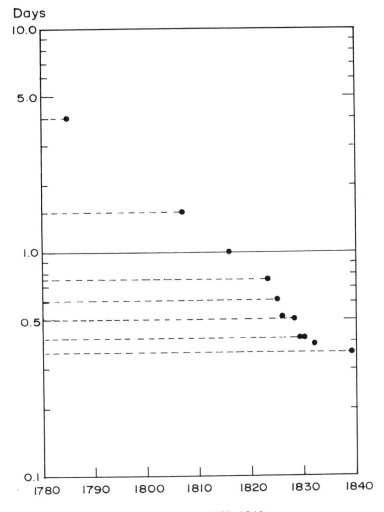

Fig. 5.4. New York-Albany travel times, 1785–1840.

Source: NWR 10, no. 23 (Aug. 3, 1816), 381; 24, no. 12 (May 24, 1823), 178; 35, no. 7 (Oct. 11, 1828), 101;
37, no. 8 (Oct. 17, 1829), 120; 39, no. 8 (Oct. 16, 1830), 126; 57, no. 4 (Sept. 21, 1839), 64; Oliver W. Holmes,
"The Stage-Coach Business," *Quarterly Journal of the New York State Historical Association* 12 (1931), 233,
239; Morrison, *History of American Steam Navigation*, pp. 24, 566; Pomerantz, *New York*, 162.

Table 5.9. Travel-time reductions between major urban pairs, 1790–1840.

Urban pair	Ratio of 1790 travel time to 1840 travel time	Average rate of time-space convergence[a] (minutes per year)	Minutes saved per 1840 route mile[b]	1840 speed (miles per hour)
New York–Philadelphia	4.0:1.0	21.6	12.4	14.5
New York–Boston	7.2:1.0	99.2	21.8	17.1
Philadelphia–Baltimore	11.6:1.0	79.0	34.3	18.5
New York–Albany	11.2:1.0	104.9	36.2	16.9

Source: HCSR 2, no. 22 (May 27, 1840), 338; 3, no. 18 (Oct. 28, 1840), 277; *New York Packet*, July 7, 1791; Holmes, "Levi Pease," pp. 241, 256; Holmes, "Stage-Coach Business," p. 233; *Pennsylvania Packet and Daily Advertiser* (Philadelphia), Oct. 16, 1790; Buckingham, *America*, I, 182; *NWR* 57, no. 4 (Sept. 21, 1839), 64; Mitchell, *Traveller's Guide*, p. 73.

a. The average rate of time-space convergence may be expressed:

$$\frac{T_{y_x} - T_{y_{x+n}}}{y_{x+n} - y_x}$$

T_{y_x} and $T_{y_{x+n}}$ are interurban travel times at two different dates, and $y_{x+n} - y_x$ is the separating interval in years.

b. Because different modes of transport were used in 1790 and 1840, route distances at those dates were not identical.

instance, to over 36 minutes per route mile in the New York-Albany instance (Table 5.9).

The New York-Philadelphia travel time reductions, although impressive, were less striking than those for New York-Boston, Philadelphia-Baltimore, and New York-Albany. There were several reasons. The New York-Philadelphia route had long been the highest priority linkage in the country, and by 1790, considerable travel-time reductions had been realized along its length. (Fig. 5.1). Moreover, much of the 1790–1840 travel-time reduction between New York and Boston, Philadelphia and Baltimore, and New York and Albany was owing to the elimination of overnight stops; but by 1790, such stops had already been eliminated on the New York-Philadelphia route. Finally, the time consumed on the 1840 New York-Philadelphia trip was lengthened by an en route change

of vehicle. Although a change from train to steamboat was also necessary on the New York-Boston route, there the time lost was spread out
over a much greater distance.

Travel times between Pittsburgh, Cincinnati, Louisville, and St. Louis
dropped off quickly in the 1820s and 1830s as ever more powerful
steamboats were introduced to service. Wood-gathering delays "were
reduced by the establishment of woodyards along the rivers" and as the
art of running at night was perfected, other time gains were made.[68]
For example, between 1819 and 1840 the more rapid downstream
Cincinnati-Louisville journey was diminished from 18 hours to 7.25
hours at best, which meant an average speed of 18.2 miles per hour
(Fig. 5.5).[69] Thus, time-space convergence between Cincinnati and
Louisville during that 21-year period was 30.7 minutes per year, and
travel time was reduced almost 5 minutes per route mile (cf. Table 5.9).
In like fashion, the 449-mile downstream trip from Pittsburgh to Cincin-
nati was cut from over 6 days in 1818 to 3.0–3.5 days in the early
1830s.[70]

Although travel between Pittsburgh, Cincinnati, Louisville, and St.
Louis was very rapid in comparison to that between lesser Western
centers which did not benefit from a location on the Ohio or Mississippi, travel-generated information often moved much more slowly
among these four cities than it did among New York, Boston, Philadelphia, and Baltimore. This was partly because the physical distances
were greater between some of the Western urban pairs and partly
because steamboats were much slower when sailing upstream (Fig. 5.5).
In addition, whereas Northeastern travel schedules were generally
reliable during the 1820s and 1830s, in the Ohio and Upper Mississippi
valleys this was true only between Cincinnati and Louisville. Between
Pittsburgh and Cincinnati and between Louisville and St. Louis, departures were frequently wanting in promptness, for captains were prone
to make postponements until the freight and passenger loads promised
a large enough profit.[71]

During the first decades of the steamboat era, travel times between
Buffalo, Cleveland, and Detroit were also reduced drastically. When
Buffalo-Detroit service began in 1818, the usual time was three days.
The trip length shrank to two days in 1828, and one day plus thirty

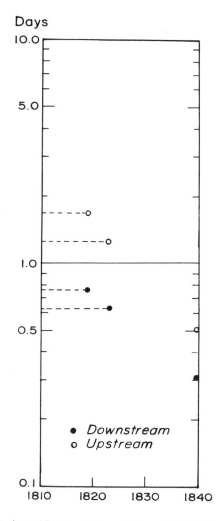

Fig. 5.5. Cincinnati-Louisville travel times, 1819–1840.

Source: NWR 25, no. 6 (Oct. 11, 1823), 95; Morrison, *History of American Steam Navigation*, p. 228.

minutes in 1834 (an average speed of 12.9 miles per hour).[72] Thus, in the course of this sixteen-year period the time-space convergence between Buffalo and Detroit was almost three hours per year. At the same time a savings of 8.7 minutes per route mile was registered (cf. Table 5.9). One journalist wrote: "Distance . . . in the neighborhood of the lakes is no longer a thing to be regarded. Detroit is virtually nearer to the city of New York, than Cumberland, Maryland is to Baltimore."[73] However, owing to the poor road conditions between Buffalo, Cleveland, and Detroit, the pace of travel-generated information flow between these places during the winter months was not comparable to that prevailing among the largest cities of the Northeast.

Even though interurban travel times in the South improved during the decades preceding 1840, they left much to be desired in many instances. In consequence, time lags in the interurban circulation of travel-generated information were usually greater than elsewhere in the country, especially in the Northeast. For example, in 1820 it was thought that considerable progress had been made when improved stagecoach service allowed a Norfolk-Charleston journey in 5.5–6.0 days, yet by the same date a Baltimore-Boston journey of approximately the same length could be accomplished in 2.5–3.0 days (Figs. 5.1–5.3). Furthermore, the steamboat-stage-railroad line that opened between Charleston and New Orleans in 1840, which cut the 1830 travel time by more than half (Map 5.2), still only provided a terminal-to-terminal running speed of 8.8 miles per hour (cf. Table 5.9). New railroad connections in 1839 made a Richmond-Charleston trip possible at an average speed of 12.1 miles per hour, and speeds around 13.0 miles per hour were realized in the late 1830s on the shorter Norfolk-Richmond, New Orleans-Mobile, and Savannah-Charleston routes. However, on the shorter as well as the longer Southern interurban routes, departures were offered at a less-than-daily frequency for most, if not all, of the 1790–1840 period. Thus, the travel-generated flow of information in the South moved even more slowly than trip times would seem to indicate.[74]

6

An Urban-System Interpretation of the Growth of Large Cities

Cities continue to grow, not because their situation is intrinsically the most advantageous, but because they have already acquired a certain growth, which of itself contains within it the elements of further increase.
—Nathan Hale (1837)

The pattern of urbanization existing in the United States by 1840 was extremely concentrated, both nationally and regionally. New York, Philadelphia, Boston, Baltimore, and New Orleans, the country's five largest urban centers, accounted for 48.3 percent of the nation's population in urban areas having over 2,500 inhabitants. These five cities, plus Charleston, Richmond, Mobile, Savannah, Norfolk, Cincinnati, Pittsburgh, Louisville, St. Louis, Buffalo, Cleveland, and Detroit, answered for almost 61 percent of the population in centers with more than 2,500 inhabitants. In the Northeast the four leading cities contained 56.9 percent of the region's urban population. In the region embracing most of the settled West, Pittsburgh, Cincinnati, Louisville, and St. Louis were together responsible for 64.4 percent of the population in all cities of over 2,500. Buffalo, Cleveland, and Detroit jointly included 90.8 percent of the total urban population of the Lake Erie region (see Map 1).[1] Perhaps even more striking is the fact that the few cities which by 1840 had become the foci of urban population concentration in three of the nation's well settled and economically integrated regions have continued to the present to occupy the highest size ranks in their respective urban subsystems.[2]

The process by which rank stability sets in among the largest cities of an urban system or subsystem under pretelegraphic conditions, or during a relatively early period of urban system development, may be illuminated by a descriptive model. Such a model also throws light on the phenomenon of extreme urban concentration. However, the model developed here is directly concerned only with the highest ranking units in an urban system or subsystem. It is not intended to cover the development of an entire urban system or subsystem, that is, the simultaneous growth of all cities, regardless of size, in a given region or country.

URBAN SYSTEMS AND SUBSYSTEMS

The various meanings attached to the term "urban system" are not always consistent with one another. At times the term has been applied to individual cities, in which case the city is seen as being comprised of interacting and interdependent components. Here, however, the term refers to a group of cities and is used interchangeably with "system of cities." More precisely, an urban system is defined as a set of cities which are interdependent in such a way that any significant change in the economic activities, occupational structure, total income, or population of one member city will directly or indirectly bring about an alteration in the economic activities, occupational structure, total income, or population of one or more other set members. An urban subsystem is defined as a physically proximate subset of cities within an urban system whose economic and demographic relationships, or interdependencies, of the same type are quite pronounced.[3]

Given these definitions, the dynamics of an urban system or subsystem could theoretically be recorded in large part by an enormous input-output table, where the major economic sectors of each city or urban region would be represented along the axes of both production (output in dollars) and purchases (input in dollars) (Table 6.1). In practice, this is not possible for past or present urban systems and subsystems, because of a variety of data-collection difficulties and the virtually insurmountable problem of coping with the changes that occur in input and production coefficients over time.[4]

The pretelegraphic urban system in the United States and its subsystems were both open and complex. They were open in at least two senses. First, the development of the system both as a whole and in its different parts was subject to international influences. Second, the

Table 6.1. Hypothetical interurban input-output flow table.

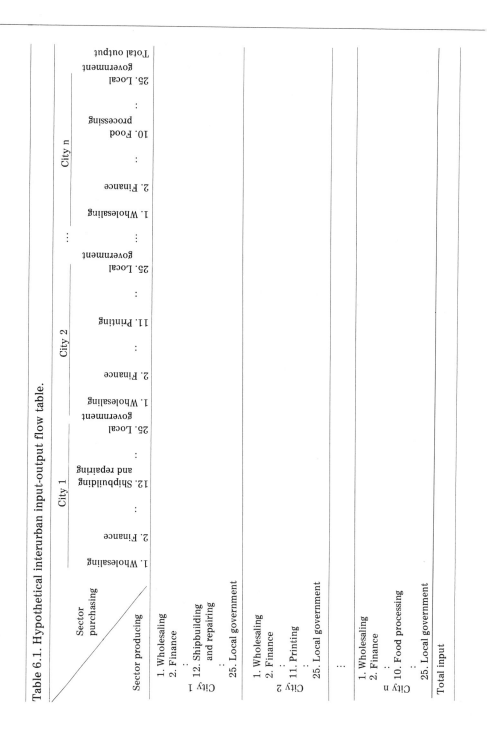

Sector purchasing	City 1						City 2						...	City n						Total output
Sector producing	1. Wholesaling	2. Finance	:	12. Shipbuilding and repairing	:	25. Local government	1. Wholesaling	2. Finance	:	11. Printing	:	25. Local government		1. Wholesaling	2. Finance	:	10. Food processing	:	25. Local government	
City 1 1. Wholesaling																				
2. Finance																				
:																				
12. Shipbuilding and repairing																				
:																				
25. Local government																				
City 2 1. Wholesaling																				
2. Finance																				
:																				
11. Printing																				
:																				
25. Local government																				
...																				
City n 1. Wholesaling																				
2. Finance																				
:																				
10. Food processing																				
:																				
25. Local government																				
Total input																				

spread of settlement from 1790 constantly added new urban units to the entire system and to certain subsystems. In the half-century or so preceding the telegraph, the urban system and its subsystems in the United States were complex in much the same way that almost any social system is complex. That is, the complete system or any one of its subsystems functioned as a "high-order, multiple-loop, nonlinear feedback structure" whose level of organization tended to become more elaborate with the passage of time.[5]

A SUBMODEL OF URBAN-SIZE GROWTH FOR THE MERCANTILE CITY

Northeastern Mercantile Cities. The principal features of the urban economies of New York, Philadelphia, Boston, and Baltimore during the initial four decades of the nineteenth century suggest that all such cities had several main features in common.[6] First, the wholesaling-trading complex and the retailing activities that were frequently intertwined with it were the two most prominent economic functions of the country's leading urban centers, which explains the appelation "mercantile city." Not only were the city's merchant middlemen (importers and shipping merchants), agent middlemen (auctioneers, brokers, commission merchants, and factors), and retailers its most important capital accumulators, but many so-called manufacturing establishments either combined small-scale production with retailing or wholesaling functions, or devoted most of their energy to the provision of repair services. The wholesaling-trading complex encompassed four principal types of commercial activity: the coastal and interregional distribution of hinterland production, the hinterland and coastal distribution of interregional and foreign imports, the foreign export of hinterland commodities, and the re-export of carrying-trade commodities. Whereas the wholesaling-trading complex as a whole dominated the urban economy, the relative importance of its four component functions varied over time and from city to city.

Second, capital shortages and the inelasticity and comparative costliness of labor supplies contributed to the limited dimensions of manufacturing in the American mercantile city. Entrepreneurs both inside and outside the wholesaling-trading complex with earnings to invest usually preferred capital outlets other than manufacturing. Mercantile profits were generally ploughed directly back into expanded wholesaling and exporting, or into closely allied ventures such as banking, insurance, and retailing. As hinterland competition intensified, a growing portion of the capital resources of the major cities was indirectly channeled into trade expansion via investments in canal, turnpike, and railroad construction projects. Frequently, enormous profits encouraged the placement of much capital in real estate, construction speculation, and related rent profiteering.[7] These profits apparently made an important contribution to urban growth.

Third, manufacturing was also curtailed in the largest mercantile cities because the state of technology limited the scale of individual establishments. Even the few production units utilizing machinery were usually characterized by a relatively small volume of undifferentiated, unspecialized outputs. Water power, the primary source of energy for driving early nineteenth-century factory machinery, was immobile and therefore could not be transferred to plants within the municipal boundaries of New York, Boston, Philadelphia, or Baltimore. Steam power was not as yet a viable alternative for large-scale production, since engines were small and inefficient and the cost of operation per unit of horsepower was high.

Finally, the vast bulk of the industrial activities located in New York, Boston, Philadelphia, and Baltimore were either directly or indirectly linked to the mercantile functions of those cities.[8] Almost all industries fell into one of three categories: entrepôt manufactures, commerce-serving manufactures, and local-market manufactures. Entrepôt manufactures were linked to the wholesaling-trading complex, since by definition they involved the processing of sugar, tobacco, leather, and other interregional and foreign raw-material imports that for the most part were in transit to other final destinations. Such industries as shipbuilding and repairing, printing, and coopering were dependent on the magnitude of demand created by the city's wholesaling-trading complex itself.[9] Local-market manufactures, which basically catered to the local construction, household, and government sectors, were indirectly linked to the wholesaling-trading complex since the aggregate demand of these three sectors was precipitated principally by the city's mercantile population and the workers serving that population. Largely on the basis of these findings, an ideal-typical model of urban-size growth for the individual mercantile city can be constructed.

Basic Structure. Imagine a mercantile city that is indiscriminately located in space and whose businessmen are uninvolved in hinterland competition with other cities. These aspatial and monopolistic conditions are assumed so as to permit concentration on that portion of the growth process which does not involve other cities.

Further imagine the occurrence in this city of a successful scale increase in at least one subsector of its middleman wholesaling-trading complex. This increase, which may assume the form of either expansion within existing mercantile concerns or the creation of new business establishments, eventually elicits an ideal-typical sequence of circularly and cumulatively caused events involving several feedback loops (Fig. 6.1).

Expanded wholesaling-trading activities give rise to an initial employment multiplier. That is, new local demand generated by mercantile units calls into being additional job opportunities for bank and insurance company employees, draymen, stevedores, weighers, hotel and boardinghouse operators, and people in other occupations.[10] The combined effect of new mercantile employment and an initial multiplier is an increase in population, or growth in urban size, and the probable attainment of one or more new local thresholds in retailing, the services, and commerce-serving and local-market industries. A threshold refers to the minimum population or volume of sales required either to support a new market-oriented establishment or to justify economically an addition to such existing facilities.[11] Since some importing activities of the wholesaling-trading complex are dependent on the size of the local or regional market, new mercantile employment and an initial multiplier may also lead to threshold fulfillment within that complex itself.[12] The fulfillment and exploitation of thresholds further augment the city's population through influencing migration streams by job opportunities.[13] New mercantile functions also add to the working force employed in manufacturing by precipitating new or expanded entrepôt industries. Any new or enlarged manufacturing, whether of the entrepôt, commerce-serving, or local-market variety,

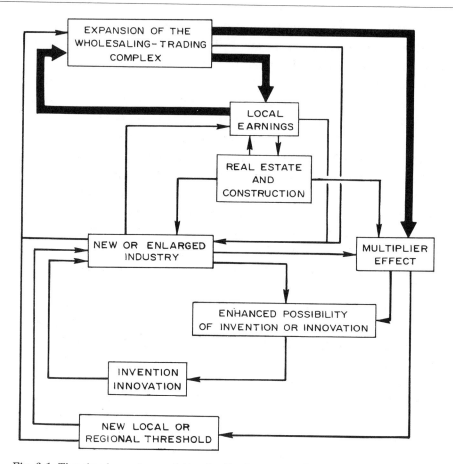

Fig. 6.1. The circular and cumulative feedback process of urban-size growth for the individual American mercantile city, 1790–1840.

generates a secondary multiplier effect and touches off a subsidiary feedback process.[14] In this process, successive low manufacturing thresholds are fulfilled, and the possibilities of invention and innovation are continuously enhanced in threshold and nonthreshold industries, owing to, among other things, increased local circulation of information pertaining to manufacturing in general and technological problems and solutions in particular.

This succession of events must grind to a halt unless it repeatedly receives new life in the form of reinvestments derived from the earnings of the new or expanded mercantile functions and other already existing profit-making enterprises within the wholesaling-trading complex. However, each reinvestment in commerce, or scale increase within the wholesaling-trading complex, brings forth another initial multiplier and the likely achievement of thresholds in other sectors of the urban economy, consequently making the growth process self-generating unless, or until, some exogenous disruptive forces appear.

The size-growth process of the mercantile city is invigorated by developments within two other sectors. First, a portion of the earnings from the wholesaling-trading complex is diverted into real-estate speculation and construction. This action is encouraged by a mounting population and causes a multiplier of its own (new jobs for construction workers, plus further labor opportunities in the building-service manufactures). It also contributes to threshold-fulfillment in retailing, local-market manufacturing, and other unrelated sectors. Moreover, a portion of the real estate and construction profits spurs growth by finding its way back into the wholesaling-trading complex and igniting another round of earnings and multiplier effects. The second group of developments affecting urban growth occur when an indeterminate fraction of industrial capital winnings wend their way back to the wholesaling-trading complex, further rejuvenating the entire size-growth process. New or expanding nonthreshold manufactures are particularly likely to contribute such additional capital for mercantile functions, because the success of such industries, whether of the footloose or the labor-oriented variety, is by definition quite independent of the size of the local market.[15] That is, they are basically export industries, either owned directly by mercantile interests or requiring the shipping services of the wholesaling-trading complex. Furthermore, entrepôt manufactures similarly stimulate growth by participating directly in commercial expansion (note the two-way arrows in Fig. 6.1 connecting the box marked "expansion of the wholesaling-trading complex" and the box labeled "new or enlarged industry"). The feedback chains from real estate, from construction, and from manufacturing, with their progressively compounded consequences, are reiterated until detoured or obstructed. Meanwhile, the functioning of the entire model is reinforced by the increasing attractiveness that the city's growing scale and array of mercantile establishments exert upon hinterland businessmen and foreigners seeking a marketing outlet or purchasing source.

Applicability to Other Mercantile Cities. Since the submodel was fashioned on the basis of empirical materials regarding New York, Boston, Philadelphia, and Baltimore, its general validity may be legitimately questioned. Specifically, it may be asked whether the submodel accurately portrays the pretelegraphic size-growth process of major cities in the Upper Mississippi and Ohio valleys, the South, and the Lake Erie region. To prove that the submodel captures the main features of the size-growth process for regional centers outside the Northeast requires establishing that the wholesaling-trading complex and related retailing activities were the growth leaders in those cities.

This leadership can be shown, although comparative data are beset with limitations and pertain only to 1840, a year in which the relative position of manufacturing should have been more prominent in large cities than in earlier decades. The six largest Southern cities, the four regionally dominant centers in the Ohio and Upper Mississippi valleys, and the three largest cities around Lake Erie had ratios of capital invested in wholesaling commission houses and retailing to capital invested in manufacturing that were for the most part well in excess of 1.0 (Table 6.2). However, the ratios for Cincinnati, Louisville, Pittsburgh, and the three Lake Erie centers were somewhat less than those for their four Northeastern counterparts. Thus, the relative importance of the wholesaling-trading complex in these low-ratio places requires some elaboration.

According to all indications, the capital investment ratios indicated understate the comparative significance of the wholesaling-trading complex in every instance. Although omissions were probably made for one or more categories in each city, owing to the poor instructions given to the 1840 census marshalls and their assistants, urban manufacturing totals were padded considerably by the inclusion of all capital invested in the construction sector, the capital of establishments whose primary function was to perform repair services, and the capital of workshops that sold directly to the household consumer.[16] Furthermore, the ratios took no account of capital invested in commercial houses in foreign trade, as such data were not tallied by the census takers. This exclusion

Table 6.2. Selected economic characteristics of major United States cities, 1840.

City	Commercial houses in foreign trade	Commission houses	Capital invested (thousands of dollars)			$\frac{A+B}{C}$
			Commission houses (A)	Retailing (B)	Manufacturing (C)	
New York[a]	417	918	45,941.2	14,648.6	11,228.9	5.4
Philadelphia[b]	182	35	1,944.5[c]	15,177.6	5,387.5	3.2
Boston[b]	142	89	11,676.0	4,184.2	2,770.3	5.7
Baltimore	70	108	4,404.5	6,708.6	2,730.0	4.1
Cincinnati	42	36	5,200.0	12,877.0	7,469.9	2.4
Louisville	1	11	191.8	2,128.4	713.7	3.2
Pittsburgh	7	32	1,241.1	4,165.2	2,058.0	2.6
St. Louis	1	24	717.0	3,875.1	674.3	6.8
Buffalo	0	23	94.0	736.3	630.3	1.3
Detroit	0	11	123.0	412.8	172.4	3.1
Cleveland	0	21	58.0	139.7	128.6	1.5
New Orleans	8	375	16,490.0	11,018.2	1,774.2	15.5
Charleston	27	34	3,563.8	3,317.5	770.5	8.9
Richmond	17	29	3,062.0	1,646.5	1,373.0	3.4
Mobile	21	93	3,129.6	1,861.7	475.6	10.5
Savannah	2	50	943.5	855.2	105.5	17.0
Norfolk	8	8	202.0	1,590.5	178.3	10.1

Source: U.S. Bureau of the Census, Aggregate Value and Produce, and Number of Persons Employed in Mines, Agriculture, Commerce, Manufactures, &c.: Sixth Census of the United States, 1841.
a. As then constituted.
b. Exclusive of suburbs.
c. This low capital figure is suspect, especially since the number of commission houses reported for the city is surprisingly small. This may have been owing either to omissions by census marshals or to their incorrect recording of "commission houses" as retail establishments or "commercial houses in foreign trade." In fact, it is improbable that Philadelphia, with a municipal population equivalent to that of Boston and one-third that of New York, had more capital invested in retailing than the latter, and more than three times as much as the former—even if Philadelphia's sizable suburbs are included.

must have considerably reduced the ratio for Cincinnati, as well as for a number of other places in and outside the Northeast.[17] Also, many commission houses were apt to have been misassigned to other categories. The term commission houses itself could include auction houses, brokerage firms, and other merchant-middleman establishments that were easily misplaced under the rubric of commercial houses in foreign trade or in the retailing category.[18]

Scattered evidence for specific cities is perhaps more convincing. During the 1820s Cincinnati "clinched her position as the leading point of concentration" for the export of surplus production from the Ohio Valley. In 1829 her merchants imported $3,800,000 worth of merchandise and exported commodities valued at $3,100,000. At this time, "industry was so weak that many businessmen feared that Cincinnati's economy was dangerously unbalanced." By 1840 the city's commerce had expanded to an extent where her dry goods wholesalers alone were doing a $4,000,000 business.[19]

During the 1820s and 1830s commerce "was the mainspring of Louisville's economy." In 1829 a Louisville paper bragged: "The people of the greater part of Indiana, all Kentucky, and portions of Tennessee, Alabama, Illinois, Missouri, &c. now resort to this place for dry goods, groceries, hardware and queensware." Contemporaries estimated the total volume of mercantile business transacted in Louisville during the year 1835 at $24,837,000, or roughly $1,600 per capita. A less precise estimate of the city's "various commercial and trading transactions" made in 1838 stood at $45,000,000, or approximately $2,300 per capita.[20] Both of these per capita figures are very high in relation to the per capita income levels of the time.[21]

From early in its development, Pittsburgh merchants accumulated considerable wealth by acting as middlemen in the distribution of Northeastern manufactures and foreign imports throughout the Ohio Valley, western Pennsylvania, and a small portion of western New York. In 1836 a perhaps overly exalted journalist pronounced: "The value of every description of foreign and domestic goods received in transit from the Eastern cities and passing through the hands of our commission merchants for all parts of the West and South may be estimated at between 60 and 70 millions of dollars." In 1839 it was said that the "annual business of Pittsburgh has been fairly estimated at about $31,590,750," of which $18,975,000 was accounted for by "mercantile sales" and "commission business," about $1,000,000 by the coal trade, and $11,606,350 by local manufactures.[22]

Buffalo and Cleveland, which had the lowest ratios of all, are both generally acknowledged to have mushroomed during the 1830s. This growth was largely the result of their dual roles as grain trade nodes and as distributing centers for goods acquired from the Northeast.[23]

The validity of the urban-size growth submodel elsewhere than in the Northeast is also suggested by the trade-related character of the manufacturing sector in large cities outside that region. In most instances, whatever industrial activity occurred in the major cities was comprised largely of entrepôt, commerce-serving, and local-market manufactures.[24] For example, Cincinnati's manufactures, in which large capital investments had been made by 1840, were dominated by entrepôt establishments engaged in pork slaughtering and various other food-processing activities. In 1826, salt pork, lard, ham, bacon, flour, and whiskey accounted for $489,500 of Cincinnati's total exports of $740,020. By 1839, pork products alone answered for 44 percent of the total exports from the city. Also important were the commerce-serving activities of printing and publishing, steamboat construction, and coopering, and such local-market manufactures as furniture production and brewing.[25]

The situation was similar in Buffalo and Cleveland, where flour milling was prominent, and in Louisville, where local-market production was complemented by meat packing, by tobacco and hemp processing (all entrepôt manufactures), and by shipbuilding. The picture differed somewhat only in Pittsburgh, where profit-making merchants sought manufacturing investment opportunities more readily than elsewhere, and entrepreneurs exploited nearby coal and iron ore resources to specialize in iron and iron-consuming industries. In 1826 Pittsburgh's production of iron and related products was estimated at $1,150,000. By 1839 the industry supposedly had an output of $5,000,000 and employed 2,305 men. Despite this specialization, 1839 estimates of Pittsburgh employment in many entrepôt, commerce-serving, and local-market industries were high by prevailing standards: 394 in furniture workshops, 210 in milling, 237 in leather processing, and 130 in printing. In addition, steamboat construction was significant.[26] Moreover, the Pittsburgh situation was not as exceptional as might first appear, for its manufacturing expansion was highly dependent on commercial profits, and its iron industry and major glass industry, which in 1839 employed an estimated 515 persons, primarily involved the conversion of hinterland raw materials into products which for the most part entered into the city's interurban trade.

A third set of conditions that indicates the applicability of the sub-model outside the Northeast is the real-estate and construction speculation associated with the soaring land values and crowded housing of those cities. Not atypically, a centrally located lot in Cincinnati "was taken for $2.00 in 1790 and sold for $800 in 1804. A small slice from the corner went for . . . $6,000 in 1819. The subdivision was sold and repurchased in 1828 for $15,000." The demand for real estate in the quickly growing cities of the West and South was such that land values in Pittsburgh could double and triple within the span of a few years, the price of lots on the main streets of Louisville could soar from $700 per lot in 1812 to $300 per foot five years later, and property values in Buffalo, New Orleans, and other Southern cities could jump "to unheard-of heights."[27]

Construction speculation was constantly spurred by the high rents made possible by overcrowded conditions in the existing housing stock. Cincinnati was representative since acute housing shortages "were reported not only in boom years but also in hard times such as the early twenties, the depression of 1834, and the 'paralyses' of 1837 to 1840." Consequently, housing construction was generally pursued at a great pace. As early as 1819, when Cincinnati had a population of only about 9,000, it had work for 560 house carpenters and joiners, brick layers, plasterers, stone masons, glaziers, painters, and street pavers, as well as 200 jobs in its brickyards. In 1831 the city saw the completion of 500 new buildings of all types, and in the economically slow year of 1840 it still provided employment for 809 construction workers. In New Orleans, despite the depressed conditions of 1840, housing construction had an aggregate value placed at $2,231,300. There were 784 construction jobs in Charleston in 1840, when the city had a population of 29,261.[28]

Although the evidence seems to show that the wholesaling-trading complex and intertwined retailing activities were the principal generators of size growth in the leading regional cities outside the Northeast, and while real estate and construction speculation were of some importance in those cities, certain reservations have to be made regarding the more general applicability of the submodel. First, to state that the submodel accurately depicts the size-growth process of large cities other than New York, Boston, Philadelphia, and Baltimore does not mean that the submodel functioned identically in all cases. Although the described investment and multiplier interrelationships were common to all large centers, in some cities the functioning of certain feedback loops was more important than others. In Pittsburgh, for example, the feedback subprocess involving manufacturing was clearly of greater relative importance than elsewhere.

Second, the submodel typically functioned more slowly in Southern cities. The feedback cycles originating with each expansion of the wholesaling-trading complex (Fig. 6.1) were dampened, particularly in Norfolk, Charleston, Savannah, Mobile, and New Orleans. In those cities wholesaling-trading profits often leaked out of the local economy, either because the mercantile activity in question was controlled directly by New York and other Northeastern business interests, or because credits had been extended to local wholesalers and retailers by New Yorkers and others. Moreover, multiplier effects in all Southern cities were depressed by the presence of large slave populations and by the generally lower wage levels than those that prevailed in leading urban centers elsewhere.[29] Finally, the feedback loops involving manufacturing were of very little relative significance in all major Southern cities other than Richmond (thus the high ratios in Table 6.2). This was so in part owing to the low level of local and regional purchasing power. Two other contributing factors were the negative attitude toward manufacturing investment widely held by Southern elites and the tradition of channeling savings into slaveholding.

Differential Growth among Mercantile Cities. If the submodel of mercantile-city size growth functioned flawlessly, and if all urban centers were isolated units not indulging in hinterland competition with one another, then each individual city would have expanded indefinitely, or at least as long as available natural resources permitted, and places that were initially similar in population would presumably have remained so. However, between 1790 and 1840 some cities grew larger more rapidly than others, both within the spatially spreading American system of cities as a whole and within regional urban subsystems. At the national level, for instance, New York, Boston, Philadelphia, and Baltimore grew faster than, and at the expense of, just about every South Atlantic coastal center. In the Northeast, Boston grew at the expense of such Massachusetts ports as Beverly, Gloucester, Marblehead, Newburyport, and Salem, while New York's rate of growth outstripped that of New Haven, New London, Hartford, Newport, and other southern New England centers with limited hinterlands.[30] In the Ohio Valley, Louisville flourished at the cost of Lexington; and on Lake Erie, Cleveland grew more quickly than Erie, Pennsylvania, and Sandusky, Ohio.

Quite clearly then, the feedback process depicted in the submodel did not unwind at nearly the same pace in all centers within the urban system and its subsystems. Instead, several factors served to hinder or retard the growth process in some centers while stimulating the growth of a limited number of larger cities, thereby contributing to an extremely concentrated pattern of urbanization. Two of these factors were transport and route developments, and agglomeration economies.

Canal construction, other internal improvements, and newly established steamboat routes had a considerable impact on the differential growth of American mercantile cities during the country's final pretelegraphic decades, for every factor "that alters the significance of a route . . . alters the importance of commercial nodes [cities]."[31] When a new line of penetration was extended inland from a coastal terminus, such as the Erie Canal from New York or the Ohio Canal from Cleveland, a train of events was usually set in motion that began with a reduction in hinterland transport costs for the terminus city, while similar costs for nonterminus centers remained unchanged. Following this cost reduction, the hinterland of the terminus city expanded. Hinterland expansion soon took on the form of hinterland piracy from nonterminus cities, as feeder lines began to spread out both from the terminus city and from previously existing and newly emerging interior urban nodes along the path of the penetration line. In short, the hinterland aggrandizement of the terminus city was compounded by the market and supply area expansion of its dependent interior centers.[32] This ideal-typical succession of events, by distending the market and commodity-source areas of the terminus city's wholesaling-trading complex at the expense of nonterminus cities, led to locational variations in the speed with which various coastal cities grew. In summary, each increment in the nodality of a mercantile city at the coastal terminus of a penetration line encouraged expansion of its wholesaling-trading complex, followed by an initial local multiplier, threshold fulfillment and exploitation in various sectors of the economy, real estate and construction speculation, and still greater inducements to investment in wholesaling-trading activities. The net result was population growth at the cost of nonterminus coastal centers.

Similarly, when a new regularly scheduled steamboat route was initiated between two termini, such as that between Louisville and Cincinnati, it generally started a sequence of events that culminated with a locational variation in the functioning of the size-growth process. That is, the terminus cities grew at the expense of intervening places and of proximate nonterminus centers.[33] This development normally included the appearance of additional or more frequently scheduled water and overland feeder services leading to the terminus cities, usurpation of the commodity supply areas and market areas of intervening places and proximate nonterminus cities, and an upsurge in the growth of the wholesaling-trading complexes of the two terminus hubs.

The differential growth of mercantile cities in the United States was also owing to the formation of agglomeration economies by wholesaling-trading complexes in the most rapidly expanding national and regional centers.[34] In cities that were drawing away from their competitors there was an increasing specialization of activities within the wholesaling-trading complex and the related financial sector. This specialization enabled wholesalers to call upon the services of one another and thereby apparently to reduce overhead costs.[35] Increasing specialization, which was largely the product of enlarged hinterland markets, attracted yet greater numbers of those seeking a market outlet or purchasing source who might otherwise have opted for smaller cities.

The broadening spectrum of wholesaling and trading establishments in the largest mercantile cities was not alone responsible for increasing the attraction exerted upon hinterland and foreign entrepreneurs. Credit extension, risk reduction, and other services attainable from banking and insurance institutions augmented the lure of the major mercantile centers. Banking and insurance institutions also encouraged hinterland aggrandizement (differential urban growth), both because their services either could not be initiated or could not mature fully in those other cities where the aggregate scale of the wholesaling-trading complex remained comparatively small, and because they were often important investors in locally terminating transportation projects. These types of agglomeration economies apparently proved self-enlarging by acting simultaneously as external economies for hinterland production. That is, by causing a greater volume of agricultural and manufactured goods to be funneled through the economy-providing mercantile city, they ultimately precipitated additional agglomeration benefits.[36] Such developments frequently were compounded by the superior trading terms offered by individual merchants who were operating on a scale that was not possible in smaller cities.

In brief, the agglomeration economies arising from increases in the scale and array of the mercantile functions of a few cities favored the propagation of fresh agglomeration economies and further expansion of the wholesaling-trading complex. Through encouraging hinterland enlargement and usurpation, these economies also curtailed the development of less diversified and inefficient centers.[37] This entire process was reinforced by urbanization economies that derived from the advantages of information availability and information circulation, which were pivotal to the maintenance of rank stability among the largest units in the American system of cities and three of its regional subsystems.

A MODEL OF LARGE-CITY RANK STABILITY FOR THE URBAN SYSTEM AND THREE SUBSYSTEMS

Inasmuch as both information circulation and interurban trade are at the core of the model, it can be brought into focus by a reformulation of some of the most salient findings to this point. During the period 1790–1840 in the United States, newspaper circulation was quite limited and was concentrated to some degree in the largest cities. Most large-city newspapers devoted a large proportion of their space to three varieties of material that were important to urban economic and locational decision making: advertising, shipping intelligence, and lists of prices current and other commercial statistics.

From perhaps as early as the beginning of the 1790s New York had the highest probability of being the first United States city to receive any specific piece of news from Europe. After 1822, and maybe even four years earlier, New York was first to come into possession of the vast bulk of economic information arriving from England and the Continent.

Foreign news usually disseminated from the New York press to the press of Boston, Philadelphia, and Baltimore, and then into the newspapers in the immediate hinterlands of these cities. Foreign news normally entered the South when the papers of its largest cities reprinted items from the New York press. Especially during the 1820s and 1830s, foreign news generally moved into the West when papers in the largest cities along Lake Erie and the banks of the Ohio and the Upper Mississippi openly plagiarized the pages of a New York, Philadelphia, or Baltimore daily.

Decreasing time-lag spatial biases in the availability of information were characteristic for all settled portions of the nation for the 1790–1840 period. However, the axis extending from Baltimore through Philadelphia and New York to Boston always remained at least one step ahead of both the remainder of the Northeast and the country as a whole in terms of speed and frequency of public information movement. Public information often moved more rapidly and more often between the four most populous Northeastern cities than between each of those places and most, if not all, subservient centers in their respective hinterlands. Within the Northeastern belt, New York increasingly became the entry point or dissemination node for information originating elsewhere in the country. Even the most closely spaced of the Southern ports were relatively distant from one another informationally for most of the period. Southern and other time-lag spatial biases grew largely out of interurban economic relationships; thus, major Southern cities often acquired information from one another via their mutual trading partner, New York. After 1820 communications between the youthful cities of the Western rivers and the Lake Erie region improved markedly.

The use of postal services was extremely small during the half-century prior to 1840. Because of the high postage rates, a very large share of the private correspondence directed through the mails was of a commercial nature. Postal use was also disproportionately concentrated in the largest cities. Throughout the entire period New York and the three other major Northeastern ports dominated private information exchange through the mails. During the 1820s and 1830s the major cities of the Upper Mississippi and Ohio valleys, the Lake Erie region, and the South dominated their respective regional patterns of mail generation. Within a sample of twenty-nine cities over the 1820–1840 period, moreover, there was an extremely high correlation between absolute urban population growth and absolute increases in postal receipts.

The Baltimore-Boston axis had the quickest and most frequent postal service throughout the 1790–1840 era. The mails usually moved more frequently and at greater speeds between New York, Philadelphia, Boston, and Baltimore than they did between each of these cities and smaller places in their individual hinterlands. During the 1820s and 1830s Pittsburgh, Cincinnati, Louisville, and St. Louis, on the one hand, and Buffalo, Cleveland, and Detroit on the other hand came to enjoy the same kind of intraregional superiority of postal service as had long been possessed by the four leading cities of the Northeast.

The South had the poorest mail service in the country. The only postal links between Charleston or Savannah and New Orleans or Mobile were indirect. Until well into the 1830s, as a result of the slowness of the Southern posts, private information of a commercial nature from the Northeast was often conveyed by means other than the mails.

At one pretelegraphic date or another the largest cities in most settled regions of the country developed a significant amount of intraregional commercial interaction with one another. Quite early a high degree of economic interdependence arose in the Northeast among New York, Boston, Philadelphia, and Baltimore, as well as Albany and Providence, with New York serving as the central node for the entire group. In the Ohio and Upper Mississippi valleys important trade relationships were developed, particularly in the 1820s and 1830s, between Pittsburgh, Cincinnati, Louisville, and St. Louis. In the Lake Erie region, Buffalo,

Cleveland, and Detroit nurtured important economic linkages with one another, especially after completion of the Erie Canal in 1825.

Only in the South was the magnitude of interurban trade occurring on an intraregional scale generally relatively small. Except for the flows between New Orleans and Mobile, the major ports of the South Atlantic seaboard and the Gulf Coast had little to do with one another in the way of commercial activity. Instead, they conducted their domestic exchanges primarily with New York, secondarily with Boston, and to a lesser extent with Philadelphia and Baltimore.

The largest cities of the Ohio and Upper Mississippi valleys, as well as Buffalo, Cleveland, and Detroit, possessed either direct or indirect trade ties with New York. Pittsburgh, Cincinnati, Louisville, and St. Louis—the four leading cities of the Ohio and Upper Mississippi valleys—were directly bound to New York as a consequence of goods imported via New Orleans. Those same four cities were also indirectly linked to New York as a result of both the transporting of Northeastern and European merchandise from Philadelphia to Pittsburgh, and the forwarding of their own shipments from New Orleans to Boston, Baltimore, and Philadelphia. The three principal Lake Erie centers were directly tied to New York, owing to the two-way traffic between Buffalo and New York.

Despite a long-run tendency for fares to decline, the costs of interurban travel by common carrier throughout the period between 1790 and 1840 were for the most part very high in terms of the prevailing wage levels. The expenses of interurban travel were greatest in the South.

Interurban travelers fell into two basic categories: merchants, other businessmen, and the economic elite in general; and post-1820 westward-bound migrants who moved at especially low one-way fares. The migrants traveled over a limited number of steamboat and canal routes, including those between New York and Albany, between Buffalo, Cleveland, and Detroit, and between the major cities of the Ohio and Upper Mississippi valleys.

In the period from 1790 to 1840, travel volumes between New York and Philadelphia, New York and Boston, and Philadelphia and Baltimore were very large in the context of the times and grew faster than would be expected from their population growth. During the 1820s and 1830s the same was apparently true of the size and growth of travel volumes between Pittsburgh, Cincinnati, Louisville, and St. Louis, and between Buffalo, Cleveland, and Detroit.

Travel volumes among the leading Southern cities were generally quite small in comparison to interurban passenger flows elsewhere in the country. Interurban travel within the South was confined largely to movement between the most closely spaced urban pairs: Richmond and Norfolk, Charleston and Savannah, and New Orleans and Mobile. However, a well-established travel network arose between these centers and New York, Philadelphia, Baltimore and Boston.

New York was the nation's major focus of interurban travel, being directly or indirectly involved in all of the eight most important interurban travel links. At the national level, therefore, the city dominated the long-distance circulation of travel-generated information.

The transportation improvements that helped to bring about a rapid increase in interurban travel volumes between the largest urban pairs in the Northeast, the Ohio and Upper Mississippi valleys, and around Lake Erie, also brought about sharply reduced travel times between the same major centers. These steadily diminishing journey times enlarged the time-lag spatial biases in information availability held by the regionally dominant cities. Because of comparatively infrequent departures, travel-generated interurban information flows in the South often moved even more slowly than the modestly improved 1840 trip times would seem to indicate.

In light of these empirical findings, the model is seen to hold for a number of situations up to the coming of the telegraph: the entire system of cities in the densely settled portion of the United States from the early 1790s on, the Northeastern regional subsystem of cities over the same period, the urban subsystem of the Ohio and Upper Mississippi valleys following the War of 1812, and the urban subsystem around Lake Erie from the late 1820s. That is, with the passage of time and the westward spread of dense settlement, the model applies to an ever-expanding area and an increasing number of large cities.

However, the model does not apply to the cities of the South if those centers are considered on a separate regional basis, as opposed to being considered a part of the national urban system. By 1840 the largest cities of the South had not yet begun to function as an interdependent regional subsystem of cities, as shown by their weak economic and informational ties with one another and their "colonial" dependence on New York and other Northeastern centers.[38] In this context it is significant that the South was the only well-populated region whose leading cities of 1840 did not register an impressive record of long-term rank stability.

The use of the early 1790s as a dividing line, though somewhat arbitrary, is justified by the fact that at the time of independence America's port cities, with their very limited hinterlands, were not participants in an urban system except insofar as they were connected with the developing system of cities in Western Europe. Although there were signs of market reorientation within the national economy during the 1780s, not until after the adoption of the Constitution did the hinterland-carving and economic specialization so characteristic of an independent urban system begin to occur in earnest. The fact that foreign trade remained a keystone in the American economy until the War of 1812 also does not invalidate the starting date of the 1790s, for the urban-size growth submodel recognizes that the relative importance of the components of the wholesaling-trading complex varied over time.

Basic Structure. Imagine a large mercantile city (C_1); i.e., one which either has already outdistanced most of its regional subsystem competitors in terms of population or, on a larger scale, has grown more populous than its national competitors. Its previous and ongoing population expansion is assumed to be basically the outcome of the urban-size growth submodel. Thus, earnings and miltiplier effects from the city's wholesaling-trading complex act as the major growth generator, and transport and route developments and agglomeration economies partially contribute to the city's outdistancing of rival centers. The urban-size growth submodel for C_1 is collapsed into a shorthand version in the lower left-hand portion of Fig. 6.2. The synopsized submodel of size growth operates simultaneously at the upper left for other large mercantile cities (C_2, C_3 ... C_n) in the same pretelegraphic urban system or subsystem.

Each increment in the wholesaling-trading complex of C_1 not only

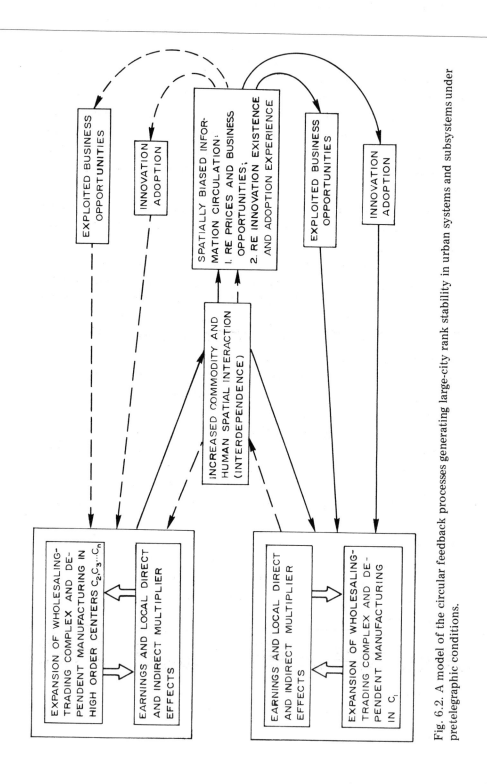

Fig. 6.2. A model of the circular feedback processes generating large-city rank stability in urban systems and subsystems under pretelegraphic conditions.

enhances that city's own size but also directly or indirectly engenders economic interdependence (interaction) with other large centers $(C_2, C_3, \ldots C_n)$ within the urban system or subsystem, thereby increasing the magnitude of their wholesaling-trading complexes and thus their populations. Direct increases in interdependence occur when expansion of the C_1 wholesaling-trading complex is owing to a larger scale of exports to C_2, C_3, or C_n of either the agricultural specialities of its hinterland or the manufacturing specialities of C_1 itself and its smaller subordinate centers.[39] Expanded interdependence also occurs directly when the wholesaling-trading complex of C_1 enlarges the scale of its operation by increasing agricultural or industrial imports originating in or passing through the hands of middlemen in C_2, C_3, or C_n. Thus, regardless of whether intraregional imports or exports are involved at C_1, there is also an increment in the wholesaling-trading complex of C_2, C_3, or C_n. Indirect growth of interdependence between C_1 and C_2, C_3 or C_n begins with population increases in the former city and terminates with a larger demand for the locally consumed agricultural and industrial goods normally received from or through the latter cities. (Such an augmentation of the demand in C_1 takes place both when the initial population increases stem from the local multiplier effects associated with direct expansion of large-city interdependence, and when the local multiplier effects are associated with other forms of domestic and foreign trade.) Likewise, indirect growth of interdependence comes about when population growth in C_2, C_3, or C_n magnifies the local demand for the agricultural produce of C_1's hinterland or the manufactured output of C_1 and its smaller urban dependents. Any enlarged commodity interaction between C_1 and C_2, C_3, or C_n is accompanied by a widening of human spatial interaction between the same cities. This is so because it was frequently necessary for merchants or their agents to travel to the purchase source or sales destination city in order to bargain and consummate business transactions.

Each increment in commodity and human spatial interaction between C_1 and C_2, C_3, or C_n contributes to spatial biases in the circulation of information. These in turn lead to yet further large-city interaction and spatially biased information flows through one of two pairs of feedback loops (Fig. 6.2). The net impact of these two feedback sequences is a continued domination of the urban system or subsystem by the same large cities. The contact-array and time-lag spatial biases in information availability triggering the two feedback loops are not generated solely by trade-linked human spatial interaction. The expansion of interdependence, or interurban trade, between C_1 and C_2, C_3 or C_n can further compound spatially biased information flows by creating an incentive to improve the quality, speed, and frequency of transport and postal linkages between the large centers; by inducing a larger volume of interurban business mail; and by causing a greater interurban movement of newspapers via passenger and freight services and the mails.

One pair of feedback loops involves information about market changes, prices, and business opportunities in general. The spatially biased flows in question operate so that any specific piece of information originating in or entering the system (or subsystem) at C_1 will have a greater probability of being acquired early and exploited by an entrepreneur in C_2, C_3, or C_n than by an entrepreneur in smaller cities within the system (subsystem), which have fewer and less frequent contacts with C_1 or have greater time lags from that city. Likewise, any economically exploitable news originating in or entering the system (subsystem) at C_2, C_3, or C_n will have a greater probability of being soon put to use in C_1 than in smaller centers within the system (subsystem), which have fewer and less frequent contacts with the information source city or have greater time lags from the source city. Should a new business opportunity be exploited at one of the large mercantile cities, such as C_1, it will eventually be synonymous with an expansion of the local wholesaling-trading complex and population growth. For one of two reasons, this in turn leads both to increased interdependence with one or more of the other large mercantile cities (C_2, C_3 ... C_n) and to reinforced spatial biases of information circulation. One reason is that the previously unexploited opportunity directly involves C_2, C_3, or C_n (or conversely, C_1), the agricultural hinterland of one of these cities, or a center subordinate to one of them. The second possibility is that the previously unexploited opportunity involves another system or foreign country (subsystem or domestic region), but the consequent population growth in C_1 (C_2, C_3, or C_n) precipitates a greater demand for locally consumed agricultural and manufactured goods normally acquired from or through C_2, C_3, or C_n (C_1). Since the probabilistic nature of these interrelationships permits any given opportunity to be exploited in one, two, three, or all of a system's (subsystem's) largest centers, the model allows for adjustment in the population ratios of C_1, C_2, C_3 ... C_n, and perhaps even for minor rank-shifting among them.[40] Population-ratio adjustments and rank-shifting would follow from both the occurrence of local multipliers in some rather than all of the system's (subsystem's) leading cities, and the consequent minor alterations in the distribution of probabilities among C_1, C_2, C_3 ... C_n for subsequent business opportunity exploitation.

The second pair of feedback loops involves information concerning the existence of commercial (organizational, financial) and industrial innovations as well as information on the experience of those who have already adopted such innovations.[41] Here, too, the spatial biases of information circulation are such that any innovation entering or originating at C_1 $(C_2, C_3,$ or $C_n)$ has a probability of being adopted first or on a larger or multiple basis at C_2, C_3, or C_n (C_1) that is greater than the probability for other places within the system (subsystem).[42] That is, the probability is lower at smaller cities within the subsystem (system), which have either fewer and less frequent contacts with the initially accepting large city, or greater time lags from that same city. For one of two reasons the consequences of adoption at C_2, C_3, or C_n (C_1) are increased interdependence with C_1 $(C_2, C_3,$ or $C_n)$ and reinforced spatial biases of information circulation. One reason is that single or multiple adoption of the innovation brings into being previously nonexistent forms of interdependence between the subsystem's (system's) largest cities. This would take place, for example, with commercial innovations such as banking and various forms of insurance. Or the adoption of new manufacturing practices in one large city could augment or create a demand for raw materials normally procured from the hinterland of another of the subsystem's (system's) dominant centers. In the second, more common, case, innovation adoptions bring about local multiplier effects in C_2, C_3, or C_n (C_1), which in turn breed a larger local demand for the agricultural and manufactured products generally imported from or through C_1 $(C_2, C_3,$ or $C_n)$. The diffusion feedback loops of the model also allow for adjustment in the population ratios of C_1, C_2, C_3 ... C_n, and perhaps even for minor rank-shifting among them. The reason is that the probabilistic character attributed to interurban diffusion permits any particular innovation to be adopted in one, some, or all of a subsystem's (system's) highest-order cities, and thus permits the occurrence of specific innovation-derived local multipliers in some, or all of these centers. Here, too, if comparable local multipliers did not occur in all of the subsystem's (system's) major centers, minor alterations would follow in the distribution of probabilities among C_1, C_2, C_3 ... C_n for subsequent innovation adoption.[43]

Nonlocal Multiplier Effects. In several different guises the model incorporates nonlocal multiplier effects. Expanded wholesaling-trading activities, newly exploited business opportunities, or the adoption of a commercial or industrial innovation at C_1 can lead to increased interaction (interdependence) with C_2, C_3, or C_n, and vice versa. To one degree or another the increased interaction stemming from events at C_1 is synonymous with greater economic activity and employment at C_2, C_3, or C_n, that is, it has a nonlocal multiplier effect. This aspect of the model is thus consistent with those interpretations of nineteenth-century American economic development that place much emphasis on nonlocal multipliers.[44] Nonetheless it differs from them in being phrased in terms of interurban multipliers at the national (system) and intraregional (subsystem) level, rather than in terms of interregional multipliers.

The nonlocal multipliers in the model are all depicted as primary, or initial, effects. But rank stability in urban subsystems and systems is apt to be further supported by secondary, or reverse, nonlocal multiplier effects. When economic actions at C_1, for example, generate nonlocal multiplier effects at C_2, C_3, or C_n, the enlarged scale of the urban economy at one or more of the latter places may in turn lead to increased imports of goods normally secured via C_1 and to nonlocal multiplier effects in C_1. As a consequence of the reverse multiplier effects at C_1, successive rounds of modest secondary nonlocal multipliers may develop in both directions between that city and C_2, C_3, or C_n.

All the model's nonlocal multiplier effects that affect C_1-C_n are positive, or employment (population) augmenting. However, on occasion negative nonlocal multiplier effects may be operative. More precisely, when there is a business failure or net decrease in the scale of the whole-saling-trading complex at C_1 (or conversely, C_2, C_3, or C_n) there may follow a decrease in economic exchange with C_2, C_3, or C_n (C_1). This will occur either because the business failure directly involved another major mercantile city, or because it brings a decrease in demand for the locally consumed agricultural and industrial products imported from one or more large centers. In either instance, decreased employment at C_1 (C_2, C_3, or C_n) is apt to precipitate a negative nonlocal multiplier, or decreased employment, at C_2, C_3, or C_n (C_1). If the negative nonlocal multiplier is short-lived, it may bring an increased rate of un-employment rather than a population decrease.

It is also possible that a positive nonlocal multiplier will be dampened on occasion. This could occur when expansion of the wholesaling-trading complex at C_1, C_2, C_3, or C_n caused an increase in local demand for at least one manufactured good sufficient to justify a total or partial substitution of local production for imports from a large sister city. Such import substitution following threshold fulfillment would probably not often be total, owing to the product variety of the already existing small manufacturing sector of each large mercantile city. Moreover, while import-replacing industrial production might diminish large-city interdependence, it should be more than compensated for in the long run by the development of new manufacturing special-ties that accompany the growth of C_1, C_2, C_3, or C_n. This is the case since the invention and innovation feedback loop of the urban-size growth submodel enables the appearance of new export or nonthreshold industries.

A distinction must be drawn between the nonlocal multipliers of pre-telegraphic mercantile cities and those of urban subsystems and systems in modern industrialized economies. Today, primary nonlocal multi-pliers are often internalized within the large multifunctional business organization. Such organizations are usually comprised of spatially dis-persed production, distribution, administrative, and research and development units, with some units functioning on a local and regional basis, others functioning on a national or international basis. Thus, an adjustment in the scale or operations within one unit leads to adjust-ments not only elsewhere in the organization but also elsewhere in space, or at other cities where units of the organization are located.[45] In contrast, most primary nonlocal multipliers prior to 1840 fell outside the simply-organized business establishments of the leading American mercantile cities. There were nevertheless exceptions. For example, some mercantile houses had offices in more than one city, and the management function of hinterland-located small-town and rural manufactures was sometimes found in the largest centers. This phenomenon was most pronounced in Boston, where wholesaling-trading entrepreneurs administered the cotton textile production of Waltham, Lowell, Lawrence, Chicopee, and Manchester, as well as other forms of hinterland manufacturing. But in Boston, as well as in New York, Philadelphia, and Baltimore, such efforts were confined to nearby hinterlands, where informational contacts were easily maintained, making it easier to cope with uncertainty. In none of these cities were "businessmen thinking of business administration on a nationwide scale, or even of administration in other than the direct . . . local, and speculative sense."[46]

The pretelegraphic nonlocal multipliers that touched any major mercantile city did not merely come from and return to other major major mercantile centers. Although not explicitly a part of the model of large-city rank stability, nonlocal multipliers involving the individual large mercantile city and lesser urban units in its hinterland merit attention. The hinterland nonlocal multipliers of cities already dominating the regional urban subsystems were of two basic types. First, some nonlocal multipliers devolved from an expanded supply of hinterland goods and were related to the local multipliers generated in large mercantile cities by the hinterland-product export component of their wholesaling-trading complexes. Insofar as any given hinterland town functioned as a point where nearby agricultural, forest, or mineral production was collected and forwarded to its mother mercantile city, an increase in that function should have brought a local multiplier to the town's economy as well as a nonlocal multiplier in the mercantile city whose wholesaling-trading complex received and further distributed the hinterland goods. These relationships held for such different cases as agricultural towns in Philadelphia's or Baltimore's hinterland, or lead-mining towns in St. Louis' hinterland. They also held when an expanded supply of hinterland production was brought about by an increase of hinterland population or an increase of demand in the hinterland's mother city itself.[47] The same kind of hinterland nonlocal multipliers were operative whenever there was an enlargement in the scale of industrial activity oriented toward water power or raw materials in hinterland centers such as Paterson, New Jersey, and the various Connecticut Valley towns whose factory production was forwarded to New York.[48]

The second type of hinterland nonlocal multiplier originated when, as the result of a local multiplier, an increased demand developed in a hinterland town for the finished products, miscellaneous services, and industrial inputs acquired from or via its dominant mercantile city. This kind of hinterland nonlocal multiplier need not have been divorced from the first type, for when a town expanded its shipments to the city in whose hinterland it was located, a local multiplier normally ensued, and an increased demand for items from the larger city should have developed.

The existence of these types of hinterland nonlocal multipliers has led to the assertion that the early nineteenth-century growth of major American port cities "was dependent not only on the physical size, population, and fertility of their hinterlands but also on the extent to which those hinterlands were commercialized, industrialized, and linked to the ports."[49] New York's emerging dominance in the national system of cities ought to be seen at least partially in this light, especially after the opening of the Erie Canal, as well as partially in light of its interdependence with other large mercantile cities controlling their own hinterlands.[50] However, the urban population of the country was highly concentrated in a few hinterland-dominating mercantile cities, and as a consequence, the magnitude of any hinterland nonlocal multiplier involving a single town was apt to be somewhat limited. Put otherwise, individual nonlocal multipliers associated with hinterland towns were usually limited by the population of those towns. Most hinterland towns were generally only a fraction of the size of the mercantile cities that dominated them. For example, in 1840 Reading and Lancaster, the two largest towns in Philadelphia's hinterland, had no more than 1/26 the population of Philadelphia.[51] The widespread absence of medium-sized hinterland cities was in itself probably related in part to the manner in which most hinterland retailing was bound directly to the concentrated wholesaling activities of the major mercantile cities. That is, wholesaling was mostly confined to the largest cities in each urban subsystem, rather than being hierarchically apportioned to cities of increasingly greater population.[52]

Interaction Increases. The model portrays commodity and human spatial interaction as self-propagating. Interaction between the most populous mercantile centers in a given system or subsystem $(C_1, C_2, C_3 \ldots C_n)$ contributes to spatial biases in the circulation of information, which then generates positive feedbacks and eventual interaction increases between those same major cities. In a sense it was already recognized by several early nineteenth-century observers that large-city interaction breeds additional large-city interaction. For example, one commentator on New York's rise to supremacy noted: "It is to be remembered also, that when once a city has acquired an established character as the great commercial emporium of a country, whether from local advantages or fortuitous circumstances, the course of trade becomes settled by flowing regularly in the same channel."[53]

Geographers have recently provided more substantial support for the validity of the self-generating manner in which large-city inter- action increases are here portrayed. One has contended that with the passage of time, "the established and dominating linkages [between cities] will tend to become more and more reinforced . . . .Since there is an interplay between internal changes in a subsystem and the intensity of interaction of this subsystem, some linkages tend to be strengthened at the expense of others." Moreover, since virtually all of the model's commodity-spatial interaction involves either the shipment of goods from a wholesaling-trading unit in one large city directly to a retailer in another large city, or the shipment of goods from a wholesaling-trading unit in one large city to a wholesaling- trading unit in another large city which then forwards the goods to local or nonlocal retailers, the following observation is highly relevent: "In the wholesaling-trading linkage the trade is repeating and formal- ized . . . [the retailer] tends to maintain particular wholesale linkages, both in type of goods sought and in sources of supply. The conduct of his business is facilitated by reducing the supply problem to a routine. To do that, the establishment of regular linkages is of great value." Thus, each increment in the scale of operations of a retailer who has already acquired goods directly or indirectly via large-city interaction should result in greater large-city interaction.[54]

More important, Donald G. Janelle specified an empirically based model in which increased interaction calls forth transport improvements, which after an indefinite lag, to allow for decision-making adjustments, result in another round of increased interaction. More precisely, and in somewhat modified form, the increasing spatial interaction among particular places where business, service, and manufacturing activities are becoming more concentrated (that is, growing large cities) "leads to further demands for increased accessibility," or demands for more varied, more frequent, and faster transport services and routes (Fig. 6.3). When these demands are satisfied through transport innovations, which may involve the application of new technology, time-space convergence occurs, "that is, the travel-time required between places decreases and distance declines in significance."[55] However, the impact of time-space convergence is rarely homogeneous, for "an increase in transport-speed on a route connecting successive places will generally result in greater convergence rates for the more distant places than for the closer or intervening ones." Or, "this declining significance of intervening space benefits the more distantly-spaced larger cities more than it benefits the smaller ones." As a consequence, there is a further concentration of economic activities in the large, growing cities, accompanied by a specialization of hinterland production, both of which precipitate increased interaction and pave the way for another cycle of the positive feedback process.[56]

Janelle's model, which may be viewed as a submodel to the model of large-city rank stability, is of particular significance in view of the evidence on interurban travel volumes and times. It is also closely related to P. Pottier's contention that economic development usually is propagated circularly and cumulatively along the major transport routes which join leading urban industrial centers.[57] Its virtues of conciseness and insight notwithstanding, however, Janelle's model does not come to grips with the process of large-city growth and dominance within a

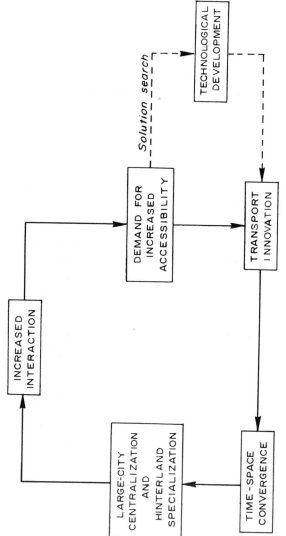

Fig. 6.3. A model of the process generating increased interaction between large cities. Modified from Donald G. Janelle "Spatial Reorganization: A Model and Concept," *Annals of the Association of American Geographers* 59 (1969), 348–364.

system-of-cities framework. Also, it gives no attention to the local and nonlocal multipliers and information circulation biases that are central to the development of urban systems and subsystems.

Spatially Biased Information Circulation and the Exploitation of Business Opportunities. The large-city rank stability model argues that the time-lag and contact-array spatial biases in the availability of information associated with major American mercantile cities positively affected the probability of new market and business opportunities being exploited in those same cities. Richard Meier similarly remarked: "Opportunities also appear at linkage points [large cities] in communications systems and entrepreneurs located there obtain access to several independent sources of information first. Thus change encourages change in the vicinity of a communications focus, and activity is piled upon activity within a small amount of space, subject only to diseconomies associated with intense land use."[58] However, the fact that the largest pretelegraphic mercantile cities were usually the first cities in their respective regions to acquire any specific piece of information regarding markets, prices, and business opportunities in general was not the only cause of the heightened probability that these cities would be the scene of opportunity exploitation.

In many instances it was presumably of greater importance for the cities in question to receive more comprehensive and redundant information pertaining to a particular opportunity. In most spatial and temporal settings, new economic decisions must generally be reached in a climate of uncertainty; and the greater the volume of varied and redundant information possessed by an economic decision maker, the greater the likelihood that he will reduce or eliminate his uncertainty and take action. Therefore, spatial biases in the availability of information give a spatial dimension to the level of uncertainty prevailing locally.[59] Thus, the individual entrepreneur or mercantile firm situated in a regionally dominant pretelegraphic city, where information advantages permitted uncertainty to be more easily reduced than elsewhere, should have been more apt to exploit certain types of new business opportunities. This advantage was considerable, because the pretelegraphic wholesaling or trading merchant was particularly susceptible to uncertainty, his entire success or failure depending on his ability to appraise nonlocal market or supply conditions which could easily change with time.[60]

On occasion, however, the information advantages of the major mercantile cities may have caused an overestimation of the business opportunities at those locales. Such an overestimation would have expressed itself either as an overcrowding of a particular wholesaling-trading market or, more important, as local investments that might just as well have been undertaken elsewhere—perhaps even at a greater profit. This possibility of unnecessarily concentrated growth-amplifying investments in the major mercantile cities follows from evidence that private entrepreneurs in newly developing economies consistently overestimate the profitability of investments in one or a few major cities vis-à-vis other places.[61]

The business opportunities exploited in the largest mercantile cities on the basis of more and earlier information were essentially of two types: those related to the performance of everyday business at relatively modest profit levels, and those involving short-range speculation and high profits. In both instances there are indications that the agglomeration (urbanization) economies provided by superior information availability contributed to the success and continued expansion of wholesaling-trading activities in the leading mercantile centers. An 1827 New York newspaper, marveling at the business advantages brought to that city by its regularly scheduled packets to England, France, and the Cotton Ports, remarked: "Nothing is more important in mercantile business than system and certainty of [information] transmission."[62] And an economic historian asserted: "The growing movement of vessels [to and from New York, Boston, Philadelphia, and Baltimore] made possible the amassing of much more commercial information than before . . . Thus . . . a general focusing of the markets [at these cities] was inevitable."[63]

It is possible to document speculative ventures, especially those resting on sharp commodity price changes, in which time lag advantages of even a few hours could be converted into lucrative profits. Several postal service reforms put into effect during the 1820s and 1830s were designed to reduce the speculative profits acquired by large-city merchants whose privately informed agents had been able to take action in distant places before the arrival of the mails.[64] New York merchants, usually being the first to learn of radical price changes for cotton in Liverpool, were often ruthless in their exploitation of the market in Charleston, Savannah, Mobile, and New Orleans, while interests in those cities, being the first in the South to acquire New York news, could make quick back-country purchases before the word on price adjustments became public property. Similarly, hastily dispatched representatives of New York mercantile houses frequently could take advantage of early news of foreign or domestic price changes in Philadelphia, Baltimore, and major interior cities, with entrepreneurs in those cities frequently repeating the process in their respective hinterlands.[65]

The large-city exploitation of business opportunities as a result of spatial biases in the availability of information is also revealed by the scattered evidence of entrepreneurial migration from one major mercantile center to another. At different times during the 1790–1840 period merchants are known to have migrated, for example, from Philadelphia, Baltimore, and Boston to New York; from Baltimore to Philadelphia; and from New York to New Orleans, Mobile, Savannah, and Charleston.[66] In other words, the knowledge that the individual merchant gained of business opportunities in other large cities, whether or not correctly perceived, was sometimes sufficient to persuade him either to migrate himself or to have one of his business associates do so. In this connection, the major mercantile cities were not only the foci of interregional information receipt within their respective urban subsystems but also the principal information dissemination nodes for their respective hinterlands. Thus, as suggested by the size-growth submodel, news of expanding job opportunities within the confines of regionally dominant cities acted also as a migration magnet to rural and urban hinterland residents. The attractive force exerted by job and other economic opportunities was particularly great in the hinterland towns at whose expense the major mercantile cities were growing. Witness, for example, the known streams of migration from Salem to Boston, and from Stamford, New Haven, New Bedford, and other small southern New England cities to New York.[67]

These migration observations, as well as the interregional feedback of migration-inducing economic-opportunity information that brought great numbers of Northeasterners (and foreigners) to Pittsburgh, Cincinnati, Louisville, St. Louis, Buffalo, Cleveland, and Detroit, are in keeping with Torsten Hägerstrand's model for predicting the number of migrants (M) from one place (a) to another (b) during the short-term time-period t_i-t_j. In this model, migration volume is determined by the density of opportunities in the place of destination and the level of information about them in the place of origin. It may be expressed:

$$M_{a \to b} = k \frac{V_b I_b}{P_b} \tag{6.1}$$

where V_b is the number of vacancies at b (estimated by the total number of in-migrants to b), P_b the population of b, I_b the number of existing private contacts between b and potential migrants in a at time t_i (estimated by the number of individuals living in b who originated from a), and k is a constant.[68]

Finally, the already existing day-to-day business operations in regionally dominant mercantile cities had the possibility of being conducted more rapidly than in smaller centers, which suffered both from longer time lags in the receipt of information from distant places and from a more limited array of direct nonlocal contacts. In a pretelegraphic environment, where the pace of business transactions was slow, merchants stood to gain greatly from completing sales deliveries and purchase acquisitions as quickly as possible, since it allowed them to avoid the unnecessary tying up of capital in goods-in-transit or goods-in-stock. Hence, where the intervals between information receipt were shorter and transport services were more frequent and rapid, the entrepreneur could in the course of a year complete a greater number of capital turn-overs, or "action cycles," than could his counterpart who had similar capital resources but operated from a smaller place. Since a greater number of action cycles could be completed in large cities, greater local earnings and a higher employment multiplier could be generated annually from a given volume of capital assets. This, in turn, could cause a more rapid functioning of the size-growth submodel, increased inter-

action with other large subsystem or system cities, and further rein-
forcement of the existing pattern of spatially biased information
circulation, all of which meant still further possibilities for completing
routinized transactions more rapidly.

Presumably, the relationships between action cycle efficiency and
time lag and contact array biases in the availability of information also
contributed to New York's complete domination of the entire American
system of cities. New York's preeminence was based in particular on the
information and shipping frequency advantages given to that city by
her packet lines to the Cotton Ports. For example, in 1840 the mean
public-information time lag separating New York and Mobile was 11.3
days, while that separating Philadelphia and Mobile was 13.0 days
(Maps 2.9 and 2.11). If the minimum action cycle time is assumed to
have been twice the mean time lag, thereby allowing for movement in
both directions (order receipt and shipment dispatch), then in theory a
New York mercantile enterprise could have completed a maximum of
16.2 turnovers of the same initial capital during one year, while a
Philadelphia wholesaling-trading establishment could have completed
only 14.0.[69]

Disturbances to Rank Stability and Population Ratio Adjustments.
Because of the probabilistic attributes given to the opportunity exploitation and innovation adoption feedbacks, and because, if so desired,
local and nonlocal multipliers can also be placed in a probabilistic framework, the proposed model of large-city rank stability is not incompat-
ible with the population ratio adjustments and the few minor large-city
rank shifts that occurred in American urban subsystems before the
coming of the telegraph. For example, between 1830 and 1840 the ratio
of New York's population to Philadelphia's population increased from
roughly 1.3:1 to 1.6:1, and between 1820 and 1830 Boston and Baltimore reversed ranks as the third and fourth largest cities in the Northeast. Furthermore, the model is not necessarily at odds with the larger
population ratio adjustments that occurred between the leading centers
of the Ohio and Upper Mississippi Valley subsystem and the Lake Erie
subsystem, on the one hand, and the older nationally and regionally
dominant cities of the Northeast on the other hand. This compatibility
exists because the model applies to an open system, characterized by

the westward spread of settlement and supposedly does not hold for the subsystem of the Ohio and Upper Mississippi valleys until after the War of 1812 and for the Lake Erie subsystem until the late 1820s.[70]

Despite such consistency, the model is not capable of accounting for all large-city population ratio adjustments and rank shifts that occurred within the American system of cities and its subsystems between 1790 and 1840. For one thing, the model cannot provide for disturbances to stability and population ratios that were political in origin, such as the Embargo Act and the War of 1812.[71] Nor does it directly account for differences in the impact of business cycle upswings and downswings on the largest mercantile cities. The model also has no explicit place for stability disturbances that were derived from large-city variations in entrepreneurial attitudes on such matters as credit extension and participation in risky ventures.

In questioning the model, some might argue that alterations in large-city rank and population relationships were owing in part to the inevitable rise of places that had both excellent physical sites and superior locational situations. Certainly, the fact that New York outdistanced other cities was somewhat related to the depth and extent of its harbor, the protection of that harbor from the wind and sea, and the city's accessibility both to the western interior via the Hudson and Mohawk valleys and to southern New England via the East River and Long Island Sound. The importance to Baltimore's growth of its harbor and its ability to tap the Susquehanna Valley is obvious, as is the significance to Louisville's expansion of its position at the Falls of the Ohio, and the development benefits gained by Pittsburgh from its position at the confluence of the Ohio, Allegheny, and Monongahela Rivers.

However, the fact that the "prototypic American metropolis . . . was a port at a strategic location on long-distance trade routes" does not justify the interpretation of urban growth prior to 1840 primarily in terms of site, situation, and physical barriers. The geographic superiority of a city relative to other points furnishes merely a "potentiality" and by no means guarantees success, just as success does not automatically mirror superior site and situation. Norfolk, for instance, lost rather than gained importance in the system of cities during the early nineteenth century, despite its excellent harbor, its position near the entrance to

Chesapeake Bay, its central location for the coastal trade, and its control of the James-Kanawha route to the interior. In 1800 Norfolk was the country's eighth largest city; by 1840 it had dropped to thirtieth place. Walter Isard even speculated that if the trans-Allegheny railroad westward from Philadelphia had been built earlier, in the 1830s, "the economic ascendency of New York City would have been less marked; perhaps her industrial and commercial supremacy would not have been achieved at all." Or as the *New York American* observed in 1823 when evaluating Mobile's rapid expansion: "[nearby] Blakely has every advantage over Mobile, except that of being begun when this was already established." And Buffalo's preeminence, although based on its position as western terminal of the Erie Canal, "was not due entirely to this geographic situation."[72] In short, site and situation do not of themselves explain urban growth and are poorly suited to identifying the processes by which rank stability sets in among the largest cities of an urban system or subsystem.

Related Models. Although the model of large-city development departs in important respects from the manner in which historians and economic historians have traditionally interpreted American urban development between 1790 and 1840, it is buttressed by a number of other models. The pivotal role of information circulation and generation in the model is in keeping with arguments of social communications theorists regarding the interrelationships between macro-level economic growth and communications development. For example, Karl Deutsch contended: "Within any geographical setting and any population, economic, social, and technological developments mobilize individuals for relatively more intensive communication." Likewise, Wilbur Schramm insisted: "Although economics and communication are both organic to society, and neither can develop to any great extent without a corresponding development in the other, still they act powerfully on one another."[73]

Furthermore, the leading role assigned to information circulation and generation is in keeping with Magoroh Maruyama's observation that interaction and information can be regarded as the dynamic counterparts of the descriptive concept of interdependence. It also conforms to his depiction of the growth of a single hypothetical city at a previously unsettled location on a homogeneous plain. When one farmer starts cultivation at a chance location on the plain, this attracts other farmers who do likewise (owing to information feedback). Then: "Someone opens a tool shop, someone else a food stand [because of information generated about demand], and gradually a village grows. The village facilitates the marketing of crops and attracts more farms [as a result of information feedback]. The increased activity and population necessitates the development of industry [another response to information generated about demand], and the village becomes a city." Maruyama concluded: "The secret of the growth of the city is in the process of deviation-amplifying mutual positive feedback networks rather than the initial condition." [74]

The specifics of the urban systems framework of the model are also consistent with John Friedmann's argument that since cities are "generators and consumers of new information," the "successful" development of urban-centered regions "requires the increased circulation of ideas." Moreover, he stated that, when once established in a given national economic setting, "the hierarchy of cities, particularly . . . the urban centers at the top . . . tend to perpetuate their relative position and functional role in organizing the pattern of economic growth in its spatial dimension." [75]

Since the model describes in essence how a few large cities, or urban regions, continuously reinforce one another's growth, it is related to those models that deal with the problem of regional growth inequalities. Gunnar Myrdal's model of this type is phrased in terms of a circular and cumulative process—just as the large-city rank stability model—and involves two basic components, "spread effects" and "backwash effects." Spread effects are akin to the nonlocal interurban multipliers and the accompanying information advantages of the large-city rank stability model. Backwash effects parallel the attractive force exerted on migrants by leading centers and the information disadvantages of cities that dominated neither the national system of cities nor a regional urban subsystem. [76] Much of the literature on regional growth processes is built on François Perroux' concept of the "growth pole," which in Boudeville's modified definition is "a set of expanding industries [activities] located in an urban area and inducing further development of economic activity throughout its zone of influence." Growth pole theorists concerned with the relationships between locations have recently argued: "Information and economic flows are interdependent (one to a large extent generates the other); thus these sets of flows tend to have similar patterns."[77]

LARGE-CITY INTERDEPENDENCE AND INNOVATION DIFFUSION

The large-city rank stability model permits commercial and industrial innovations to diffuse from any major subsystem (system) city to any other leading subsystem (system) center, regardless of their population relationships. This means that in 1840, for example, an innovation could have been regionally introduced in either Pittsburgh, Cincinnati, Louisville, or St. Louis, and then diffused to the other three in any order or sequence, with less important urban subsystem members having a smaller probability of early adoption but not being definitively excluded from early adoption. In contrast, the prevailing models of interurban diffusion require that an innovation first be accepted in the largest subsystem (system) city and then pass downward through the urban hierarchy—in other words, that the sequence of spread be an orderly one from the most populous city to cities of successively smaller size. This would mean that in 1840 an innovation could only have been regionally introduced to the Ohio and Upper Mississippi valleys at Cincinnati, the largest subsystem city. The innovation could then have passed only to the subsystem's second-ranking city, Pittsburgh, then on to the third-ranking Louisville, and from either of those places or from Cincinnati only to the subsystem's fourth largest city, St. Louis. Only then could it have moved on to smaller subsystem members. There are a number of inadequacies in these prevailing models. However, it is possible to devise an alternative which is not completely contradictory to them and at the same time make the innovation-adoption component of the large-city rank stability model mathematically specific.

Christallerian Interurban Diffusion Models. Virtually all theoretical statements to date regarding the interurban diffusion of innovations have been framed in the hierarchical terminology of Christaller's central place theory.[78] Most such thinking can be traced to Hägerstrand's observation: "The urban hierarchy canalizes [channels] the course of diffusion." He later reformulated this concept: "A closer analysis shows that the spread along the initial 'frontier' is led through the urban hierarchy. The point of introduction in a new country is its primate city; sometimes some other metropolis. Then centers next in rank follow. Soon, however, this order is broken up and replaced by one where the neighborhood effect dominates over the pure size succession."[79]

The "filtering" of innovations downward through a central place hierarchy has been stated most formally by John Hudson, whose key assumption in his stochastic model is: "A message [or innovation] emanating from a single center of order m diffuses downward through the [central place] hierarchy such that in the first interval of time, Δt, after a center has heard the message, it in turn tells every [definitionally smaller] place that it directly dominates. Thus, the message eventually reaches all q^{m-1} places." Or: "Once a center has heard a message, it is equally likely to pass this in the next period to any of the towns that it directly dominates."[80]

The shortcomings of such hierarchical diffusion schemes become clear when the hierarchical dominance structure and some of the other direct linkages (information flows paths) are diagramed for the four highest order places in a Christallerian central place system where $k = 3$ (Fig. 6.4).[81] One unsatisfactory feature is the impossibility of lateral diffusion between members of different nesting arrangements; that is, each nest culminating at the single first-order place is a closed diffusion system. In other words, the next to largest places in an urban system or subsystem cannot exchange innovation-relevant information with one another. Another weakness is that not even in the same nesting arrangement is there any possibility of lateral diffusion between places of identical order. Under no circumstances can an innovation diffuse from one place of a given population to another place of roughly the same population. Furthermore, diffusion from a lower order place to a higher order place is precluded even within the framework of a single nested subsystem. Thus, it is impossible for an innovation to diffuse from one place of a given population to another place of a larger population, even where the separating distance is small. Another less critical shortcoming, which is applicable to some but not all models, is the requirement that diffusion always start in the largest city.

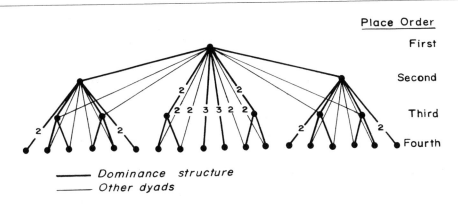

Place Order

First

Second

Third

Fourth

——— Dominance structure
——— Other dyads

Fig. 6.4. The dominance structure and other interaction dyads in a Christallerian central-place system where $k = 3$.
The only undiagramed linkages involve the procurement of highest- or first-order goods and services from the single first-order place by the six left-most and six right-most fourth-order places. Numbers refer to the number of orders of goods and services procured by lower-order places from higher-order places. Unnumbered dyads involve only one order of goods.

As a result, in most urban systems and subsystems the interdependencies governing the economy and size of individual cities are not confined to central place activities, or the so-called tertiary sector. Rather than constituting the entire set of interdependencies within an urban system or subsystem, hierarchically ordered tertiary activities, as well as related market-oriented industrial activities, are usually responsible for a subset of such interdependencies. In most urban systems and large subsystems other interurban interaction and nonhierarchical interdependencies are generated by the shipment of geographically specialized agricultural commodities, the flow of inputs and outputs associated with footloose and labor-oriented manufacturing, and private and public administrative functions. For example, if the four largest cities of the Northeast in 1820–1840 were organized in accord with Christaller's theory, the only possible economic flows would have been those from New York to Philadelphia, Boston, and Baltimore, as well as those from the second-ranked Philadelphia to the roughly equal-sized Boston and Baltimore, and none of the four would have in any way been dependent on smaller places. Instead, the 1820 and 1840 data show that considerable economic interaction occurred in both directions between every possible pair of the four centers, and each of the four received large quantities of agricultural and industrial products from smaller urban places in their respective hinterlands. In fact, the total pattern of inter-urban economic exchange of a nonhierarchical character was relatively complex, even before individual urban economies or the American economy as a whole had become highly industrialized and thus capable of generating much larger, more varied input and output flows.[82]

Thus, the generally held view of interurban innovation diffusion needs to be modified. In particular, it must be allowed that nonhierarchical as well as hierarchical economic interdependencies between cities nondeter-ministically influence the diffusion of innovations within an urban system or subsystem. In at least one sense this was especially true of pre-telegraphic urban systems and subsystems, for most long-distance infor-mation flows—whether by newspaper, the post, or travel—came about as a result of the information acquisition and exchange of the numerically limited economic elite who were conducting or attempting to initiate nonlocal business.

To place all interurban diffusion within a Christallerian central place framework, and thereby erroneously equate all central place systems with all urban systems, is to ignore Christaller's own reservations. In evaluating the version of his theory in which $k = 3$, he stated that it "is chiefly and uncontestedly valid for the largely agricultural provinces." In assessing his theory more generally, Christaller noted that he had "disregarded, above all, the entire complex of the determination of urban development through industrialization."[83] Moreover, although Christaller-based interurban diffusion models lack general applicability on logical grounds, they are probably still valid under special circum-stances. Such circumstances might include the diffusion of economic innovations whose successful adoption requires the presence of a potential market of a minimum size, or the fulfillment of threshold conditions.[84] They might also include the diffusion of innovations in feudal agricultural economies organized along strict hierarchical lines.

A Löschian Alternative. Some of the objections to hierarchical dif-fusion models can be overcome by proposing that interurban infor-mation flows are channeled by the interdependencies existing in a central place system of the type formulated by August Lösch, which includes market-oriented manufacturing establishments as well as retailing and service activities.[85] Here, in order to remain consistent with Hudson-like formulations, one has to assume that once a given center receives an innovation-relevant message, it can pass this information in the next time period to any city, regardless of size, which is dependent on it for secondary or tertiary goods and services.

One possible set of conditions that could arise under these circumstances is depicted in a pair of diagrams (Figs. 6.5 and 6.6). These diagrams are confined to 27 places so as to remain comparable with Fig. 6.4. The first diagram shows the location of seven orders of activity (designated by vertically arranged numbers) in cities (designated by letters). The population of each of these cities (designated by horizontally arranged numbers) is proportional to the number of other centers, or market area (designated by sloping lines), served by each locally present economic activity.[86] The second diagram indicates the interaction dyads, or information flow paths, existing in the system. Here lateral diffusion between places of roughly the same population can occur because in a Löschian central place system, urban size does not automatically define the array of activities locally present. For the same reason there can be diffusion from a center of given population to another of larger population, although most cases would yield diffusion from a larger to a smaller place. Nonetheless, this Löschian scheme is unsatisfactory insofar as it does not permit the exchange of information between the largest places in an urban system, or for that matter between any pair of places that do not belong to the same contiguous subsystem. In Fig. 6.6 there is a complete absence of contact between the five largest cities as well as between all places to the left and right of A.

A Model Incorporating Large-City Interdependence. Any highly realistic model designed to describe the process of diffusion within an urban system or subsystem ought to combine the Christallerian hierarchical spread of existing models, the lateral and smaller-to-larger-place dissemination allowed by a Löschian scheme, and some degree of information exchange between places belonging to the size classes just below the system's or subsystem's largest city (Fig. 6.7). Moreover, any model of interurban innovation diffusion aspiring to realism ought to allow that information also flows in the opposite direction to the movement

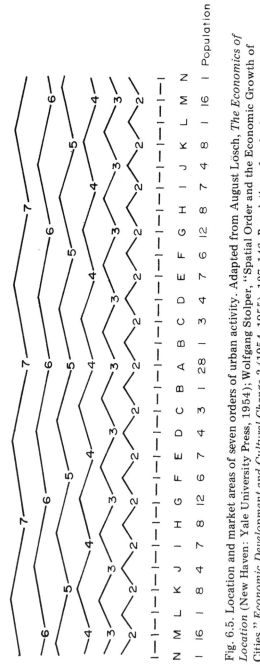

Fig. 6.5. Location and market areas of seven orders of urban activity. Adapted from August Lösch, *The Economics of Location* (New Haven: Yale University Press, 1954); Wolfgang Stolper, "Spatial Order and the Economic Growth of Cities," *Economic Development and Cultural Change* 3 (1954-1955), 137-146. Population of each place acquired by adding the numbers above it, that is, by summing each order of economic activity locally present.

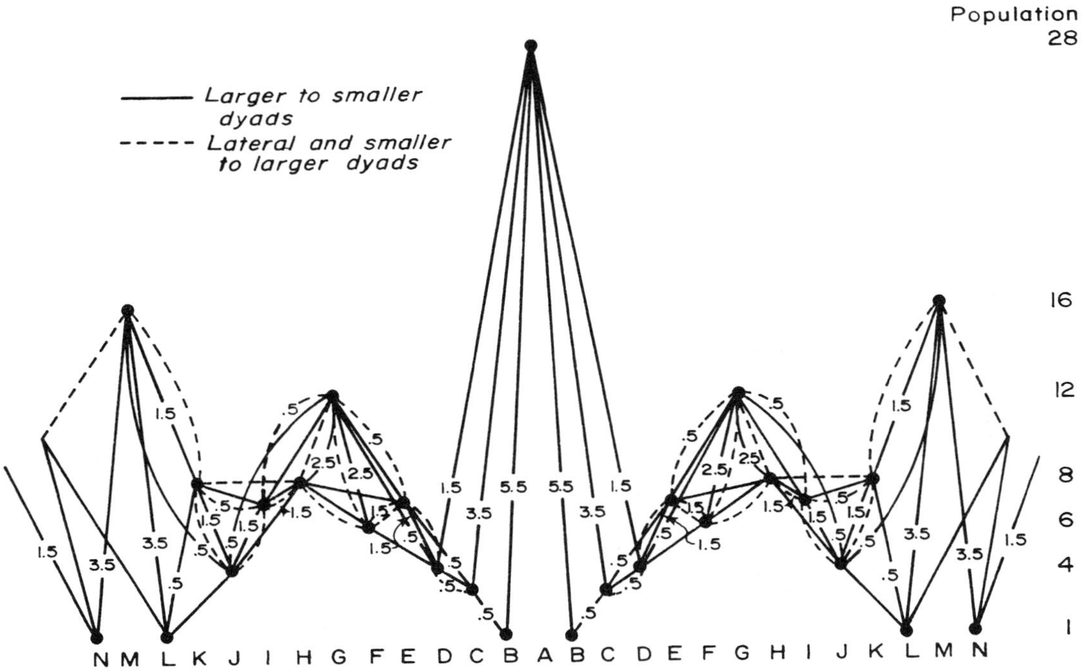

Fig. 6.6. Interaction dyads in Stolper's modified Löschian central-place system. Numbers refer to the number of sets of goods and services procured from one place by another. Unnumbered dyads involve only one set of goods and services.

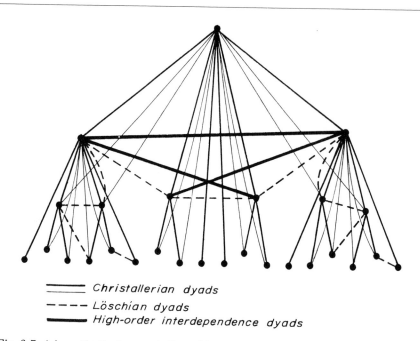

    ———— Christallerian dyads
    – – – – Löschian dyads
    ▬▬▬▬ High-order interdependence dyads

Fig. 6.7. A hypothetical permutation of interaction, or information flow, dyads in an urban system (subsystem) with Christallerian and Löschian qualities as well as large-city interdependence. The diagram is confined to 27 places to make it comparable with Figs. 6.4. and 6.6. Undiagramed are dyads connecting the largest place with the six left-most and six right-most places of the smallest size shown.

of goods and services along any interaction dyad within the urban system or subsystem. An allowance for the two-way flow ought to be made, for example, because information-bearing household consumers, wholesale purchasers, or factory representatives often go to the goods or input source, or because order requests often precede actual shipment to the consuming center.[87]

In view of these requirements, it is suggested that once a city (i) has received a message or adopted an economic innovation, it can pass the information on in the next time period (Δt) to any smaller, larger, or similarly sized city (j) either to which it sends goods and services or from which it receives goods and services. Thus, during Δt, the probability of message receipt or innovation adoption at the jth city via i ($A_{i \to j}$) is:

$$A_{i \to j} = \frac{f\left[(P_i G_{j \to i}),(P_j G_{i \to j})\right]}{d_{ij}^b} \qquad (6.2)$$

where P_i is the population of i, P_j is the population of j, $G_{j \to i}$ and $G_{i \to j}$ are the number of goods and services totally or fractionally supplied by j to i and i to j, d_{ij} is the distance separating i and j, and b is an empirically derived exponent.[88] If the product of P_i and $G_{j \to i}$ is a rough measure of the total volume of goods and services from j marketed via i, or the total volume of trade moving from j to i ($T_{j \to i}$), and the product of P_j and $G_{i \to j}$ is similarly a rough measure of the total volume of trade moving from i to j ($T_{i \to j}$), then formula (6.2) becomes:[89]

$$A_{i \to j} = \frac{f(T_{j \to i}, T_{i \to j})}{d_{ij}^b} \qquad (6.3)$$

Since city i is simultaneously indulging in interurban trade with several places, the probability that the jth city will be the first place to receive innovation-relevant information from i, or to have a person or firm influenced toward adoption from i ($I_{i \to j}$), is:[90]

$$I_{i \to j} = \frac{f(T_{j \to i}, T_{i \to j})}{d_{ij}^b} \bigg/ \sum_{j=1}^{n} \frac{f(T_{j \to i}, T_{i \to j})}{d_{ij}^b} \qquad (6.4)$$

Since the numerator mirrors economic flow, a distance factor is already built into the expressions. The distance denominator, however, is meant to capture the time lag effects of pretelegraphic information circulation. Under modern technology the denominator probably can be eliminated.[91] The assumed extra deterrent of time lags, and thereby distance, in pretelegraphic times is strengthened by the knowledge that in any setting, redundant and experience-based information is usually required by the potential innovator (individual or firm) before adoption actually occurs. Hence, in many pretelegraphic interurban diffusion processes there should have been, at least initially, a marked spatial clustering of innovation acceptances. In many such instances the configuration of this "neighborhood effect" was almost surely influenced by physical barriers, such as rivers. Physical barriers ought to have inhibited diffusion by obstructing frequent contact between places on their opposite sides and by lengthening the time lag of information flows that did occur.[92]

In short, expressions (6.2), (6.3), and (6.4) state that within an urban system or subsystem economic innovations diffuse in a probabilistic manner by being passed from one urban information field to another, that is, by being passed from one city to a unit in its set of direct nonlocal contacts (mean information field), and from the recipient city to a unit among its often overlapping set of direct nonlocal contacts (Fig. 6.8). The mean information field for any city i would be arrived at either by solving (6.2) or (6.3) for all j's with which direct contact occurred, then converting all those solutions into percentages, or by solving (6.4) for all j's.[93] Owing to the character of small-city information fields and expression (6.2), regardless of where an innovation had originated or entered an urban subsystem (system), it would be very likely to jump quickly to the largest cities. That is, even if an innovation did not originate or first enter an urban subsystem (system) at one of a few regionally (nationally) dominant cities, those places would tend to be early to receive or adopt it because of their high contact probabilities with a number of other places. These high contact probabilities would stem from their own population and the variety of their economic contacts. In cases where diffusion within the subsystem (system) did begin at a comparatively small city, other small centers, unless close to a major city, would tend to be bypassed and to receive information or adopt an innovation late because of their limited population and relatively narrow array of economic contacts. It is also clear that within a probabilistic information-field framework, large cities benefit additionally from indirect contacts.[94] This is in keeping with the fact that communications and information-flow advantages normally increase

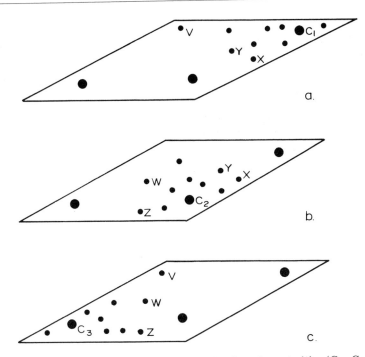

Fig. 6.8. Hypothetical information fields for the three largest cities (C_1, C_2, and C_3) in a regional urban subsystem. Adapted from Torsten Hägerstrand, *Innovation Diffusion* (Chicago: University of Chicago Press, 1967), p. 239. The nonlocal contacts of each city are shown in three different planes covering the same geographic area (C_1 in a plane a, C_2 in plane b, and C_3 in plane c). In accord with what has been said of large-city interdependence, all three leading cities fall within each other's information field. There are other common elements in the sets of nonlocal contacts: C_1 and C_2 both have direct contacts with the smaller cities X and Y; C_1 and C_3 both have direct contacts with the less populous V; and C_2 and C_3 share direct contacts with the lesser centers W and Z. The interregional contacts of C_1, C_2, and C_3 are not shown.

with urban size. More precisely, because of their high frequency of direct contact with one another, large cities may be quick to snap up innovations originating or entering at smaller centers with which they do not have direct contact, but which lie within each other's sphere of influence.[95] Ironically, the resulting sequence of innovation acceptances is not completely at odds with those often interpreted as the outcome of a hierarchical diffusion process.

Finally, since business-opportunity exploitation as well as the inter-urban diffusion of economic innovations is supposedly related to spatial biases in the availability of information, formulas (6.2), (6.3), and (6.4) ought to apply equally as well to the business-opportunity exploitation component of the large-city rank stability model. That is, $A_{i \to j}$ in (6.2) and (6.3) can also express the probability that the jth city will receive information from i permitting exploitation of business opportunities during time period Δt. Similarly, $I_{i \to j}$ in (6.4) can also express the probability that the jth city will be the first place to receive new business opportunity information from i.

7

Pretelegraphic Patterns of Interurban Innovation Diffusion

The entire body of received knowledge necessarily limits what inventions [and innovations] are possible at any given time.
—Jacob Schmookler

The large-city rank stability model is not a conceptual castle in the sky. Instead, it is derived in large measure from empirical evidence on the long-distance flow of information through newspapers, on postal services, on interurban commodity flows, and on interurban travel. Because of this evidence, spatial biases in the availability of information are assigned a pivotal role in the model. Yet if the model is to be accepted as a reasonable ideal-typical depiction of large-city development, it remains to be demonstrated that pretelegraphic patterns of interurban innovation diffusion were in accord with the prevailing pattern of information circulation. If the model is correct, an examination of specific interurban innovation diffusion processes should reveal that the largest cities in the American urban system and its regional subsystems were usually very early to receive or adopt innovations, frequently being the points of innovation origin or entry, and that those same cities were often the scene of large-scale or multiple adoptions when adoptions were nonexistent or limited in smaller cities. Moreover, the dissection of particular interurban diffusion processes should demonstrate that more than hierarchical spread was often involved; that the sequence of adoptions was not always an orderly one, proceeding progressively from the largest cities to ones of smaller population. If the model is valid, it should also become apparent that lateral diffusion between large cities frequently occurred; that innovations occasionally proceeded from smaller to larger cities; and that, owing to the strong "distance-decay" of information, acceptance patterns sometimes were highly concentrated or evidenced a pronounced "neighborhood effect."

In any environment the process of innovation diffusion may be depicted as being comprised of two subprocesses: an information-spread subprocess, in which news of the existence of an innovation is disseminated; and an adoption subprocess, in which the individual or organization that has become aware of an innovation passes through a series of ideal-typical stages leading to innovation acceptance or rejection. It has been established empirically that at each of the stages—usually termed awareness, interest, evaluation, trial, and adoption—the actor is likely to be intentionally or unintentionally exposed to decision-influencing private or public information. It has also been shown that information concerning the experience of previous adopters is often crucial to eventual acceptance.[1]

Thus, in both subprocesses, information circulation is critical. Under any circumstances, spatial biases in the availability of information ought to influence the locational sequence of innovation adoptions. Given the demonstrated magnitude of time-lag and contact-array spatial biases in the availability of information, this should have been particularly true for pretelegraphic interurban diffusion in the United States. It should have been even more true for commercial and industrial innovations in that environment, for most pretelegraphic long-distance information flows came about as a result of the information acquisition and exchange of the economic elite who were conducting or attempting to initiate nonlocal business.

BANKING

The diffusion of banking in the United States after 1781 had two aspects of particular interest here: the very early pattern of acceptance at the national level, and the diffusion sequence in Massachusetts.[2] On the final day of 1781, the Bank of North America was incorporated in Philadelphia, then the largest city in the country. The opening of this first bank was attributable largely to the initiative taken by Alexander Hamilton, who was much influenced by European banking practices.

The second bank to open, in July 1784, was the Bank of New York, in what was then the nation's second largest city. This financial institution had also been promoted by Hamilton. But the banking innovation did not diffuse merely from Philadelphia to New York, for during the campaign for the bank's founding a New York paper reported that the "banks of Venice, Amsterdam, London and Philadelphia are cited as examples."[3] Later in 1784, a third bank was opened independently in Boston, whose population was surpassed only by Philadelphia and New York. By then, support for the organization of a bank was also beginning to accumulate in Baltimore, which ranked behind Charleston as the fifth largest city. The major stimulus there came from Robert Morris, who had also played a pivotal role in establishing Philadelphia's bank. However, difficulties in obtaining financial support prevented Baltimore from obtaining a chartered bank until 1790. Thus, the first four banks in the United States were founded in four of its five leading cities, with the order of acceptance parallelling their population size and with both domestic and foreign interurban information flows influencing adoption decisions.[4] These features are consistent with the large-city rank stability model. In particular, the influence of foreign information is in keeping with the local economic dominance of foreign trade in all four cities. That is, their foreign trade volumes gave them a high probability of being early recipients of new and redundant information from Europe.

The advent of the federally chartered Bank of the United States, and the imitative appearance of state-affiliated banks shortly thereafter, quickly brought the national total to 38 banks by 1800. Although by the turn of the century, banking had spread to Albany, Providence, New Orleans, Charleston, Savannah, and a number of lesser cities in the Northeast, activities still remained highly concentrated in New York, Philadelphia, Boston, and Baltimore, which in that order were then the country's largest cities and its four greatest banking centers. By 1805, each of the four major Northeastern cities had three banks, or innovation adoptions, and six years later their institutions held 64 percent of all American bank capital. Moreover, their banks were playing a key part in circulating economic information among the four cities, for they "were constantly in touch with one another." Gradually the spread of settlement in the West and South, with the accompanying need for agricultural and other credit, helped blanket most of the more densely populated areas of the country with banks. In 1840, when the United States had 901 banks, a pattern of dispersed concentration prevailed. Over 100 banks (adoptions) existed in New York, Philadelphia, Boston, and Baltimore; another 18 were in New Orleans, then the fifth-ranked city; and Cincinnati, Pittsburgh, Louisville, St. Louis, Buffalo, Detroit, and Cleveland all had achieved some prominence as regional banking centers.[5] Thus, as the large-city rank stability model suggests, multiple adoptions were numerous in the largest units of three regional urban subsystems.

The locational sequence of bank diffusion in Massachusetts from 1784 to 1826 reveals that in four of the first five cases, adoption occurred in the largest city previously lacking the innovation. Boston, Salem, Newburyport, and Gloucester were in "the right order" with respect to one another; but Nantucket, scene of the third adoption, was "too early." However, only one of the next thirteen adoptions took place in the largest town currently without a bank, and in one instance (Dedham), adoption occurred when there were thirty larger bank-free communities. Hence, there was not an orderly progression of acceptance downward through the urban-size hierarchy. Admittedly, factors other than spatial biases in the availability of information were probably at work in producing this "disorderly" process. But none of these, including the supposed desire of most bankers to capture a larger market area, seems to provide more than an ancillary explanation.[6]

HORSE-DRAWN OMNIBUSES AND INTRAURBAN STREET RAILWAYS

Until the late 1820s no American city possessed any intraurban transportation services that ran on prescribed routes or fixed schedules. Hackney coaches were available for public hire in some cities, having been first introduced in New York in 1786, but they carried few passengers and had no fixed routes. In 1827 regular service was inaugurated with a twelve-passenger vehicle on New York's Broadway. The next decade saw the initial appearance of both the larger omnibus and the faster horse-drawn street railway.[7]

The omnibus was basically a high-capacity stagecoach, allowing for the movement of twenty or more persons. It first appeared in Paris in 1828 and was taken up in London one year later. The establishment of omnibus service in London "had a direct bearing on the establishment of a similar omnibus service in New York in 1831." This diffusion process in the United States began, not unexpectedly, in the largest city, which was also the place receiving information most quickly and in the largest quantities from both London and Paris. Since the omnibus clearly required a minimum market population, or threshold, one would expect that its diffusion, if any, would follow a hierarchical path. Indeed, the records show that there was a strong relationship between population size-rank and the date of omnibus adoption. However, the sequence of urban acceptance was not a duplicate of the population ranks prevailing at the start of the diffusion process (Table 7.1). More-

Table 7.1. Inception of pretelegraphic omnibus services.

City	Date of inception	Population[a]	1830 size rank
New York	1831	228,390	1
Philadelphia	1831–1833	173,101	2
New Orleans	1831–1832	57,304	5
Boston	1835	91,467	3
Springfield	1839	10,565	34
Newark	1840[b]	17,290	16
Albany	C. 1840	33,721	8
Troy	C. 1840	19,334	15
New Haven	1840–1842	13,699	18
Baltimore	1842	115,661	4

Source: Arthur J. Krim, "The Innovation and Diffusion of the Street Railway in North America," M.A. thesis, University of Chicago, 1967, p. 38; George Rogers Taylor, "American Urban Growth Preceding the Railway Age," *Journal of Economic History* 27 (1967), 311–315; *Census of Population: 1960* I, pt. A, 1-66–1-67.

a. New York population includes Brooklyn. Philadelphia population includes Kensington, Moyamensing, Northern Liberties, Spring Garden, and Southwark. Boston population includes Cambridge, Charlestown, Roxbury, and Dorchester. Populations for these three cities, New Orleans, Springfield, and Baltimore are interpolated from nearest census-date populations.

b. May have been somewhat earlier.

over, second-order cities such as Newark, New Haven, and Springfield had omnibus services before fourth-ranked Baltimore, and there was an apparent "neighborhood effect" in the vicinity of New York, which resulted not only in the "early" entry of Newark and possibly New Haven but also in the 1834 adoption in Brooklyn (which is not shown in Table 7.1 because of that suburb's inclusion in New York).

The horse-drawn intraurban street railway was essentially an omnibus on rails. However, many of its early adoptions were no more than animal-powered railroads operating on the right of way of interurban railroads, for frequently there was strong local opposition to the operation of steam locomotives in densely settled urban areas. Some street railways stopped on downtown streets and then ran on to relatively distant and physically discrete residential areas. The latter was the case with the New York and Harlem Railroad, which began in 1832 and is usually acknowledged to have been the first intraurban street railway in the United States. However, in 1831 the Baltimore and Ohio Railroad, in seeking to quell the public's fear of locomotive boiler explosions, employed horse-drawn railroad cars on the Baltimore streets leading to its terminal. This venture may well have influenced New York decision-makers. If so, the diffusion process began by passing upward from one of the largest units in the national urban system to its most populous unit, or in a manner complying with the large-city rank stability model. Further pretelegraphic diffusion was limited to four adoptions. The failure of the street railway to gain wider acceptance probably was owing in part to its unrefined technology. The need for quick, frequent stops and its other specialized demands required a technology different from that developed for interurban railways.[8] High fares were also likely to inhibit diffusion, just as they curtailed the spread of the omnibus.[9] One other scene of acceptance was New Orleans, where services were begun in 1835, long before they commenced in the larger Boston.[10] Cleveland and Buffalo acquired intraurban street railway lines in 1834, only to have them cease operations during the Panic of 1837. Although both of these Lake Erie ports were much smaller than numerous other places that failed to adopt until the 1850s, events at the two cities conformed to the theoretical framework because of the large volume of commodities funneled through Buffalo to and from

New York, and the numerous business travelers and migrants moving between those same cities via Albany. That is, it may be speculated that the probability of Cleveland or Buffalo receiving early information "hits" from New York was of a high intermediate value owing to their economic interdependence with that city. Furthermore, the fact that Cleveland and Buffalo were the first adopting cities within their regional urban subsystem is also consistent with the large-city rank stability model.

THE CHOLERA EPIDEMIC OF 1832

In the summer and fall of 1832 a cholera epidemic swept the United States. Although not an economic or cultural innovation, cholera could sweep its scythe of death over a large area only through the movement of people.[11] Therefore, it is quite possible that the 1832 spread of the disease contained some features that were representative of other interurban diffusion processes involving the movement of travelers or migrants.

In 1831 the cholera epidemic had begun to spread across Europe from Asia via Russia and Poland. Repeated word of this pestilence caused alarm in New York and elsewhere. As early as September 17, 1831, "Mayor Walter Browne of New York announced that he had made arrangements for a special depot for . . . quarantining all goods and passengers from infected ports in Russia and the Baltic."[12] Significantly, in terms of the requirements of the large-city rank stability model, this action was imitated quickly in Boston, Philadelphia, Charleston, and Baltimore; that is, in the third, second, sixth, and fourth leading cities of the time.

According to a report of the United States Surgeon General's Office published in 1875, the 1832 epidemic entered the country from Canada, first appearing between June 11 and 14 in Plattsburgh and White Hall, New York, and Burlington, Vermont—all three towns having a population below 5,000. The same report indicates that New York recorded its first case on June 26, thereby becoming the fifth city to be infected. But other sources suggest: "There is some confusion within the literature as to whether cholera did or did not first appear in New York City in April 1832. [Or, instead of coming from Europe, it] may simply have traveled down the Hudson River from Canadian sources in the summer [June] of that year." This last is questionable, as Albany is not officially credited with a cholera case until July 3. Regardless of whether the disease first came from Canada or Europe, it "was firmly established in New York by late June, and it apparently moved up the Hudson Valley from that city. It then followed the Erie Canal to western New York State in the wake of the Canadian wave. The movement continued with traffic down the Ohio Canal to the Ohio and Mississippi Rivers, eventually to strike Baton Rouge and New Orleans in November. . . . The third path of cholera movement was outward from New York along the Atlantic Coast. The epidemic apparently spread from New York through New Jersey to Philadelphia and on to Baltimore, Virginia, and eventually Charleston [most likely by a vessel in the New York-Charleston traffic]. It also spread north to Boston and New England."[13]

After analyzing the time sequence of cholera outbreaks along these various paths of supposed movement, Gerald Pyle concluded that "cholera struck larger cities and subsequently showed up in small cities immediately adjacent to the larger cities," and that interurban distance was a more important diffusion determinant than city size.[14] Again, the early appearance in large regional centers and the pronounced neighborhood effects conform to the innovation diffusion component of the large-city rank stability model.

THE SUSPENSION OF SPECIE PAYMENTS DURING THE PANIC OF 1837

In almost every empirical study of interurban diffusion there is the assumption that a high correlation between city size and adoption date reflects a hierarchical diffusion process. The fact that less than perfect correlations infer some nonhierarchical channels of spread is usually ignored. That is, the underlying information circulation paths and influence linkages are only inferred or guessed. The continued dominance of strictly hierarchical diffusion models in the literature doubtlessly largely stems from this lack of empirical work on information circulation and influence linkages. Fortunately, this empirical lacuna can be filled to some degree with many of the particulars of the diffusion of the cessation of specie payments by banks during the Panic of 1837. Some of the key details of this process are available because newspapers reported the public resolutions in favor of suspension made by local businessmen or bankers. These resolutions, and the discussions surrounding them, usually mentioned the sources of diffusion influence.

Domestically, the 1837 monetary crisis had its roots in a widespread overinvestment in internal improvement projects and a speculative mania connected with the occupation and sale of public lands. Overly enthusiastic public works construction had tied up millions of dollars in ventures that frequently would be unproductive for many years. At the same time the federal government had been selling large quantities of land, mainly in the fertile Mississippi and Ohio valleys, at the modest price of $1.25 per acre. Much of this land was gobbled up by speculators, who were catered to by a rapidly multiplying number of unsoundly operated banks that were practically free of restraints: "Each bank could count the notes of other banks as reserves and expand its loans accordingly; with the general result that the more the banks lent the more they mutually augmented their reserves and the more they were able to lend [for speculation]." The financial situation worsened in 1836 when the secretary of the treasury issued the "specie circular," requiring federal land agents to accept only gold or silver payments for public lands. This action "produced absurd disorder," because the government was simultaneously distributing its surplus funds to the states, which required the transferral of much gold and silver from banks holding disproportionately large federal deposits.[15]

Events in England also hastened the panic. Large import surpluses from that country in the 1830s had put both private businesses and individual states in tremendous debt to English investors. Shortly after word of the specie circular was recieved, the Bank of England instructed her Liverpool agent "to reject the paper of certain houses with American interests . . . [which] annihilated the credit of those houses and shook the whole [Anglo-American] trade." In ensuing months the English demand for cotton dwindled, and prices fell sharply. This brought a rash of failures to American merchants, who were unable to acquire enough from their cotton sales to cover their purchasing expenses. By the spring of 1837 money had become scarce, while the

British "had stopped buying, had stopped lending, and expected payment of what was due them."[16]

The interplay of information circulation within the national urban system during the final pre-panic months was also a contributory cause. That is, the interurban flow of both accurate information and unfounded rumors helped create the atmosphere which precipitated the Panic of 1837. In March, three of New York's cotton firms failed for over $9.0 million immediately after the city had received news of the collapse of three New Orleans firms for $2.5 million. In April a Charleston resident wrote to a New Yorker: 'The blighting effects of the present state of affairs in your city have affected this place, and business is completely at a stand."[17] Throughout late April and early May the New Orleans press was filled with dismal business and money market forecasts as well as stories of failures in New York, Boston, and Providence.[18] Rumors coursed back and forth between New Orleans and Mobile to the effect that the suspension of specie payments was imminent.[19] In Philadelphia it was reported: "The *Cleveland Herald* contradicts the rumor that the Cleveland bank, the Commercial bank of Lake Erie, [and] Canton and Massillon banks, had suspended specie payments for sixty days."[20] Similar accounts of the spread of information from small cities to large ones and vice versa abound in the April and May 1837 newspapers of numerous other urban centers.

When the Panic struck, banks did not close their doors to every manner of business but merely refused to convert deposits and banknotes into coin. Some banks suspended payments because they lacked the specie to cover local demands. Others wished to prevent the depletion of reserves by nonlocals attempting to cash paper money that had been issued elsewhere. Whatever the facts, the latter reason was almost always given publicly. In Baltimore, bankers spoke of "their own protection and the interests of the whole community."[21] In Charleston it was a matter of "self-defence," a fear that their vaults would be "speedily drained of every dollar."[22] Philadelphia financiers contended that "arrangements are now making to drain the specie from the vaults of our banks."[23] Similar alibis were paraded out by Richmond and Hartford bankers.[24]

New York banks suspended specie payment on May 10, 1837, and the stoppage of payments by banks in the rest of the country over the next few weeks is usually depicted as having spread from that place.[25] In great measure this was true, for in Providence, Boston, Albany, Rochester, Detroit, and a host of smaller cities, word of specie-payment suspension in New York resulted in almost immediate local imitation (Maps 7.1–7.3).[26] However, the process was much more complicated, with numerous situations where information and diffusion influence flowed from smaller to larger cities, or from one large city to another.

The decision of New York bankers did not occur in a vacuum. The suspension of specie payments had been anticipated locally "for a number of weeks" when word was published on May 8 that "the operation of all the banks of Buffalo will by this time have been suspended by injunction . . . on the ground of alleged violations of charter by each of them." On that same day the Dry Dock Bank of New York was forced to cease operations after depositors had made a run on its specie reserves.[27] New York's banking community itself appears to have been influenced by specie-suspension rumors from the less populous Baltimore, for on May 9 a Baltimore newspaper expressly contradicted "the report mentioned in some of the New York papers that the Banks of Baltimore intended to suspend payments in specie."[28]

Furthermore, New York's action was taken several days after gold and silver payments had been brought to a halt in two much smaller places and on the same day that such a decision was reached independently in a much smaller city. On May 4 specie payments were suspended by banks in Natchez, Mississippi, which had a population in 1840 of 3,612.[29] Two days later the Union Bank in Tallahassee, Florida, with an 1840 population of under 2,500, stopped metallic payments.[30] On May 10 the Alabama State Bank at Montgomery, whose population in 1840 was 2,179, also "refused to pay specie for its bills."[31] All three Southern towns were probably hard hit by falling cotton prices. Moreover, banking interests in all three places shared the misery of relative informational isolation from the remainder of the country. Given the uncertainty of the economic situation, businessmen in these informational backwaters may have been driven to this extreme decision so early because their awareness of their own ignorance of developments elsewhere either made the environment seem especially threatening or

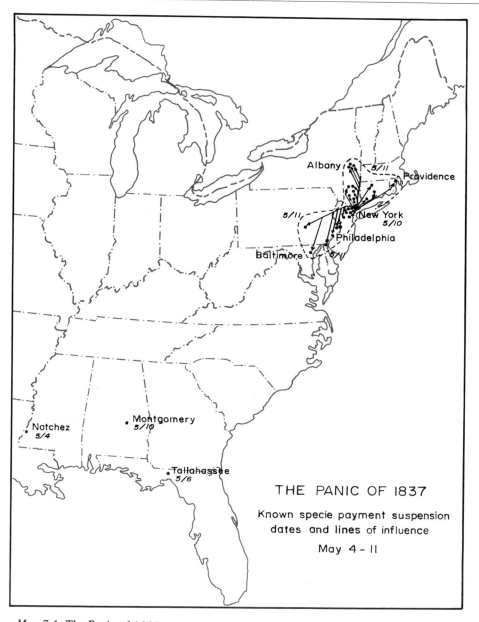

Map 7.1. The Panic of 1837: known specie payment suspension dates and lines of influence, May 4–11. Here and in Maps 7.2. and 7.3., lines of influence do not necessarily represent actual routes of information circulation.

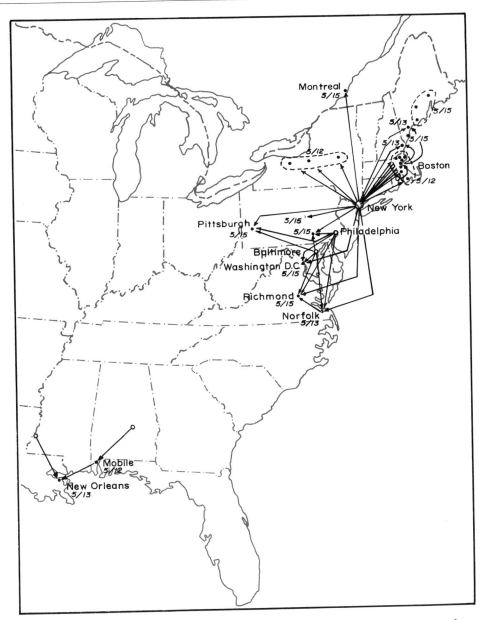

Map 7.2. The Panic of 1837: known specie payment suspension dates and lines of influence, May 12–15. Here and in Map 7.3., open dots refer to cities with earlier suspensions that influenced other urban centers during this period.

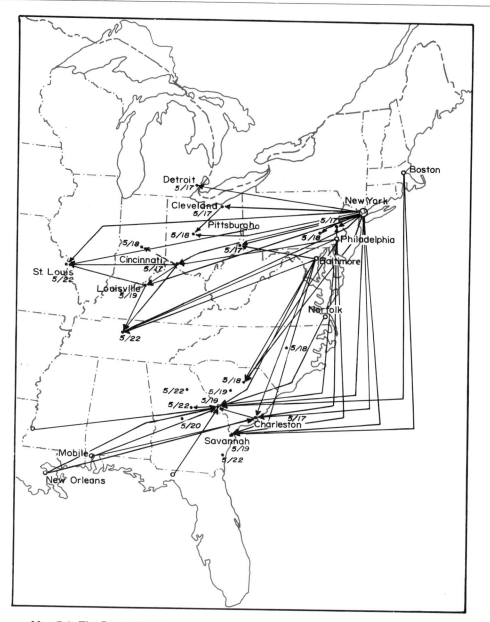

Map 7.3. The Panic of 1837: known specie payment suspension dates and lines of influence, May 16–22.

put them in a state of high stress.[32] In Natchez, where cotton price news from New York and Liverpool was usually quite dated, the pressure probably was brought to a head when "the Government . . . made a draft of $130,000 in specie upon the Agricultural Bank in that city."[33]

Once specie payment suspension was a fact in New York, a torrent of such suspensions swept the Northeast. Within a day, gold and silver payments were cut off in the major cities of New Jersey and Connecticut, in the Hudson Valley ports, in Providence, in scattered middle-sized towns of southeastern Pennsylvania and Delaware,[34] and in Philadelphia and Baltimore (Map 7.1). With the major exceptions of Philadelphia and Baltimore, the sole cause of this pronounced neighborhood effect was the receipt of news regarding New York suspensions. The bankers of Philadelphia acted both on false reports that the banks of the somewhat smaller city of Baltimore had ceased specie payments and on accurate accounts from New York.[35] Rumors from Cleveland and lesser Ohio cities may also have had an impact. Ironically, Baltimore, which had unwittingly influenced both New York and Philadelphia, did not reach a decision until receiving information of specie-payment suspensions in those two centers.[36]

During the next four days (May 12–15) the panic spread over a wider area and developed more intricate patterns of influence (Map 7.2). The neighborhood effect originating in New York encompassed Boston, Lynn, Lowell, New Bedford, and lesser Massachusetts cities on May 12.[37] In Boston, some influence was also apparently exerted by the smaller Providence and perhaps even by less important Connecticut centers.[38] New York-inspired suspensions occurred along the route of the Erie Canal, in Montreal, and in Pennsylvania.[39] New York and Boston jointly influenced events in New Hampshire and Maine.[40] New York, Philadelphia, and Baltimore together helped precipitate specie payment suspension in Pittsburgh, which was the first city in the Ohio and Upper Mississippi valley subsystem to join the diffusion process.[41] New York, Philadelphia, and Baltimore actions also had an impact in Washington, D.C., Norfolk, and Richmond, although no decision was reached in Richmond, with an 1840 population of 20,153, until it was known that sister banks had followed suit in Norfolk, with an 1840 population of 10,920.[42] In the Deep South, specie payment suspensions soon moved up to the largest cities. Banks in Mobile took action on May 12 after hearing of suspensions in the more diminutive Montgomery.[43] Events in the considerably smaller Natchez, as well as in Mobile, had a clear impact on the May 13 stoppage of coin payments in New Orleans.[44]

In the course of the subsequent week the Panic reached most of the remaining densely settled areas of the country (Map 7.3). Suspensions entered the Lake Erie urban subsystem at Cleveland and Detroit.[45] The influence of New York, Philadelphia, and Baltimore was felt west of the Alleghenies at such places as Wheeling and Nashville,[46] as well as at Cincinnati, Louisville, and St. Louis.[47] There was some mutual influence among the last three cities and Pittsburgh as well; that is, among the largest cities of the Ohio and Upper Mississippi valley urban subsystem.[48] Entire state bank systems simultaneously ceased paying gold and silver in many states, including North Carolina and Indiana (represented in Map 7.3 by single dots at Raleigh and Indianapolis).[49] At Savannah, Augusta,[50] and other points in the South the influence exerted by New York, Philadelphia, and Baltimore was compounded by information from Boston. The news of earlier Southern suspensions had by then drifted to Georgia and South Carolina; as a result, the bankers of Charleston were influenced by knowledge acquired from the smaller Mobile,[51] just as the bankers of Augusta were persuaded to specie payment cessation in part by word from the less populous centers of Natchez and Tallahassee.[52]

Even in a diffusion process so widespread as the Panic of 1837, evidence of innovation resistance is found frequently. For example, the bank in Gettysburg at first offered fierce resistance to the thought of suspending and held out until May 27 before doing so.[53] In other diffusion processes involving less pressing situations, economic, psychological, or political resistance to a specific economic innovation often resulted in no local adoption whatsoever.

It is thus clear that the spread of specie payment suspensions had characteristics that validate the diffusion component of the large-city rank stability model, including nonhierarchical as well as hierarchical acceptance sequences, early acceptance by the leading cities of the national urban system, large-city first acceptances within the two western urban subsystems, and a strongly expressed neighborhood effect.

Only the speed with which the panic spread may be regarded as unrepresentative of pretelegraphic interurban diffusion processes in general.

DAILY NEWSPAPERS AND THE PENNY PRESS

Although newspapers had been published in colonial cities since 1704, not until 1784 did the first successful daily newspaper appear in Philadelphia, then the largest city in the country.[54] The diffusion process of the next sixteen years gave superficial indications of being dominated by a spread downward through the highest echelons of the urban hierarchy. In 1785, dailies appeared in New York and Charleston, at the time the nation's second and fourth cities respectively. By 1790 there were four daily newspapers in Philadelphia, three in New York, and one in Charleston. In 1787 a newspaper had also been unsuccessfully started in fifth-ranked Baltimore. At the turn of the century there were six dailies (adoptions) in Philadelphia, five in New York, three each in Charleston and Baltimore, and five or six in and around the new capital, Washington, D.C. Thus, in accord with the probabilistic aspect of the model, multiple acceptances occurred in some large cities before initial adoptions occurred in lesser places. During the 1790–1800 interval, short-lived dailies had operated in Boston (third-ranked in 1790) and Richmond (sixteenth-ranked in 1790), as well as in each of the cities where successful publications still survived.[55]

It is not easy to establish how many late eighteenth-century daily newspapers were started as the result of information and influence from Philadelphia, and how many as the result of something other than direct hierarchical diffusion from Philadelphia. However, it is known that one paper moved from Philadelphia to Washington, D.C., and that at least two papers were diffused because of migration from one large place to an even larger place—from New York to Philadelphia, and from Richmond to Charleston.[56] Moreover, the innovation was passed in one way or another between large centers, each of which (except Washington, D.C.) presumably dominated its own hinterland hierarchically, with no adoptions occurring in subservient smaller centers where newspapers appearing less frequently were already published. Admittedly, there might have been a minimum market or threshold requirement. However, the circulation necessary to sustain a daily with the limited technology available in 1790–1800 was quite small, perhaps no more than 400. New York's three dailies had an estimated combined circulation of 1,200 per day in 1790, and the average circulation per issue of all American dailies in 1810 is estimated to have been no more than 550.[57] Publication on such a small scale could prove profitable since newspaper production was normally combined with several other printing functions.

As of 1828, daily newspapers sold for between 6 and 12.5 cents per copy, which were very high prices given the wage levels of approximately $1.00 per day for urban laborers. The largest daily in the country, the *New York Courier and Enquirer*, reached a circulation of 4,500 in 1833. Prior to that, broader circulation and lower prices were hampered by expensive newsprint and hand-powered production equipment. However, between 1828 and 1832, Fourdrinier paper-making machines slashed newsprint costs, and Napier-type, steam-powered presses, which were first adopted in New York, then in Philadelphia, accelerated production time. The Napier press was capable of delivering 3,000 papers per hour, which made possible a cheaper form of journalism.[58]

The first successful one-cent paper was established in September 1833 in New York, then the most populous city by a wide margin, when Benjamin Day founded the *New York Sun*. Nonetheless, diffusion did not really start at the top of the urban hierarchy, for Day's decision was reached with the apparent knowledge of a short 1830 experiment with penny journalism in second-ranked Philadelphia, as well as two abortive efforts during August 1833 in third-ranked Boston. Furthermore, the Boston attempts to market penny papers had been encouraged by the local publication of relatively cheap dailies beginning in 1830, which in turn were influenced by the 1829 appearance of a daily that charged $4 per annual subscription in Portland, Maine, a city having an 1830 population of 12,598.[59]

The *New York Sun* quickly gained a wider audience by breaking "sharply with the traditional American news concept" and printing "whatever was interesting and readable regardless of its wide significance or recognized importance." The paper's circulation leaped to 10,000 by November 1834. This increase induced a number of local imitators of varying fortune to spring up—two in 1834, at least one in 1835, and at least a dozen for the entire 1834–1837 period.[60] Thus, here too manifold duplication occurred in a large center long before initial acceptances appeared in most other places.

Between 1835 and 1837, viable penny papers were begun in Philadelphia, Boston, and fourth-ranked Baltimore in an order consistent both with the large-city rank stability model and with strictly hierarchical diffusion models. Philadelphia's first one-cent dailies appeared in 1835 and 1836. In the later year the *Philadelphia Public Ledger* was started by acquaintances of Benjamin Day who had moved from New York. Baltimore joined the penny press ranks in 1837 when the *Baltimore Sun* was established by the same trio that had founded the *Philadelphia Public Ledger*.[61]

Not untypically, the diffusion of one economic innovation soon generated the start of an interdependent diffusion process. The demand for the more successful penny papers shortly outstripped their production capacity. Eighteen months after its inception, for example, the *Philadelphia Public Ledger* claimed a daily circulation of 20,000. In 1835 the *New York Sun* adopted a newly invented steam press, which increased its printing capacity to 22,000 copies per eight-hour production period.[62] The subsequent spread of the steam press within the urban system must have been largely steered by the existing locational pattern of the penny press.

STEAM ENGINES

Because of the wide variety of uses to which steam engines were put, their spread involved several diffusion processes rather than one. It is possible to reconstruct a few of the details of three of these processes, namely, steamboat diffusion, the diffusion of industrially employed steam engines, and the diffusion of steam-engine production itself.

John Fitch designed a steam-propelled boat as early as 1785. Two experimental versions were built at Philadelphia in 1787 and 1788, and in 1790 a third of Fitch's steamboats offered what was then the nation's largest city regular service to Trenton and occasional Sunday excursions to Wilmington and Chester. But the boat was "laid up in the fall and never used afterwards, as operations were conducted at a loss.'' When the diffusion process began in earnest, it at first exhibited hierarchical features. New York had just surpassed Philadelphia in population when Fulton began his successful steamboat ventures at New York in 1807. Two years later steamboat operations were established more permanently in Philadelphia by a competitor of Fulton's, who had been barred from sailing between New Jersey towns and New York because of the traffic monopoly granted to Fulton. Baltimore, the third-ranking city in the United States as of 1810, became fourth in line as a base of steamboat sailings in 1813 when a New York vessel was brought there to operate in the neighborhood. By this date New York had nine steam-powered ferries and boats, while Philadelphia had a total of six. Fourth-ranked Boston's first experience with the steamboat did not occur until 1817, with a run between that city and Salem, but it lasted only a short time. Long before the Boston misadventure, the sequence in which steamboat service took hold nationally had acquired nonhierarchical qualities. New Orleans, sixth ranked in 1810, had a steamboat line to Natchez by 1812; and Pittsburgh, ranked only twenty-eighth in 1810, had experienced several steamboat efforts by 1814. In the years immediately after 1817, relatively small Western cities, such as Cincinnati, Louisville, St. Louis, Buffalo, and Detroit, became the foci of steamboat firms. Diffusion to and within the two Western urban subsystems, however, was in accord with the large-city rank stability model, for regionally large towns were the first to adopt and they soon influenced one another.[63]

The diffusion of steam engines for manufacturing purposes began in New York in 1803 when a steam-powered sawmill was introduced. This event was given newspaper publicity in Philadelphia, where a small establishment soon began to utilize an engine for grinding plaster of paris. In 1803 an industrially employed steam engine also began operating in fourth-ranked Boston.[64] The precise sequence of ensuing adoptions is not readily identified. However, it is apparent that a hierarchical pattern did not prevail. Pittsburgh probably became the next city to have a steam engine operating in a local industrial facility. By 1809 at least one of Pittsburgh's flour mills had turned to steam, and within a few years the city had become a major center of steam-driven industry, having six steam-powered factories in 1815 and eight in 1816. By 1812 Oliver Evans of Philadelphia had managed to sell high-pressure wood-burning engines in such widespread places as Lexington, Kentucky, Marietta, Ohio, Middletown, Connecticut, Natchez, Mississippi, Manchacks, Louisiana, and a small settlement in Florida, as well as in Philadelphia and Pittsburgh. Cincinnati also joined the list of cities with steam-powered manufacturing in 1812.[65]

Because of notorious census deficiencies, nothing conclusive is known of the subsequent diffusion of steam engines for manufacturing purposes until 1838, when the secretary of the treasury completed a national survey of all steam engines. His report, which was not without data shortcomings, asserted that 1,860 generally very small engines averaging less than 20 horsepower were then "used in manufactories of various kinds."[66] Despite the report's omission of details for New York State, it shows that repeated adoptions occurred with the greatest frequency in and around the major cities of the urban subsystems of the Northeast and the Ohio and Upper Mississippi valleys. If it is assumed that only a small fraction of the plants had more than one engine, then about 25 percent of the nation's industrial establishments with steam engines were located in four places: 165 in Philadelphia and its physically integrated manufacturing suburbs, 87 in Pittsburgh, 48 in Boston plus at least as many in nearby industrial towns, and 45 in Baltimore.[67] The neighborhood effects around Philadelphia and Pittsburgh[68] were probably encouraged by comparatively cheap coal supplies.[69] In addition, by 1838 steam-engine usage in some manufacturing categories was far more extensive than in others.[70] Hence, the diffusion of industrial steam engines really ought to be considered as several quasi-independent processes.

Although adoption-sequence specifics are almost totally lacking, it is unlikely that the diffusion of steam-engine production was completely divorced from the diffusion of steam engines for manufacturing and steamboat purposes. In fact, it is most probable that there was considerable feedback between these processes. Wherever steam engines were produced, there should have been relatively large amounts of adoption-encouraging information available to manufacturers. Wherever steam engines and their parts were in demand, foundries and other unspecialized establishments should have been encouraged to take up their production. Significantly, by 1808 the first regular steam-engine production in the United States had been undertaken in Philadelphia and Pittsburgh, with individual engines having been built in Philadelphia as early as 1801.[71] Both cities soon established themselves as leading steam-engine manufacturing centers. The number of production units in Pittsburgh, for example, grew steadily from three in 1815, to six in 1825, and ten in 1839.[72] By 1817 steam engines also were being turned out in Cincinnati, Louisville, New York, Baltimore, and other Eastern cities. Cincinnati acquired special stature as a producer, its 1830 output apparently outstripping that of Pittsburgh.[73] According to one analysis of the 1838 report on steam engines, steam-engine production was "a small-scale business carried on for a predominantly local market." In that year the number of steam-engine makers who had produced more than a single engine was only 119; another 131 unspecialized multiproduct manufacturers had built only one engine each.[74] In short, the pattern of diffusion acceptance of steam-engine production, as well as consumption, was most intense around the leading cities of the Northeast and the Ohio Valley, and thereby conforms with the large-city rank stability model.

OTHER INTERURBAN DIFFUSION PROCESSES

The initial adoption of the steam engine for manufacturing purposes in New York was representative of what happened with most economic innovations of European origin. Especially after 1800, the first acceptance usually occurred in New York. When it did not, Philadelphia, Boston, and Baltimore were the most frequent sites of first adoption. One survey of late eighteenth and early nineteenth century manufacturing in the nation concluded that the four major Northeastern ports "were the centers for the introduction and diffusion of new industries." Also, auctions in the leading Northeastern ports, most particularly those in New York, "served to introduce new goods" and "assisted in forming new tastes on the part of the consumer."[75] The repeated start of interurban diffusion processes in New York, Philadelphia, Boston, or Baltimore was in keeping both with New York's role in the receipt and dissemination of foreign information, and with the foreign trade volumes of all four cities. The pattern of immigrant entrances to the country also contributed to this repetitive phenomenon.

Before the opening of the National Road and the Erie Canal, the Appalachians severely limited direct trade and information exchange between the Northeast and the West; that is, they acted as a physical barrier, often slowing down the westward interurban diffusion of innovations already prevailing in New York, Philadelphia, and lesser Northeastern cities. However, both before and after the Appalachians were opened up to travel, most of the economic innovations passing between Pittsburgh, Cincinnati, Louisville, and St. Louis came from one of the four principal cities of the Northeast. Examples like the Panic of 1837 are legion (Maps 7.2 and 7.3). The recessed business conditions immediately following the War of 1812 were first felt in the leading Atlantic ports, from which they spread westward via Pittsburgh. Moreover, Pittsburgh, Cincinnati, Louisville, and St. Louis businessmen, "yearly visitors in the East, brought marketing techniques and promotion from there." This repeated diffusion from the largest cities in one urban subsystem to the largest units of another subsystem bears out a national-level interpretation of the large-city rank stability model. The influence of Philadelphia, by means of its links with Pittsburgh, was particularly great in the realm of urban planning and administration. For instance, the dominant units of the Ohio and Upper Mississippi urban subsystem aped Philadelphia's street plan, street widths, landings, location of market houses, techniques for fire fighting and police protection, street lighting, and water works. Occasionally, innovations came directly from sources other than the Northeastern metropolises. The architecture of St. Louis, for example, was influenced greatly by that of New Orleans. However, given the commerce between these two Mississippi River ports, this exception fits perfectly within the diffusion framework of the large-city rank stability model.[76]

Neighborhood effects frequently were sharply outlined in the diffusion of "footloose" manufactures. The economic reasons are simple. By definition, footloose manufactures were insensitive to transport costs, so that individual establishments could serve extensive nonlocal as well as local markets and, theoretically, could locate as profitably in one city as in another. Thus, once a footloose industry had begun to diffuse, the number of imitations of observed success could be increased indefinitely in the initial adoption center, subject only to the accrual of inordinate diseconomies of concentration, or exhaustion of the market. The concentration of costume and other jewelry production in Providence was a case in point. Although various silver- and gold-plating activities existed in Providence prior to 1800, only after that date did local entrepreneurs turn to the production of jewelry in relatively large quantities. "In 1805 there were four firms making jewelry in that city, and five years later the number of workmen employed . . . was 100." By 1827, when the city shared dominance of the national market with New York, Newark, and Philadelphia, Providence had 19 "extensive" producers who gave "constant employment" to over 300 persons; and within another nine years the city's directory listed 155 jewelers, at which time employment in the industry may have neared 1,000.[77] This concentration, like that in so many other footloose industries, provided various agglomeration economies which encouraged additional local adoptions and made profitable competition from most other places difficult. Other extreme neighborhood effects in the diffusion of footloose industries were centered at large cities—such as the production of saws in Philadelphia and of printing equipment in New York—at intermediate-sized cities—such as the manufacture of edge tools in Hartford—and in smaller cities—such as the brass products industry in and near Waterbury, Connecticut.[78] When these concentrations occurred at places with only a moderate or small probability of developing such agglomerations, the medium- and smaller-cized cities in question could make relatively rapid progress through the middle or lower ranks of their regional urban subsystem.

THE LOCATIONAL PATTERN OF INVENTIONS

Despite many acknowledged weaknesses, patent data provide perhaps the most telling evidence against any strictly hierarchical interpretation of pretelegraphic interurban innovation diffusion.[79] United States government patent records for 1790–1793 and 1805–1840 reveal that only a fraction of inventive activity for any single date or subperiod transpired in the largest urban unit (Tables 7.2–7.6). The same was doubtless true for 1794–1804, although patent-grant sources did not adequately specify the residential location of inventors. In 1831, for example, 573 patents were issued to domestic residents, of which 67 went to New York, 38 to Philadelphia, 28 to Boston, 26 to Baltimore, and the remaining 414 to lesser places.[80] During the arbitrarily delimited subperiods of 1805–1810, 1811–1820, 1821–1830, and 1831–1840, although New York dominated the country's inventions, in no case did its inventors secure more than 13.3 percent of the total number of patents granted (Tables 7.3–7.6). Only during the early 1790s, when Philadelphia was first ranked and the number of patents involved was extremely small, did as much as a third of the country's registered inventive activity fall to its largest city (Table 7.2). In that particular instance the percentage was probably so high because the seeking of patent grants was itself an innovation still in its earliest phases of diffusion, not having spread extensively from its point of governmental

Table 7.2. Patent data for selected major United States cities, 1790–1793.

Location	Patents granted, 1790–1793	Percentage of U.S. population, 1790 (A)	Percentage of patents granted, 1790–1793 (B)	Location quotient B/A
United States	66[a]	100.00	100.00	1.0
Philadelphia	22	1.12[b]	33.33	29.8
New York	8	.84	12.12	14.4
Boston	4	.47	6.06	12.9
Baltimore	2	.34	3.03	8.9
Albany	2	.09	3.03	33.7
Richmond	1	.10	1.52	15.2

Source: Henry L. Ellsworth, A Digest of Patents, Issued by the United States, from 1790 to January 1, 1839 (Washington, D.C., 1840); U.S. House, Letter from the Secretary of State Transmitting A List of All Patents Granted by the United States, Document No. 50, 21st Cong., 2nd sess., 1831; Taylor, "American Urban Growth," pp. 311–315; Census of Population: 1960; Historical Statistics, pp. 8, 608.
a. Excluding one 1792 patent granted to a foreign resident.
b. Philadelphia population includes Southwark and Northern Liberties.

origin in Philadelphia, the nation's capital. In fact, 15 of the first 36 grants issued went to Philadelphians.

The locational pattern of inventive activity strongly suggests that, at least in the early stages of interurban diffusion processes, innovations frequently spread from smaller to larger places and between large cities of roughly the same size. This conclusion assumes that among the subset of inventions which actually were practically implemented, and thereby became innovations, the great bulk were first put to such use in the city of invention. This means that for any year or subperiod between 1805 and 1840, little more than 10-13 percent of all technological innovations could have been first accepted in New York. Therefore, in only 10-13 percent of the cases could the entire interurban diffusion sequence have been in full accord with a hierarchical diffusion model based solely on Christaller's central place theory. In the other cases where inventions of non-

Table 7.3. Patent data for selected major United States cities, 1805-1810.

Location	Patents granted, 1805-1810	Percentage of U.S. population, 1810 (A)	Percentage of patents granted, 1805-1810 (B)	Location quotient B/A
United States	580	100.00	100.00	1.0
New York	77	1.39[a]	13.28	9.6
Philadelphia	56	1.21[b]	9.66	8.0
Baltimore	36	.64	6.21	9.7
Boston	51	.53[c]	8.79	16.6
Albany	8	.15	1.38	9.2
Providence	5	.14	.86	6.1
Pittsburgh	1	.07	.17	2.4
Louisville	2	.02	.34	17.0
Charleston	6	.34	1.03	3.0
New Orleans	1	.24	.34	1.4
Richmond	4	.13	.69	5.3

Source: See Table 7.2.
a. New York population includes Brooklyn.
b. Philadelphia population includes Southwark and Northern Liberties.
c. Boston population includes Charlestown.

local origin were adopted in New York, it would have been necessary for them either to have "jumped" from small cities or villages, or to have spread from another major center of lesser population. Both of these alternatives would be expected within the framework of the large-city rank stability model. The assumption that the city of invention and the city of initial implementation were usually identical is supported by the fact that almost all pretelegraphic invention was the product of individual rather than corporate or institutionalized efforts. Individuals usually had neither the surplus capital nor the time necessary for gathering information on alternative nonlocal implementation

Table 7.4. Patent data for selected major United States cities, 1811–1820.

Location	Patents granted, 1811–1820	Percentage of U.S. population, 1820 (A)	Percentage of patents granted, 1811–1820 (B)	Location quotient B/A
United States	1,928[a]	100.00	100.00	1.0
New York	208	1.36[b]	10.79	7.9
Philadelphia	176	1.13[c]	9.13	8.1
Baltimore	78	.65	4.05	6.2
Boston	114	.56[d]	5.91	10.6
Albany	24	.13	1.24	9.5
Providence	19	.12	.99	8.3
Cincinnati	5	.10	.26	2.6
Pittsburgh	6	.08	.31	3.9
Detroit	1	.01	.05	5.0
New Orleans	4	.28	.21	.8
Charleston	7	.26	.36	1.4
Richmond	10	.13	.52	4.0
Norfolk	3	.09	.16	1.8
Savannah	1	.08	.05	.6

Source: See Table 7.2.
a. Not including two patents granted to foreign residents.
b. New York population includes Brooklyn.
c. Philadelphia population includes Kensington, Spring Garden, Southwark, and Northern Liberties.
d. Boston population includes Charlestown and Roxbury.

sites. When they did, they were still most likely to decide to implement in their city of residence, where they were best able to cope with the manifold uncertainties and risks normally associated with industrial innovations.[81]

Although the locational pattern of innovation origins was far more dispersed than hierarchical diffusion theory permits, the comparatively

Table 7.5. Patent data for selected major United States cities, 1821–1830.

Location	Patents granted, 1821–1830	Percentage of U.S. population, 1830 (A)	Percentage of patents granted, 1821–1830 (B)	Location quotient B/A
United States	3,069[a]	100.00	100.00	1.0
New York	384	1.67[b]	12.51	7.5
Philadelphia	175	1.25[c]	5.70	4.6
Boston	115	.67[d]	3.75	5.6
Baltimore	96	.63	3.13	5.0
Albany	23	.19	.75	4.0
Providence	55	.13	1.79	13.8
Cincinnati	18	.19	.59	3.1
Pittsburgh	17	.10	.55	5.5
Louisville	7	.08	.23	2.9
Buffalo	3	.07	.10	1.4
Detroit	2	.02	.07	3.5
Cleveland	1	.01	.03	3.0
New Orleans	6	.36	.20	.6
Charleston	14	.24	.46	1.9
Richmond	15	.12	.49	4.1
Norfolk	12	.08	.39	4.9
Savannah	1	.06	.03	.5
Mobile	1	.02	.03	1.5

Source: See Table 7.2; U.S. House, *Letter from the Secretary of State Transmitting a List of Patents Granted for Useful Inventions During the Year 1830*, Document No. 49, 21st Cong., 2nd sess., 1831.

a. Excluding 17 patents granted to foreign residents.

b. New York population includes Brooklyn.

c. Philadelphia population includes Kensington, Moyamensing, Northern Liberties, Spring Garden, and Southwark.

d. Boston population includes Cambridge, Charlestown, Roxbury, and Dorchester.

Table 7.6. Patent data for selected major United States cities, 1831–1840.

Location	Patents granted, 1831–1840	Percentage of U.S. population, 1840 (A)	Percentage of patents granted, 1831–1840 (B)	Location quotient B/A
United States	5,519[a]	100.00	100.00	1.0
New York	595	2.04[b]	10.78	5.3
Philadelphia	301	1.29[c]	5.45	4.2
Boston	273	.70[d]	4.95	7.1
Baltimore	168	.60	3.04	5.1
Albany	35	.20	.63	3.2
Providence	29	.17	.53	3.1
Cincinnati	41	.27	.74	2.7
Louisville	11	.12	.20	1.7
Pittsburgh	36	.12	.65	5.4
St. Louis	6	.10	.11	1.1
Buffalo	16	.11	.29	2.6
Detroit	4	.05	.07	1.4
Cleveland	3	.04	.05	1.3
New Orleans	13	.60	.24	.4
Charleston	12	.17	.22	1.3
Richmond	23	.12	.42	3.5
Mobile	2	.07	.04	.6
Savannah	5	.07	.09	1.3
Norfolk	14	.06	.25	4.2

Source: See Table 7.2; U.S. Senate, Report from the Commissioner of Patents Showing the Operations of His Office During the Year 1839, Document No. 111, 26th Cong., 1st sess., 1840; U.S. Senate, Report from the Commissioner of Patents Showing the Operations of the Patent Office During the Year 1840, Document No. 152, 26th Cong., 2nd sess., 1841.
a. Excluding 61 patents granted to foreign residents.
b. New York population includes Brooklyn.
c. Philadelphia population includes Kensington, Moyamensing, Northern Liberties, Spring Garden, and Southwark.
d. Boston population includes Cambridge, Charlestown, Roxbury, and Dorchester.

small number of patent grants involved was nevertheless extremely concentrated. (The total of 11,918 patents issued to residents during the entire 1790–1840 period was fewer than have been issued in any single year since 1875.)[82] In every subperiod between 1805 and 1840, New York, Philadelphia, Boston, and Baltimore together accounted for at least 24.3 percent, and as much as 38.0 percent, of all registered inventions, while at no time did they represent more than 4.6 percent of the nation's population (Tables 7.3–7.6). In other words, these four cities were at various times responsible for anywhere from 4.2 to 16.6 times as much inventive activity as would be expected from their populations. (The nation's entire population, rather than just its urban population, is used as a reduction base, since so much manufacturing of this period was of the rural household variety). Two other important Northeastern cities, Albany and Providence, repeatedly accounted for a percentage of the total patents granted that was several times greater than their percentage of the national population. After the War of 1812, Cincinnati and Pittsburgh became disproportionately important as invention centers;[83] and in a less pronounced way this became so for Louisville, Buffalo, Detroit, and Cleveland during the 1820s and 1830s. Richmond, the most industrialized Southern city, and Norfolk also had more inventive activity than their populations would indicate; but between 1811 and 1840 the Cotton Ports frequently had fewer patent grants than their populations would lead one to anticipate. The low levels of inventive activity in New Orleans, Savannah, Mobile, and Charleston were probably owing in large part to the agricultural orientation of their socially and economically elite groups, to negative local attitudes toward manufacturing, to comparatively strict class lines and limited social mobility, and to the large populations of uneducated blacks in these cities.

In general, then, inventive activity was concentrated in the largest and most rapidly growing units in the American urban system. In fact, data for thirty-eight important cities shows a consistently high correlation between the number of patents granted to a place and its absolute population growth: for the period 1810–1820, $r = .9241$ ($R^2 = 85.39\%$); for the period 1820–1830, $r = .8447$ ($R^2 = 71.36\%$); and for the period 1830–1840, $r = .8974$ ($R^2 = 80.54\%$).[84] This large-city concentration was recognized by contemporaries. Since perception of demand, problem awareness, and the interindustry transferability of problem solutions are usually viewed as the major sources of inventive activity, and since all three variables are information linked, this pattern of large-city concentration is consistent with the extreme spatial biases in information availability characteristic of pretelegraphic times.[85]

The variable of problem awareness presumably underlies the concentration in time and space of very specialized types of patent grants, such as patents for cotton textile machinery in Providence during the late 1820s, patents related to tobacco processing in Richmond during the 1820s and 1830s, patents for stoves and other heating equipment in Philadelphia during the first two decades of the nineteenth century, printing-trade patents in New York during the 1830s, and patents limited to one or two industries in innumerable medium-sized cities and small towns of New England.[86] Moreover, since some activities are more problem-prone than others, it is quite likely that some of the city-to-city variation in inventive activity evident from Tables 7.3–7.6 is attributable to city-to-city variations in industrial composition.

IMMIGRATION AND FOREIGN TRAVEL

Immigrants and travelers who have been abroad for a lengthy period of time sometimes bear ideas and experiences that result in the national introduction of innovations. Owing to less uncertainty under certain circumstances, immigrants may find it easier than others to adopt an innovation. These circumstances might include either their own previous adoption in another setting, or their observation of a successful adoption by others before departure. As a result, international migration is frequently pivotal to the international diffusion of technological and other economic innovations, especially when numbers of potential innovators share the same occupation or geographic origin and settle at a common destination.[87] (Settlement at a common destination heightens the probability of face-to-face information exchange and the spread of uncertainty-reducing influence among potential innovators.) However, only a small minority of immigrants and foreign travelers disembarking at pretelegraphic ports in the United States were capable of initiating interurban innovation diffusion processes. Many arrivals were merely in transit, proceeding to other cities, to public works projects, or most commonly, to rural destinations.[88] Immigrants who did remain at their port of disembarkation often adhered to the values of a traditional society and therefore were not innovation prone. Even when they did possess innovation-relevant information, they were frequently inhibited from taking action by language and social barriers.[89]

Whatever the relative extent to which interurban innovation diffusion processes were set in motion by immigrants and foreign travelers, the phenomenon ought to have been most common in absolute terms after the War of 1812. Estimates for the 1790–1812 period place the annual average of immigrant arrivals between 4,000 and 6,000. The surge of immigration following the end of the war resulted in at least 22,240 passengers arriving from foreign ports in 1817 (Table 7.7).[90]

From 1817 on, if not earlier, New York dominated the immigrant and foreign traveler traffic.[91] Its total passenger arrivals fluctuated upward with the city's foreign trade volume along a curve that was slightly out of phase with changes in the general economic climate.[92] New York's share of the total stream grew from a range of 34.7 to 59.6 percent for the years 1820–1825, to a range of 55.2 to 72.4 percent for the years 1835–1840.[93] Hence, even on the unrealistic assumption that every eventual diffusion-process initiator who landed at New York adopted his innovation there and not elsewhere, it is evident that in any given year the city could have been the starting site of many, but by no means all, immigration-linked interurban diffusion processes. At best, there was a probability varying from roughly 35 to 72 percent that any specific immigration-linked process would start in the country's largest city between 1820 and 1840. Therefore, many such processes could not have been in complete accord with hierarchical diffusion models. Moreover, in other immigration-linked processes that eventually reached New York, there must have been some diffusion from smaller to larger places of the type depicted in the large-city rank stability model. In addition, while New York was particularly attractive to Europeans and managed to retain comparatively large numbers of them, during the 1820s and 1830s droves of immigrants departed the city via the Hudson Valley and Erie Canal for Western destinations.[94] Consequently, the probability of immigration-linked interurban diffusion processes beginning in New York must have been somewhat lower.

It is evident that the disembarkation patterns of certain types of immigrants and travelers are particularly valid for assessing starting-point probabilities for diffusion processes of foreign origin. Of the various categories present in the secretary of the treasury's annual report on alien passengers and immigrants, three appear to have been more innovation-prone than others: "merchants," who may have been willing to sink capital in new projects; "mechanics" and "engineers," who may have come with completely new skills, techniques, and kinds of problem-awareness;[95] and returning United States citizens, many of whom had been abroad on business and were thus exposed to new possibilities. Although the data on these three categories suffer from incompleteness and other imperfections, they again indicate that New York dominated but did not monopolize the configuration of disembarkations (Tables 7.8–7.10).[96] In fact, if it is assumed that the probability of a city being the starting point of a foreign-based diffusion process was a function of its share of disembarking merchants, technicians, and citizens, then there was a substantial percentage of instances in which initial adoption did not occur in the largest city. That is, there were numerous instances in which the adoption sequence contained some nonhierarchical elements of the type called for in the large-city rank stability model.

The immigration data also are revealing in connection with an earlier observation that supported the high adoption probabilities ascribed to large cities in the rank stability model; namely that European economic innovations, when they did not enter the system of cities via New York, were introduced most frequently via Philadelphia, Boston, and Baltimore. In this connection, at least 77.5 percent of all immigrants and alien passengers arrived at these four ports in nineteen of the twenty-two data years 1817 and 1820–1840 (Table 7.7). Moreover, in five or six sample years the four ports in combination accounted for about four-fifths of all entering mechanics and engineers (Table 7.9).[97] However, the percentage totals of merchants were somewhat lower (Table 7.8), largely because a sizable share of those passengers went to New Orleans. That city, however, was seldom the scene of first adoptions from

Table 7.7. Aliens and immigrants arriving at major United States ports: 1817, 1820–1840 (percentages in italics).

Period	New York	Philadelphia	Boston[a]	Baltimore	Providence	New Orleans	Charleston	Norfolk[b]	Savannah	Mobile	U.S. total
1817	7,634	7,085	2,200	1,187	—	879	747	520	163	—	22,240[c]
	34.3	*31.9*	*9.9*	*8.2*		*4.0*	*3.4*	*2.3*	*.7*		*100.0*
1820[d]	3,834	2,050	861	1,262	7	911	385	164	86	—	10,311
	37.2	*19.9*	*8.4*	*12.2*	*.1*	*8.8*	*3.7*	*1.6*	*.8*		*100.0*
1821[d]	4,038	1,783	1,013	1,409	29	591	867	267	188	—	11,644
	34.7	*15.3*	*8.7*	*12.1*	*.2*	*5.1*	*7.4*	*2.3*	*1.6*		*100.0*
1822[d]	4,116	802	1,002	730	13	438	561	125	76	—	8,549
	48.1	*9.4*	*11.7*	*8.5*	*.2*	*5.1*	*6.6*	*1.5*	*.9*		*100.0*
1823[d]	4,247	463	672	562	27	1,058	402	70	26	—	8,265
	51.4	*5.6*	*8.1*	*6.8*	*.3*	*12.8*	*4.9*	*.8*	*.3*		*100.0*
1824[d]	4,889	1,273	737	610	12	1,014	158	132	20	—	9,627
	50.8	*13.2*	*7.7*	*6.3*	*.1*	*10.5*	*1.6*	*1.4*	*.2*		*100.0*
1825[d]	7,662	1,363	858	1,365	160	429	447	92	23	—	12,858
	59.6	*10.6*	*6.7*	*10.6*	*1.2*	*3.3*	*3.5*	*.7*	*.2*		*100.0*
1826[d]	6,908	2,275	1,170	1,434	23	1,100	325	116	17	—	13,908
	49.7	*16.4*	*8.4*	*10.3*	*.2*	*7.9*	*2.3*	*.8*	*.1*		*100.0*
1827[d]	12,602	3,556	1,858	1,706	4	1,341	341	127	—	—	21,777
	57.9	*16.3*	*8.5*	*7.8*	*.02*	*6.2*	*1.6*	*.6*			*100.0*
1828[d]	19,860	3,500	1,496	1,951	—	1,958	349	96	—	—	30,184
	65.8	*11.6*	*4.8*	*6.5*		*6.5*	*1.2*	*.3*			*100.0*
1829[d]	14,814	1,468	1,595	1,691	29	3,044	231	242	—	—	24,513
	60.4	*6.0*	*6.5*	*6.9*	*.1*	*12.4*	*.9*	*1.0*			*100.0*
1830[d]	13,748	1,890	1,520	3,943	—	2,287	152	523	—	—	24,837
	55.3	*7.6*	*6.1*	*15.9*		*9.2*	*.6*	*2.1*			*100.0*

Year																			
1831[d]	10,737		3,808		1,417		3,711		—		3,191		107		552		—		23,880	
	45.0		15.9		5.9		15.5				13.4		.4		2.3				100.0	
1832[e]	35,246		4,747		3,344		9,979		27		4,397		—		191		231		61,654	
	57.2		7.7		5.4		16.2		.04		7.1				.3		.4		100.0	
1833	39,440		4,216		3,240		4,619		27		4,785		214		187		—		59,925	
	65.8		7.0		5.4		7.7		.05		8.0		.4		.3				100.0	
1834	46,053		4,170		2,931		6,913		64		4,035		89		200		—		67,948	
	67.8		6.1		4.3		10.2		.1		5.9		.1		.3				100.0	
1835	32,715		1,705		3,168		3,566		6		3,552		280		33		—		48,716	
	67.2		3.5		6.5		7.3		.01		7.3		.6		.1				100.0	
1836	58,617		2,507		3,258		6,129		47		4,966		328		163		—		80,972	
	72.4		3.1		4.0		7.6		.1		6.1		.4		.2				100.0	
1837	51,676		4,194		3,673		6,632		90		6,683		393		146		—		84,959	
	60.8		4.9		4.3		7.8		.1		10.2		.5		.2				100.0	
1838	24,935		2,159		2,070		5,234		36		7,434		477		32		—		45,159	
	55.2		4.8		4.6		11.6		.1		16.5		1.1		.1				100.0	
1839	47,688		3,949		3,046		6,081		30		10,306		545		11		—		74,666	
	63.9		5.3		4.1		8.1		.04		13.8		.7		.01				100.0	
1840	60,609		4,079		5,361		7,271		19		11,085		224		247		—		92,207	
	65.7		4.4		5.8		7.9		.02		12.0		.2		.3				100.0	

Source: Seybert, *Statistical Annals*, p. 29; U.S. Treasury Department, *Tables Showing Arrivals of Alien Passengers and Immigrants in the United States*, 1889, pp. 108–109.

a. Includes suburb of Charlestown.
b. Includes nearby port of Portsmouth.
c. Includes Perth Amboy, New Jersey, and Wilmington, Delaware. As the figure excludes several other ports where immigrants probably landed, it is probably low. Another 1817 estimate that placed the total at 30,000 appears high, in view of the proportion of immigrants landing at Seybert's unlisted ports in subsequent years. *NWR* 13, no. 3 (Sept. 3, 1817), 35–36.
d. Twelve-month period ending Sept. 30.
e. Fifteen-month period ending Dec. 31, 1832.

Table 7.8. Merchants arriving at major United States ports: 1821, 1823, 1825–1840 (percentages in italics).

Period	New York	Phila-delphia	Boston[a]	Baltimore	Provi-dence	New Orleans	Charles-ton	Nor-folk[b]	Savan-nah	Mobile	U.S. total
1821[c]	519	161	180	167	7	82	118	24	56	—	1,441
	36.0	*11.5*	*12.5*	*11.6*	*.5*	*5.7*	*8.2*	*1.7*	*3.9*		*100.0*
1823[c]	665	76	96	109	11	317	84	10	6	—	1,427
	46.6	*5.3*	*6.7*	*7.6*	*.8*	*22.2*	*5.9*	*.7*	*.4*		*100.0*
1825[c]	1,036	225	124	62	61	114	88	8	13		1,841
	56.3	*12.2*	*6.7*	*3.4*	*3.3*	*6.2*	*4.8*	*.4*	*.7*		*100.0*
1826–1830[d]	3,190[e]	1,093	645	378	22	3,674	407	49	5		10,435
	35.4[e]	*10.5*	*6.2*	*3.6*	*.2*	*35.2*	*3.9*	*.5*	*.05*		*100.0*
1831–1835[f]	7,959	781	857	357[g]	16	5,939	141	69	—	13	19,601
	40.6	*4.0*	*4.4*	*2.3[g]*	*.1*	*30.3*	*.7*	*.4*		*.1*	*100.0*
1836–1840	7,814	701	1,572	812[h]	9	8,193	507	32	—	—	22,280
	35.1	*3.1*	*7.1*	*4.4[h]*	*.04*	*36.8*	*2.3*	*.1*			*100.0*

Source: U.S. Customs Office, *Passengers Who Arrived in the U.S. During the Year . . .* , submitted to Congress by the Secretary of State, 1821, 1823, 1825–1840; *Historical Statistics*, p. 61.
a. Includes suburb of Charlestown.
b. Includes nearby port of Portsmouth.
c. Twelve-month period ending Sept. 30.
d. Five-year period ending Sept. 30, 1830.
e. Subtotal for 1825–1829 (1830 data unavailable). Percentage based on U.S. total for 1825–1829.
f. Period of Oct. 1, 1830–Dec. 31, 1835.
g. Subtotal for 1831–1834 (1835 data unavailable). Percentage based on U.S. total for 1831–1834.
h. Subtotal exclusive of 1838 (data unavailable). Percentage based on U.S. total for 1836–1837, 1839–1840.

Table 7.9. Mechanics and Engineers arriving at major United States ports, 1821–1840 (percentages in italics).

Period	New York	Philadelphia	Boston[a]	Baltimore	Providence	New Orleans	Charleston	Norfolk[b]	Savannah	Mobile	Ten-port total
1821[c]	28	7	2	9	1	2	—	—	15	—	64
	43.8	*10.9*	*3.1*	*14.1*	*1.6*	*3.1*			*23.4*		*100.0*
1825[c]	73	34	33	4	1	8	7	1	—	—	171
	42.7	*19.9*	*19.3*	*2.3*	*.6*	*4.7*	*4.1*	*.6*			*100.0*
1828[c]	127	162	2	137	—	50	6	—	—	—	484
	26.2	*33.5*	*.4*	*28.3*		*10.3*	*1.2*				*100.0*
1833	2,134	216	30	173	—	359	8	—	—	—	2,920
	73.1	*7.4*	*1.0*	*5.9*		*12.3*	*.3*				*100.0*
1837	4,399	432	288	35	6	777	45	23	—	—	6,005
	73.3	*7.2*	*4.8*	*.6*	*.1*	*12.9*	*.7*	*.4*			*100.0*
1840	6,500	362	422	638	1	1,268	29	24	—	—	9,244
	70.3	*3.9*	*4.6*	*6.9*	*.01*	*13.7*	*.3*	*.3*			*100.0*

Source: Passengers Who Arrived in the U.S., 1821, 1825, 1828, 1833, 1837, and 1840.
a. Includes suburb of Charlestown.
b. Includes nearby port of Portsmouth.
c. Twelve-month period ending Sept. 30.

Table 7.10. Returning citizens arriving at major United States ports, 1821–1840 (percentages in italics).[a]

Period	New York	Phila- delphia	Boston[b]	Baltimore	Provi- dence	New Orleans	Charles- ton	Nor- folk[c]	Savan- nah	Mobile	Ten-port total
1821[d]	785 *35.4*	168 *7.6*	356 *16.1*	297 *13.4*	28 *1.3*	274 *12.4*	182 *8.2*	55 *2.5*	72 *3.2*	—	2,217 *100.0*
1825[d]	1,346 *53.8*	292 *11.7*	336 *13.4*	158 *6.3*	35 *1.4*	153 *6.1*	134 *5.4*	38 *1.5*	12 *.5*	—	2,504 *100.0*
1828[d]	1,706 *62.6*	511 *18.7*	246 *9.0*	200 *7.3*	—	—	41 *1.5*	23 *.8*	—	—	2,727[e] *100.0[e]*
1834	1,111 *55.3*	315 *15.7*	416 *20.7*	124 *6.2*	26 *1.3*	—	—	18 *.9*	—	—	2,010[e] *100.0[e]*
1837	2,030 *61.4*	469 *14.2*	651 *19.7*	131 *4.0*	10 *.3*	—	—	15 *.5*	—	—	3,306[f] *100.0[f]*
1840	3,119 *63.4*	312 *6.4*	1,425 *29.0*	63 *1.3*	1 *.02*	—	—	—	—	—	4,920[f] *100.0[f]*

Source: Passengers Who Arrived in the U.S., 1821, 1825, 1828, 1834, 1837, and 1840.
a. Because of incomplete data, the years in this table do not coincide fully with those in Table 7.9.
b. Includes suburb of Charlestown.
c. Includes nearby port of Portsmouth.
d. Twelve-month period ending Sept. 30.
e. Excludes New Orleans.
f. Excludes New Orleans and Charleston.

abroad—perhaps because many of the merchants landing there were European cotton dealers paying only temporary visits, perhaps because of the negative local attitude toward manufacturing, or perhaps because of a combination of these and other factors.

VARIATIONS IN BUSINESS ATTITUDES AND BEHAVIOR

If the impressionistic accounts of historians can be believed, there were pronounced city-to-city differences in prevailing business attitudes during the final pretelegraphic decades. In the early nineteenth century, "Almost every foreign visitor asserted in the most positive terms the belief that New York exhibited more entrepreneurial daring than any other city." Throughout the 1790–1825 period the economic writings of New Yorkers were also generally marked by a "vision of the city as the coming integrated [commercial and financial] cosmopolis," while similar views were "largely absent in the works of residents of other major cities."[98] A few years prior to the War of 1812 it was observed that Philadelphia was dominated by Quakers who had "given a tone to the manners of the people different from what is to be found in most places of equal extent. They are industrious and sober, and, though sufficiently commercial, they do not conduct their business in the same *dashing* style which is done by some commercial cities; but confine themselves within bounds, and secure what they gain." Over two decades later the *New York Journal of Commerce* remarked: "Our brothers of Philadelphia are renowned for their prudence; they never break the Sabbath, or their own necks, scrambling after news, nor burn their fingers by laying hold of it before it gets cool."[99] Boston's mercantile entrepreneurs were on the whole more sympathetic toward manufacturing investments than were their New York counterparts. Thus, also in contrast to New Yorkers, they became increasingly outspoken advocates of protective tariffs during the 1820s and 1830s.[100] Baltimore's financiers have been depicted as conservative in their banking practices following the War of 1812, and the city possessed many businessmen who reiterated the Southern line of reasoning on low tariffs. Providence's entrepreneurs were supposedly more willing to diversify and absorb risks than were merchants and investors in other cities. During the 1830s most New Orleans businessmen, unlike their confreres in major Northeastern cities, apparently refused to believe that canals or railroads offered a real alternative to river transportation. In turn-of-the-century Charleston, "No gentleman . . . connected himself with trade."[101]

In any specific instance, of course, the attitude toward risk, or any other business-related attitude, was not necessarily uniform within a city's entrepreneurial community. The largely noncorporate entrepreneurs of any mercantile city could have differed on particular matters because, among other reasons, individuals were in different stages of the life cycle or in different branches of trade or industry.[102] Nonetheless, it is probable that the spectrum of business-related attitudes did not vary appreciably among major pretelegraphic cities, but that the distribution and clustering of entrepreneurs along that spectrum did vary from center to center. This more cautious view of interurban variations in business attitudes and derived behaviors requires interpretation. It is here speculated that the nature of pretelegraphic information circulation contributed greatly to the locally circumscribed diffusion of business attitudes and risk-taking behavior patterns.

It is a social-psychological commonplace that when "a number of persons are in interaction over an extended period of time, mutual expectations and norms develop for their behavior, and their actions are not independent of these norms and expectations."[103] Likewise, "exchange theorists" argue: "Individuals do not assess rewards and costs, and make decisions or choices, as independent monads in a Hobbesian situation, but rather as 'selves' in an interpersonal matrix or field of at least partly matched or common symbols and intimate exchanges of information."[104] The "intimate exchanges of information" made by pretelegraphic entrepreneurs, like those made by modern business executives, usually consisted of local, regional or national, and international components.[105] However, given the relatively small volume of pretelegraphic long-distance information flow, the local component was probably more important in relative terms between 1790 and 1840 than it is today. If so, and if group "influentials" affected information receipt and attitude formation, while membership in informal and formal face-to-face groups tended to be locally restricted, then entrepreneurial attitudes in a pretelegraphic city ought to have resembled one another to the extent that group memberships, or private-information fields, overlapped one another.[106] Moreover, the time lag aspect of pretelegraphic information circulation quite likely sharply limited the diffusion of business attitudes. Time-lag spatial biases in the availability of information meant that, except when traveling, local reactions and opinions on any economic or business matter were heard first by the individual entrepreneur. According to social psychologists, although being heard first does not make a message more likely to be remembered, it "does make it more likely to be believed; one side of an argument tends to be persuasive provided we have not heard the other side. [And once] they have been influenced, many persons make up their minds and are no longer interested in other communications on the same issue."[107] Therefore, once attitudes toward risk or any other general issue were established in an entrepreneurial community, they were not likely to be altered by information from another city. This resistance to change must have been especially strong where individual confidence required a reduction in uncertainty, in the form of frequent attitude validation and confirmation, or redundant information, from others.

The above interpretation of interurban variations in business attitudes rests on the assumption that information of local origin was received by individual entrepreneurs primarily from their own peers in various groups. One form of inferential support for this assumption comes from the fact that United States mercantile cities at the end of pretelegraphic times were extremely compact. Even the largest were of very modest physical extent. The area contained within the built-up portion of Philadelphia, including its suburbs, was under ten square miles. The same was true of Baltimore; and the developed area of Boston was entirely within a two-mile radius from City Hall. Manhattan's 1840 population was mostly packed into the area south of Fourteenth Street, little more than one-fourth of the island's land mass being allocated to urban land uses. Under these circumstances of very small separating distances, members of any formal or informal group were likely to encounter one another frequently on face-to-face terms.[108]

Moreover, the most important entrepreneurs and businessmen were especially likely to meet each other, for their places of work were usually clustered on one or a few proximate streets. In describing New York's lower East Side, an 1833 observer wrote: "Pearl-street . . . is the principal seat of the [wholesale] dry goods and hardware business. Front and Water streets . . . are occupied principally by the wholesale grocers, commission merchants, and mechanics associated with the shipping business. South street . . . contains the warehouses and offices of most of the principal shipping merchants. Wall Street . . . is occupied by the Banks, Insurance Companies, Merchants' Exchange, Newspapers, and Brokers offices." In Boston, "the city's most important enterprises, its docks and markets, offices and counting houses, stores and workshops," were concentrated in an area "extending from the water front westward to Washington Street and from Water Street north to Ann." Such functional agglomeration was also true of the smaller major cities. Norfolk, for example, had most of its wholesaling and commercial activities on Water Street.[109]

The likelihood of entrepreneurial and merchant group members verbally exchanging information and influencing one another was enhanced by their widespread practice of gathering almost daily in taverns, coffeehouses, and inns, whose clientele was usually socially or occupationally specialized, in newspaper reading rooms to look at out-of-town papers, and in merchant exchanges.[110] General evidence from the late eighteenth century in the United States and elsewhere also demonstrates "that elites or leading classes are not horizontal slices off the top of some uniform cake, but that they are the result of connections growing in time and clustering in space."[111]

A Specific Case. Probably the best documented study of interurban variations in business attitudes and behavior patterns is Julius Rubin's investigation of events in Philadelphia, Baltimore, and Boston following the 1825 opening of the Erie Canal. In all three cities there was alarm over the implications of the canal for New York's future share of the Western trade, and it was realized that transportation countermeasures must be implemented in order even to hold pace with New York's growth: "The uncertainty associated with the railroad confronted New York's rivals with a difficult choice. Should they use the tried and tested method of canals in a geographic situation entirely unsuited to that method or should they turn to the new and untried? Should they imitate or innovate? Of course, a third alternative was possible: they could postpone a decision, avoid investment in either railroad or canal, and wait for the railroad to prove itself. But in the meantime New York was monopolizing the western trade. Delay required coolness and great objectivity. The pressure was for immediate action in a deteriorating situation."[112]

In this stress-filled situation, whose uncertainty stemmed from the great capital risks involved as well as from an unfamiliarity with railroad technology, performance, and construction and operating costs, quite different responses emerged in Baltimore, Philadelphia, and Boston. The business community of Baltimore risked its own capital and moved comparatively rapidly, by February 1827, being "willing to accept the [barely tested] railroad as an alternative to the canal." Construction of the Baltimore and Ohio Railroad began in July 1828. Philadelphians lacked such daring and were unwilling to invest their own capital. In the absence of experience, business interests there would not tolerate any project westward comprised solely of railroad facilities. Instead, they quickly turned to legislative support for their Mainline scheme, which initially assumed a full-length canal to Pittsburgh but was later modified to include a railroad link and extra transshipment costs to cross the mountains between Hollidaysburg and Johnstown. The Mainline bill was passed by the Pennsylvania legislature in 1826, but not until 1831, over four years after canal construction had commenced, did the legislature authorize the building of a railroad portage. In sharp contrast, Boston entrepreneurs resorted to the common strategy of procrastination to cope with the uncertainty of the situation. The canal was rejected, and the railroad project was postponed for a decade, despite the need for a trans-Appalachian line that was felt at least as urgently in Boston as in the other two cities. Only in May 1832 was a private company organized to construct a simple railroad line to Worcester. Extension of the line to Albany required the formation of a new corporation in 1836 and the immediate acquisition of a state subsidy.[113]

With respect to these highly dissimilar decision-making responses, Rubin noted:

These striking differences in behavior seem completely out of proportion to the small discrepancies in the situation of these three closely similar regions. For these were all commercialized coastal areas of the same country; all were subject to the competitive pressure created by the success of the Erie Canal; all were confronted with the problem of crossing a mountain range; all had access to almost identical technical information on canals and railroads; and all made their decisions at almost the same time. Is it possible that extremely small disparities in situation, [technical] information, and timing could have produced such large differences in response? . . . this is highly improbable. If so, the differences in behavior are to be explained by attitudinal rather than situational factors; by divergencies in the history and traditions of the three regions which produced differences in the attitudes that the decision-making groups brought to the common problem rather than by differences in the problem itself. Since that problem involved a choice between a tried and untried method and between immediate action and postponement, differences in attitude toward uncertainty and delay must account for those remarkable differences in behavior.[114]

Although Rubin does not make the argument himself, the attitudes and behavior patterns in question probably were closely related to the nature of nonlocal and local pretelegraphic information circulation. That is, the interplay of predominantly local face-to-face contacts, time-lag spatial biases in the availability of information, and group conformity processes greatly curtailed the diffusion of local business attitudes and behavior patterns. In Philadelphia, a small organization with from forty-four to forty-eight members who were in frequent, informal and formal contact with one another helped to mold local opinion. The attitudes of that group itself were under the sway of a single influential figure, Mathew Carey. In Baltimore, railroad interest was ignited at an informal dinner attended by a few of the city's economic elite. Events gathered momentum as the result of "much" private discussion and the informal gathering of twenty-five of the city's well-acquainted "leading citizens." This group, whose attitude formation apparently was steered by a few opinion leaders, soon gained support. Shortly after the group's second meeting the *Baltimore American* commented that the favorable reception of the railroad proposal flowed "as well from the character of the promoters, as from the evidence recently accumulated from various quarters, on the efficacy and cheapness of rail-road communication." In Boston, a single newspaper editor, Nathan Hale, was largely responsible for gathering railroad support. However, he was far more cautious in his stance than were either Mathew Carey or the citizens of Baltimore, even being in favor of delaying construction. Thus, the railroad met a generally cold reception among the small coterie of Boston's wealthiest merchants. Their mutually reinforcing attitudes were so negative that, as late as 1835, most of them still did not regard a rail line to Albany as a "money-making enterprise" and were unwilling to risk more than very small sums in shares for such a project.[115]

Although these circumstances can in no way be taken as conclusive proof of the validity of the proposed relationships between pretelegraphic information circulation and interurban variations in entrepreneurial attitudes toward risk-taking and related matters, they do have a bearing on the large-city rank stability model. That model made no explicit place for such a phenomenon, but it implied that large-city variations in entrepreneurial attitudes may have elicited different reactions to specific business opportunities and thereby, at least partly, have accounted for large-city population-ratio adjustments and minor rank shifts. As Herman Krooss concluded, after examining the varying aggressiveness and risk-taking proclivities of bankers in early nineteenth century New York, Philadelphia, Baltimore, and Boston: "a daring generalizer would say that these slight differences had something to do with the way the four cities grew. Just how much, however, even a daring generalizer would not dare to say."[116] It can indeed be asserted, in an admittedly daring manner, that there was a causal relationship of indefinable proportions between spatial biases in information availability, entrepreneurial attitudes and behavior and the differential growth of leading urban system and subsystem units.

8

Modern Policy Ramifications

To fulfil their tasks, or even to state them well, social scientists must use the
materials of history. Unless one assumes some trans-historical theory of the nature
of history, or that man in society is a non-historical entity, no social sicence can be
assumed to transcend history.
—C. Wright Mills

Transport costs and times have fallen radically since 1840. Since that
date, information gathering and circulation have been revolutionized by
electronic media and computer technology. Nevertheless, it is possible
that the large-city rank stability model has some relevance for both
well-established and developing systems of cities in the 1970s.[1] In
particular, the basic components of the model remain valid for a
variety of modern situations, with two important modifications. First,
the circular and cumulative submodel of size growth for individual
cities now takes different forms, with manufacturing or the tertiary
sector and administrative activities usually providing the principal
stimulus to the self-reinforcing rounds of multiplier effects and earnings. Second, the means by which urban interdependencies generate
spatial biases in the availability of economically significant information
are now more complicated. Although a modern version of the model
cannot be made explicit here and given empirical substantiation, studies
have begun to stress the role of innovation diffusion in the development
of urban systems.[2]

If the time is indeed ripe "to call attention to the informational
aspects of regional development," then in some circumstances the
present form of the model should be able to provide insights for locational and regional planners.[3] A number of applications can be suggested, although it is fully realized that there is great danger in facile
translations, and that no sketched policy proposal can hold either for

all cultural and institutional frameworks, or for all political and resource settings. First, if planners in newly independent former colonies are confronted with the problem of allocating resources and activities among several urban-regional alternatives, they should keep in mind that some of their largest port cities, by nature of their commodity flows and service dependencies, remain outliers of the urban system of the former "mother" country. Thus, investments in such large cities, unless wisely selected and accompanied by the development of new interurban transport facilities, probably will not foster the same kind of domestic nonlocal multipliers and urban interdependencies as large-city investments in other countries. That is, such investments in and of themselves probably will not aid as much as possible in the development of an integrated and stable national urban system.[4]

In a related vein, the long-run success of newly planned urban complexes, or "growth poles," in developing countries would appear to be best ensured by the early, large-scale establishment of types of activity whose very existence can set in motion interdependencies with existing large cities or other newly planned units. Such activities are much more likely than others to generate subsequent interdependencies and growth.[5] Similarly, those wishing to rectify regional inequalities, or to stimulate regionally lagging economies such as those of Appalachia, the Mezzogiorno in Italy, or Sweden's Norrland, would be well advised to promote urban activities that give rise not only to regional exports but to intraregional urban interdependencies as well.

Planners intent upon discouraging the growth of already large metropolitan areas by assigning new activities to "rural growth centers, market towns, [and] small cities" ought to be cautioned that their actions may not have the clear-cut affect they anticipate, because large-city expansion is not easily halted. For example, new activities in small urban units can contribute to the growth of large cities by creating new interdependencies with them. Moreover, when the consequent multipliers unfold in the large cities, they may trigger additional and unexpected interdependencies between those major centers and yet other cities.[6] Since these and other undesired effects associated with the foregoing policy suggestions are apt to be self-perpetuating, it would seem wise for regional policy makers to try at least roughly to establish what immediate urban interdependencies will follow from any specific locational decisions.

The assertion that a model designed for the pretelegraphic American system of cities and its regional subsystems could have relevance for planners in the 1970s might at first sound bizarre. However, this position is based on the assumption that "it is not possible to deal with any complex phenomena except over long time periods."[7] It is also based on the conviction that policy-making requires the comprehension of processes, or general feedback mechanisms, which allow the components of specific patterns and structures at one point in time to have a probabilistic impact on the components of subsequent patterns and structures. Yet the only large-scale processes that lend themselves to such study are those which have already transpired. On the basis of this study and other findings, it is contended that, regardless of the particular historical or technological setting, the process of city-system growth and development always involves intricate feedbacks between nonlocal or interurban multiplier effects, spatial biases in the availability of specialized information, the interurban diffusion of economic innovations, and the day-to-day exploitation of opportunities by job-providing units. This process point of view is not compatible with the views held by urban historians or urban and historical geographers who devote themselves to the "unique." It is in line, however, with the views of geographers, other social scientists, and historians who maintain that the "particular possesses significance only in the context of the general."[8] In short, the argument for using analyses of the past as inputs in the development of regional planning policies can be put quite simply: History does not repeat itself, but processes do.

Notes and Index

Abbreviations

ARJ   *American Railroad Journal and Advocate of Internal Improvements*
HCSR   *Hazard's United States Commercial and Statistical Register*
HMM   *Hunt's Merchants' Magazine*
NYSL   *New York Shipping and Commercial List*
NWR   *Niles' Weekly Register*

Notes

Introduction

1. Richard L. Meier, *A Communications Theory of Urban Growth* (Cambridge: M.I.T. Press, 1962), p. 43.

2. See Edgar M. Hoover and Raymond Vernon, *Anatomy of a Metropolis* (Cambridge: Harvard University Press, 1959), esp. pp. 62–73; Gunnar Törnqvist, *Contact Systems and Regional Development*, Lund Studies in Geography, ser. B, Human Geography, no. 35 (Lund, 1970). For related theoretical statements, see Thomas Marschak, "Centralization and Decentralization in Economic Organizations," *Econometrica* 27 (1959), 399–430; Walter Isard, *General Theory: Social, Political, Economic and Regional* (Cambridge: M.I.T. Press, 1969), pp. 57–115; Bertil Thorngren, "How Do Contact Systems Affect Regional Development?" *Environment and Planning* 2 (1970), 409–427.

3. Walter Buckley, *Sociology and Modern Systems Theory* (Englewood Cliffs, N.J.: Prentice-Hall, 1967), p. 82.

4. This book is a sequel to an earlier work of mine, which dealt with the locational dynamics of American urban-industrial growth over a much longer period of time and which promised to be "a prelude to more detailed studies to be carried out in the future." Allan R. Pred, *The Spatial Dynamics of U.S. Urban-Industrial Growth, 1800–1914: Interpretative and Theoretical Essays* (Cambridge: M.I.T. Press, 1966), p. 7.

5. In another context Buckley similarly stated: "Process, then, focuses on the actions and interactions of the components of an ongoing [sociocultural] system, such that varying degrees of structuring arise, persist, dissolve, or change." Buckley, *Sociology*, p. 18.

6. See, e.g., Sam B. Warner, Jr., *Streetcar Suburbs: The Process of Growth in Boston, 1870–1900* (Cambridge: Harvard University Press and M.I.T. Press, 1962); Sam B. Warner, Jr., *The Private City: Philadelphia in Three Periods of Its Growth* (Philadelphia: University of Pennsylvania Press, 1968); Robert Greenhalgh Albion, *The Rise of New York Port, 1815–1860* (New York: Charles Scribner's Sons, 1939); Sidney I. Pomerantz, *New York: An American City, 1783–1803: A Study of Urban Life* (New York: Columbia University Press, 1938).

7. See, e.g., Wyatt Winton Belcher, *The Economic Rivalry Between St. Louis and Chicago, 1850–1880* (New York: Columbia University Press, 1947); Leonard P. Curry, *Rail Routes South: Louisville's Fight for the Southern Market, 1865–1872* (Lexington: University of Kentucky Press, 1969); Charles N. Glaab, *Kansas City and the Railroads* (Madison: University of Wisconsin Press, 1962).

8. See, e.g., Carl Bridenbaugh, *Cities in Revolt: Urban Life in America, 1743–1776* (New York: Alfred A. Knopf, 1955); David T. Gilchrist, ed., *The Growth of the Seaport Cities, 1790–1825* (Charlottesville: University Press of Virginia, 1967);

Richard C. Wade, *The Urban Frontier: Pioneer Life in Early Pittsburgh, Cincinnati, Lexington, Louisville, and St. Louis* (Chicago: University of Chicago Press, 1964).

9. See, e.g., Blake McKelvey, *The Urbanization of America, 1860-1915* (New Brunswick: Rutgers University Press, 1963); Charles N. Glaab and A. Theodore Brown, *A History of Urban America* (New York: Macmillan, 1967); Arthur Meier Schlesinger, *The Rise of the City, 1878-1898* (New York: Macmillan, 1933). See also Charles N. Glaab, "The Historian and the American City: A Bibliographic Survey," in Philip M. Hauser and Leo F. Schnore, eds., *The Study of Urbanization* (New York: John Wiley, 1965).

10. See, e.g., Jeffrey G. Williamson and Joseph A. Swanson, "The Growth of Cities in the American Northeast," *Explorations in Entrepreneurial History*, 2nd ser. 4, no. 1 (1966-1967); Eugene Smolensky and David Ratajczak, "The Conception of Cities," *Explorations in Entrepreneurial History*, 2nd ser. 2 (Winter 1965), 90-131; Eric E. Lampard, "The History of Cities in the Economically Advanced Areas," *Economic Development and Cultural Change* 3 (1954-1955), 81-136; Lampard, "The Evolving System of Cities in the United States: Urbanization and Economic Development," in Harvey S. Perloff and Lowdon Wingo, Jr., eds., *Issues in Urban Economics* (Baltimore: Johns Hopkins Press, 1968), pp. 81-139.

11. Leo F. Schnore, "Problems in the Quantitative Study of Urban History," in H. J. Dyos, ed., *The Study of Urban History* (New York: St. Martin's Press, 1968), pp. 189-208; S. G. Checkland, "Toward a Definition of Urban History," in Dyos, *Study of Urban History*, pp. 343-361; Sam Bass Warner, Jr., "If All the World Were Philadelphia: A Scaffolding for Urban History, 1774-1930," *American Historical Review* 74 (October 1968), 26-43; Stephen Thernstrom, "Reflections on the New Urban History," *Daedalus*, Spring 1971, pp. 359-375.

12. See, e.g., Olof Wärneryd, *Interdependence in Urban Systems* (Göteborg: Regionkonsult Aktiebolag, 1968); Brian J. L. Berry, "Cities As Systems Within Systems of Cities," in John Friedmann and William Alonso, eds., *Regional Development and Planning* (Cambridge: M.I.T. Press, 1964), pp. 116-137; Brian J. L. Berry and Frank E. Horton, *Geographic Perspectives on Urban Systems* (Englewood Cliffs, N.J.: Prentice-Hall, 1970).

13. See, e.g., John R. Borchert, "American Metropolitan Evolution," *Geographical Review* 47 (1967), 301-332; Richard L. Morrill, *Migration and the Spread and Growth of Urban Settlement*, Lund Studies in Geography, ser. B, Human Geography, no. 26 (Lund, 1965); David Ward, *Cities and Immigrants: A Geography of Change in Nineteenth Century America* (New York: Oxford University Press, 1971); James E. Vance, Jr., *Geography and Urban Evolution in the San Francisco Bay Area* (Berkeley: University of California, Institute of Governmental Studies, 1964); Peter G. Goheen, *Victorian Toronto, 1850 to 1900: Pattern and Process of Growth*, University of Chicago, Department of Geography Research Paper no. 128 (Chicago, 1970).

14. Carl H. Madden, "On Some Indications of Stability in the Growth of Cities in the United States," *Economic Development and Cultural Change* 4 (1955-1956), 236-252. The rank-size rule, originally formulated by George Kingsley Zipf

[*National Unity and Disunity* (Bloomington, Ind.: Principia Press, 1941); *Human Behavior and the Principal of Least Effort* (Reading, Mass.: Addison-Wesley, 1949)],

can be expressed: $P_r = \dfrac{P_1}{r^q}$. This means that "the population of the rth ranking city P_r equals the population of the largest city P_1 divided by rank r raised to an exponent q . . . which generally has a value very close to unity." Rank-size regularities have been observed not only in the U.S. but in other economically advanced countries with integrated systems of cities. Berry and Horton, *Geographic Perspectives*, pp. 64, 66–75. See also Berry, "Cities As Systems," pp. 118–120; Brian J. L. Berry, "An Inductive Approach to the Regionalization of Economic Development," in Norton Ginsburg, ed., *Essays on Geography and Economic Development*, University of Chicago, Department of Geography Research Paper no. 62 (Chicago, 1960), pp. 78–107; Rutledge Vining, "A Description of Certain Spatial Aspects of an Economic System," *Economic Development and Cultural Change* 3 (1954–1955), 147–195.

15. Fred Lukermann, "Empirical Expressions of Nodality and Hierarchy in a Circulation Manifold," *East Lakes Geographer* 2 (1966), 18–20.

16. Washington, D.C., was arbitrarily excluded from the northeastern regional urban subsystem because its growth sprang largely from political rather than economic functions. In any event, its inclusion would have had no appreciable affect on the stability observation, for Washington's 1840 rank would have been either sixth as then constituted, or fifth as presently constituted (including Georgetown and other former suburbs), whereas its 1960 regional metropolitan-area rank would have been fourth.

17. The comparison of 1790–1840 city populations with 1960 metropolitan-area populations is based on the fact that a comparison of functional urban units is more meaningful than one of politically defined urban units. Modern metropolises are usually regarded as economically integrated functional units, in part because of their journey-to-work patterns. Even where municipalities that were once economically and physically independent have been engulfed, the processes that have generated the present scale of metropolitan areas ought to be seen as inseparable from the processes that generated the growth of their central-city forebears.

18. See John G. Clark, *The Grain Trade in the Old Northwest* (Urbana: University of Illinois Press, 1966), pp. 61, 18–19. See also comments on the early "Lakes" and "River" alignment of Western cities in James E. Vance, Jr., *The Merchant's World: The Geography of Wholesaling* (Englewood Cliffs, N.J.: Prentice-Hall, 1970), p. 158.

19. These rankings are exclusive of several metropolitan areas in central and southern Florida—including Miami and Tampa-St. Petersburg—which were larger than Charleston and Savannah in 1960.

20. In 1840, Chicago's exports took their first great leap, to $228,635, while its imports that year amounted to $562,106. [*HMM* 18 (February 1848), 168; Israel Andrews, *Report . . . on the Trade and Commerce of the British North American Colonies*, U.S. Senate Document No. 112, 32nd Cong., 1st sess., 1853, p. 175]. "In 1839 the hinterland of Chicago was sparsely settled [and lacking transportation

facilities]. The region from Rock River was described as a desolate waste and the region between Chicago and Springfield was virtually unsettled." Clark, *Grain Trade*, p. 85.

21. See, e.g., Douglass C. North, *The Economic Growth of the United States, 1790-1860* (New York: W. W. Norton, 1966); William N. Parker and Franklee Whartenby, "The Growth of Output Before 1840," in *Trends in the American Economy in the Nineteenth Century* (Princeton: Princeton University Press, 1960), pp. 191-216; Paul A. David, "The Growth of Real Product in the United States Before 1840: New Evidence, Controlled Conjectures," *Journal of Economic History* 27 (1967), 151-197.

22. Contrary to the popular impression, agricultural settlement did not drag behind it a train of urban development. Instead, "on the Ohio Valley frontier, towns were established around the Great Lakes far in advance of any agricultural development in the area," because "towns were the necessary bases from which the farmers could move out and begin to subdue the new land to their purposes." Glaab and Brown, *History of Urban America*, pp. 45, 29. See also Wade, *Urban Frontier*.

23. U.S. Bureau of the Census, *Historical Statistics of the United States, Colonial Times to 1957*, 1960, pp. 8, 13. For the adjustments in population distribution during 1790-1840, see Charles O. Paullin and John K. Wright, ed., *Atlas of the Historical Geography of the United States* (Washington, D.C.: Carnegie Institution of Washington, 1932), plate 76.

24. *Historical Statistics*, pp. 8, 14. The Bureau of the Census figures probably understate the 1840 urban population, since they refer solely to places with a population exceeding 2,500. Cities, particularly in the early stages of economic growth, ought to be defined in terms of their functions, not of arbitrary demographic limits.

25. George Rogers Taylor, "American Urban Growth Preceding the Railway Age," *Journal of Economic History* 27 (1967), 309. Cf. remarks on changes in the nodal structure of U.S. economic activity, 1790-1830, in John G. B. Hutchins, "Trade and Manufactures," in Gilchrist, *Growth of the Seaport Cities*, pp. 86-87.

1. Pretelegraphic Information Circulation: A Prelude

1. See Robert Luther Thompson, *Wiring a Continent: The History of the Telegraph in the United States, 1832-1866* (Princeton: Princeton University Press, 1947).

2. Colin Cherry, *On Human Communication*, 2nd ed. (Cambridge: M.I.T. Press, 1966), p. 22.

3. Frank Luther Mott, *American Journalism: A History of Newspapers in the United States Through 250 Years, 1690 to 1940* (New York: Macmillan, 1941), pp. 154-155.

4. I. N. Phelps Stokes, *The Iconography of Manhattan Island* (New York: Robert H. Dodd, 1918), IV, 765; Mott, *American Journalism*, p. 101.

5. *NWR* 37, no. 21 (Jan. 16, 1830), 339; 53, no. 2 (Sept. 9, 1837), 17.

6. Torsten Hägerstrand, *Innovation Diffusion As a Spatial Process*, trans. and postscript by Allan R. Pred (Chicago: University of Chicago Press, 1967), p. 138.

7. Elihu Katz and Paul F. Lazarsfeld, *Personal Influence: The Role Played by People in the Flow of Mass Communications* (Glencoe: Free Press, 1955), p. 32. See also Elihu Katz, "The Two-Step Flow of Communications: An Up-to-Date Report on an Hypothesis," *Public Opinion Quarterly* 21 (1957), 61-78.

8. Cf. Nicolas Rashevsky, *Looking at History Through Mathematics* (Cambridge: M.I.T. Press, 1968), pp. 150-158.

2. The Long-Distance Flow of Information Through Newspapers

1. Until the appearance of the penny press in a few cities, the high cost of newspapers restricted circulation largely to the economically well-to-do. However, the number of readers per copy through 1840 was high by modern standards because of the availability of newspapers in taverns, coffee houses, and other public places.

2. Frank Luther Mott, *American Journalism: A History of Newspapers in the United States Through 250 Years, 1690 to 1940* (New York: Macmillan, 1941), p. 48.

3. Joseph T. Buckingham, *Specimens of Newspaper Literature* (Boston, 1852), p. 12; Richard L. Merritt, *Symbols of American Community, 1735-1775* (New Haven: Yale University Press, 1966), pp. 62, 82; Mott, *American Journalism*, p. 114.

4. Based on a seasonally stratified sample of 48 issues of the Philadelphia *Gazette of the United States and Daily Evening Advertiser* from 1794.

5. *New York Spectator*, Oct. 4, 1797; George Rogers Taylor, *The Transportation Revolution, 1815-1860* (New York: Holt, Rinehart and Winston, 1951), p. 10.

6. Merritt, *Symbols*, p. 6.

7. Mott, *American Journalism*, p. 196.

8. Frederic Hudson, *Journalism in the United States, from 1690 to 1872* (New York, 1873), p. 91; Alfred McClung Lee, *The Daily Newspaper in America: The Evolution of a Social Instrument* (New York: Macmillan, 1937), pp. 31, 57; Frank Presbrey, *The History and Development of Advertising* (New York: Doubleday, Doran, 1929), p. 161.

9. Lee, *Daily Newspaper*, pp. 59, 316; Mott, *American Journalism*, p. 157; 1790 issues of the *Boston Independent Chronicle* and *Columbian Centinel*; 1794 issues of the Philadelphia *Gazette of the United States and Daily Evening Advertiser* and the *American Mercury and New York Evening Advertiser*.

10. Mott, *American Journalism*, p. 201; Lee, *Daily Newspaper*, pp. 318, 391; *NWR* 28, no. 11 (May 14, 1825), 176; 42, no. 7 (Apr. 7, 1832), 111. The comparison between New York and Great Britain and Ireland must be tempered by the fact that newspaper advertisements were taxed in the United Kingdom.

11. Mott, *American Journalism*, p. 294; Presbrey, *History and Development of Advertising*, p. 154.

12. Presbrey, *History and Development of Advertising*, p. 181.

13. Arthur L. Jensen, *The Maritime Commerce of Colonial Philadelphia* (Madison: State Historical Society of Wisconsin, 1963), p. 45.

14. Catherine Elizabeth Reiser, *Pittsburgh's Commercial Development, 1800–1850* (Harrisburg: Pennsylvania Historical and Museum Commission, 1951), p. 136; Robert Greenhalgh Albion, *Square-Riggers on Schedule: The New York Sailing Packets to England, France, and the Cotton Ports* (Princeton: Princeton University Press, 1938), p. 180.

15. Taylor, *Transportation Revolution*, p. 151.

16. Richard C. Wade, *The Urban Frontier: Pioneer Life in Early Pittsburgh, Cincinnati, Lexington, Louisville, and St. Louis* (Chicago: University of Chicago Press, 1964), p. 26; Thomas Senior Berry, *Western Prices Before 1861: A Study of the Cincinnati Market* (Cambridge: Harvard University Press, 1943), pp. 16–17.

17. Albion, *Square-Riggers*, pp. 317, 200; Robert Greenhalgh Albion, *The Rise of New York Port, 1815–1860* (New York: Charles Scribner's Sons, 1939), p. 51; *NWR* 35, no. 21 (Jan. 17, 1829), 344; 58, no. 1 (Mar. 7, 1840), 1.

18. Adam Seybert, *Statistical Annals: Embracing Views of the Population, Commerce, Navigation . . . of the United States of America* (Philadelphia, 1818), pp. 425–437, 321; Sidney I. Pomerantz, *New York: An American City, 1783–1803: A Study of Urban Life* (New York: Columbia University Press, 1938), p. 159; *American Minerva and New York Evening Advertiser*, Jan. 8, 1794; *NWR* 55, no. 24 (Feb. 9, 1839), 371.

19. C. W. Janson, *The Stranger in America* (London, 1807), p. 92; Seybert, *Statistical Annals*, pp. 430–432.

20. Seybert, *Statistical Annals*, p. 436. For the period March 1815–July 1816, inclusive, gross import duty revenues were: New York, $9.9 million; Philadelphia, $5.0 million; Boston, $3.6 million; Baltimore, $3.3 million. *New York Evening Post*, Oct. 2, 1817.

21. Albion, *Rise of New York Port*, p. 393.

22. Albion, *Square-Riggers*, pp. 174, 20.

23. Albion, *Square-Riggers*, p. 47. Boston packet owners claimed that their operations were undermined by their New York counterparts. New Yorkers "charged $10 a ton for fine freight from Europe, but on shipments for Boston merchants they reduced the price to $8 to lure the business in their direction." *Ibid.*

24. Lee, *Daily Newspaper*, p. 481; *NWR* 37, no. 22 (Jan. 23, 1830), 356; Albion, *Square-Riggers*, pp. 177–178. See also James Flint, *Letters from America* (Edinburgh, 1822), p. 5.

25. Lee, *Daily Newspaper*, pp. 482, 491; Hudson, *Journalism in the U.S.*, p. 446; Albion, *Square-Riggers*, pp. 174–175, 178–179.

26. *New York Daily Advertiser*, Jan. 4, 1805. Signal poles had previously been operated at the southern end of Manhattan.

27. *New York Evening Post*, June 20, 1815; Albion, *Rise of New York Port*, p. 217; Lee, *Daily Newspaper*, pp. 482–483; *ARJ* 3, no. 49 (Dec. 13, 1834), 778.

28. *HCSR* 2, no. 12 (Mar. 18, 1840), 182–183; and *HMM* 2 (April 1840), 342–

344. With the aid of westerly winds the packets competed somewhat better in sailings to England: 33 of 56 sailings in 1839 were completed in 17–22 days.

29. *NWR* 38, no. 11 (May 8, 1830), 205.

30. *NWR* 2, no. 45 (July 11, 1812), 320.

31. *NWR* 18, no. 22 (July 29, 1820), 385.

32. Lee, *Daily Newspapers*, pp. 711–714.

33. *NWR* 41, no. 25 (Feb. 18, 1832), 447. See also Ralph H. Brown, *Historical Geography of the United States* (New York: Harcourt, Brace, 1948), p. 102.

34. Edward C. Kirkland, *Men, Cities and Transportation: A Study in New England History, 1820–1900* (Cambridge: Harvard University Press, 1948), 19; Albion, *Square-Riggers*, p. 69.

35. The Boston-to-Philadelphia mean time lag was 12.0 days; the Philadelphia-to-Boston lag was 12.1 days. This appears to reflect well on the validity of the sampling procedure.

36. Mott, *American Journalism*, p. 154.

37. The 1794 ten-day isoline encompasses a larger area than the 1790 fifteen-day isoline.

38. In both Philadelphia and New York the receipt of news from the immediate hinterland, however, was often remarkably slow. Contrast the 1.6-day New York-to-Philadelphia time lag with the 4.0-day Lancaster-to-Philadelphia delay, despite Lancaster's greater proximity by about thirty miles.

39. In 1820 there were at least 79 shipping arrivals from Norfolk in New York, but only 26 from Norfolk at Philadelphia. On the average, a vessel from Norfolk docked in New York once every 4.6 days, in Philadelphia once every two weeks. Thus, Philadelphia papers were apt to receive their Norfolk stories via New York or by an overland route, and Norfolk was more likely to receive foreign and nonlocal news from New York than from Philadelphia. In 1820 there were 111 New York shipping arrivals in Norfolk, a mean of one every 3.3 days, but only 29 from Philadelphia, a mean of one every 12.6 days. The discrepancy between Norfolk arrivals in New York [79] and New York arrivals in Norfolk [111] was owing to the tendency of vessels from New York to continue beyond Norfolk to other ports and consequently to be recorded as arriving back in New York from their last port of call rather than from Norfolk. Data derived from an examination of all 104 1820 issues of *NYSL*.

40. Baltimore was also known to receive New Orleans news via New York and thus to have a greater time lag, both because of the very slow overland mail service in the South and because the number of shipping departures from New Orleans for New York in 1816 was at least triple that for Baltimore (43 to 14). *NWR* 13, no. 10 (Nov. 1, 1817), 160; 12, no. 5 (Mar. 29, 1817), 70.

41. If the data is assumed to be representative as well as accurate, Baltimore information was often published in New York before it was published in Philadelphia, which had a 2.7-day mean public-information time lag from the Maryland city. Thus, newsworthy information must have moved directly through Philadelphia via stage and steamboat to New York. Yet undoubtedly, this peculiarity arose in

part because the New York paper sampled appeared in the evening, which meant that it sometimes could print material that had passed through Philadelphia too late to make the morning deadline.

42. The Savannah-to-Charleston stage-route distance was 106 miles, while the Philadelphia-to-New York distance over the main stage and steamboat route was 100 miles. H. S. Tanner, *The American Traveller; or Guide Through the United States*, 2nd ed. (Philadelphia, 1836), pp. 85, 113.

43. According to samples of the *Charleston Courier* in 1817, New Orleans-to-Charleston time lags were 27-65 days.

44. *NYSL*. At this date, New Orleans was also apt to receive news channeled via New York before it acquired information from other major Southern ports, for in 1816 New Orleans was visited by 67 vessels from New York (an average of one every 5.4 days), seven from Charleston (an average of one every 52.1 days), and two from Savannah. *NWR* 12, no. 5 (Mar. 29, 1817), 70.

45. A survey of event-to-publication time lags in 27 issues of the *Inquisitor and Cincinnati Advertiser*, June–December 1818, revealed: New York-to-Cincinnati, 21.0 days; Boston-to-Cincinnati, 23.0 days; and Norfolk-to-Cincinnati, 30.0 days.

46. Other mean public-information time lags for Cincinnati in 1818 were Nashville, 13.7 days; St. Louis, 34.3 days; and Detroit, 37.5 days. Significantly, the prevalent path of commodity movement from Cincinnati to New Orleans resulted in a time lag of only 34.5 days, although the intervening physical distance was considerably more than twice that from Cincinnati to either St. Louis or Detroit.

47. Lee, *Daily Newspaper*, pp. 715-717; Clarence S. Brigham, *History and Bibliography of American Newspapers, 1690-1820* (Worcester: American Antiquarian Society, 1947).

48. Hudson, *Journalism in the U.S.*, pp. 365, 608; *History of the Railway Mail Service*, U.S. Senate Executive Document No. 40, 48th Cong., 2nd sess., 1885, pp. 12, 16, 20; Lee, *Daily Newspaper*, pp. 484-485; *NWR* 49, no. 18 (Jan. 2, 1836), 299.

49. Lee, *Daily Newspaper*, p. 486; *New York Evening Post*, July 6, 1839; *Boston Evening Transcript*, June 15, 1841.

50. *NWR* 44, no. 6 (Apr. 6, 1833), 81; Hudson, *Journalism in the U.S.*, p. 365; Lee, *Daily Newspaper*, p. 485; *Boston Evening Transcript*, Apr. 2, 1841; Harold A. Innis, *The Bias of Communication* (Toronto: University of Toronto Press, 1951), p. 175.

51. J. S. Buckingham, *America: Historical, Statistic, and Descriptive* (New York, 1841), II, 347.

52. In 1841 the mean Charleston-to-New York news delay was 5.5 days, while that for Charleston-to-Philadelphia was 6.6 days. Similarly, the average Savannah-to-New York time lag was 6.3 days, but that from Savannah-to-Philadelphia was 7.7 days.

53. See, e.g., *NWR* 53, no. 2 (Sept. 9, 1837), 17; 55, no. 15 (Dec. 8, 1838), 225.

54. *NWR* 43, no. 23 (Feb. 2, 1833), 371; Lee, *Daily Newspaper*, p. 485; Albion, *The Rise of New York Port*, p. 315; *NWR* 56, no. 5 (Mar. 30, 1839), 80.

55. Albion, *Square-Riggers*, pp. 57-61, 66; *NWR* 58, no. 2 (Mar. 14, 1840), 32; and 56, no. 16 (June 15, 1839), 244. Until the signing of new mail-carrying contracts in 1835, "express" mails under good conditions required almost two weeks to go from New York to New Orleans. In 1835 those same mails consumed almost 18 days in their passage via a western route, in itself a considerable improvement. In comparison, packets built in the 1830s made the New York-to-New Orleans run in from 10 to 35 days, with most of them averaging well under 18 days. That is, the overland information route to the South probably was not of real importance until after 1835. Albion, *Square-Riggers*, pp. 290-295; *NWR* 53, no. 20 (Jan. 13, 1838), 319-320.

56. *Cincinnati Daily Gazette*, Dec. 16, 1836, in Berry, *Western Prices*, p. 13.

57. Lee, *Daily Newspaper*, p. 486.

58. Arthur H. Cole, *Wholesale Commodity Prices in the United States, 1700-1861* (Cambridge: Harvard University Press, 1938), pp. 94-96, 103. See also Berry, *Western Prices*, pp. 99-101.

59. Mott, *American Journalism*, pp. 50-51.

60. Buckingham, *Specimens of Newspaper Literature*, II, 77; *Boston Evening Transcript*, Dec. 2, 1841.

61. S. N. D. North, *History and Present Condition of the Newspaper and Periodical Press of the United States* (Washington, D.C., 1884), p. 141. The Postal Act of 1792 had granted newspaper publishers exemption from postage when mailing copies to each other. This privilege was not terminated until 1845. "It is difficult to see how the western papers, above all others, could have existed without free exchanges. Not only were they more dependent on them, owing to their distance from the sources of information in the older districts, but the slender resources of most western papers would have been seriously taxed had the exchanges been subjected to postage." Julian P. Bretz, "Some Aspects of Postal Extension into the West," *Annual Report of the American Historical Association for the Year 1909* (Washington, D.C.: Government Printing Office, 1911), p. 147.

62. *NWR* 44, no. 12 (May 18, 1833), 178.

63. Wesley E. Rich, *The History of the United States Post Office to the Year 1829* (Cambridge: Harvard University Press, 1924), pp. 78-80; *History of the Railway Mail Service*, p. 13.

64. *NWR* 26, no. 11 (May 15, 1824), 178; Lee, *Daily Newspaper*, p. 728; Hudson, *Journalism in the U.S.*, p. 512. Even if one were to make the unrealistic assumption that Philadelphia dailies had a circulation in 1824 comparable to that of 1836, and even if one were to amplify that total 40 or 50 percent by allowing for the circulation of semiweeklies, triweeklies, and weeklies, the 1824 weekly mailing of 12,500 copies would still appear sizable.

65. *NWR* 28, no. 11 (May 14, 1825), 167. The number of Richmond editions per week may be inaccurate, because it is for not 1825 but 1828, as derived from "Daniel Hewitt's List of Newspapers," p. 377. The number of papers published nationally in 1825 was arrived at by interpolating the 1820 and 1828 data. The estimate of those receiving Richmond papers is based on the assumption that the daily was sent to as many editors as the average for the five weeklies.

66. *NWR* 35, no. 8 (Oct. 18, 1828), 118; 44, no. 9 (Apr. 27, 1833), 132. The one-million per month claim was consistent with an earlier statement: "The annual number of newspapers which pass through the New York post office is estimated at eleven million eight hundred thousand." *NWR* 44, no. 1 (Mar. 2, 1833), 4.

67. *History of the Railway Mail Service*, p. 39; *NWR* 53, no. 20 (Jan. 13, 1838), 320. The combined total of 29,000,000 papers moved by the Post Office in 1837 approached the volume of postage-paying letters delivered that year (29,360,992; another 3,000,000 dead and free letters were also carried). In 1840 the postmaster general indicated: "It will not be far from the truth to estimate the printed matter as constituting ninety-five per cent. of the whole [weight of the] mails." *HCSR* 3, no. 26 (Dec. 23, 1840), 414.

68. "Postage on Newspapers and Periodicals, Communicated to the House of Representatives on the 13th Feb., 1832," *American State Papers*, Class VII, *Post Office Department*, 1834, pp. 341-343. Many cities had specialized agricultural papers with far-flung circulations.

69. North, *Newspaper and Periodical Press*, pp. 137, 141; Rich, *History of the Post Office to 1829*, pp. 137-142. See also Innis, *Bias of Communication*, pp. 165-166.

70. Lee, *Daily Newspaper*, pp. 302, 261, 382; Brigham, *History and Bibliography of American Newspapers*. In 1820 country editions also originated from Boston, Albany, Alexandria, Lynchburg, Norfolk, Richmond, Charleston, Savannah, Mobile, St. Louis, and New Orleans. They should not be confused with the specialized agricultural papers printed in some of the same cities.

71. For the original formulation of the "potential" concept, see John Q. Stewart, "Empirical Mathematical Rules Concerning the Distribution and Equilibrium of Population," *Geographical Review* 37 (1947), 461-485. See also Walter Isard, *Methods of Regional Analysis* (Cambridge: M.I.T. Press, 1960), pp. 493-568.

72. The use of editions-per-week data rather than circulation data, which exists only in extremely scattered and often unreliable forms, is consistent with editorial exchange practices.

73. Arnold Court noted the different self-potential results obtained when a uniform rather than a conical intra-areal (intracounty) distribution is assumed. See Leslie J. King, *Statistical Methods in Geography* (Englewood Cliffs, N.J.: Prentice-Hall, 1969), pp. 96-97.

74. Innis, *Bias of Communication*, p. 157; Brigham, *History and Bibliography of American Newspapers*.

75. In 1820 four dailies were in operation in Charleston and three in New Orleans.

76. New York's public-information accessibility also would have achieved a higher 1840 value if newspaper editions had been weighted as to size (inches of column space) as well as frequency of publication. To a lesser degree this would have been true of Boston, Philadelphia, and a few other large cities.

77. In 1840 nine dailies were published in New Orleans, and another two in its immediate suburbs. U.S. Bureau of the Census, *Aggregate Value and Produce, and Number of Persons Employed in Mines, Agriculture, Commerce, Manufactures, &c.: Sixth Census of the United States, 1840*, 1841.

3. Postal Services and Long-Distance Information Flows

1. Wesley Rich, *The History of the United States Post Office to the Year 1829* (Cambridge: Harvard University Press, 1924), pp. 58-62, 64, 69, 182-184; Sidney I. Pomerantz, *New York: An American City, 1783-1803: A Study of Urban Life* (New York: Columbia University Press, 1938), p. 164.

2. Rich, *History of the United States Post Office*, pp. 182-183. Rich's source was Pliny Miles, *Postal Reform: Its Urgent Necessity and Practicability* (New York: 1855), of whose data Rich noted (p. 108): "These figures represent at best an estimate only, and are based in part, at least, on the receipts for postage." Apparently the only other estimate for any date through 1829 was made by Henry Adams, who assumed that ten letters were carried for every dollar of postage receipts, from which he concluded: "the whole number of letters was 2,900,000—about one a year for every grown inhabitant." Henry Adams, *The United States in 1800* (Ithaca: Cornell University Press, 1955), pp. 43-44. This is likely a high approximation, since postage rates at that date ranged from 8 to 35 cents per single sheet of paper, with no letter that moved over 90 miles costing less than 10 cents. Thus, with multiple rates being charged for each extra sheet of paper, and long-distance mail exercising a disproportionate influence on the average cost, it is almost certain that far fewer than ten letters were carried for every dollar of receipts.

3. *NWR* 53, no. 20 (Jan. 13, 1838), 320. The ratio is based on an 1837 population estimated provided in U.S. Bureau of the Census, *Historical Statistics of the United States, Colonial Times to 1957*, 1960, p. 7.

4. Daniel Roper, *The United States Post Office* (New York: Funk & Wagnalls), p. 52; Adam Seybert, *Statistical Annals: Embracing Views of the Population, Commerce, Navigation . . . of the United States of America* (Philadelphia, 1818), pp. 374-375; Stuart Weems Bruchey, *Robert Oliver, Merchant of Baltimore, 1783-1819* (Baltimore: Johns Hopkins Press, 1956), pp. 132-135; *HCSR* 3, no. 8 (Aug. 19, 1840), 119.

5. Rich, *History of the United States Post Office*, pp. 137-140; *Historical Statistics*, p. 498. Actually, packets in excess of one ounce were charged even more in proportion to their weight.

6. Stanley Lebergott, "Wage Trends, 1800-1900," in *Trends in the American Economy in the Nineteenth Century* (Princeton: Princeton University Press, 1960), pp. 462, 471-473, 482-484; Richard A. Easterlin, "Interregional Differences in Per Capita Income, Population, and Total Income, 1840-1950," in *Trends in the American Economy*, pp. 97-98. By comparison, a contemporary estimate put the 1840 annual income of individuals employed in commerce in New York, Boston, Philadelphia, Baltimore, and New Orleans at $1,000, and of persons elsewhere employed in business at $600. Ezra C. Seaman, *Essays on the Progress of Nations* (New York, 1852), p. 459.

7. "In 1840, the head of the family was asked for the total number of illiterates in each family, a method which undoubtedly led to some understatement." *Historical Statistics*, p. 206.

8. Ralph H. Brown, *Historical Geography of the United States* (New York: Harcourt, Brace, 1948), p. 99; Seybert, *Statistical Annals*, p. 374; U.S. Senate, *History of the Railway Mail Service*, Executive Document No. 40, 48th Cong., 2nd sess., 1885, pp. 20-28. Although contracts had previously been signed by the post office and individual railroads, not until 1838 did Congress enact legislation declaring every railroad a post road. The mobile railroad post office did not make its first appearance until 1840.

9. Rich, *History of the United States Post Office*, pp. 94, 96; *History of the Railway Mail Service*, p. 34; HCSR 3, no. 27 (Dec. 30, 1840), 431.

10. Seybert, *Statistical Annals*, p. 376; *NYSL* May 24, 1816; John H. Morrison, *History of American Steam Navigation* (New York: W. F. Sametz, 1903), pp. 169, 266; *NWR* 16, no. 4 (Mar. 20, 1819), 78.

11. U.S. Senate, *Report [by] the Committee on the Post Office and Post Roads*, Executive Document No. 422, 23rd Cong., 1st sess., 1834, pp. 329-341; *History of the Railway Mail Service*, pp. 12, 16, 19, 20, 22; *NWR* 49, no. 7 (Oct. 17, 1835), 101; 51, no. 9 (Oct. 29, 1836), 135; 58, no. 20 (July 18, 1840), 320; Morrison, *History of American Steam Navigation*, p. 342; *New York Evening Post*, July 9, 1840; HCSR 3, no. 27 (Dec. 30, 1840), 431; Wheaton J. Lane, *From Indian Trail to Iron Horse: Travel and Transportation in New Jersey, 1620-1860* (Princeton: Princeton University Press, 1939), pp. 300-301.

12. Philadelphia *Gazette of the United States and Daily Evening Advertiser*, Oct. 17, 1794; *History of the Railway Mail Service*, pp. 20, 28; *Report [by] the Committee on the Post Office*, pp. 321-325, 327, 329-341.

13. Rich, *History of the United States Post Office*, p. 96; *Philadelphia Aurora for the Country*, Feb. 1, 1805; *NWR* 48, no. 9 (May 2, 1835), 145; 27, no. 25 (Feb. 19, 1825), 389; 41, no. 25 (Feb. 18, 1832), 147; *History of the Railway Mail Service*, p. 13; Frank Luther Mott, *American Journalism: A History of Newspapers in the United States Through 250 Years, 1690 to 1940* (New York: Macmillan, 1941), p. 306.

14. Julian P. Bretz, "Some Aspects of Postal Extension into the West," *Annual Report of the American Historical Association for the Year 1909* (Washington, D.C.: Government Printing Office, 1911), p. 143-146; Rich, *History of the United States Post Office*, pp. 68-70, 92-93; Roper, *United States Post Office*, p. 94.

15. Bretz, "Some Aspects of Postal Extension," p. 128; Rich, *History of the United States Post Office*, p. 77.

16. Rich, *History of the United States Post Office*, p. 74; Balthasar H. Meyer, ed., *History of Transportation in the United States Before 1860* (Washington, D.C.: Carnegie Institution of Washington, 1917), p. 121; Seymour Dunbar, *A History of Travel in America* (Indianapolis: Bobbs-Merrill, 1915), III, 759; *NWR* 14, no. 26 (Aug. 22, 1818), 439; 53, no. 20 (Jan. 13, 1838), 319-320; U.S. Senate, *Letter from the Postmaster General . . . Failures and Delays of the United States Mail Between Washington City and Wheeling, Va.*, Executive Document No. 97, 17th Cong., 1st sess., 1822, p. 1; U.S. Senate, *United States Mail—Washington and Wheeling*, Executive Document No. 348, 25th Cong., 2nd sess., 1838, p. 1. The improvements claimed by the post office in 1837 were substantial, for in 1835 the

fastest mails from New York to Cincinnati had taken 5.7 days, to Louisville—7.75 days, and to St. Louis—13.4 days.

17. Rich, *History of the United States Post Office*, pp. 86-87; *Report [by] the Committee on the Post Office*, pp. 334, 351-356; Almon E. Parkins, *The Historical Geography of Detroit* (Chicago: University of Chicago Libraries, 1918), p. 260. The *Cleveland Gazette* on Aug. 31, 1837, still claimed: "The land [as opposed to steamboat] mail between this and Detroit crawls at a snail's pace."

18. Dunbar, *History of Travel*, III, 759; *NWR* 12, no. 19 (July 5, 1817), 304; *Report [by] the Committee on the Post Office*, pp. 347, 352-357.

19. Louis C. Hunter, *Steamboats on the Western Rivers* (Cambridge: Harvard University Press, 1949), pp. 336-337; *NWR* 52, no. 7 (Apr. 15, 1837), 102; *HCSR* 3, no. 27 (Dec. 30, 1840), 431; *Historical Statistics*, p. 13. A thrice-weekly steamboat mail between Pittsburgh and Cincinnati operated briefly in 1835.

20. In 1790 Virginia and North Carolina were the first and third most populous states in the Union. In the 1820 census the total population of Ohio, Kentucky, and Tennessee first surpassed the 1790 total attained by Virginia and both Carolinas. *Historical Statistics*, pp. 12-13.

21. Rich, *History of the United States Post Office*, p. 78; *NWR* 36, no. 12 (May 16, 1829), 178; 59, no. 4 (Sept. 26, 1840), 64; *Boston Evening Transcript*, Feb. 1, 1841.

22. *NWR* 28, no. 13 (May 28, 1825), 194; Meyer, *History of Transportation*, p. 420.

23. Rich, *History of the United States Post Office*, pp. 80-84; *NWR* 27, no. 18 (Jan. 1, 1825), 279; Meyer, *History of Transportation*, pp. 62-63.

24. *NWR* 53, no. 20 (Jan. 13, 1838), 319. In the spring of 1833 the *Mobile Advertiser* claimed that no paper from Charleston was less than 15 days old and that five daily mails were due from New Orleans. *NWR* 44, no. 12 (May 18, 1833), 178.

25. *NWR* 30, no. 18 (July 1, 1826), 320; 55, no. 2 (Sept. 8, 1838), 32; 56, no. 5 (Mar. 30, 1839), 80; 56, no. 20 (July 13, 1839), 320; *HCSR* 2, no. 3 (June 3, 1840), 363. The 2.6-day New York-Charleston delivery time was not recorded until 1840. In the late 1830s New Orleans' postal contacts with the Ohio Valley were also noticeably better, owing partly to the 1837 introduction of expresses as far as Nashville on the Louisville–New Orleans route, and partly to the 1838 establishment of previously frustrated steamboat mails between Louisville and New Orleans. Hunter, *Steamboats*, pp. 336-337; *NWR* 54, no. 26 (Aug. 25, 1838), 416.

26. Rich, *History of the United States Post Office*, p. 69; *Report [by] the Committee on the Post Office*, p. 273.

27. This would need not be so if receipts for the latter date were reported on a net basis and those for the earlier date on a gross basis.

28. U.S. Senate, *Postage Accruing in the Year 1835*, Executive Document No. 262, 24th Cong., 1st sess., 1836; *NWR* 48, no. 12 (May 23, 1835), 216. The data for Boston and Philadelphia include figures for post offices in subsequently incorporated suburbs. The greater volume for Boston conforms with the expectedly high prevalence of short-distance mail flow, given the high population density of the city's immediate hinterland, for in 1840 half of Massachusetts' population was

within a 29-mile radius. Jesse Chickering, "Progress of Population in Boston," *HMM* 13 (December 1845), 556.

29. The same difficulty is not usually associated with comparing receipt data for a single place at different dates. This is so because it is assumed that the relative distribution of a city's postal contacts at various distances is normally stable over fairly lengthy periods of time, or that the contact-array spatial biases of a city are in most instances relatively stable, and thus a city's postal receipts usually reflect changes in its contact intensities on the whole rather than major alterations in its array of postal destinations. The assumption is consistent with Hägerstrand's observation that "information and influences travel in a system of communication with a rather stable spatial configuration." Torsten Hägerstrand, "Aspects of the Spatial Structure of Social Communication and Diffusion of Information," *Papers and Proceedings of the Regional Science Association* 16 (1966), 27–42.

30. "List of Post Offices and the Receipts and Expenditures for the Year Ending Oct. 5, 1791," *American State Papers*, Class VII, *Post Office Department*, 1834, pp. 13–14. In 1791 the total postage collected was $42,255.14, of which $9,674.40 came from Philadelphia (then the country's largest city), $5,537.18 from New York, $3,936.81 from Baltimore, and $3,694.75 from Boston.

31. The comparison between 1822 local postal receipts (the earliest post-1791 data available) and 1820 population levels is justified since 1822 receipts at the national level ($1,108,309.54) were almost identical with those of 1820 ($1,111,927.00).

32. U.S. House, *Letter from the Postmaster General Transmitting a Statement of the Nett Amount of Postage Accruing at Each Office in Each State and Territory of the United States for the Year Ending 31st March, 1827*, Document No. 60, 20th Cong., 1st sess., 1828; U.S. House, *Letter from the Postmaster General Transmitting a Statement of the Amount of Postages Accruing in the United States for One Year Prior to 31st March, 1829*, Document No. 61, 21st Cong., 1st sess., 1830; U.S. House, *Letter from the Postmaster General Transmitting a Statement of the Nett Amount of Postage Accruing to Each Post Office in Each State and Territory of the United States, for One Year, Ending March 31st, 1830*, Document No. 119, 21st Cong., 2nd sess., 1831; U.S. House, *Postage Accruing for Year Ending March 31, 1831*, Document No. 262, 22nd Cong., 1st sess., 1832; U.S. Senate, *Postage for One Year Ending March 31, 1832*, Executive Document No. 18, 22nd Cong., 2nd sess., 1833; U.S. Senate, *Postage Accruing in 1833*, Executive Document No. 63, 23rd Cong., 1st sess., 1834; U.S. Senate, *Postage Accruing in the Year 1834*, Executive Document No. 176, 23rd Cong., 2nd sess., 1835; U.S. Senate, *Postage Accruing in the Year 1835*, Executive Document No. 262, 24th Cong., 1st sess., 1836.

33. The correlation of 1822–1840 receipt increases with 1820–1840 population advances is permissible because of the similarity between the value of postage fees collected nationally in 1820 and 1822.

34. A correct interpretation of the growth of postal receipts requires that it be known that the 1840–41 data are on a net basis, and that during 1839–1841 the

depression caused a decrease in postal revenues at the national scale. *Historical Statistics*, p. 497; *HCSR* 3, no. 8 (Aug. 19, 1840), 119.

35. *NWR* 35, no. 8 (Oct. 18, 1828), 118; 44, no. 9 (Apr. 27, 1833), 132; Rich, *History of the United States Post Office*, p. 183; U.S. House, *Letter from the Postmaster General Transmitting a Statement of the Amount of Postage Accruing in the United States for One Year Prior to 31st March, 1829*, Document No. 61, 21st Cong., 1st sess., 1830; U.S. Senate, *Postage Accruing in the Year 1834*, Executive Document No. 176, 23rd Cong., 2nd sess., 1835.

36. Rich, *History of the United States Post Office*, p. 36; Pomerantz, *New York*, p. 161; Robert Greenhalgh Albion, *Square-Riggers on Schedule: The New York Sailing Packets to England, France, and the Cotton Ports* (Princeton: Princeton University Press, 1938), p. 17. Mail-carrying arrangements were formalized between the United States Post Office and the various New York packet lines long before the demise of the British postal brigs. This was true not just of the packets to Liverpool and London, for in 1827 it was announced: "From the first of October a mail for France will be regularly made up at the New York post office." *NWR* 33, no. 4 (Sept 22, 1827), 56.

37. Roper, *United States Post Office*, p. 366; *NWR* 19, no. 26 (Feb. 24, 1821), 432; 30, no. 14 (June 3, 1826), 239; 39, no. 13 (Nov. 20, 1830), 205; 50, no. 1 (Mar. 5, 1836), 4; 58, no. 12 (May 23, 1840), 192.

38. New York's population—excluding Brooklyn and its other lesser suburbs, most of which had their own post offices—was 1.28 percent of the country's total in 1820, and 1.83 percent of its total in 1840. Inasmuch as the foreign-mail destination data is not specific for any post office other than New York, it was not possible to aggregate that data for the functional city.

39. That the percentage of incoming foreign mail via New York was higher than the percentage of outgoing foreign mail leaving the port is suggested by the fact that 240,548 letters arrived in New York Jan. 1–June 30, 1838, while only 65,667 left the port during the overlapping period of Apr. 16–July 17. *NWR* 54, no. 23 (Aug. 4, 1838), 367. However, other factors, such as seasonal fluctuations in business orders from abroad and correspondence time lags, might also explain why the three-month outgoing volume fell short of 120,000, or about half the six-month incoming total.

40. New York merchants could often send mail overseas on vessels other than their own by repairing to the Tontine Coffee House, where the private letter bags of ships about to depart were usually hung. A list of the ships for which the bags were hung, accompanied by an indication of their intended destinations, was frequently published in the *NYSL* and other commercially oriented newspapers.

4. Interurban Commodity Flows and Long-Distance Information Circulation

1. Clarence H. Danhof, *Change in Agriculture: The Northern United States, 1820–1870* (Cambridge: Harvard University Press, 1969), p. 30. See also Fred Mitchell Jones, *Middlemen in the Domestic Trade of the United States, 1800–*

1860, Illinois Studies in the Social Sciences, vol. 21, no. 3 (Urbana: University of Illinois Press, 1937), pp. 45–57, 66–67; John G. Clark, *The Grain Trade in the Old Northwest* (Urbana: University of Illinois Press, 1966), pp. 41–42; Lewis E. Atherton, *The Pioneer Merchant in Mid-America* (Columbia: University of Missouri Press, 1939).

2. George Rogers Taylor, "American Urban Growth Preceding the Railway Age," *Journal of Economic History* 27 (1967), 328; Douglass C. North, *The Economic Growth of the United States, 1790–1860* (New York: W. W. Norton, 1966), pp. 46, 233; Gordon C. Bjork, "Foreign Trade," in David T. Gilchrist, ed., *The Growth of the Seaport Cities: 1790–1825* (Charlottesville: University of Virginia Press, 1967), p. 54. The resurgence of foreign trade after the War of 1812 was erratic. Exports rose rapidly during 1815–1818, then a recession set in until 1830, followed by six years of renewed rapid expansion. Irregular export fluctuations characterized the final years of the pretelegraphic period.

3. Henry Adams, *The United States in 1800* (Ithaca: Cornell University Press, 1955), pp, 8, 10, 6.

4. *HMM* 25 (September 1851), 381–382; U.S. Bureau of the Census, *Historical Statistics of the United States, Colonial Times to 1957*, 1960, p. 427; Taylor, "American Urban Growth;" p. 334. See also George Rogers Taylor, *The Transportation Revolution, 1815–1860* (New York: Holt, Rinehart & Winston, 1962).

5. Emory R. Johnson, T. W. Van Metre, G. G. Heubner, and D. S. Hanchett, *History of the Domestic and Foreign Commerce of the United States* (Washington, D.C.: Carnegie Institution, 1915), I, 230–231.

6. For the view that the South had a large food deficit and therefore sizable agricultural imports from the West, see North, *Economic Growth*, pp. 67–68, 101–121; Clark, *Grain Trade*, pp. 32–51; Louis B. Schmidt, "Internal Commerce and the Development of the National Economy Before 1860," *Journal of Political Economy* 47 (1939), 798–822. However, Fishlow contended that while 49 percent of the West's agricultural exports were shipped via New Orleans, only 18 percent of such exports were actually consumed in the South. Albert Fishlow, *American Railroads and the Transformation of the Ante-Bellum Economy* (Cambridge: Harvard University Press, 1965), p. 284. See also Isaac Lippincott, "Internal Trade of the United States, 1700–1860," *Washington University Studies* IV, pt. 2, no. 1 (1916), 63–150; Donald L. Kemmerer, "The Pre-Civil War South's Leading Crop, Corn," *Agricultural History* 23 (1949), 236–239.

7. North, *Economic Growth*, p. 105; Fishlow, *American Railroads*, p. 275; Albert Fishlow, "Antebellum Interregional Trade Reconsidered," *American Economic Review* 54 (1964), 352–364. Not until 1847 did tonnage from the Western states through the Erie Canal exceed that originating in western New York.

8. Fishlow, *American Railroads*, p. 271.

9. Johnson et al., *History of the Domestic and Foreign Commerce*, I, 202; cf. I, 208; II, 8; Tench Coxe, *A View of the United States of America* (Philadelphia, 1794), pp. 340–341.

10. Taylor, *Transportation Revolution*, p. 133; Thomas Senior Berry, *Western*

Prices Before 1861: A Study of the Cincinnati Market (Cambridge: Harvard University Press, 1943), pp. 71-87.

11. Taylor, *Transportation Revolution*, pp. 133, 134.

12. Kent T. Healy, "Transportation As a Factor in Economic Growth," *Journal of Economic History* 7 (1947), 84. Those willing to bear railroad carrying and transshipment costs must have gained a saving in time, for long-distance wagon movements were extremely time-consuming. During the War of 1812, for example, summer wagon shipments "required 26 days to go from Boston to Baltimore, 10 days from Baltimore to Richmond [less than 160 miles], and 33 days from Baltimore to Augusta (Ga.). From New York to Augusta required 50 days, and from Philadelphia to Augusta, 45 days. In the winter and spring, however, transportation was far less expeditious." Balthasar H. Meyer, ed., *History of Transportation in the United States Before 1860* (Washington, D.C.: Carnegie Institution, 1917), p. 59.

13. Taylor, *Transportation Revolution*, pp. 132-133; *NWR* 40, no. 12 (May 21, 1831), 207; 31, no. 3 (Sept. 23, 1826), 58; Clark, *Grain Trade*, p. 9; Berry, *Western Prices*, pp. 78, 80-81; Stephen Salsbury, *The State, the Investor, and the Railroad: The Boston & Albany, 1825-1867* (Cambridge: Harvard University Press, 1967), p. 27; Louis C. Hunter, *Steamboats on the Western Rivers* (Cambridge: Harvard University Press, 1949), pp. 374-377, 658-659; Healy, "Transportation As a Factor," p. 84.

14. Julius Rubin, *Canal or Railroad? Imitation and Innovation in the Response to the Erie Canal in Philadelphia, Baltimore, and Boston, Transactions of the American Philosophical Society*, n. s. 51, pt. 7 (Philadelphia, 1961), 6; Fishlow, *American Railroads*, p. 295; F. A. Michaux, *Travels to the West of the Allegheny Mountains . . . Undertaken in the Year 1802* (London, 1805), pp. 126-127; Thaddeus Morton Harris, *The Journal of a Tour into the Territory Northwest of the Allegheny Mountains* (Boston, 1805), p. 343; Berry, *Western Prices*, p. 81; *NWR* 31, no. 3 (Sept. 23, 1826), 58.

15. Yet the impact of the 1840 depression on shipping between these major ports was considerable. In 1835, a pre-depression year, Boston arrivals in New York totaled 494 (751 weighted), almost half again as many as in 1840. Robert G. Albion, *The Rise of New York Port, 1815-1860* (New York: Charles Scribner's Sons, 1939), p. 397.

16. Of the 1,607,492 bushels of corn that arrived in Boston in 1839, 475,236 were from Baltimore, 231,390 from New York, and 201,701 from Philadelphia. Of the 487,674 bushels of oats and rye received that same year, 115,272 were from New York, 82,616 from Baltimore, and 79,627 from Philadelphia. Of Boston's 1839 flour imports of 451,667 barrels, 153,450 came from New York, 61,093 from Baltimore, and 25,872 from Philadelphia. *HCSR* 2, no. 6 (Feb. 5, 1840), 95.

17. The demand for leather in Boston's hinterland was great. In 1810, 100,000 pairs of women's shoes were manufactured in Lynn alone. *American State Papers, Class II, Finance*, 1834, p. 426.

18. Edward C. Kirkland, *Men, Cities and Transportation: A Study in New England History, 1820–1900* (Cambridge: Harvard University Press, 1948), pp. 11–15. In Boston, anthracite began to replace wood imported for fuel purposes during the 1820s. Of the 96,365 tons of domestic and foreign coal arriving in Boston in 1839, Philadelphia provided 72,488. *HCSR* 2, no. 6 (Feb. 5, 1840), 95.

19. Kirkland, *Men, Cities and Transportation*, I, 14; Albion, *Rise of New York Port*, pp. 127, 189; J. S. Buckingham, *America: Historical, Statistic, and Descriptive* (New York, 1841), I, 360. As New York packet service expanded, English manufacturers became increasingly inclined to ship their merchandise to Boston and other major coastal ports via New York.

20. Rubin, *Canal or Railroad?* pp. 18–19.

21. Albion, *Rise of New York Port*, p. 134; *NWR* 43, no. 15 (Dec. 8, 1832), 240.

22. Rubin, *Canal or Railroad?* pp. 18–19; Kirkland, *Men, Cities and Transportation*, II, 229; I, 14.

23. Albion, *Rise of New York Port*, p. 127; Fishlow, *American Railroads*, pp. 270–271; Berry, *Western Prices*, p. 78.

24. Pennsylvania anthracite was first burned in New York in 1810, but the city's consumption did not grow significantly until the 1820s. In 1825, anthracite output from eastern Pennsylvania reached almost 34,000 tons, of which roughly one-third was shipped from Philadelphia to New York. By 1840, production was over 865,000 tons. Although the Philadelphia-to-New York coal trade was soon shared with the Delaware and Raritan, Morris, and Delaware and Hudson canals, it continued to grow in importance. In 1822 the Philadelphia coal fleet consisted of only four vessels, but by 1834, 1,614 colliers departed from the port, and in 1839 "perhaps nine-tenths" of the vessels arriving in Philadelphia were employed in the anthracite trade. I. N. Phelps Stokes, *The Iconography of Manhattan Island, 1498–1909* (New York: Robert H. Dodd, 1915–1928), I, 407; *NWR* 28, no. 13 (May 28, 1825), 195; 56, no. 20 (July 13, 1839), 320; *HCSR* 3, no. 7 (Aug. 12, 1840), 103; *HMM* 4 (March 1841), 286; Kirkland, *Men, Cities and Transportation*, I, 15; Albion, *Rise of New York Port*, p. 136.

25. *HMM* 18 (April 1848), 434; Albion, *Rise of New York Port*, p. 134; George Armroyd, *A Connected View of the Whole Internal Navigation of the United States* (Philadelphia, 1830), p. 99. By comparison, overland freight movements across New Jersey between Philadelphia and New York probably never had exceeded the 1822 and 1830 estimates of 10,000 tons. Armroyd, *A Connected View*, p. 99; Wheaton J. Lane, *From Indian Trail to Iron Horse: Travel and Transportation in New Jersey, 1620–1860* (Princeton: Princeton University Press, 1939), p. 206.

26. The amount of coal carried on the Delaware and Raritan Canal in 1840 was 113,078 tons, or over 65 percent of the canal's total traffic. *HMM* 18 (April 1848), 433.

27. James W. Livingood, *The Philadelphia-Baltimore Trade Rivalry, 1780–1860* (Harrisburg: Pennsylvania Historical and Museum Commission, 1957), pp. 96, 98; *HCSR* 6, no. 25 (June 22, 1842), 400. The traffic on the Chesapeake and Delaware Canal accounted in part for the surprisingly small volume of coastal shipping between Philadelphia and Baltimore in Table 4.4. During the 1820s the volume of

trade moving coastwise between the two ports was apparently exceeded by that moving via a route which included two waterborne links and a land leg over the Delmarva Peninsula. (Armroyd, *A Connected View*, pp. 160-161). This makes the small volume of Baltimore-Philadelphia interaction shown in Table 4.3 more understandable.

28. Taylor, *Transport Revolution*, p. 154.

29. Livingood, *Philadelphia-Baltimore Trade Rivalry*, p. 162.

30. *HMM* 21 (July 1849), 54; J. Finch, *Travels in the U.S.A. and Canada* (London, 1833), in Stokes, *Iconography of Manhattan Island*, V (1926), 1,707.

31. In 1835 there were 137 arrivals in Boston from Albany. Four years later, Albany provided Boston with almost 40,000 tons of flour and nearly 47,000 tons of oats and other grains. Albion, *Rise of New York Port*, p. 128; *HCSR* 2, no. 6 (Feb. 5, 1840), 95.

32. In 1816, of New Orleans' 387 foreign and domestic arrivals, only seven came from Charleston and two from Savannah. In that same year Charleston had only six arrivals from New Orleans, and Savannah had only one. *NWR* 12, no. 5 (Mar. 29, 1817), 70.

33. The discrepancy between New Orleans arrivals at Mobile and Mobile arrivals at New Orleans is primarily because New Orleans vessels often proceeded beyond Mobile before returning home and were therefore recorded as arriving from another port.

34. *HMM* 22 (May 1850), 501. The remaining domestic arrivals at Charleston, however, were not necessarily from outside the South, for the city received many vessels from lesser Southern ports, such as Wilmington, North Carolina. The total of 1,461 was also swollen by the inclusion of passenger vessels not tallied by the *NYSL*, the source for Table 4.6.

35. Diane Lindstrom, "Southern Dependence upon Interregional Grain Supplies: A Review of the Trade Flows, 1840-1860," *Agricultural History* 44 (1970), 101-113. According to Lindstrom, in 1841-1842 only 3.2 percent of New Orleans domestic flour and corn exports went to Gulf Coast ports and 3.0 percent to South Atlantic ports.

36. *HMM* 5 (November 1841), 471. In 1821-1822, 7,059 of the 45,423 bales exported from Mobile were freighted to New Orleans; in 1823-1824, 13,094 of the 40,182 bales sent from Mobile were destined for New Orleans. *NWR* 24, no. 2 (Mar. 15, 1823), 21; 27, no. 10 (Nov. 6, 1824), 149.

37. For example, cotton exports from Mobile to Liverpool were 250,844 bales in 1839-1840, while those from New Orleans to Liverpool reached 465,183 bales in 1837-1838. *HMM* 3 (November 1840), 454; 13 (November 1845), 422.

38. Albion, *Rise of New York Port*, pp. 95-96. Not all the cotton shipped to New York from Charleston, Savannah, Mobile, and New Orleans was transferred to transatlantic packets. Much of it found its way to textile mills in southern New England after having been freighted from New York to Providence. Providence had 60 coastal arrivals from New York in 1820 and 78 arrivals (82.5 weighted) in 1840, exclusive of frequently docking passenger steamers.

39. "The average [cotton] planter was inclined to be at least one year in debt, receiving from the [New York or Northeastern] factor, at a substantial rate of

interest, a considerable part of the value of his next year's crop." Albion, *Rise of New York Port*, p. 112. On cotton sales and purchases, see Norman Sydney Buck, *The Development of the Organization of Anglo-American Trade, 1800–1850* (New Haven: Yale University Press, 1925), pp. 66–97.

40. Albion, *Rise of New York Port*, p. 100.

41. For example, in 1822, New York packets were an average of two days quicker in reaching Charleston than were ordinary vessels from Baltimore and Philadelphia and six days quicker than Boston vessels completing the same trip. Robert G. Albion, *Square-Riggers on Schedule: The New York Sailing Packets to England, France, and the Cotton Ports* (Princeton: Princeton University Press, 1938), p. 54.

42. *NWR* 56, no. 22 (July 27, 1839), 349.

43. Albion, *Square-Riggers*, p. 73.

44. In addition to her other cotton imports, Boston acquired between 7,159 and 22,889 bales per year from Charleston and from Savannah between 5,668 and 11,123 bales per year during the 1830s. *HMM* 10 (May 1844), 425.

45. Of the 1,607,492 bushels of corn unloaded in Boston in 1839, 274,886 were from New Orleans, 96,823 from Norfolk, and 22,863 from Richmond. Of the 451,667 barrels of flour shipped to Boston that year, 55,086 were from Richmond, 47,871 from New Orleans, and only 3,576 from Norfolk. *HCSR* 2, no. 6 (Feb. 5, 1840), 95.

46. Philadelphia's coal shipments to Boston in 1839 were about 14 times those from Richmond. *HCSR* 2, no. 6 (Feb. 5, 1840), 95.

47. In the 1790s, Philadelphia played a relatively more important role than in later years in redistributing European imports to Southern ports. Jedidiah Morse, *The American Geography; or a View of the Present Situation of the United States of America*, 2nd ed. (London, 1792), p. 335.

48. Richmond dominated the New York coal market between the end of the War of 1812 and the rapid development of Pennsylvania anthracite mining in the 1820s. Flour shipments from Richmond to New York declined sharply in importance with the opening of the Erie Canal. Albion, *The Rise of New York Port*, pp. 135, 136, 138.

49. In 1840, Richmond's arrivals from New York were roughly twice those of Norfolk; while in 1820, Norfolk's trade with New York exceeded that between Richmond and New York. This change occurred largely in the late 1820s, when steam-powered vessels of light draft began to ascend the James River and thus bypassed Norfolk.

50. In a Christallerian central place system for 1840, goods from Cincinnati could only move to each of the three ports just below it in the urban-size hierarchy, and from the roughly equal-sized Pittsburgh or Louisville to the smaller St. Louis; yet in reality goods were exchanged in both directions by all six possible port couples.

51. John H. Morrison, *History of American Steam Navigation* (New York: W. F. Sametz, 1903), pp. 228, 230; Hunter, *Steamboats*, pp. 35–37, 318, 326, 644; Richard C. Wade, *The Urban Frontier: Pioneer Life in Early Pittsburgh, Cincinnati, Lexington, Louisville, and St. Louis* (Chicago: University of Chicago Press, 1964),

p. 191; Frank Haigh Dixon, *A Traffic History of the Mississippi River System*, National Waterways Commission Document No. 11 (Washington, D.C., 1909), p. 15; *ARJ* 3, no. 51 (Dec. 27, 1834), 807; Timothy Pitkin, *A Statistical View of the Commerce of the United States of America* (New Haven, 1835), p. 356.

52. Louisville persisted as a transshipment and break-in-bulk center during the 1830s and early 1840s because the Louisville and Portland Canal could accommodate no craft over 180 feet and was frequently choked with mud in the springtime. Transshipment allowed for sorting of goods bound for Cincinnati from those bound for Pittsburgh, Wheeling, and lesser upper Ohio ports.

53. See Leonard P. Curry, *Rail Routes South: Louisville's Fight for the Southern Market, 1865-1872* (Lexington: University of Kentucky Press, 1969), p. 9; Berry, *Western Prices*, pp. 216-220; Clark, *Grain Trade*, p. 17. Clark noted: "Until the mid-1820's flour was Cincinnati's most valuable export . . . In 1830, with the Miami and Erie Canal completed to Dayton, exports of flour jumped to about 130,000 barrels." However, the pork packing and processing industry expanded at a more rapid rate: "In 1825 the value of pork exports formed 30 per cent of Cincinnati's total exports, and in 1839 44 per cent."

54. Hunter, *Steamboats*, pp. 35-37. Boats to and from Pittsburgh often stopped at Wheeling and sometimes at lesser ports. If some of the steamboats recorded as arriving in Cincinnati from Wheeling in reality originated in Pittsburgh, then Pittsburgh accounted for more than one-third of Cincinnati's incoming steamboats. *NWR* 56, no. 6 (Apr. 6, 1839), 96.

55. Catherine Elizabeth Reiser, *Pittsburgh's Commercial Development, 1800-1850* (Harrisburg: Pennsylvania Historical and Museum Commission, 1951), pp. 45-46.

56. Between 1818 and 1824 about 30,000 tons of merchandise arrived annually at Pittsburgh by overland freight from Philadelphia. Even after the Mainline had usurped much of the Philadelphia-to-Pittsburgh traffic, winter freezing of the canals forced the continued use of overland transport. Estimates for the volume of goods carried in 1837 and 1838 by wagon from Philadelphia and other Eastern cities are 13,500 tons or higher. Reiser, *Pittsburgh's Commercial Development*, p. 77; Wade, *Urban Frontier*, p. 193; *NWR* 55, no. 25 (Feb. 16, 1839), 391.

57. In 1825-1826, Pittsburgh's total downriver exports amounted to $2,781,276, of which $480,000 was for imported dry goods, and $525,000 for "groceries and foreign liquors." In the late 1820s half of all Cincinnati's imports were estimated to be dry goods acquired via Pittsburgh. One specific estimate of Cincinnati's 1826 commerce placed the city's total imports at $1,931,290, and its imports of dry goods at $1,100,000. Reiser, *Pittsburgh's Commercial Development*, p. 46; Wade, *Urban Frontier*, pp. 196-197; Ralph H. Brown, *Historical Geography of the United States* (New York: Harcourt, Brace, 1948), p. 235.

58. In 1825-1826, the value of other leading downriver exports from Pittsburgh was: iron, $398,000; nails, $210,000; castings, $88,000; glass, $105,000; and paper, $55,000. In 1826, Cincinnati's imports of bar, cast, and pig iron supposedly exceeded $225,000. The value of Pittsburgh's steam engine exports stood at $100,000, of cotton yarns and cloth at $160,324. Reiser, *Pittsburgh's Commercial*

Development, p. 46. However, neither of these last items were significant in the Cincinnati trade.

59. *HCSR* 2, no. 4 (Jan. 22, 1840), 62. In 1837 a Pittsburgh newspaper reported that coal exports by flatboat were worth $1 million. *ARJ* 6, no. 47 (Nov. 25, 1837), 646.

60. In 1835, over 5,000,000 pounds of bacon originating in Cincinnati were moved eastward from Pittsburgh via the Mainline. By 1839 this total exceeded 7,000,000 pounds. Berry, *Western Prices*, p. 220.

61. *NWR* 47, no. 24 (Feb. 14, 1835), 413; Hunter, *Steamboats*, pp. 35, 315–316, 327–328; Reiser, *Pittsburgh's Commercial Development*, p. 44. Of the 1,764 steamboats departing in 1837 from Pittsburgh, 523 were scheduled to terminate in Louisville.

62. Wade, *Urban Frontier*, pp. 191, 201; Hunter, *Steamboats*, pp. 315–316, 328, 644; Berry, *Western Prices*, p. 19.

63. Berry, *Western Prices*, pp. 23–24; Dixon, *A Traffic History*, p. 14; Harry N. Scheiber, "The Ohio-Mississippi Flatboat Trade: Some Reconsiderations," in David M. Ellis, ed., *The Frontier in American Development: Essays in Honor of Paul Wallace Gates* (Ithaca: Cornell University Press, 1969), pp. 277–298.

64. Dixon, *A Traffic History*, p. 14; William F. Switzler, *Report on the Interior Commerce of the United States*, U.S. House of Representatives Executive Document No. 6, pt. 2, 50th Cong., 1st sess., 1888, p. 199.

65. *ARJ* 3, no. 51 (Dec. 27, 1834), 807; Pitkin, *A Statistical View*, p. 356.

66. Berry, *Western Prices*, p. 29; *ARJ* 6, no. 47 (Nov. 25, 1837), p. 646. In 1811, a speed record of 78 days was set by a barge on the New Orleans-to-Cincinnati route. "Keelboat rates from New Orleans to Louisville before 1820 were for the most part $5.00 a hundred pounds . . . By 1820 [when steamers had begun to take over] freight was carried from New Orleans to Louisville for as low as 2 cents a pound and three years later from New Orleans to Pittsburgh at $1.00 per hundred." Berry, *Western Prices*, p. 56; Hunter, *Steamboats*, pp. 25–26.

67. Curry, *Rail Routes South*, pp. 9–11, 13; Reiser, *Pittsburgh's Commercial Development*, p. 47; James Flint, *Letters from America* (Edinburgh, 1822), p. 149; Berry, *Western Prices*, pp. 19, 253. The annual volume of goods moving south from the Ohio River between 1820 and 1830 was said to include 200,000–300,000 barrels of flour, 30,000–50,000 barrels of pork, 200,000 bushels of corn and oats, and 75,000 barrels of whiskey. Clark, *Grain Trade*, p. 15. In the late 1830s some of this southbound trade was diverted to the Northeast via the Ohio and Erie Canals.

68. Based on data in Fishlow, *American Railroads*, p. 278. Virtually all of the remainder of New Orlean's receipts were in cotton.

69. In the early 1840s, 36.1 percent of New Orleans' corn receipts, and 30.5 percent of her flour receipts were forwarded to New York, Boston, Philadelphia, and Baltimore. Lindstrom, "Southern Dependence," pp. 103–104.

70. Clark, *Grain Trade*, p. 118; Brown, *Historical Geography*, p. 280; Pitkin, *A Statistical View*, p. 576.

71. *NWR* 14, no. 1 (Feb. 28, 1818), 15; 15, no. 6 (Oct. 3, 1818), 92; 48, no. 12

(May 23, 1835), 205; 51, no. 6 (Oct. 8, 1836), 82; Almon E. Parkins, *The Historical Geography of Detroit* (Lansing: Michigan Historical Commission, 1918), pp. 244-245, 261-263; Morrison, *History of American Steam Navigation*, p. 366; *HCSR* 2, no. 12 (Mar. 18, 1840), 188; 2, no. 13 (Mar. 25, 1840), 197.

72. Israel D. Andrews, *Report . . . on the Trade and Commerce of the British North American Colonies*, U.S. Senate Document No. 112, 32nd Cong., 1st sess., 1853, p. 278; Albion, *Rise of New York Port*, p. 90; Pitkin, *A Statistical View*, p. 576; U.S. Senate, *Preliminary Report of the Inland Waterways Commission*, Document No. 325, 60th Cong., 1st sess., 1908, p. 226; U.S. Senate, *Statistics of Foreign and Domestic Commerce*, Executive Document No. 55, 38th Cong., 1st sess., 1864, p. 133.

73. Johnson et. al., *History of the Domestic and Foreign Commerce*, I, 230-231; Pitkin, *A Statistical View*, p. 576; Clark, *Grain Trade*, pp. 65, 117; U.S. Senate, *Statistics of Foreign and Domestic Commerce*, Executive Document No. 55, 38th Cong., 1st sess., p. 161; Andrews, *Report . . . on the Trade and Commerce*, p. 84. The generation of new grain trade rather than the diversion of old may have been the most important repercussion of the Ohio Canal. After the canal went into operation, "Cleveland's area of supply covered virtually the entire northeastern quarter of Ohio . . . Several lateral or feeder canals connected the Ohio Canal with areas on either side and served to extend the territory from which Cleveland derived its cereals . . . a connection with the Pennsylvania canals was completed in 1839." Clark, *Grain Trade*, p. 61. Much of Cleveland's breadstuff exports bypassing Buffalo went to Lake Ontario ports and Montreal.

74. Brown, *Historical Geography*, p. 283; Parkins, *Historical Geography of Detroit*, p. 162; Clark, *Grain Trade*, pp. 75, 77, 105.

75. John Adams Dix, *Sketch of the Resources of the City of New-York* (New York, 1827), p. 75; *HMM* 10 (May 1844), 423.

76. U.S. House, *Commerce and Naviagation of the United States*, Document No. 122, 26th Cong., 2nd sess., 1841, pp. 284-287. While the use of New York foreign-trade vessels for coastal shipping purposes has been frequently documented, the volume involved is extremely difficult to assess. Quite probably it was not great, for "registered" vessels were forced to pay the same duties at each and every entry that "licensed" vessels paid per annum.

5. Interurban Travel and Long-Distance Information Circulation

1. Stanley Lebergott, "Wage Trends, 1800-1900," in *Trends in the American Economy in the Nineteenth Century* (Princeton: Princeton University Press, 1960), pp. 462, 471-473, 482-484.

2. Henry Adams, *The United States in 1800* (Ithaca: Cornell University Press, 1955), p. 10; Balthasar H. Meyer, ed., *History of Transportation in the United States Before 1860* (Washington, D.C.: Carnegie Institution of Washington, 1917), p. 74; Alice Morse Earle, *Stage-Coach and Tavern Days* (New York: Macmillan, 1901), pp. 270-271; *HCSR* 2, no. 22 (May 27, 1840), p. 338.

3. Meyer, *History of Transportation*, p. 76; *HCSR* 2, no. 22 (May 27, 1840), 338; *NWR* 56, no. 18 (June 29, 1839), 288.

4. Richard A. Easterlin, "Interregional Differences in Per Capita Income, Population, and Total Income, 1840-1950," in *Trends in the American Economy*, pp. 97-98. These estimates pertain to workers employed outside of commerce.

5. Isaac Holmes, *An Account of the United States of America* (London, 1823), p. 335; Robert Greenhalgh Albion, *The Rise of New York Port, 1815-1860* (New York: Charles Scribner's Sons, 1939), p. 118; Fred Mitchell Jones, *Middlemen in the Domestic Trade of the United States, 1800-1860*, Illinois Studies in the Social Sciences, vol. 21, no. 3 (Urbana: University of Illinois Press, 1937), pp. 11, 14-15, 16.

6. Jones, *Middlemen*, pp. 9-11; Norman S. Buck, *The Development of the Organization of Anglo-American Trade, 1800-1860*, Illinois Studies in the Social Press, 1925), p. 149.

7. Albion, *Rise of New York Port*, p. 410; Jones, *Middlemen*, pp. 64, 70, 33; *NWR* 36, no. 5 (Mar. 28, 1829), 67; James Flint, *Letters from America* (London, 1822), pp. 33-34.

8. Jones, *Middlemen*, pp. 18, 24, 52; Buck, *Development of the Organization of Anglo-American Trade*, p. 84.

9. Jones, *Middlemen*, pp. 16, 24, 33, 65-66.

10. Louis C. Hunter, *Steamboats on the Western Rivers* (Cambridge: Harvard University Press, 1949), p. 421.

11. George Rogers Taylor, *The Transportation Revolution, 1815-1860* (New York: Holt, Rinehart & Winston, 1962), p. 146; *NWR* 28, no. 11 (May 14, 1825), 161; *ARJ* 6, no. 51 (Dec. 23, 1837), 674-675. The 1837 estimate is exclusive of passengers who migrated to western New York and took the canal packets no farther west than Rochester.

12. As of 1800, 4 miles per hour was the average stagecoach speed on existing routes. Distances of more than 40 miles were seldom covered in a day, and progress was even slower when the roads or the weather were poor. Subsequently, on good roads, "stagecoaches appear to have averaged from about 6 to 8 miles an hour, though, apparently, faster time was sometimes obtained on important routes where competition was keen. Thus, between New York and Philadelphia stagecoaches were reported in 1819 to be travelling 11½ miles an hour." Adams, *United States in 1800*, p. 8; *NWR* 51, no. 9 (Oct. 29, 1836), 135; Taylor, *Transportation Revolution*, p. 210.

13. Seymour Dunbar, *A History of Travel in America* (Indianapolis: Bobbs-Merrill, 1915), II, 530, 722; Charles W. Janson, *The Stranger in America, 1793-1806* (New York: The Press of the Pioneers, 1935), pp. 177-178.

14. Emory R. Johnson, T. W. Van Metre, G. G. Heubner, and D. S. Hanchett, *History of the Domestic and Foreign Commerce of the United States* (Washington, D.C.: Carnegie Institution of Washington, 1915), II, 8; Christopher Colles, *A Survey of the Roads of the United States of America, 1789*, ed. Walter W. Ristow (Cambridge: Harvard University Press, 1961), p. 97; Meyer, *History of Transportation*, pp. 41, 50-63.

15. Taylor, *Transportation Revolution*, pp. 17-28; Meyer, *History of Transportation*, p. 52.

16. Dunbar, *History of Travel*, III, 3, pp. 744-746; Stephen Salsbury, *The State, the Investor, and the Railroad: The Boston & Albany, 1825-1867* (Cambridge: Harvard University Press, 1967), p. 26; *Philadelphia Public Ledger*, Apr. 15, 1840; *NWR* 54, no. 26 (Aug. 25, 1838), 416.

17. Albert Gallatin, *Report of the Secretary of the Treasury on . . . Public Roads and Canals* (Washington, D.C., 1808), p. 37; Dunbar, *History of Travel*, III, 752. See also Ulrich Bonnell Phillips, *A History of Transportation in the Eastern Cotton Belt to 1860* (New York: Columbia University Press, 1939).

18. Sidney I. Pomerantz, *New York: An American City, 1783-1803: A Study of Urban Life* (New York: Columbia University Press, 1938), pp. 162, 161; Dunbar, *History of Travel*, II, 405; I, 324; Samuel Eliot Morison, *The Maritime History of Massachusetts, 1783-1860*, rev. ed. (Boston: Houghton Mifflin, 1961), p. 231.

19. Morison, *Maritime History*, p. 232; Ralph H. Brown, *Historical Geography of the United States* (New York: Harcourt Brace, 1948), p. 127; Robert Greenhalgh Albion, *Square-Riggers on Schedule: The New York Sailing Packets to England, France, and the Cotton Ports* (Princeton: Princeton University Press, 1938), p. 229; Edward Chase Kirkland, *Men, Cities and Transportation: A Study in New England History* (Cambridge: Harvard University Press, 1949), I, 9.

20. Hunter, *Steamboats*, p. 421; James Grant Wilson, *The Memorial History of the City of New York* (New York, 1893), III, 335; *NWR* 30, no. 14 (June 3, 1826), 241; 50, no. 1 (Mar. 5, 1836), 4; 56, no. 20 (July 13, 1839), 320; J. S. Buckingham, *America: Historical, Statistic, and Descriptive* (New York, 1841), I, 167, 459.

21. U.S. Bureau of the Census, *Historical Statistics of the United States, Colonial Times to 1957*, 1960, p. 427; Meyer, *History of Transportation*, p. 573; Albert Fishlow, *American Railroads and the Transformation of the Ante-Bellum Economy* (Cambridge: Harvard University Press, 1965), pp. 6, 269; Oliver W. Holmes, "The Stage-Coach Business in the Hudson Valley," *Quarterly Journal of the New York State Historical Association* 12 (1931), 255.

22. Pomerantz, *New York*, p. 163.

23. *New York Daily Advertiser*, May 22, 1804.

24. If the average load figure is somewhat high, it is probably compensated for by the extra vehicles used during periods of heavy demand.

25. *NYSL*, May 24, 1816. At this time stage routes were longer during winter months, owing to river ice. Wheaton J. Lane, *From Indian Trail to Iron Horse: Travel and Transportation in New Jersey, 1620-1860* (Princeton: Princeton University Press, 1939), p. 195.

26. George Armroyd, *A Connected View of the Whole Internal Navigation of the United States* (Philadelphia, 1830), p. 99; *NWR* 30, no. 12 (May 20, 1826), 201; 35, no. 1 (Aug. 30, 1828), 4.

27. Lane, *From Indian Trail to Iron Horse*, pp. 201-202, 289. This estimate agrees with another 1833 evaluation placing annual steamboat traffic between New York and New Jersey in excess of 125,000 persons. *ARJ* 2, no. 25 (June 22, 1833), 387. By 1833 the number of passengers making the New York-Philadelphia trip by sailing vessel must have been negligible.

28. Lane, *From Indian Trail to Iron Horse*, pp. 290-291; Meyer, *History of Transportation*, pp. 364-365.

29. The number of one-way trips per 1,000 persons of both cities is not an ideal measure, for it suggests an equal number of trips in both directions. Pretelegraphic travel between specific urban pairs was sometimes heavier in one direction than another, either because of businessmen who were calling on contacts in more than one place and therefore did not return to their city of residence by the same route on which they had left, or because of migrants who did not make the return trip. Thus, if data permitted, it would be more meaningful to compute two ratios, one for each direction of movement.

30. Oliver W. Holmes, "Levi Pease, The Father of New England Stage-Coaching," *Journal of Economic and Business History* 3 (1930-1931), 241-245, 256; Dunbar, *History of Travel*, I, 187-188. In the early 1790s New York and Boston newspapers frequently advertised passenger berths on vessels sailing between both places as well as between New York and Providence. The ratio of sailing passengers to stagecoach passengers between New York and Boston in 1794 has been set higher than that for New York and Philadelphia in 1790 because the Providence-New York sailing route was not devious, as was the passage around the southern tip of New Jersey.

31. Albion, *Square-Riggers*, p. 18; John H. Morrison, *History of American Steam Navigation* (New York: W. F. Sametz, 1903), pp. 265, 270-271; Dunbar, *History of Travel*, III, 743-744; Meyer, *History of Transportation*, p. 74; Kirkland, *Men, Cities and Transportation*, I, 22; *Badger & Porter's Stage Register*, no. 6 (1826), 3, 18-19.

32. *ARJ* 3, no. 44 (Nov. 8, 1834), 689; *Badger & Porter's Stage Register*, no. 65 (1836), 4, 18, 22, 29, 30; H. S. Tanner, *American Traveller; or Guide Through the United States* (Philadelphia, 1836), p. 43; Samuel Mitchell, *Traveller's Guide Through the United States* (Philadelphia, 1838), pp. 60-61.

33. Morrison, *History of American Steam Navigation*, pp. 270, 272, 276; Buckingham, *America*, II, 484; *NWR* 56, no. 20 (July 13, 1839), 320; Albion, *Rise of New York Port*, p. 155; Kirkland, *Men, Cities and Transportation*, II, 245-247; Meyer, *History of Transportation*, p. 327; *Badger & Porter's Stage Register*, no. 65 (1836), 4; *HCSR* 2, no. 22 (May 27, 1840), 338; 2, no. 15 (Apr. 8, 1840), 229. No 1839 estimate could be made because the revenue figures for the Boston and Providence Railroad included way passengers who were not coming from or going to New York, but were only making the short journey between Providence and Boston.

34. J. Thomas Scharf and Thompson Westcott, *History of Philadelphia, 1609-1884* (Philadelphia, 1884), III, 2,156, 2,161.

35. *NWR* 9, no. 6 (Oct. 7, 1815), 96; 16, no. 22 (July 28, 1819), 357.

36. Dunbar, *History of Travel*, IV, 1,387; *NWR* 44, no. 14 (June 1, 1833), p. 222; Tanner, *American Traveller*, p. 99; Meyer, *History of Transportation*, pp. 392-393.

37. In 1839 the Washington branch of the Baltimore and Ohio Railroad carried 80,000-85,000 passengers. *HMM* 23 (July 1850), 45. The 1839 Philadelphia-Baltimore figure suggests that the later New York-Philadelphia and New York-Boston estimates may have been conservative.

38. Albion, *Square-Riggers*, p. 144; Morrison, *History of American Steam Navigation*, pp. 24-25; *New York Public Advertiser*, Dec. 1, 1809; Dunbar, *History of Travel*, I, 398.

39. Morrison, *History of American Steam Navigation*, pp. 46, 63; Albion, *Square-Riggers*, p. 153; *ARJ* 1, no. 19 (May 5, 1832), 293; 2, no. 27 (July 6, 1833), 419.

40. Kirkland, *Men, Cities and Transportation*, I, 55; *Badger & Porter's Stage Register*, no. 6 (1826), 2-5; no. 65 (1836), 1-3; Stephen Salsbury, *The State, the Investor, and the Railroad: The Boston & Albany, 1825-1867* (Cambridge: Harvard University Press, 1967), pp. 26-27.

41. Scharf and Westcott, *History of Philadelphia*, III, 2,156-2,157, 2,170; Dunbar, *History of Travel*, I, 189.

42. Dunbar, *History of Travel*, I, 308.

43. Morrison, *History of American Steam Navigation*, p. 228. Although this estimate may be high, it does not take account of overland passenger traffic between the two cities during the winter months.

44. Hunter, *Steamboats*, p. 326.

45. Morrison, *History of American Steam Navigation*, p. 230. Although the estimate may be high, it does not take into account the traffic that moved either by overland means or by the numerous steamers running between the cities on an irregular basis.

46. Meyer, *History of Transportation*, p. 96; Thomas Senior Berry, *Western Prices Before 1861: A Study of the Cincinnati Market* (Cambridge: Harvard University Press, 1943), p. 27; Catherine Elizabeth Reiser, *Pittsburgh's Commercial Development, 1800-1850* (Harrisburg: Pennsylvania Historical and Museum Commission, 1951), p. 44; Hunter, *Steamboats*, pp. 327-328.

47. Israel Andrews, *Report . . . on the Trade and Commerce of the British North American Colonies*, U.S. Senate Document No. 112, 32nd Cong., 1st sess., 1853, p. 660.

48. *NWR* 42, no. 9 (Apr. 28, 1832), 154.

49. *HMM* 6 (May 1842), 448; Timothy Pitkin, *A Statistical View of the Commerce of the United States of America* (New Haven, 1835), p. 576. From 1820 to 1840 Buffalo's entries and departures grew from 120 to 4,061. By 1833, Cleveland's passenger steamboat arrivals had risen to 705.

50. Dunbar, *History of Travel*, II, 404; *NWR* 29, no. 9 (Oct. 29, 1825), 144. The predominance of migrants among Detroit's arriving passengers is indicated in *NWR* 30, no. 14 (June 3, 1826), 341. The 9,000 estimate is supported by a claim that 4,000 persons had arrived by July. Brown, *Historical Geography*, p. 284.

51. *NWR* 38, no. 16 (June 12, 1830), 293; 44, no. 13 (May 25, 1833), 198; *HMM* 6 (February 1842), 189; U.S. Bureau of the Census, *Census of Population: 1960* (Washington, D.C. 1961).

52. *ARJ* 6, no. 6 (Feb. 11, 1837), 85; *Rochester Democrat*, May 31, 1837; *HMM* 6 (February 1842), 189; Andrews, *Report on the Trade and Commerce*, p. 658. The 1837 estimate actually came to 200,000 but included 12,000 sailing on freight vessels and 5,600 traveling by wagon.

53. Meyer, *History of Transportation*, p. 420; Guy Stevens Callender, *Selections from the Economic History of the United States, 1765–1860* (Boston: Ginn and Company, 1909), pp. 411–412.

54. Tanner, *American Traveller*, pp. 23, 69–70, 78–80, 108–109, 113; *NWR* 44, no. 14 (June 1, 1833), 222. The only other Southern urban pair to develop noteworthy passenger traffic was Charleston and Augusta, Georgia, which occurred only after the opening of the South Carolina Railroad.

55. Dunbar, *History of Travel*, III, 961, 971; Tanner, *American Traveller*, p. 73.

56. *NWR* 16, no. 13 (May 22, 1819), 223; 29, no. 17 (Dec. 24, 1825), 263; 44, no. 12 (May 18, 1833), 178; 46, no. 20 (July 12, 1834), 332; Mitchell, *Traveller's Guide*, pp. 62, 73; J. Thomas Scharf, *The Chronicles of Baltimore* (Baltimore, 1874), pp. 420, 429; Scharf and Westcott, *History of Philadelphia*, III, 2,156–2,157; Brown, *Historical Geography*, p. 127.

57. New York *L'Oracle*, Jan. 27, 1808; Albion, *Square-Riggers*, pp. 35, 303–304; *NWR* 23, no. 9 (Nov. 2, 1822), 130; 42, no. 7 (Apr. 14, 1832), 111. Also carrying New York passengers more or less regularly in the mid-1830s, but not included in Table 4.14, were 7 brigs to Charleston, 8 brigs and 11 schooners to Savannah, 8 ships to New Orleans, and 6 ships to Mobile.

58. Albion, *Square-Riggers*, p. 219.

59. Albion, *Square-Riggers*, p. 75.

60. *Badger & Porter's Stage Register*, no. 45 (1836), 30; Buckingham, *America*, I, 167.

61. Andrew T. Goodrich, *The Picture of New-York and Stranger's Guide to the Commercial Metropolis of the United States* (New York, 1828), quoted in James Grant Wilson, *The Memorial History of New York* (New York, 1893), III, 355. Goodrich's estimate excluded travel associated with foreign ports and the "immense number" moving by "ships, sloops and coasters" between New York and Southern and Eastern ports.

62. Albion, *Rise of New York Port*, p. 164.

63. *ARJ* 2, no. 27 (July 6, 1833), 419.

64. *NWR* 45, no. 2 (Sept. 7, 1833), 17; 49, no. 7 (Oct. 17, 1835), 116. New York's rooming facilities for travelers were considerable by European standards.

65. Buckinghan, *America*, I, 47.

66. All times presented in this section were subject to some seasonal variation.

67. On time-space convergence, see Donald G. Janelle, "Central Place Development in a Time-Space Framework," *Professional Geographer* 20, no. 1 (January 1968), 5–10; Donald G. Janelle, "Spatial Reorganization: Model and Concept," *Annals of the Association of American Geographers* 59 (1969), 348–364. One property of "time-space convergence" rates is that the greater the route length, the greater the minutes saved per year for any specific improvement in transportation technology.

68. Hunter, *Steamboats*, p. 22.

69. Morrison, *History of American Steam Navigation*, p. 228.

70. William Cobbett, *A Year's Residence in the United States of America* (London, 1818), pt. 3, pp. 460–463; Hunter, *Steamboats*, p. 24. Upstream steamboat travel times from New Orleans to Louisville were sliced from 25.0 days in

1817 to 8.17 days in 1828 and 5.64 days in 1840. In 1814 the identical trip required four months. Morrison, *History of American Steam Navigation*, p. 208; Dunbar, *History of Travel*, II, 396; *NWR* 32, no. 14 (June 2, 1827), 229. Downstream times from Cincinnati to New Orleans were decreased from 8.0 days in 1823 to 4.9 days in 1840. *NWR* 35, no. 6 (Oct. 11, 1823), 95; 59, no. 13 (Nov. 28, 1840), 208.

71. Hunter, *Steamboats*, p. 319.

72. Dunbar, *History of Travel*, II, 404; *NWR* 35, no. 7 (Oct. 11, 1828), 101; 47, no. 11 (Nov. 15, 1834), 163. The Lake Erie route from Buffalo to Detroit took 5-10 days before the steamboat.

73. *NWR* 29, no. 12 (Nov. 29, 1825), 180. In the brief interval 1825-1828, New York-Detroit travel times fell from 5.5 days to 4.5 days. *NWR* 29, no. 6 (Oct. 8, 1825), 96; 35, no. 7 (Oct. 11, 1828), 101; *New York Evening Post*, Oct. 10, 1825.

74. *NWR* 18, no. 16 (June 17, 1820), 288; 48, no. 21 (July 25, 1835), 365; Dunbar, *History of Travel*, II, 961, 971; I, 329.

6. An Urban-System Interpretation of the Growth of Large Cities

1. U.S. Bureau of the Census, *Historical Statistics of the United States, Colonial Times to 1957*, 1960, p. 14; U.S. Bureau of the Census, *Census of Population: 1960*, 1961, I, pt. A, 1-66, 1-67; George Rogers Taylor, "American Urban Growth Preceding the Railway Age," *Journal of Economic History* 27 (1967), 311-315. By 1840 the country had a total of 1,845,055 people dwelling in "urban places," that is nonrural settlements containing at least 2,500 residents. In these calculations the populations of New York, Philadelphia, Boston and Pittsburgh have been allowed to include subsequently annexed suburbs. The degree of concentration indicated by the national and regional percentages is exaggerated to the extent that the Bureau of the Census had neglected places that were urban in function but had fewer than the arbitrary 2,500 persons.

2. Similar long-run patterns of rank stability have been noted in urban systems and subsystems of varying magnitude. Friedmann, for example, remarked about urban development in Venezuela since the beginning of its modern economic growth: "one cannot fail but be impressed by the remarkable stability in the general order of relative dominance of cities." John Friedmann, *Regional Development Policy: A Case Study of Venezuela* (Cambridge: M.I.T. Press, 1966), p. 146.

3. Cf. Olof Wärneryd, *Interdependence in Urban Systems* (Göteborg: Regionkonsult Aktiebolag, 1968), pp. 16-19; Brian J. L. Berry, "Cities As Systems Within Systems of Cities," in John Friedmann and William Alonso, eds. *Regional Development and Planning: A Reader* (Cambridge: M.I.T. Press, 1964), pp. 116-137.

4. For the terminology and limitations of interregional or interurban input-output analysis, see Walter Isard, *Methods of Regional Analysis: An Introduction to Regional Science* (Cambridge: M.I.T. Press, 1960), pp. 309-374.

5. For the terminology of complex social systems, see Walter Buckley, *Sociology and Modern Systems Theory* (Englewood Cliffs, N.J.: Prentice-Hall, 1967).

6. Allan R. Pred, *The Spatial Dynamics of U.S. Urban-Industrial Growth, 1800–*

1914: Interpretive and Theoretical Essays (Cambridge: M.I.T. Press, 1966), pp. 146-177.

7. Mercantile capital also responded frequently to the temptation of land purchases in upstate New York and in the developing agricultural areas west of the Alleghenies.

8. See John G. B. Hutchins, "Trade and Manufactures," in David T. Gilchrist, ed., *The Growth of the Seaport Cities, 1790-1825* (Charlottesville: University of Virginia Press, 1967), pp. 81-91.

9. The size of the local shipbuilding industry was dependent on the scale of the wholesaling-trading complex because most ship-purchasing merchants "preferred to order vessels from builders who were known to them, and whose yard they could visit," in order to dictate structural specifications and cut costs. John G. B. Hutchins, *The American Maritime Industries and Public Policy, 1789-1914* (Cambridge: Harvard University Press, 1941), p. 194.

10. Inns, hotels, and boardinghouses were numerous in mercantile cities, primarily because of the need to accommodate hinterland purchasers and commercial representatives from other cities, as well as foreign business agents.

11. Because of entrepreneur-to-entrepreneur and firm-to-firm variations in perception of the market and in profit aspiration level, new establishments or additions may in some cases have occurred considerably before or after the fulfillment of theoretical threshold conditions.

12. Increases in the size of the local or regional market could also lead to greater specialization within the wholesaling-trading complex. That is, some multifunctional mercantile enterprises could be split up to operate more efficiently on an independent basis. Cf. George J. Stigler, "The Division of Labor Is Limited by the Size of the Market," *Journal of Political Economy* 59 (June 1951), 185-193; James E. Vance, Jr., *The Merchant's World: The Geography of Wholesaling* (Englewood Cliffs, N.J.: Prentice-Hall, 1970), p. 55.

13. Knowledge of the labor market and of destinations of previous migrants, who themselves may have been influenced by job opportunities, are normally two of the most important determinants of individual migration decisions. See, e.g., Allan R. Pred, *The External Relations of Cities During "Industrial Revolution,"* Department of Geography Research Paper no. 76 (Chicago: University of Chicago, 1962), pp. 57-68; Gunnar Olsson, *Distance and Human Interaction* (Philadelphia: Regional Science Research Institute, 1965), pp. 23-42. More specifically Easterlin suggested that migration in response to economic opportunities was a key factor in the population expansion of New York, Boston, Philadelphia, and Baltimore from 1790 to 1825. Richard Easterlin, "Discussion," in Gilchrist, *Growth of the Seaport Cities*, pp. 80-81.

14. This subsidiary process is viewed as a low metabolic version of a model of urban-size growth for individual cities during periods of rapid industrialization in general, and for large American cities in particular from the early 1860s to 1910 or shortly thereafter. In the 1790-1840 period, unlike the post-Civil War period, the nature of urban manufacturing was such that the threshold and invention cycles were incapable of sustaining themselves independently without constant prodding

from wholesaling-trading sources. For the rapid industrialization urban-size growth model, see Pred, *Spatial Dynamics*, pp. 24-46.

15. "Footloose" manufactures usually include industries that are essentially insensitive to transportation costs. Individual establishments in these high-value-per-unit-weight industries can therefore serve large market areas and, *ceteris paribus*, may locate as economically in one area or city as another.

16. See Meyer H. Fishbein, "The Censuses of Manufactures, 1810-1890," *National Archives Accessions*, no. 57 (June 1963), 7-9. In view of the nearly comparable populations of Louisville and Pittsburgh, large across-the-board omissions must have been made by enumerators in Louisville.

17. If an investment is allocated for each "commercial house in foreign trade" equal to the national average invested in "commission houses" ($41,000), the 1840 ratio of mercantile to local industrial investments for Cincinnati rises to 2.7:1. If, alternatively, average investments in "commercial houses in foreign trade" were on a par with those in local "commission houses," the ratio for Cincinnati nearly reaches 3.3:1. See Theodore F. Marburg, "Income Originating in Trade, 1799-1869," in *Trends in the American Economy in the Nineteenth Century* (Princeton: Princeton University Press, 1960), p. 318.

18. Cf. Fred Mitchell Jones, *Middlemen in the Domestic Trade of the United States, 1800-1860*, Illinois Studies in the Social Sciences, vol. 21, no. 3 (Urbana: University of Illinois Press, 1937), p. 29. The marshals of Cincinnati, e.g., were apparently guilty of much misassignment. In view of that city's known trading pattern, it is highly questionable that Cincinnati possessed more "commercial houses in foreign trade" than "commission houses."

19. Richard C. Wade, *The Urban Frontier: Pioneer Life in Early Pittsburgh, Cincinnati, Lexington, Louisville, and St. Louis* (Chicago: University of Chicago Press, 1964), pp. 55, 196-197; Thomas S. Berry, *Western Prices Before 1861: A Study of the Cincinnati Market* (Cambridge: Harvard University Press, 1943), p. 409; Jones, *Middlemen*, p. 15.

20. Wade, *Urban Frontier*, pp. 198-200; *NWR* 49, no. 22 (Jan. 30, 1836), 361; 53, no. 26 (Feb. 24, 1838), 416.

21. Total annual income per capita for the country as a whole in 1840 is estimated to have been $65. Total annual income per worker in nonagricultural occupations, including commercial employment, is estimated to have been $437. Corresponding figures for Kentucky are placed at $52 and $357. Richard A. Easterlin, "Interregional Differences in Per Capita Income, Population, and Total Income," in *Trends in the American Economy*, pp. 97-98.

22. George Armroyd, *A Connected View of the Whole Internal Navigation of the United States* (Philadelphia, 1830), p. 360; Wade, *Urban Frontier*, pp. 44-45; Catherine E. Reiser, *Pittsburgh's Commercial Development* (Harrisburg: Pennsylvania Historical and Museum Commission, 1951), p. 152; *NWR* 35, no. 25 (Feb. 16, 1839), 391.

23. See John G. Clark, *The Grain Trade in the Old Northwest* (Urbana: University of Illinois Press, 1966).

24. North portrayed most Western urban manufacturing as market-oriented.

Douglass C. North, *The Economic Growth of the United States, 1790-1860* (New York: W. W. Norton, 1966), pp. 194-195.

25. Ralph H. Brown, *Historical Geography of the United States* (New York: Harcourt, Brace, 1948), p. 235; Clark, *Grain Trade*, p. 17; Wade, *Urban Frontier*, p. 197; James Flint, *Letters from America* (Edinburgh, 1822), pp. 239-240; Constance McLaughlin Green, *American Cities in the Growth of the Nation* (New York: Harper & Row, 1965), p. 47.

26. Wade, *Urban Frontier*, p. 69; Reiser, *Pittsburgh's Commercial Development*, pp. 25, 27, 203; *HCSR* 3, no. 24 (Dec. 9, 1840), 375-376; 6, no. 22, (June 1, 1842), 346; John H. Morrison, *History of American Steam Navigation* (New York: W. F. Sametz, 1903), p. 220.

27. Berry, *Western Prices*, p. 10; *NWR* 12, no. 9 (Apr. 26, 1817), 131; 56, no. 7 (Apr. 13, 1839), 113; Wade, *Urban Frontier*, p. 164; Reginald Charles McGrane, *The Panic of 1837: Some Financial Problems of the Jacksonian Era* (Chicago: University of Chicago Press, 1934), p. 48.

28. Berry, *Western Prices*, p. 8; Flint, *Letters from America*, p. 241; *NWR* 29, no. 12 (Nov. 19, 1825), 182; 41, no. 25 (Feb. 18, 1832), 447; *Aggregate Value and Produce, and Number of Persons Employed in Mines, Agriculture, Commerce, Manufactures, &c.: Sixth Census of the United States, 1840*, 1841; Ezra C. Seaman, *Essays on the Progress of Nations* (New York, 1852), p. 465.

29. In 1840 the percentage of local population accounted for by slaves was 53.6 in Charleston, 41.7 in Savannah, and 34.0 in Norfolk. U.S. Bureau of the Census, *Sixth Census or Enumeration of the Inhabitants of the United States*, 1841. See also Richard C. Wade, *Slavery in the Cities: The South, 1820-1860* (New York: Oxford University Press, 1964).

30. Taylor, "American Urban Growth," pp. 311-313, 331. See Samuel Eliot Morison, *The Maritime History of Massachusetts, 1783-1860*, rev. ed. (Boston: Houghton Mifflin, 1961), pp. 215-216; Pred, *Spatial Dynamics*, pp. 187-188.

31. William Henry Dean, Jr., *The Theory of the Geographic Location of Economic Activities* (Ann Arbor: Edwards Brothers, 1938), p. 39.

32. For details of this type of hinterland expansion process, see Edward J. Taaffe, Richard L. Morrill, and Peter R. Gould, "Transport Expansion in Underdeveloped Countries," *Geographical Review* 53 (1963), 503-529; Pred, *Spatial Dynamics*, pp. 186, 189-191. For the impact of successive transportation improvements on the hinterland sales of an individual terminus-city merchant, see Elva Tooker, *Nathan Trotter, Philadelphia Merchant, 1787-1853* (Cambridge: Harvard University Press, 1953), pp. 118-131.

33. The steamboat services of Louisville and Cincinnati, e.g., are generally credited with making Lexington's inland position commercially untenable. Cf. Wade, *Urban Frontier*, pp. 182-187; John Borchert, "American Metropolitan Evolution," *Geographical Review* 57 (1967), 303-304.

34. Agglomeration economies subsume scale economies to the individual entrepreneur as well as two forms of "external economies"—"localization" and "urbanization" economies: "Localization economies [occur] for all firms in a single industry [activity] consequent upon the enlargement of the total output of

that industry [activity] at that location . . . Urbanization economies [occur] for all firms in all industries [activities] at a single location, consequent upon the enlargement of the total economic size (population, income, output, or wealth), of that location, for all industries [activities] taken together." Walter Isard, *Location and Space-Economy* (New York: John Wiley and Sons, 1956), p. 173.

35. For such specialization in New York, Boston, Philadelphia, and Baltimore, see Hutchins, "Trade and Manufactures," p. 87. For specialization in Cincinnati, Pittsburgh, Louisville, and St. Louis, see Wade, *Urban Frontier*, p. 307.

36. North stressed "the role of the nodal center in providing external economies for the export industries" of its hinterland. Douglass C. North, "Location Theory and Regional Economic Growth," *Journal of Political Economy* 63 (June 1955), 257.

37. Although agglomeration economies are emphasized, it should be evident from the overall structure of the size-growth submodel that external economies are only one of a number of keys to the understanding of city development.

38. Friedmann suggested that the cities of a colonial economy generally do not knit themselves into a system, that they "frequently have closer commercial and even social ties with centers in the mother country than among themselves." Friedmann, *Regional Development*, p. 9. Rubin also noted the "inhibited urbanization" of the South during 1790-1825. Julius Rubin, "Urban Growth and Regional Development," in Gilchrist, *Growth of the Seaport Cities*, pp. 14-15, 20.

39. The similarity of hinterland agricultural specialities and the virtual absence of export-oriented manufacturing activities were at the heart of the poorly developed interdependence of the largest Southern cities.

40. Similarly, the probabilistic nature of these interrelationships sometimes permits opportunity exploitation in low-probability smaller centers at the same time that exploitation is limited in other comparably sized low-probability cities as well as $C_1, C_2, C_3, \ldots C_n$. This feature on occasion can enable a city to make rapid progress through the lowest or even middle ranks of an urban system or subsystem.

41. Because of the uncertainty to be overcome and the risk-taking frequently involved, adoption of an economic innovation is not apt to be undertaken by an entrepreneur or firm immediately upon receipt of information regarding its existence. Additional information concerning the experience of previous adopters is often crucial to the potential adopter's decision to accept or reject.

42. In instances where successful adoption requires the fulfillment of threshold conditions that can be met only in large cities $(C_1, C_2, C_3, \ldots C_n)$, diffusion cannot proceed to smaller centers except where poorly based decision-making leads to ill-fated short-term acceptances.

43. The probabilistic qualities ascribed to interurban diffusion can on occasion enable a small city to make rapid progress through the lowest or middle ranks of an urban system or subsystem. This would happen when a commercial or industrial innovation was adopted successfully in a low-probability small center at the same time that its adoption was limited in other comparably sized low-probability cities as well as in $C_1, C_2, C_3, \ldots C_n$. Progress would be accounted for by a sizable and

temporally concentrated local multiplier, increased interaction with other cities, and higher probabilities at later dates.

44. See, e.g., Arthur M. Johnson and Barry E. Supple, *Boston Capitalists and Western Railroads: A Study in the Nineteenth-Century Railroad Investment Process* (Cambridge: Harvard University Press, 1967), p. 3.

45. Cf. Wärneryd, *Interdependence in Urban Systems*, pp. 18–31.

46. Hutchins, "Trade and Manufactures," pp. 89–91; Morison, *Maritime History*, pp. 214–215, 226.

47. Mounting demands for hinterland products were at the heart of transportation developments that led to hinterland expansion and piracy and contributed to the differential growth of mercantile cities. See North, *Economic Growth*, pp. 50–51.

48. In some larger hinterland centers, such as New York's Rochester and Philadelphia's Reading, nonlocal multipliers were associated with the shipment of both local manufactures and nearby agricultural products. See Taylor, "American Urban Growth," pp. 333, 337; Rubin, "Urban Growth," pp. 11, 20.

49. Rubin, "Urban Growth," p. 8.

50. New York City's hinterland during the first four decades of the nineteenth century is usually depicted as including the entire state of New York, the eastern half of New Jersey, and much of western New England. If it is conservatively regarded as embracing New York State's population, half of New Jersey's, and a third of Connecticut's, "the population of New York's hinterland numbered about 1,170,000 in 1810 and 1,600,000 in 1820," or roughly one-sixth of the national total for each year. Within five years of the opening of the Erie Canal the towns along its length mushroomed in population; e.g., Utica grew from 2,972 in 1820 to 8,323 in 1830, while Troy went from 5,264 to 11,556. By 1840 New York State's population alone was greater than that of all of New England. Robert Greenhalgh Albion, *The Rise of New York Port, 1815–1860* (New York: Charles Scribner's Sons, 1939), p. 77; Taylor, "American Urban Growth," p. 314.

51. Nonlocal multipliers involving hinterland towns were even more modest in the South, where interior urbanization was limited. Rubin, "Urban Growth," p. 20.

52. Cf. Vance, *Merchant's World*, pp. 83–85.

53. John A. Dix, *Sketch of the Resources of the City of New York* (New York, 1827), pp. 55–57.

54. Wärneryd, *Interdependence in Urban Systems*, pp. 29, 46; Vance, *Merchant's World*, pp. 21, 76.

55. Donald G. Janelle, "Spatial Reorganization: A Model and Concept," *Annals of the Association of American Geographers* 59 (1969), 348–364. Although Janelle does not make the point, the demands for increased accessibility may also derive from a desire for improved information-flow conditions.

56. Donald G. Janelle, "Central Place Development in a Time-Space Framework," *Professional Geographer* 20 (January 1968), 8–9. Janelle's model and the self-compounding character of commodity and human spatial interaction are both consistent with Ohlin's observation that the "improvement of transport relations through a local concentration of economic activity where they are already good tends to concentrate population and production [and trade] still further."

Bertil Ohlin, *Interregional and International Trade* (Cambridge: Harvard University Press, 1933), p. 203.

57. P. Pottier, "Axes de communication et développement économique," *Revue économique* 13, no. 1 (1963), 70-128. For the role of information circulation biases in the development of modern urban systems and subsystems, see Gunnar Törnqvist, *Contact Systems and Regional Development*, Lund Studies in Geography, ser. B, Human Geography, no. 35 (Lund, 1970).

58. Richard L. Meier, *A Communications Theory of Urban Growth* (Cambridge: M.I.T. Press, 1962), p. 43. Vance also noted: "Improvement in intelligence flows [when exploited] will tend to expand the trade areas of the larger wholesale center at the expense of the smaller." Vance, *Merchant's World*, p. 156.

59. On the relationships between information circulation and the spatial distribution of uncertainty, see Julian Wolpert, "The Decision Process in Spatial Context," *Annals of the Association of American Geographers* 54 (1964), 537-558.

60. See Vance, *Merchant's World*, pp. 147-149.

61. Albert O. Hirschman, *The Strategy of Economic Development* (New Haven: Yale University Press, 1958), p. 185; Friedmann, *Regional Development*, p. 15.

62. Robert G. Albion, *Square-Riggers on Schedule: The New York Sailing Packets to England, France, and the Cotton Ports* (Princeton: Princeton University Press, 1938), p. 138. Because of the convenience and reliability of New York's packet service, much of the European business with leading coastal and interior cities was conducted via New York, thereby increasing the interdependence (interaction and information flows) between those cities and New York.

63. Hutchins, "Trade and Manufactures," p. 87.

64. Wesley Everett Rich, *The History of the United States Post Office to the Year 1829* (Cambridge: Harvard University Press, 1924), pp. 100-101; Julian P. Bretz, "Some Aspects of Postal Extension into the West," *Annual Report of the American Historical Association for the Year 1909* (Washington, D.C.: Government Printing Office, 1911), p. 148. In 1825, e.g., the postmaster general notified mail contractors on the route from Petersburg, Virginia, to Augusta, Georgia, that it was their duty, "on occasions of great importance to the commercial community, to send express mails on their lines, at the rate of 11 miles an hour, and thus, by affording to all the news of important changes in the markets, to put a stop to the system of speculation which has lately been so extensively practiced by individuals of one commercial town on those of another." *NWR* 28, no. 13 (May 28, 1825), 194.

65. Albion, *Rise of New York Port*, pp. 53, 114-115; Albion, *Square-Riggers*, pp. 112, 180-183.

66. Julius Rubin, *Canal or Railroad? Imitation and Innovation in the Response to the Erie Canal in Philadelphia, Baltimore, and Boston, Transactions of the American Philosophical Society*, n. s. 51, pt. 7, (Philadelphia, 1961), 19; J. Thomas Scharf, *The Chronicles of Baltimore* (Baltimore, 1874), p. 445; Albion, *Rise of New York Port*, pp. 105, 236-237. Although such interurban migration was important in terms of its economic repercussions, there is serious doubt that the numbers involved were large.

67. Morison, *Maritime History*, p. 217; Johnson and Supple, *Boston Capitalists*, p. 15; Albion, *Rise of New York Port*, p. 242; Albion, *Square-Riggers*, p. 157; Robert Ernst, *Immigrant Life in New York City, 1825–1863* (New York: King's Crown Press, 1949), pp. 15–16.

68. Torsten Hägerstrand, "Migration and Area: Survey of a Sample of Swedish Migration Fields and Hypothetical Considerations on Their Genesis," in David Hannerberg, Torsten Hägerstrand, and Bruno Odeving, eds., *Migration in Sweden*, Lund Studies in Geography, ser. B, no. 13 (Lund: 1957), pp. 27–158. See also remarks on economic opportunities and United States urban in-migration, 1790–1825, in Easterlin, "Discussion," pp. 80–81.

69. See Albion, *Square-Riggers*, pp. 38, 75.

70. Subsystem population ratios among the four major cities of the Northeast were affected by the different patterns of interregional interaction developed between them and leading centers of the new Western subsystems. Ratio adjustments also stemmed from the fact that the relative growth rates of the largest cities in newly settled regions are usually very high, and the relative growth rates of older cities tend to decline, even if their absolute population increments per annum are increasing somewhat.

71. E.g., the War of 1812 affected the growth of the major Atlantic Coast cities more than it did the newly emerging cities of the interior. It also slowed the expansion of some Atlantic Coast centers more than others.

72. Brian J. L. Berry, *Theories of Urban Location* (Washington, D.C.: Association of American Geographers, 1968), p. 5; Dean, *Theory of the Geographic Location*, p. 38; Albion, *Rise of New York Port*, p. 375; Taylor, "American Urban Growth," pp. 311–314; Rubin, "Urban Growth," pp. 17–18; *NWR* 24, no. 19 (July 12, 1823), 295; Clark, *Grain Trade*, p. 119.

73. Karl W. Deutsch, *Nationalism and Social Communication: An Inquiry into the Foundations of Nationality*, 2nd ed. (Cambridge: M.I.T. Press, 1966), p. 126; Wilbur Schramm, "Communication Development and the Development Process," in Lucien Pye, ed., *Communications and Political Development* (Princeton: Princeton University Press, 1963), p. 35.

74. Magoroh Maruyama, "The Second Cybernetics: Deviation-Amplifying Mutual Causal Processes," *American Scientist* 51 (1963), 164–179.

75. Wärneryd, *Interdependence in Urban Systems*, p. 56; Friedmann, *Regional Development*, pp. 64, 151.

76. Gunnar Myrdal, *Economic Theory and Underdeveloped Regions* (London: Duckworth, 1957). Myrdal's "spread effects" include the establishment of markets in rapidly growing regions for raw materials available in backward, or lagging, regions. His "backwash effects" include the out-migration of capital and skilled labor from backward regions and the saturation of backward regions with industrial products from rapidly expanding regions.

77. François Perroux, "Note sur la notion de pôle de croissance," *Economique appliquée* 7 (1955), 307–320; J. R. Boudeville, *Problems of Regional Economic Planning* (Edinburgh: Edinburgh University Press, 1966), p. 11; Hamilton Tolosa and Thomas A. Reiner, "The Economic Programming of a System of Planned

Poles," *Economic Geography* 46 (1970), 451. However, in most of its formulations the "growth pole" concept tends to obscure both the interdependencies existing between large cities and other important urban systems characteristics.

78. Walter Christaller, *Central Places in Southern Germany* (Englewood Cliffs, N.J.: Prentice-Hall, 1966). See also Brian J. L. Berry and Allan Pred, *Central Place Studies: A Bibliography of Theory and Applications*, 2nd ed. (Philadelphia: Regional Science Research Institute, 1965); Brian J. L. Berry, *Geography of Market Centers and Retail Distribution* (Englewood Cliffs, N.J.: Prentice-Hall, 1967).

79. Torsten Hägerstrand, *The Propagation of Innovation Waves*, Lund Studies in Geography, ser. B, no. 4 (Lund, 1952), p. 8; Torsten Hägerstrand, "Aspects of the Spatial Structure of Social Communications and the Diffusion of Information," *Papers of the Regional Science Association* 16 (1966), 40.

80. John C. Hudson, "Diffusion in a Central Place System," *Geographical Analysis* 1 (1969), 45-58. Cf. Poul Ove Pedersen, "Innovation Diffusion Within and Between National Urban Systems," *Geographical Analysis* 2 (1970), 223-224.

81. Christaller proposed three ideal distributions of central places and central place activities. One was based on the "marketing principle," according to which all parts of a region "are supplied from the minimum possible number of functioning central places." His empirical work led him to conclude that "the marketing principle is the primary and chief law of distribution of central places." Christaller, *Central Places*, pp. 72, 192. In a central place system organized according to the "marketing principle," $k = 3$. This means that every third place providing a given array of tertiary goods and services also provides the other two (and their trade areas) with additional goods and services of the next highest order (goods requiring a larger market, or threshold), and is therefore of larger population.

82. Manufacturing probably accounted for only 17 percent of the value of all commodity output in the United States in 1839. Robert E. Gallman, "Commodity Output, 1839-1899," in *Trends in the American Economy*, p. 26.

83. Christaller, *Central Places*, pp. 190, 198. See also Michael F. Dacey, "A Probability Model for Central Place Locations," *Annals of the Association of American Geographers* 56 (1966), pp. 550-568.

84. See Pred, *Spatial Dynamics*, pp. 136-138; Pedersen, "Innovation Diffusion," pp. 206, 219-220.

85. August Lösch, *The Economics of Location* (New Haven: Yale University Press, 1954).

86. Wolfgang Stolper, "Spatial Order and the Economic Growth of Cities," *Economic Development and Cultural Change* 3 (1954-1955), 137-146. Stolper's modified Löschian scheme, which is diagrammatically confined to centers located on a straight line passing through the system's largest metropolis (A), requires that it "be imagined that the distribution of production schematized . . . exists also in all directions" (p. 139).

87. The claimed existence of two-way information flows along any interaction dyad is supported by recently gathered evidence involving the Swedish urban system. See Bengt Sahlberg, *Interregionala kontaktmönster: Personkontakter inom svenskt*

näringsliv (Lund: Gleerups, 1970); Björn Hedberg, *Kontaktsystem inom svenskt näringsliv: En studie av organisationers externa personkontakter* (Lund: Gleerups, 1971).

88. For a related formulation where only P_i and P_j appear in the numerator, see Pedersen, "Innovation Diffusion," pp. 216-217.

89. To replace $P_iG_{j \to i}$ with $T_{j \to i}$, and $P_jG_{i \to j}$ with $T_{i \to j}$, does not mean that all goods arriving at i or j are consumed by their own local populations or activities, for often some portion of the goods arriving at i from j, or at j from i, are further shipped to their respective hinterlands. But insofar as the populations of i and j partly reflect the population of their market areas, the replacement of $P_jG_{i \to j}$ seems reasonable.

90. Expressions (6.3) and (6.4) would be more complicated if it were assumed that entrepreneurs or other potential innovators were present in unequal proportions in each jth place. Cf. Pedersen, "Innovation Diffusion," pp. 218-219.

91. Pedersen observed, e.g., that the distance decay of interurban diffusion in Chile was much stronger during the pretelegraphic phases of economic growth than during the twentieth century. Pedersen, "Innovation Diffusion," pp. 224-226.

92. Cf. Torsten Hägerstrand, "A Monte Carlo Approach to Diffusion," *Archives européennes de sociologie* 6, no. 1 (1965), 43-67; Deutsch, *Nationalism*, p. 100. See also Robert S. Yuill, *A Simulation Study of Barrier Effects in Spatial Diffusion Problems*, Michigan Inter-University Community of Mathematical Geographers, Discussion paper no. 5 (Ann Arbor, 1965).

93. Obviously, for any i, the sum of all solutions to (6.4) would be 1.0. On the concept of the mean information field, see Torsten Hägerstrand, *Innovation Diffusion as a Spatial Process* (Chicago: University of Chicago Press, 1967), pp. 235-238; Richard L. Morrill and Forrest R. Pitts, "Marriage, Migration, and the Mean Information Field," *Annals of the Association of American Geographers* 57 (1967), 401-422.

94. See Meier, *Communications Theory*, p. 43; Pedersen, "Innovation Diffusion," p. 228.

95. There is much twentieth-century evidence of such diffusion from smaller to larger places. For example, in a study of the spread of liquid propane gas tanks in an area of Wisconsin "dominated by lower-order central places," it was found that "diffusion does *not* follow the central place hierarchy, although it does maintain the characteristic of short-circuiting to the more important places at a greater distance"; that is, innovation diffusion "jumps from one location to another, ignoring the area in between." Lawrence Brown, *Diffusion Dynamics*, Lund Studies in Geography, ser. B, no. 29 (Lund, 1968), p. 31. See also findings on the diffusion of hospitals, waterworks, and radio stations in Chile in Pedersen, "Innovation Diffusion," pp. 208-213.

7. Pretelegraphic Patterns of Interurban Innovation Diffusion

1. "At the *awareness* stage the individual is exposed to the innovation but lacks complete information about it . . . At the *interest* stage the individual becomes

interested in the new idea and seeks additional information about it . . . At the *evaluation* stage the individual mentally applies the innovation to his present and anticipated future situation, and then decides whether or not to try it . . . At the *trial* stage the individual uses the innovation on a small scale [if possible] in order to determine its utility in his own situation . . . At the *adoption* stage the individual decides to continue the full use of the innovation." Everett M. Rogers, *The Diffusion of Innovations* (New York: Free Press, 1962), pp. 81-87. See also H. F. Lionberger, *Adoption of New Ideas and Practices* (Ames: Iowa State University Press, 1960), pp. 21-32. The adoption subprocess of the individual or organization may be affected by a variety of psychological, social, and economic variables.

2. Peter David Girling, "The Diffusion of Banks in the United States from 1781 to 1861" (M.S. thesis, The Pennsylvania State University, 1968).

3. *New York Packet*, Feb. 12, 1784.

4. There had also been an unsuccessful movement to establish a bank in Charleston.

5. Girling, *Diffusion of Banks*, pp. 34-56; Curtis P. Nettels, *The Emergence of a National Economy, 1775-1815* (New York: Holt, Rinehart and Winston, 1962), pp. 295-297; Herman E. Krooss, "Financial Institutions," in David T. Gilchrist, ed., *The Growth of the Seaport Cities, 1790-1825* (Charlottesville: University Press of Virginia, 1967), pp. 104-143; U.S. Bureau of the Census, *Historical Statistics of the United States, Colonial Times to 1957*, p. 624.

6. Girling, *Diffusion of Banks*, pp. 79-83. Girling contended that some early Massachusetts banks may have been placed so as to capture a larger rural market area and to be at a distance from competitors. However, such an argument might at best explain only six of the first thirteen "deviant" cases. More likely, as is often the case in the early stages of spatial processes involving economic decisions, the misuse of information or inadequate information resulted in poor locational choices.

7. Arthur J. Krim, "The Innovation and Diffusion of the Street Railway in North America" (M.A. thesis, University of Chicago, 1967). See also George Rogers Taylor, "The Beginnings of Mass Transportation in Urban America: Part I," *The Smithsonian Journal of History*, Summer 1966, pp. 40-48.

8. Krim, "Innovation and Diffusion of the Street Railway," pp. 58-59.

9. For fare costs and their impact on street railway and omnibus traffic, see Allan R. Pred, *The Spatial Dynamics of U.S.Urban-Industrial Growth, 1800-1914: Interpretive and Theoretical Essays* (Cambridge: M.I.T. Press, 1966), pp. 211-213.

10. The New Orleans street railway consisted of horse-drawn access to its railroad terminal. This was also true of the street railway obtained by second-ranked Philadelphia in 1832. Boston was without a street railway until 1854. Krim, "Innovation and Diffusion of the Street Railway," pp. 56-57.

11. See Gerald F. Pyle, "The Diffusion of Cholera in the United States in the Nineteenth Century," *Geographical Analysis* 1 (1969), 59-75; Charles E. Rosenberg, *The Cholera Years: The United States in 1832, 1849, and 1866* (Chicago: University of Chicago Press, 1962); L. Dudley Stamp, *The Geography of Life and Death* (London: Collins, 1964).

12. Rosenberg, *Cholera Years*, pp. 79, 14-15.

13. Pyle, "Diffusion of Cholera," pp. 61-64.

14. Pyle, "Diffusion of Cholera," pp. 65-66.

15. Bray Hammond, *Banks and Politics in America, from the Revolution to the Civil War* (Princeton: Princeton University Press, 1957), pp. 452-453, 455-457. Western banks were hardest hit, because government funds "had accumulated in them to an amount double what they could keep under the distribution, and suddenly they were called on to surrender the excess in specie to be shipped east." Hammond, *Banks and Politics*, p. 457.

16. Hammond, *Banks and Politics*, pp. 457, 459. For the origins of the panic of 1837, see also Reginald Charles McGrane, *The Panic of 1837: Some Financial Problems of the Jacksonian Era* (Chicago: University of Chicago Press, 1924); Peter Temin, *The Jacksonian Economy* (New York: W. W. Norton, 1969).

17. *NWR* 52, no. 8 (Apr. 22, 1837), 114

18. *The Picayune* (New Orleans), Apr. 25, 26, 28, 29, May 2, 5, 6, 7, 10, 1837.

19. *Edgefield Advertiser* (South Carolina), May 25, 1837; *Charleston Courier*, May 15, 1837.

20. *Philadelphia Public Ledger*, May 10, 1837.

21. *Baltimore American*, May 12, 1836; *Baltimore Patriot*, May 12, 1837.

22. *Charleston Mercury*, May 18, 1837; *Edgefield Advertiser*, May 25, 1837.

23. *Philadelphia Inquirer*, May 11, 1837.

24. *Richmond Whig and Public Advertiser*, May 16, 1837; *New York Journal of Commerce*, May 13, 1837.

25. McGrane, *Panic of 1837*, p. 93.

26. *Boston Evening Transcript*, May 12, 1837; *Daily Albany Argus*, May 12, 15, 17; *Rochester Democrat*, May 13, 1837; *New York Journal of Commerce*, May 27, 1837.

27. *New York Journal of Commerce*, May 10, 1837; *New York Daily Express*, May 8, 9, 10, 1837; *Rochester Democrat*, May 11, 1837.

28. *Baltimore Transcript*, May 9, 1837; *Philadelphia Public Ledger*, May 11, 1837.

29. *The Picayune*, May 12, 1837; *Boston Evening Transcript*, May 22, 1837.

30. *Charleston Mercury*, May 22, 1837.

31. *Charleston Courier*, May 16, 1837; *Annapolis Maryland Gazette*, May 18, 1837.

32. Awareness of insufficient information is a common cause of individual and group "stress," which frequently terminates with nonadaptive behavior or behavior that is less adaptive than normal. That stress did not lead to similar early action in other cotton-forwarding centers is perhaps attributable to locational variations either in the perception of threat from the economic environment or in the ability to cope with stress. See Richard S. Lazarus, *Psychological Stress and the Coping Process* (New York: McGraw-Hill, 1966).

33. *New York Journal of Commerce*, May 19, 1837.

34. *Newark Daily Advertiser*, May 11, 1837; *New York Journal of Commerce*, May 12, 13, 1837; *New York Daily Express*, May 12, 13, 1837; *Boston Evening Transcript*, May 12, 1837; *Daily Albany Argus*, May 12, 13, 1837; *Harrisburg Pennsylvania Telegraph*, May 11, 1837.

35. *Philadelphia Public Ledger*, May 11, 1837; *Philadelphia Inquirer*, May 11, 1837.

36. *Baltimore American*, May 12, 13, 1837; *Baltimore Patriot*, May 12, 1837.

37. *Boston Evening Transcript*, May 12, 1837; *Richmond Enquirer*, May 23, 1837 (citing the *New Bedford Gazette*); *Daily Albany Argus*, May 15, 18, 1837; *New York Journal of Commerce*, May 15, 1837.

38. *Boston Atlas*, May 12, 1837.

39. *Daily Albany Argus*, May 17, 18; *Rochester Democrat*, May 13, 1837; *Boston Evening Transcript*, May 20, 1837; *Harrisburg Pennsylvania Telegraph*, May 18, 1837.

40. *Portland Advertiser* (Maine), May 16, 23, 1837; *New York Journal of Commerce*, May 17, 1837. The May 15 suspensions shown in Map 7.2 for Augusta, Bangor, and other points in Maine were reported in the *Portland Advertiser*, May 23, 1837. That paper gave no indication of the sources of influence.

41. *Pittsburgh Mercury*, May 17, 1837.

42. *Richmond Whig and Public Advertiser*, May 16, 1837; *Annapolis Maryland Gazette*, May 18, 1837; *Richmond Enquirer*, May 16, 1837.

43. *Richmond Enquirer*, May 19, 1837; *New York Journal of Commerce*, May 20, 1837. Mobile residents did not learn of events in New York, Philadelphia, and Baltimore until May 16. *New York Journal of Commerce*, May 24, 1837.

44. *The Picayune*, May 12, 14; *New Orleans True American*, May 13, 1837.

45. *Richmond Enquirer*, May 26, 1837; *New York Journal of Commerce*, May 27, 1837. The diffusion process could not enter the Lake Erie subsystem at Buffalo because its banks had already been forced to close.

46. *Richmond Enquirer*, May 26, 1837; *The Union* (Nashville), May 23, 25. When on May 22 the Nashville business community moved toward specie-payment suspension, it expressed fear that the banks of New Orleans would soon have to imitate the policy of their Northeastern counterparts. That is, they were unaware of what had already transpired in New Orleans nine days earlier.

47. *New York Journal of Commerce*, May 25, 1837; *Richmond Enquirer*, May 26, 1837.

48. *The Union*, May 23, 1837; *St Louis Republican*, May 23, 1837; *The Sangamo Journal* (Springfield, Ill.), May 27, 1837.

49. *Richmond Enquirer*, May 26, 1837; *New York Journal of Commerce*, June 1, 1837. The suspension of specie payments in Cincinnati apparently influenced the decision in Indianapolis. However, there is no indication of the full array of information sources affecting Indianapolis.

50. *Charleston Mercury*, May 19, 22, 1837.

51. *Charleston Mercury*, May 15, 18, 1837.

52. *Milledgeville Federal Union* (Georgia), May 23, 1837 (citing the *Augusta Constitutionalist*, May 19, 1837). For other specie-payment suspensions shown in Map 7.3 but not discussed in the text, see *Augusta Constitutionalist*, May 19, 1837; *Edgefield Advertiser*, May 25, 1837; *Charleston Courier*, May 24, 27, 1837; *Philadelphia Public Ledger*, May 19, 22, 29, 1837; *Richmond Enquirer*, May 26, 1837.

53. *Philadelphia Public Ledger*, May 23, 1837; *Richmond Whig and Public Advertiser*, May 30, 1837.

54. Alfred McClung Lee, *The Daily Newspaper in America: The Evolution of a Social Instrument* (New York: Macmillan, 1937), pp. 43, 55.

55. All dates of daily newspapers are from Clarence S. Brigham, *History and Bibliography of American Newspapers, 1690-1820* (Worcester: American Antiquarian Society, 1947), 2 vols.

56. Brigham, *History and Bibliography of American Newspapers*, 2 vols.

57. Lee, *Daily Newspaper*, pp. 728, 730. If there was any minimum population requirement for daily newspaper publication, the threshold was perhaps higher in the South because of the high rate of illiteracy among the slave subpopulation.

58. Lee, *Daily Newspaper*, p. 259; Frank Luther Mott, *American Journalism: A History of Newspapers in the United States Through 250 Years, 1690 to 1940* (New York: Macmillan, 1941), pp. 202-204; "Daniel Hewitt's List of Newspapers and Periodicals in the United States in 1828," *Proceedings of the American Antiquarian Society* 44 (1934), 365-396; S. N. D. North, *History and Present Condition of the Newspaper and Periodical Press of the United States*, U.S. Department of the Interior, Census Office, 1884, p. 101.

59. Mott, *American Journalism*, pp. 220, 239, 238, 216-217.

60. Mott, *American Journalism*, pp. 224, 228-229; Harold A. Innis, *The Bias of Communication* (Toronto: Toronto University Press, 1951), p. 160

61. Mott, *American Journalism*, pp. 238-241.

62. Mott, *American Journalism*, p. 240; Innis, *Bias of Communication*, p. 160; North, *History . . . of the Newspaper and Periodical Press*, p. 101.

63. Wheaton J. Lane, *From Indian Trail to Iron Horse: Travel and Transportation in New Jersey, 1620-1860* (Princeton: Princeton University Press, 1939), pp. 174-175; John H. Morrison, *History of American Steam Navigation* (New York: W. F. Sametz, 1903), pp. 24, 36-37, 202-206, Seymour Dunbar, *A History of Travel in America* (Indianapolis: Bobbs-Merrill, 1915), II, 397, 398, 404; *NWR* 4, no. 12 (May 22, 1813), 200; 4, no. 14 (June 5, 1813), 232; Louis C. Hunter, *Steamboats on the Western Rivers: An Economic and Technological History* (Cambridge: Harvard University Press, 1949), pp. 1-27.

64. Victor S. Clark, *History of Manufactures in the United States* (New York: McGraw-Hill, 1929), I, 408; *Philadelphia Aurora*, Apr. 2, 1802; Henry Adams, *The United States in 1800* (Ithaca: Cornell University Press, 1955), p. 49.

65. Richard C. Wade, *The Urban Frontier: Pioneer Life in Early Pittsburgh, Cincinnati, Lexington, Louisville, and St. Louis* (Chicago: University of Chicago Press, 1964), p. 47; *NWR* 1, no. 22 (Feb. 1, 1812), 406-407; 3, no. 7 (Oct. 17, 1812), 110-111; 8, no. 9 (Apr. 29, 1815), 141; 48, no. 17 (June 27, 1835), 298; 49, no. 3 (Sept. 19, 1835), 35; Catherine E. Reiser, *Pittsburgh's Commercial Development, 1800-1850* (Harrisburg: Pennsylvania Historical and Museum Commission, 1951), p. 20; Clark, *History of Manufactures*, I, 409.

66. Levi Woodbury, *Report on Steam Engines*, U.S. House Document No. 21, 25th Cong., 3rd sess., 1838, pp. 3, 10. On data shortcomings, see Allen H. Fenichal, "Growth and Diffusion of Power in Manufacturing, 1838-1919," in *Output,*

Employment, and Productivity in the United States after 1800 (New York: Columbia University Press, 1966), p. 462; Peter Temin, "Steam and Waterpower in the Early Nineteenth Century," *Journal of Economic History* 26 (1966), 190.

67. Woodbury, *Report on Steam Engines*, pp. 159-167, 191-194, 41-44, 210-211.

68. A large number of steam-driven establishments in close proximity to Pittsburgh were not included in the 1838 total of 87. As early as 1833 there were 89 industrially employed steam engines in Pittsburgh and "its immediate vicinity." *NWR* 45, no. 11 (Nov. 9, 1833), 165; 45, no. 14 (Nov. 30, 1833), 165.

69. Temin argued that in 1838 the "direct costs of steam power were higher than costs for waterpower." Temin, "Steam and Waterpower," pp. 196-199, 204. Hence, the adoption of the steam engine made greatest sense where waterpower was scarce and where coal or wood could be acquired with low transport costs. Of the 90-100 engines functioning in Philadelphia in 1831, approximately 60 were already fueled by anthracite coal. *NWR* 40, no. 20 (July 16, 1831), 344.

70. See Temin, "Steam and Waterpower," pp. 199-204.

71. J. Thomas Scharf and Thompson Westcott, *History of Philadelphia, 1609-1884* (Philadelphia, 1884), III, 2,262-2,263; Wade, *Urban Frontier*, pp. 46-47.

72. *NWR* 8, no. 9 (Apr. 29, 1815), 141; 29, no. 12 (Nov. 19, 1825), 180; 55, no. 25 (Feb. 16, 1839), 391.

73. Clark, *History of Manufactures*, I, 409. In the spring of 1830 it was asserted that 103 engines had been constructed in Cincinnati "in the last twelve months." *NWR* 38, no. 16 (June 12, 1830), 293. Another report maintained that in 1830, "Pittsburgh alone produced one hundred engines, and Cincinnati one hundred fifty." Stuart Bruchey, *The Roots of American Economic Growth, 1607-1861: An Essay in Social Causation* (New York: Harper & Row, 1965), p. 86.

74. Temin, "Steam and Waterpower," pp. 190-192.

75. Dorothy S. Brady, "Manufactures," in Gilchrist, *Growth of the Seaport Cities*, p. 92; Fred Mitchell Jones, *Middlemen in the Domestic Trade of the United States, 1800-1860*, Illinois Studies in the Social Sciences, vol. 21, no. 3 (Urbana: University of Illinois Press, 1937), p. 65; Norman S. Buck, *The Development of the Organization of Anglo-American Trade, 1800-1850* (New Haven: Yale University Press, 1925), p. 149.

76. Reiser, *Pittsburgh's Commercial Development*, p. 21; Wade, *Urban Frontier*, pp. 314-319.

77. Clark, *History of Manufactures*, I, 527-528; *NWR* 33, no. 4 (Sept. 22, 1827), 56; 51, no. 15 (Dec. 10, 1836), 240. Employment in Providence's jewelry industry reached 1,400 by 1850.

78. Brady, "Manufactures," p. 93; Robert G. LeBlanc, *Location of Manufacturing in New England in the 19th Century*, Geography Publications at Dartmouth, No. 7 (Hanover, 1969), pp. 34-36.

79. For a number of reasons caution is necessary when employing patent records as an indicator of the location of inventive activity. Not all patents were for technological inventions, and especially before the practice of seeking patent grants had been widely diffused, not all technological inventions were patented. There is also some danger in assigning the same unit value to every patent issued, even

within a relatively brief time span, for within a single industry, patents can vary tremendously in their technological and economic impacts. However, if a sufficiently large number of closely dated patents are used, it is possible that "the disparate significance of patent-units may resolve itself into compensating errors fluctuating at random about . . . [some] mean 'unit-value.' " Robert K. Merton, "Fluctuations in the Rate of Industrial Invention," *Quarterly Journal of Economics* 49 (1935), 56. See also Jacob Schmookler, "The Interpretation of Patent Statistics," *Journal of the Patent Office Society*, February 1950, pp. 123–146; Jacob Schmookler, "The Utility of Patent Statistics," *Journal of the Patent Office Society*, June 1953, pp. 407–412.

80. Henry L. Ellsworth, *A Digest of Patents, Issued by the United States, from 1790 to January 1, 1839* (Washington, D.C., 1840).

81. On the relationships between uncertainty reduction and the choice of locations for invention implementation, see Pred, *Spatial Dynamics*, pp. 98–101. On the variety of risks that might confront the industrial innovator, see W. Paul Strassman, *Risk and Technological Innovation: American Manufacturing Methods During the Nineteenth Century* (Ithaca: Cornell University Press, 1959).

82. Ellsworth, *Digest of Patents*; U.S. Senate, *Report from the Commissioner of Patents Showing the Operations of the Patent Office During the Year 1840*, Document No. 152, 26th Cong., 2nd sess., 1841; U.S. Bureau of the Census, *Historical Statistics of the United States, Colonial Times to 1957*, 1960, pp. 607–608. The limited quantity of inventive activity during 1790–1840 is consistent with the then limited significance of urban manufacturing.

83. Ten of the eleven patents shown for Cincinnati and Pittsburgh in Table 7.4 were registered after the termination of the War of 1812.

84. The sample of 38 cities used in all three computations included the 19 centers listed in Table 7.6 as well as Augusta (Ga.), Harrisburg, Hartford, Lancaster, Lexington (Ky.), Lowell, Nashville, New Haven, Newport (R.I.), Portland, Portsmouth (N.H.), Raleigh, Rochester, Springfield (Mass.), Troy, Washington, D.C., Wheeling, Wilmington (Del.), and Worcester.

85. For the relationship between perception of demand and invention, see Jacob Schmookler, *Invention and Economic Growth* (Cambridge: Harvard University Press, 1966). When depressed economic conditions set in during 1837 and demand was thereby seen by many as falling off, the number of patented inventions fell to 426 from a level of 702 in 1836. The problem awareness route to invention is given a classic Gestalt-psychology description in Abbott Payton Usher, *A History of Mechanical Inventions*, rev. ed. (Cambridge: Harvard University Press, 1954), pp. 64–66. On the interindustry transferability of problem solutions and the occurence of inventions, see Nathan Rosenberg, "Technological Change in the Machine Tool Industry, 1840–1910," *Journal of Economic History* 23 (1963), 422–440.

86. Ellsworth, *Digest of Patents*; *Letter from the Secretary of State*.

87. See, e.g., Warren C. Scoville, "Minority Migrations and the Diffusion of Technology," *Journal of Economic History* 11 (1951), 347–360.

88. On the tendency of immigrants landing in Boston during the 1820s and 1830s to move farther westward, see Oscar Handlin, *Boston's Immigrants: A Study in Acculturation* (Cambridge: Harvard University Press, 1959), pp. 37, 51.

89. Cf. Handlin, *Boston's Immigrants*, p. 25; Everett E. Hagen, *On the Theory of Social Change: How Economic Growth Begins* (Homewood, Ill.: Dorsey Press, 1967), pp. 242-243.

90. Adam Seybert, *Statistical Annals: Embracing Views of the Population, Commerce, Navigation . . . of the United States of America* (Philadelphia, 1818), pp. 28-29. The European wars that began in 1792 as well as the high cost of transoceanic travel supposedly helped keep pre-1816 immigration totals relatively low.

91. In view of the generally low estimates of immigration for the 1790s, New York may already have been the nation's leading port of disembarkation: "As for arrivals at the port of New York, one estimate has it that 3,000 persons came each year from 1789 to 1794; another, that the British immigrants alone numbered 1,500 to 2,000 annually from 1784 to 1794. The lack of data on the subject makes any conclusion extremely hazardous." Sidney I. Pomerantz, *New York: An American City, 1783-1803: A Study of Urban Life* (New York: Columbia University Press, 1938), pp. 202-203.

92. See Robert G. Albion, *The Rise of New York Port, 1815-1860* (New York: Charles Scribner's Sons, 1939), pp. 336-337. On the correlation between United States business cycles and the volume of emigration from Europe, see Brinley Thomas, *Migration and Economic Growth* (Cambridge, Eng.: Cambridge University Press, 1954), pp. 83-122.

93. The low for the 1835-1840 period was reached in 1838, immediately after the panic of 1837. Since migration decisions were greatly influenced by private and public information from the United States, and since New York was the principal node of information export as well as import, immigration flows to that city in 1838 fell off more rapidly than at most other ports. See Robert Ernst, *Immigrant Life in New York, 1825-1863* (New York: King's Crown Press, 1949), p. 10.

94. See Ernst, *Immigrant Life*, pp. 40-41, 187; Everett S. Lee and Michael Lalli, "Population," in Gilchrist, *Growth of the Seaport Cities*, p. 33.

95. In this report, "mechanics" and "engineers" were actually classified separately.

96. The custom's officials responsible for collecting the data varied in diligence, for apparently there were inconsistencies in the assignment of immigrants and alien passengers to various categories. See Marian Davis, "Critique of Official United States Immigration Statistics," in Walter F. Wilcox, ed., *International Migrations* (New York: National Bureau of Economic Research, 1929-1931), II, App. 2. The inadequacies of the data are responsible for the varying temporal composition of Tables 7.8-7.10.

97. Although the percentages for mechanics and engineers in Table 7.9 are based only on ten ports, the four-fifths claim for the national total cannot be far from correct, because in all but one of the five years the same ten ports were responsible for 95.1 percent or more of all immigrants and alien passengers.

98. Krooss, "Financial Institutions," pp. 114-115, 127; Joseph Dorfman, "Economic Thought," in Gilchrist, *Growth of the Seaport Cities*, p. 157.

99. John Melish, *Travels in the United States of America in the Years 1806-1807 and 1809-1811* (Philadelphia, 1812), I, 153, cited in James Weston Livingood, *The Philadelphia-Baltimore Trade Rivalry, 1780-1860* (Harrisburg: Pennsylvania

Historical and Museum Commission, 1947), p. 2; Robert Greenhalgh Albion, *Square-Riggers on Schedule: The New York Sailing Packets to England, France, and the Cotton Ports* (Princeton: Princeton University Press, 1938), pp. 174–175.

100. Dorfman, "Economic Thought," pp. 160–161, 176–177. In Philadelphia, where a favorable attitude toward heavy industry developed relatively early, protectionist views were of longer standing than in Boston.

101. Krooss, "Financial Institutions," pp. 119–120; Dorfman, "Economic Thought," pp. 170–171, 177; Adams, *United States in 1800*, p. 108. Peter Coleman, *The Transformation of Rhode Island, 1790–1860* (Providence: Brown University Press, 1963); Merl E. Reed, *New Orleans and the Railroads: The Struggle for Commercial Empire, 1830–1860* (Baton Rouge: Louisiana State University Press, 1966), pp. 7–8, 21; Adams, *United States*, p. 108.

102. The "life cycle" is usually defined as commencing when an individual sets out on his own. It is normally divided into single, married, and solitary survivor stages, with the marriage phase including substages for no children, dependent children, and independent children. Studies with varying foci have shown that people are more prone to risk-taking and innovative behavior early in the cycle than in later stages.

At different points in time, prevailing attitudes and patterns of business behavior in a city may also differ. For example, Baltimore's financiers were supposedly "reckless" between 1805 and 1812, but generally conservative after the War of 1812. Krooss, "Financial Institutions," pp. 119–20. Such changes can be viewed as the result of experience-based negative feedback.

103. C. P. Marsh and A. L. Coleman, "Group Influences and Agricultural Innovations: Some Tentative Findings and Hypotheses," *American Journal of Sociology* 61 (1956), 589.

104. George C. Homans, "Contemporary Theory in Sociology," in Robert E. L. Faris, ed., *Handbook of Modern Sociology* (Chicago: Rand McNally & Co., 1964), pp. 967–970; Walter Buckley, *Sociology and Modern Systems Theory* (Englewood Cliffs, N.J.: Prentice-Hall, 1967), pp. 105–113.

105. Cf. Torsten Hägerstrand, "A Monte Carlo Approach to Diffusion," *Archives européennes de sociologie* 6 (1965), 457.

106. The "two-step" hypothesis holds that "messages originating outside of the individual's face-to-face group do not impinge on him directly, but are mediated by a few members of his group [influentials] who expose themselves to messages from the outside more often than their confrères," Herbert Menzel and Elihu Katz, "Social Relations and Innovation in the Medical Profession: The Epidemiology of a New Drug," *Public Opinion Quarterly* 19 (1955), 36. See also Elihu Katz, "The Two-Step Flow of Communications: An Up-to-Date Report on an Hypothesis," *Public Opinion Quarterly* 21 (1957), 61–78. On the need for considering group membership in urban historical research, see Leo F. Schnore, "Problems in the Quantitative Study of Urban History," in H. J. Dyos, ed., *The Study of Urban History* (New York: St. Martin's Press, 1968), pp. 194–195.

107. Arthur R. Cohen, *Attitude Change and Social Influence* (New York: Basic Books, 1964), pp. 15, 132.

108. In late eighteenth-century Philadelphia, "the crowded living of the age encouraged a street and tavern life which more resembled the social habits of the later nineteenth and early twentieth-century immigrant ghettos than the isolated private family life of today's working class and middle class." Sam Bass Warner, Jr., *The Private City: Philadelphia in Three Periods of Its Growth* (Philadelphia: University of Pennsylvania Press, 1968), p. 17.

109. Edwin Williams, *New-York As It Is, in 1833* (New York, 1833), p. 13; Handlin, *Boston's Immigrants*, pp. 91, 93; Thomas J. Wertenbaker, *Norfolk: Historic Southern Port* (Durham: Duke University Press, 1931), p. 92.

110. See, e.g., Alice Morse Earle, *Stage-coach and Tavern Days* (New York: Macmillan, 1901); W. Harrison Bayles, *Old Taverns of New York* (New York: Frank Allaben Genealogical Co., 1915); Wade, *Urban Frontier*, p. 205; Samuel Eliot Morison, *The Maritime History of Massachusetts, 1783-1860*, rev. ed. (Boston: Houghton Mifflin Company, 1961), pp. 131-132. Albion remarked: "In the absence of telephones, the business men of New York made it a custom to gather daily at the Merchants Exchange at a specific hour so that, with the whole commercial community present, they might transact in a few minutes what would have taken hours in going from one counting house to another." Albion, *Square-Riggers*, p. 111.

111. Karl W. Deutsch, *Nationalism and Social Communication: An Inquiry into the Foundations of Nationality*, 2nd ed. (Cambridge: M.I.T. Press, 1966), p. 36.

112. Julius Rubin, *Canal or Railroad? Imitation and Innovation in the Response to the Erie Canal in Philadelphia, Baltimore, and Boston*, Transactions of the American Philosophical Society, n. s. 51, pt. 7, (Philadelphia, 1961), pp. 48-49, 79, 80, 8.

113. Rubin, *Canal or Railroad?* pp. 13, 58, 72-76, 88, 92-95. Once positive investment results were obtained in the late 1830s, and uncertainty thereby diminished, Boston's formerly reluctant mercantile aristocracy turned increasingly to railroad projects "in an ever-widening geographical area." Arthur M. Johnson and Barry E. Supple, *Boston Capitalists and Western Railroads: A Study in the Nineteenth-Century Railroad Investment Process* (Cambridge: Harvard University Press, 1967), p. 56.

114. Rubin, *Canal or Railroad?* p. 9.

115. Rubin, *Canal or Railroad?* pp. 19, 28, 69-71, 76, 84, 93-94.

116. Krooss, "Financial Institutions," p. 135. See also Rubin, *Canal or Railroad?* p. 14.

8. Modern Policy Ramifications

1. This is not to suggest that modern communications technology has homogenized the structure of information-circulation processes in both highly industrialized and newly developing economies. On the contrary, there are "fundamental differences in the volume, speed, and accuracy with which information is transmitted" in traditional, transitional, and modern communications systems. Lucien Pye, "Models of Traditional, Transitional, and Modern Communications Systems,"

in Pye, ed., *Communications and Political Development* (Princeton: Princeton University Press, 1963), pp. 24–29.

2. Poul Ove Pedersen, "Innovation Diffusion Within and Between National Urban Systems," *Geographical Analysis* 2 (1970), 203–254; R. P. Misra, "The Diffusion of Information in the Context of Development Planning," in Antoni R. Kuklinski and Torsten Hägerstrand, eds., *Information Systems for Regional Development: A Seminar*, Lund Studies in Geography, ser. B, Human Geography, no. 37 (Lund, 1971), pp. 119–136; J. R. Lasuén, "Multi-Regional Economic Development: An Open-System Approach," in Kuklinski and Hägerstrand, *Information Systems*, pp. 169–211; Tormod Hermansen, "Development Poles and Development Centres in National Regional Development—Elements of a Theoretical Framework," in Antoni R. Kuklinski, ed., "A Review of the Concepts and Theories of Growth Poles and Growth Centres," mimeographed (Geneva: United Nations Research Institute for Social Development, 1970), pp. 10–12, 75–82. For the most part, the models and hypotheses contained in these items are stated in a strictly Christallerian framework. They also suffer generally from a failure to include the other components of the large-city rank stability model. See also Barry J. Riddell, *The Spatial Development of Modernization in Sierra Leone* (Evanston: Northwestern University Press, 1970); Peter R. Gould, "Tanzania 1920–63: The Spatial Impress of the Modernization Process," *World Politics* 22 (January 1970), 141–70. For a version of the model applying to modern, highly industrialized economies, see Allan R. Pred, "The Growth and Development of Systems of Cities in Advanced Economies," forthcoming in Lund Studies in Geography, ser. B, 1973.

3. Torsten Hägerstrand, "Introduction," in Kuklinski and Hägerstrand, *Information Systems*, p. vi. The use of the historical record to draw conclusions for local and regional planners is not unprecedented. Johnson argued—largely on the basis of materials about England in the sixteenth century, the rise of Belgian towns, the late nineteenth and early twentieth-century rural transformation of Japan, and over a century of changes in the American Midwest—that underdeveloped countries "cannot create tolerably satisfactory market economies without a spatially dispersed hierarchy of rural growth centers, market towns, small cities, and other central places that collectively can counterbalance the pull of their voracious metropolitan centers." E. A. J. Johnson, *The Organization of Space in Developing Countries* (Cambridge: Harvard University Press, 1970).

4. Particularly in West Africa there are large port cities that function basically as economic couplings between their interior hinterlands and one or a few foreign powers, but have little to do with major sister ports. They thus reflect a classical colonial situation where regions interact more with the overseas power than they do with each other. If the objective is to integrate the national urban system by creating interdependencies between these cities, major transport improvements between them are usually required. Cf. M. I. Logan, "The Process of Regional Development and Its Implications for Planning," *Journal of the Geographical Association of Nigeria* 13 (1970), 109–120.

5. Cf. the "center-periphery" arguments regarding the influence of already successful urban regions on economically backward areas in, e.g., John Friedmann,

Regional Development Policy: A Case Study of Venezuela (Cambridge: M.I.T. Press, 1966).

6. See William Alonso, "Urban and Regional Imbalances in Economic Development," *Economic Development and Cultural Change* 17 (1968), 1–14.

7. Comment by Samuel H. Beer in "New Trends in History," *Daedalus*, Fall 1969, p. 910.

8. Robert F. Berkhofer, *A Behavioral Approach to Historical Analysis* (New York: Free Press, 1969), p. 246.

Index

INDEX

Input-output relationships, 187-88
Insurance, 190-91, 201-202, 211
Interaction increases between large
cities, 216-19
Interdependence of cities, 187, 209-13,
215, 225, 229-30, 245, 284-86. *See
also* Innovation diffusion
Inventions, 192, 213, 239; causes of,
269; locations, 263-69; patent data for,
262-69. *See also* Boston; Baltimore;
New York City; Urban-size growth
Iowa, 82
Isard, Walter, 225

Jackson, Andrew, 13
James River Valley, 225
Janelle, Donald G., 217-18
Jefferson, Thomas, 63
Jersey City, 159
Johnstown (Pa.), 281

Kanawha River Valley, 225
Kennedy, John F., 12
Kentucky, 88, 90, 109, 133, 138, 196
Kingston (N. Y.), 119, 166
Knoxville (Tenn.), 48, 88, 92
Krooss, Herman, 283

Lackawanna Valley, 117
Lake Erie, 91, 138, 152, 244. *See also*
Lake Erie subsystem of cities;
Steamboats
Lake Erie subsystem of cities, 4, 6, 8,
90, 93, 108, 186, 194, 200, 203-206,
223-24, 242, 245, 254, 258-59. *See
also* Buffalo; Cleveland; Commodity
flows; Detroit
Lake Michigan, 138
Lake Ontario, 138
Lake Superior, 138
Lancashire (Eng.), 131
Lancaster (Pa.), 87, 215
Lancaster Turnpike, 119
Large-city rank-stability model, 10-11,
203-14, 216-17, 219, 223-24, 226-
27, 238-39, 241-42, 244-46, 254,
258, 260-61, 265, 270-71, 283;
applicability of, 206-207; basic
structure, 207-12; feedback loops,

209-213, 216, 223; related models,
225-27; under modern conditions, 284
Latin America, 117
Lawrence (Mass.), 214
Lebanon (Pa.), 87
Le Havre, 29, 34, 128
Lehigh Canal, 118
Lehigh Valley, 117-18
Lexington (Ky.), 39, 48, 89, 200,
259
Lexington (Mass.), 13
Liverpool (Eng.), 27, 29-30, 32, 34, 113,
128, 221, 247, 253
Location quotients, 95-99, 263-67
London, 13, 29, 34, 128, 131, 241, 243
Long Island, 108
Long Island Sound, 46, 85, 155, 162,
167, 224
Lösch, August, 230, 232. *See also* In-
novation diffusion
Louisiana, 99
Louisiana Purchase, 92
Louisville, 4, 25, 49, 141, 150, 155,
186, 200-201, 222, 224, 227, 242,
254, 258, 260-61, 268; economy,
194-98; interurban travel volumes,
167-69, 173-74, 206; postal services
and receipts, 89-91, 95, 204; public
information accessibility, 73; trade,
132-37, 204-205; travel times to and
from, 183-84
Louisville and Portland Canal, 133
Lowell (Mass.), 7, 87, 131, 214, 253
Lower Sandusky (O.), 90
Lukermann, Fred, 3
Lynn (Mass.), 61, 116, 253

McLean, John, 78, 81
Madden, Carl H., 3
Mails. *See* Postal services
Maine, 118-19, 253
Mainline, 119, 134, 152, 281
Manchacks (La.), 259
Manchester (N. H.), 214
Manhattan (New York City), 138,
142, 279
Manufacturing, 209, 211, 214-16, 227,
229, 261-62, 268, 284; in mercantile
cities, 189-94, 196-97, 199, 202, 213,

342

Harvard Studies in Urban History